MICROSOFT AZURE AI ENGINEER ASSOCIATE

- ✓ MASTER THE EXAM (AI-102)
- ✓ 10 PRACTICE TESTS
- ✓ 500 RIGOROUS QUESTIONS
- ✓ 490+ EXAM FOCUSED TIPS
- ✓ 495+ CAUTION ALERTS
- ✓ GAIN WEALTH OF INSIGHTS
- ✓ EXPERT EXPLANATIONS AND
- ✓ ONE ULTIMATE GOAL

2025 UPGRADED EDITION | PASS ON YOUR FIRST TRY

ANAND M

AMEENA PUBLICATIONS

ISBN: 9798875800573

DEDICATION

To the Visionaries in My Professional Odyssey

This book is dedicated to the mentors and leaders who guided me through triumph and adversity in my professional universe. Your guidance has illuminated the path to success and taught me to seize opportunities and surmount obstacles. Thank you for imparting the advice to those who taught me the value of strategic thinking and the significance of innovation to transform obstacles into stepping stones. Your visionary leadership has inspired my creativity and motivated me to forge new paths.

Thank you for sharing the best and worst of your experiences with me, kind and severe employers. As I present this book to the world, I am aware that you have been my inspiration. All of your roles as mentors, advisors, and even occasional adversaries have helped me become a better professional and storyteller.

This dedication is a tribute to your impact on my journey, a narrative woven with threads of gratitude, introspection, and profound gratitude for the lessons you've inscribed into my story.

With deep gratitude and enduring respect,
Anand M

FROM TECH TO LIFE SKILLS – MY EBOOKS COLLECTION

Dive into my rich collection of eBooks, curated meticulously across diverse and essential domains.

***Pro Tips and Tricks Series**: Empower yourself with life-enhancing skills and professional essentials with our well-crafted guides.*

***Hot IT Certifications and Tech Series**: Stay ahead in the tech game. Whether you're eyeing certifications in AWS, PMP, or prompt engineering, harnessing the power of ChatGPT with tools like Excel, PowerPoint, Word, and more!, we've got you covered!*

***Essential Life Skills**: Embark on a journey within. From yoga to holistic well-being, Master the art of culinary, baking, and more delve deep and rediscover yourself.*

Stay Updated & Engaged

For an entire world of my knowledge, tips, and treasures, follow me on Amazon ***https://www.amazon.com/author/anandm***

Your Feedback Matters!

Your support, feedback, and ratings are the wind beneath my wings. It drives me to curate content that brings immense value to every aspect of life. Please take a moment to share your thoughts and rate the books. Together, let's keep the flame of knowledge burning bright!

Best Regards,

ANAND M

INTRODUCTION

*In today's rapidly advancing technological landscape, artificial intelligence (AI) stands as a cornerstone of innovation, with Microsoft Azure leading the charge in AI-driven solutions. Welcome to "**Microsoft Azure AI Engineer Associate: Master the Exam (AI-102)**," your ultimate guide to mastering the AI-102 certification exam, a key achievement for those aspiring to excel in Azure-powered AI technologies.*

This comprehensive guide is meticulously designed to equip you with the knowledge and skills essential for navigating the multifaceted world of Azure AI services and applications. More than just a preparation tool, it immerses you in a deep exploration of Azure's AI engineering capabilities, ensuring you're not only exam-ready but fully prepared to implement AI solutions within the Azure ecosystem.

*Within these pages, you'll find a carefully curated selection of **500 challenging questions**, each crafted to test and enhance your understanding of Azure AI concepts. The questions go beyond rote memorization, focusing on your ability to apply AI technologies in practical, real-world Azure environments. Accompanying each question, our expert explanations provide not only the rationale behind the correct answer but also deeper insights that enrich your grasp of Azure's AI tools and services.*

In a world increasingly driven by AI, proficiency in Azure AI engineering has become indispensable for professionals looking to make their mark in fields such as machine learning, data science, and AI-driven analytics.

Let's break down the essentials of the AI-102 exam:

- ***Duration:** The exam allows a comprehensive 180 minutes to thoroughly assess your grasp of Azure AI concepts.*
- ***Cost:** The enrollment cost is $165, with potential regional tax variations.*
- ***Format:** The exam features a mix of multiple-choice and multiple-response questions in a structured, professional testing environment.*
- ***Prerequisites:** While not mandatory, a foundational understanding from the Azure Fundamentals (AZ-900) and AI-900 exams is highly beneficial, providing a solid grounding in Azure's core principles and AI technologies.*

This eBook is your roadmap to success. Beyond helping you pass the AI-102 exam, it serves as a transformative learning journey into the world of Azure AI engineering, giving you the confidence to excel in the exam and in your professional career.

Start your journey to mastering Azure AI engineering with this comprehensive guide as your steadfast companion. With diligent preparation and this book by your side, your success in the AI-102 exam is well within reach.

ADVANTAGES OF CERTIFICATION

As you set out on the path to earning the Microsoft Azure AI Engineer Associate (AI-102) Certification, it's essential to understand the profound impact this credential can have on your career. Below are the key advantages of obtaining this certification:

Prestigious Recognition in the AI Industry: *In a world where artificial intelligence is driving innovation across all sectors, possessing expertise in Azure AI engineering makes you a highly sought-after professional. The AI-102 certification not only validates your proficiency with Azure's cutting-edge AI technologies but also positions you as a leader in the rapidly expanding AI ecosystem. It's more than a certification—it's a mark of your advanced skills in a critical area of technology.*

Catalyst for Career Growth: *This certification is a game-changer for your career. Whether you're aiming to advance in AI strategy, machine learning model development, or managing complex AI-driven projects on Azure, the AI-102 certification opens the door to higher-level roles and career advancement. It signifies your readiness for more challenging, impactful, and lucrative positions within the AI and cloud technology fields.*

Elevated Earning Potential: *Certified professionals are often rewarded with increased earning potential, and this certification is no exception. Employers recognize the value of Azure AI expertise, and being certified affirms that you possess a skillset that is in high demand. This can lead to not only salary increases but also enhanced job stability in a competitive market.*

Enhanced Professional Visibility: *In the increasingly competitive job market, standing out is vital. The Azure AI Engineer Associate certification boosts your professional credibility, making you a more attractive candidate for potential employers. It gives you an edge in AI and cloud technology roles, ensuring that your expertise is recognized and valued in both your current role and future career opportunities.*

Mastery of Practical and Theoretical Knowledge: *The AI-102 certification is designed to ensure that you have both a deep understanding of Azure AI concepts and the ability to apply those concepts in real-world scenarios. By completing this certification, you'll possess the practical skills needed to design, implement, and manage AI solutions on Azure, setting you apart from peers who lack this specialized knowledge.*

In summary, the ***Microsoft Azure AI Engineer Associate (AI-102)*** *certification is a powerful tool for advancing your career in the AI and cloud computing space. It not only strengthens your technical foundation but also enhances your marketability and sets you on a path for continuous growth in Azure AI engineering. The opportunities that come with this certification are vast, and achieving it is a key milestone in your professional journey.*

EXAM OBJECTIVE

*Welcome to the **Microsoft Azure AI Engineer Associate** question bank, your comprehensive guide to mastering the AI-102 exam. Below is a detailed breakdown of the exam domains and their respective weightings:*

Exam Section & Weightage

Domain	*Weightage*
Plan and manage an Azure AI solution	*15–20%*
Implement content moderation solutions	*10–15%*
Implement computer vision solutions	*15–20%*
Implement natural language processing solutions	*30–35%*
Implement knowledge mining and document intelligence solutions	*10–15%*
Implement generative AI solutions	*10–15%*

Domain 1: Plan and manage an Azure AI solution (15–20%): *This domain focuses on planning and overseeing Azure AI solutions. You'll learn to architect AI-driven applications on Azure, manage AI services efficiently, and evaluate business requirements to align AI capabilities with organizational needs. Mastering this domain will ensure that you can manage the complete lifecycle of AI projects, from inception to deployment and monitoring.*

Domain 2: Implement content moderation solutions (10–15%): *In this domain, you will explore how to implement content moderation using Azure AI services such as Azure Content Moderator. You'll gain proficiency in detecting inappropriate content across various media types and automating content filtering in real-time applications to maintain a safe and compliant user experience.*

Domain 3: Implement computer vision solutions (15–20%): *This domain focuses on leveraging Azure's computer vision services. You'll learn to build AI solutions capable of analyzing visual content, including object detection, image classification, and optical character recognition (OCR). Understanding how to implement computer vision on Azure will help you create innovative solutions in industries ranging from retail to healthcare.*

Domain 4: Implement natural language processing solutions (30–35%): *As one of the most critical domains, this section dives into building AI systems that understand, interpret, and respond to human language. You'll cover key areas such as speech recognition, language translation, and text analytics using Azure Cognitive Services. Proficiency in NLP is vital for creating AI systems that enhance customer interactions, automate text-based tasks, and power intelligent applications.*

Domain 5: Implement knowledge mining and document intelligence solutions (10–15%): *In this domain, you'll explore Azure AI's ability to extract, organize, and analyze data from unstructured documents using tools like Azure Form Recognizer and Azure Cognitive Search. Knowledge mining allows for better data-driven decision-making by revealing insights hidden in vast amounts of data, enabling AI solutions that improve efficiency in business processes.*

Domain 6: Implement generative AI solutions (10–15%): *This domain highlights the integration of generative AI models within Azure. You'll learn to deploy and fine-tune models that create new data such as text, images, and other media forms. Generative AI has wide-ranging applications, including content generation, creative arts, and even automated problem-solving. Mastery of this domain enables you to stay ahead in the AI innovation curve.*

QUESTION BANK AND EXAM OBJECTIVE MAP

This question bank is meticulously aligned with the Microsoft Azure AI Engineer Associate (AI-102) exam syllabus, providing in-depth coverage of key concepts related to AI-powered solutions on Azure. Each question is crafted to simulate real-world scenarios, showcasing the practical application of Azure AI technologies in a variety of settings.

The questions in this book aim to build a clear and focused understanding of Azure AI principles. They are designed to help you quickly grasp essential topics, identify areas for improvement, and effectively apply your knowledge in real-world AI implementations. As you work through the questions, you'll strengthen your ability to plan, develop, and manage Azure AI solutions, while gaining confidence in your proficiency with Azure's cognitive services, machine learning, and natural language processing tools.

In addition, each question is accompanied by expert exam tips and caution alerts within the explanations. These insights are crafted to enhance your exam performance by focusing on critical concepts, key considerations, and common pitfalls encountered in Azure AI engineering. This ensures that you are thoroughly prepared to tackle the exam with confidence and precision.

The following table links each question to the relevant knowledge areas as outlined in the AI-102 exam syllabus, ensuring that your preparation is both comprehensive and strategically aligned for success.

DOMAIN 1 - PLAN AND MANAGE AN AZURE AI SOLUTION (15-20%)

Note: P indicates Practice Test and Q indicates Question

S.No	KNOWLEDGE AREA	MAPPED QUESTIONS
1	Computer Vision Solutions	P1Q1,P2Q1,P3Q1,P4Q1,P5Q1
2	Natural Language Processing Solutions	P6Q1,P7Q1,P8Q1,P9Q1,P10Q1
3	Decision Support Solutions	P1Q2,P2Q2,P3Q2,P4Q2,P5Q2
4	Speech Solutions	P6Q2,P7Q2,P8Q2,P9Q2,P10Q2
5	Generative AI Solutions	P1Q3,P2Q3,P3Q3,P4Q3,P5Q3
6	Document Intelligence Solutions	P6Q3,P7Q3,P8Q3,P9Q3,P10Q3
7	Knowledge Mining Solutions	P1Q4,P2Q4,P3Q4,P4Q4,P5Q4
8	Meeting Responsible AI principles	P6Q4,P7Q4,P8Q4,P9Q4,P10Q4
9	Creating an Azure AI resource	P1Q5,P2Q5,P3Q5,P4Q5,P5Q5
10	Default endpoint determination for a service	P6Q5,P7Q5,P8Q5,P9Q5,P10Q5
11	Integrating Azure AI services with CI/CD pipelines	P1Q6,P2Q6,P3Q6,P4Q6,P5Q6
12	Container deployment planning and implementation	P6Q6,P7Q6,P8Q6,P9Q6,P10Q6
13	Configuring diagnostic logging	P1Q7,P2Q7,P3Q7,P4Q7,P5Q7
14	Monitoring Azure AI resources	P6Q7,P7Q7,P8Q7,P9Q7,P10Q7
15	Managing Azure AI service costs	P1Q8,P2Q8,P3Q8,P4Q8,P5Q8
16	Managing account keys and secure authentication	P6Q8,P7Q8,P8Q8,P9Q8,P10Q8

DOMAIN 2 - IMPLEMENT DECISION SUPPORT SOLUTIONS (10-15%)

Note: P indicates Practice Test and Q indicates Question

S.No	KNOWLEDGE AREA	MAPPED QUESTIONS
17	Data Monitoring with Azure AI Metrics Advisor	P1Q9,P2Q9,P3Q9,P4Q9,P5Q9
18	Content Delivery Strategies	P6Q9,P7Q9,P8Q9,P9Q9,P10Q9
19	Text Moderation with Azure AI Content Safety	P1Q10,P2Q10,P3Q10,P4Q10,P5Q10
20	Image Moderation with Azure AI Content Safety	P6Q10,P7Q10,P8Q10,P9Q10,P10Q10
21	Decision Support System Integration	P1Q11,P2Q11,P3Q11,P4Q11,P5Q11
22	Monitoring and Improving Decision Support Performance	P6Q11,P7Q11,P8Q11,P9Q11,P10Q11
23	Security and Compliance in Decision Support	P1Q12,P2Q12,P3Q12,P4Q12,P5Q12
24	User Experience Optimization	P6Q12,P7Q12,P8Q12,P9Q12,P10Q12
25	Scalability and Deployment	P1Q13,P2Q13,P3Q13,P4Q13,P5Q13
26	Best Practices and Case Studies	P6Q13,P7Q13,P8Q13,P9Q13,P10Q13

DOMAIN 3 - IMPLEMENT COMPUTER VISION SOLUTIONS (15-20%)

Note: P indicates Practice Test and Q indicates Question

S.No	KNOWLEDGE AREA	MAPPED QUESTIONS
27	Visual Features Selection	P1Q14,P2Q14,P3Q14,P4Q14,P5Q14
28	Object Detection	P6Q14,P7Q14,P8Q14,P9Q14,P10Q14
29	Image Tagging	P1Q15,P2Q15,P3Q15,P4Q15,P5Q15
30	Image Analysis Response Interpretation	P6Q15,P7Q15,P8Q15,P9Q15,P10Q15
31	Text Extraction from Images	P1Q16,P2Q16,P3Q16,P4Q16,P5Q16
32	Handwritten Text Conversion	P6Q16,P7Q16,P8Q16,P9Q16,P10Q16
33	Image Classification Models	P1Q17,P2Q17,P3Q17,P4Q17,P5Q17
34	Object Detection Models	P6Q17,P7Q17,P8Q17,P9Q17,P10Q17
35	Model Training and Labeling	P1Q18,P2Q18,P3Q18,P4Q18,P5Q18
36	Model Evaluation	P6Q18,P7Q18,P8Q18,P9Q18,P10Q18
37	Model Publishing and Consumption	P1Q19,P2Q19,P3Q19,P4Q19,P5Q19
38	Video Insights Extraction	P6Q19,P7Q19,P8Q19,P9Q19,P10Q19
39	Spatial Analysis	P1Q20,P2Q20,P3Q20,P4Q20,P5Q20
40	Live Stream Analysis	P6Q20,P7Q20,P8Q20,P9Q20,P10Q20
41	Custom Video Models	P1Q21,P2Q21,P3Q21,P4Q21,P5Q21
42	Video Indexer Integration	P6Q21,P7Q21,P8Q21,P9Q21,P10Q21

DOMAIN 4 - IMPLEMENT NATURAL LANGUAGE PROCESSING SOLUTIONS (30-35%)

Note: P indicates Practice Test and Q indicates Question

S.No	KNOWLEDGE AREA	MAPPED QUESTIONS
43	Extracting Key Phrases	P1Q22,P2Q22,P3Q22,P4Q22,P5Q22
44	Entity Extraction	P6Q22,P7Q22,P8Q22,P9Q22,P10Q22
45	Sentiment Analysis	P1Q23,P2Q23,P3Q23,P4Q23,P5Q23
46	Language Detection	P6Q23,P7Q23,P8Q23,P9Q23,P10Q23
47	PII Detection	P1Q24,P2Q24,P3Q24,P4Q24,P5Q24
48	Text-to-Speech (TTS)	P6Q24,P7Q24,P8Q24,P9Q24,P10Q24
49	Speech-to-Text (STT)	P1Q25,P2Q25,P3Q25,P4Q25,P5Q25
50	SSML	P6Q25,P7Q25,P8Q25,P9Q25,P10Q25
51	Custom Speech Solutions	P1Q26,P2Q26,P3Q26,P4Q26,P5Q26
52	Intent Recognition	P6Q26,P7Q26,P8Q26,P9Q26,P10Q26
53	Keyword Recognition	P1Q27,P2Q27,P3Q27,P4Q27,P5Q27
54	Text Translation	P6Q27,P7Q27,P8Q27,P9Q27,P10Q27
55	Document Translation	P1Q28,P2Q28,P3Q28,P4Q28,P5Q28
56	Speech Translation	P6Q28,P7Q28,P8Q28,P9Q28,P10Q28
57	Custom Translation Models	P1Q29,P2Q29,P3Q29,P4Q29,P5Q29
58	Language Model Creation	P6Q29,P7Q29,P8Q29,P9Q29,P10Q29
59	Utterance Addition and Management	P1Q30,P2Q30,P3Q30,P4Q30,P5Q30
60	Entity Creation and Enhancement	P6Q30,P7Q30,P8Q30,P9Q30,P10Q30
61	Model Training and Evaluation	P1Q31,P2Q31,P3Q31,P4Q31,P5Q31
62	Deployment and Consumption	P6Q31,P7Q31,P8Q31,P9Q31,P10Q31
63	Model Optimization	P1Q32,P2Q32,P3Q32,P4Q32,P5Q32
64	Language Model Backup and Recovery	P6Q32,P7Q32,P8Q32,P9Q32,P10Q32
65	Project Creation for QA	P1Q33,P2Q33,P3Q33,P4Q33,P5Q33
66	Manual Addition of Q&A Pairs	P6Q33,P7Q33,P8Q33,P9Q33,P10Q33
67	Source Import and Management	P1Q34,P2Q34,P3Q34,P4Q34,P5Q34
68	Training and Testing Knowledge Bases	P6Q34,P7Q34,P8Q34,P9Q34,P10Q34
69	Publishing Knowledge Bases	P1Q35,P2Q35,P3Q35,P4Q35,P5Q35
70	Multi-Turn Conversations	P6Q35,P7Q35,P8Q35,P9Q35,P10Q35
71	Alternate Phrasing and Chit-Chat	P1Q36,P2Q36,P3Q36,P4Q36,P5Q36
72	Knowledge Base Export and Multi-Language Support	P6Q36,P7Q36,P8Q36,P9Q36,P10Q36
73	Model Fine-Tuning	P1Q37,P2Q37,P3Q37,P4Q37,P5Q37
74	Custom Model Deployment	P6Q37,P7Q37,P8Q37,P9Q37,P10Q37
75	Bot Framework Integration	P1Q38,P2Q38,P3Q38,P4Q38,P5Q38
76	Voice Assistants and Channels	P6Q38,P7Q38,P8Q38,P9Q38,P10Q38
77	App and Workflow Integration	P1Q39,P2Q39,P3Q39,P4Q39,P5Q39
78	Multilingual Applications	P6Q39,P7Q39,P8Q39,P9Q39,P10Q39
79	Sentiment Analysis Trends	P1Q40,P2Q40,P3Q40,P4Q40,P5Q40
80	Ethical Considerations	P6Q40,P7Q40,P8Q40,P9Q40,P10Q40

DOMAIN 5 - IMPLEMENT KNOWLEDGE MINING AND DOCUMENT INTELLIGENCE SOLUTIONS (10-15%)

Note: P indicates Practice Test and Q indicates Question

S.No	KNOWLEDGE AREA	MAPPED QUESTIONS
81	Provisioning a Cognitive Search Resource	P1Q41,P2Q41,P3Q41,P4Q41,P5Q41
82	Creating Data Sources	P6Q41,P7Q41,P8Q41,P9Q41,P10Q41
83	Creating and Managing Indexes	P1Q42,P2Q42,P3Q42,P4Q42,P5Q42
84	Defining Skillsets	P6Q42,P7Q42,P8Q42,P9Q42,P10Q42
85	Implementing Custom Skills	P1Q43,P2Q43,P3Q43,P4Q43,P5Q43
86	Creating and Running Indexers	P6Q43,P7Q43,P8Q43,P9Q43,P10Q43
87	Querying an Index	P1Q44,P2Q44,P3Q44,P4Q44,P5Q44
88	Knowledge Store Projections	P6Q44,P7Q44,P8Q44,P9Q44,P10Q44
89	Using Prebuilt Models for Data Extraction	P1Q45,P2Q45,P3Q45,P4Q45,P5Q45
90	Implementing Custom Document Models	P6Q45,P7Q45,P8Q45,P9Q45,P10Q45

DOMAIN 6 - IMPLEMENT GENERATIVE AI SOLUTIONS (10-15%)

Note: P indicates Practice Test and Q indicates Question

S.No	KNOWLEDGE AREA	MAPPED QUESTIONS
91	Provisioning Azure OpenAI Service	P1Q46,P2Q46,P3Q46,P4Q46,P5Q46
92	Deploying Azure OpenAI Models	P6Q46,P7Q46,P8Q46,P9Q46,P10Q46
93	Generating Natural Language	P1Q47,P2Q47,P3Q47,P4Q47,P5Q47
94	Generating Code	P6Q47,P7Q47,P8Q47,P9Q47,P10Q47
95	Image Generation with DALL-E	P1Q48,P2Q48,P3Q48,P4Q48,P5Q48
96	Controlling Generative Behavior	P6Q48,P7Q48,P8Q48,P9Q48,P10Q48
97	Prompt Engineering Techniques	P1Q49,P2Q49,P3Q49,P4Q49,P5Q49
98	Using Custom Data	P6Q49,P7Q49,P8Q49,P9Q49,P10Q49
99	Fine-tuning Azure OpenAI Models	P1Q50,P2Q50,P3Q50,P4Q50,P5Q50
100	Integrating Generative AI into Solutions	P6Q50,P7Q50,P8Q50,P9Q50,P10Q50

CONTENTS

PRACTICE TEST 1 - QUESTIONS ONLY

QUESTION 1

You are tasked with implementing a natural language processing (NLP) solution for a customer service application. The solution should enable the application to understand customer queries, extract key information, and provide relevant responses. You need to select the appropriate Azure AI service for this scenario. Which Azure service should you choose? Select all answers that apply.

A) Azure Cognitive Services Language Understanding (LUIS)
B) Azure Bot Services
C) Azure Cognitive Services Text Analytics
D) Azure QnA Maker
E) Azure Machine Learning

QUESTION 2

Your organization is developing a decision support solution to monitor data for anomalies and deliver real-time insights to stakeholders. The solution requires continuous monitoring and automated alerts for deviations from expected patterns. Which Azure AI service should you select to implement the data monitoring aspect effectively?

A) Azure AI Metrics Advisor
B) Azure AI Content Moderator
C) Azure AI Video Indexer
D) Azure AI Text Analytics
E) Azure AI Language Understanding (LUIS)

QUESTION 3

Which Azure CLI command can be used to retrieve diagnostic logging configuration for an Azure AI resource?

```
A) az monitor diagnostic-settings list
B) az monitor diagnostic-settings show
C) az monitor log-profiles list
D) az monitor log-profiles show
E) az monitor metrics list
```

QUESTION 4

Which methods can be used to authenticate to Azure AI Services?

A) SAML token
B) Subscription key
C) Microsoft Entra ID
D) Kerberos
E) Azure Active Directory (AAD)

QUESTION 5

Your organization is planning to deploy a new Azure AI solution to automate the processing of customer inquiries received through various communication channels, including email, chat, and social media. As part of the deployment process, you are tasked with creating an Azure AI resource to host the required services. The solution should be scalable, cost-effective, and comply with Responsible AI principles.

Which steps should you follow to create the Azure AI resource while ensuring scalability, cost optimization, and compliance with Responsible AI principles? Select all answers that apply.

A) Choose an appropriate pricing tier and region for the Azure AI resource.
B) Configure network security settings, including virtual network integration and firewall rules.
C) Define resource tags to categorize and track usage and costs.
D) Specify the required Azure AI services, such as natural language processing and text analytics.
E) Enable encryption at rest and in transit to protect data privacy and security.

QUESTION 6

You need to ensure secure access to Azure AI services from an on-premises network. What is the recommended approach to achieve this while minimizing exposure to the public internet?

A) Configure Azure AD authentication for the services.
B) Set up a VPN gateway between the on-premises network and Azure virtual network.
C) Use shared access signatures (SAS) for authentication.
D) Whitelist the on-premises network IP range in Azure AI services firewall settings.
E) Use OAuth 2.0 authentication with Azure Active Directory.

QUESTION 7

Your team is responsible for managing and securing Azure AI services for a critical project. You need to configure diagnostic logging to ensure comprehensive monitoring and troubleshooting capabilities. Which action is essential for setting up diagnostic logging for Azure AI resources?

A) Enabling Azure Monitor Logs
B) Installing third-party logging agents
C) Disabling diagnostic data collection
D) Configuring Azure Application Insights
E) Utilizing built-in AI diagnostics

QUESTION 8

Your team is responsible for managing the costs of Azure AI services in a large-scale project. Which technique can help estimate and optimize Azure AI service costs effectively?

A) Reviewing past invoices
B) Utilizing Azure Cost Management and Billing
C) Guessing based on project requirements
D) Adjusting resource allocation randomly
E) Ignoring cost implications

QUESTION 9

You are tasked with configuring authentication for an Azure App Services web app named App2. The app needs to authenticate using Microsoft Entra ID with the least administrative effort. What is the most appropriate action to take?

A) Configure App2 to use Azure AD single sign-on (SSO).
B) Enable Azure Active Directory (Azure AD) authentication and configure App2 to use it.
C) Implement OAuth 2.0 authentication with Azure AD and grant App2 access to Microsoft Entra ID.
D) Enable Managed Service Identity (MSI) for App2 and assign RBAC permissions to Microsoft Entra ID.
E) Generate a client secret and store it securely for App2 authentication.

QUESTION 10

Your company is developing a social media platform and wants to ensure user-generated content is appropriately moderated to maintain a positive user experience. As an Azure AI engineer, you are tasked with setting up text moderation using Azure Content Moderator. Which approach aligns best with this requirement?

A) Utilize a basic keyword filter to flag potentially inappropriate content
B) Implement a complex machine learning model for text analysis
C) Manually review all user-generated content without AI assistance
D) Ignore text moderation and rely solely on user reports
E) Combine Azure Content Moderator with custom text classification models for enhanced accuracy

QUESTION 11

Your company is implementing a decision support system (DSS) to analyze customer behavior and provide personalized recommendations in real-time. Which integration strategy ensures seamless connectivity between the DSS and existing databases and analytics services?

A) Implementing Azure Data Factory pipelines for data ingestion and transformation.
B) Utilizing Azure Logic Apps for orchestrating data workflows and triggers.
C) Integrating Azure Event Hubs for real-time data streaming and processing.
D) Leveraging Azure Data Lake Storage for scalable data storage and analytics.
E) Configuring Azure Stream Analytics for near-real-time analytics on streaming data.

QUESTION 12

You are configuring diagnostic logging for an Azure AI Service resource. Which two Azure services are required as prerequisites for diagnostic logging?

A) Log Analytics workspace
B) Azure Cosmos DB for NoSQL account
C) Azure Key Vault
D) Azure SQL database
E) Azure Storage account

QUESTION 13

Your team is tasked with designing a decision support system (DSS) for a rapidly growing e-commerce platform. How should you plan for scalability in the design of the DSS?
Select all answers that apply.

A) Implement distributed computing architecture to handle increasing data volume and processing demands.
B) Utilize Azure Functions for serverless computing to scale automatically based on workload.
C) Design microservices architecture to decouple components and scale independently.
D) Opt for a monolithic architecture to simplify deployment and management at scale.
E) Implement caching mechanisms to improve performance and reduce load on backend services.

QUESTION 14

You are developing an AI-driven solution for an e-commerce platform that requires analyzing product images to extract visual features for recommendation purposes. The solution aims to improve user experience by providing accurate product suggestions based on visual similarity. Which factors should you consider when selecting visual features for image analysis in Azure Computer Vision? Select all answers that apply.

A) Color histograms
B) Texture analysis

C) Object detection
D) Shape detection
E) Facial recognition

QUESTION 15

While developing an AI solution using Azure AI Services containers, you encounter a "Connection Error" message indicating a failure to connect to the Azure AI Services resource. What should you do to troubleshoot and resolve this issue?

A) Confirm that the API key is for the correct region.
B) Confirm that the API key is for the correct resource type.
C) Confirm that the Azure AI Services resource is online.
D) Upgrade the Azure AI Services resource to a higher tier.
E) Check the network configurations and firewall settings to ensure connectivity to the Azure AI Services resource.

QUESTION 16

You are developing an AI solution for a document management system that requires extracting text from images of various documents. Which method is commonly used for text extraction from images, especially when dealing with complex backgrounds and layouts?

A) Optical Character Recognition (OCR)
B) Azure AI Form Recognizer
C) Rule-based parsing
D) Semantic analysis
E) Azure AI Computer Vision API

QUESTION 17

You are developing an image classification model for a retail company. The model needs to accurately classify images of clothing items into various categories. Which approach should you take to design an effective image classification model?

A) Utilize transfer learning with a pre-trained model
B) Train the model from scratch using raw image data
C) Use a shallow neural network for faster training
D) Apply unsupervised learning techniques
E) Implement a rule-based classification system

QUESTION 18

While deploying a language translation solution using Azure AI Translator service, you encounter an error indicating "Resource not available." Which actions should you consider to troubleshoot and resolve this issue?

A) Check if the Azure AI Translator service is enabled in the Azure portal.
B) Review the subscription limits for the Azure AI Translator service.
C) Verify the API endpoint configuration in the application code.
D) Ensure that the correct region is specified for the Azure AI Translator service.
E) Upgrade the Azure AI Translator service to a higher tier.

QUESTION 19

You are tasked with publishing a custom computer vision model developed using Azure AI Vision for integration into an existing web application. What are the necessary steps to ensure successful model publishing and consumption in your application environment?

A) Export the trained model from Azure AI Vision and deploy it directly to the web server.
B) Publish the model as a Docker container and deploy it to Azure Kubernetes Service (AKS).
C) Generate a Docker image of the model and host it on a secure Docker registry.
D) Create an API endpoint for the model using Azure Functions and consume it in the web application.
E) Copy the model files to the web server directory and configure the application to load the model at runtime.

QUESTION 20

Your company is developing an AI-powered traffic management system for a smart city project. The system needs to analyze video feeds from surveillance cameras installed at various intersections to monitor vehicle flow and detect traffic congestion in real-time. You are tasked with selecting the appropriate Azure AI service to implement spatial analysis for people movement to optimize traffic flow. Which Azure AI service should you recommend based on the requirements and the need for accuracy and real-time processing?

A) Azure AI Video Indexer
B) Azure Cognitive Services - Computer Vision
C) Azure Cognitive Services - Video Analyzer
D) Azure AI Vision Spatial Analysis
E) Azure AI Metrics Advisor

QUESTION 21

While working on a natural language processing task, you encounter an API request with the command: `POST https://<resource-name>.cognitiveservices.azure.com/text/analytics/v3.0/languages`. What does this request aim to achieve?

A) Detecting the language used in the provided text.
B) Extracting key phrases from the provided text.
C) Analyzing sentiment in the provided text.
D) Summarizing the provided text.
E) Translating the provided text to multiple languages.

QUESTION 22

Your team is developing a text analysis solution to extract key phrases from customer reviews for a retail company. The solution needs to accurately identify key phrases in various languages and dialects to gain insights into customer preferences and sentiments. Which Azure service should you recommend for implementing the key phrase extraction functionality, considering the need for multilingual support and accuracy?

A) Azure Text Analytics
B) Azure AI Language - Key Phrase Extraction
C) Azure Cognitive Search
D) Azure Machine Learning - Natural Language Processing
E) Azure Translator

QUESTION 23

You are developing an AI solution for a social media analytics platform to analyze customer sentiment. The solution needs to accurately detect nuanced sentiments across various languages. Which approach should you recommend to ensure effective sentiment analysis across different linguistic nuances and cultural contexts?

A) Rule-based sentiment analysis
B) Custom sentiment analysis models

C) Pre-trained sentiment analysis models
D) Frequency-based sentiment analysis
E) Sentiment lexicon-based analysis

QUESTION 24

You are integrating the Azure AI Anomaly Detector service into your application to identify irregular patterns in data. However, you notice that the service is not providing accurate anomaly detection results. What action should you consider to improve the accuracy of anomaly detection?

A) Increasing the confidence threshold for anomaly detection.
B) Adjusting the sensitivity parameters of the anomaly detection model.
C) Training the anomaly detection model with more historical data.
D) Enabling real-time anomaly detection mode.
E) Switching to a different anomaly detection algorithm.

QUESTION 25

You are developing a real-time speech-to-text (STT) application that will be used in a call center environment. The application needs to accurately transcribe customer calls, including handling various accents and dialects. Which technique can improve the accuracy of speech recognition in this scenario?

A) Implementing speaker diarization to differentiate between speakers.
B) Utilizing transfer learning with a pre-trained model on a diverse dataset.
C) Increasing the audio sampling rate for higher fidelity.
D) Applying post-processing techniques such as language modeling.
E) Using reinforcement learning to adapt to different speech patterns.

QUESTION 26

You are developing a custom speech recognition solution for an enterprise application. The application requires accurate recognition of technical jargon and domain-specific terms. Which approach is most suitable for improving the accuracy of the custom speech model?

A) Collecting a diverse dataset encompassing various accents and dialects.
B) Incorporating domain-specific vocabulary and language models.
C) Utilizing generic pre-trained speech models without customization.
D) Implementing a low-quality audio filter to reduce background noise.
E) Training the model with non-relevant data to increase variability.

QUESTION 27

You are developing an application that utilizes Azure AI Vision to identify objects in images. However, you notice that the current implementation struggles with accurately detecting small objects. What should you consider to enhance the performance of object detection?

A) Enabling object tracking for moving objects.
B) Switching to a more advanced object detection algorithm.
C) Increasing the image resolution for input images.
D) Fine-tuning the object detection model with additional labeled data.
E) Adjusting the confidence threshold for object detection.

QUESTION 28

Your company is expanding globally and needs to translate a large volume of technical documents into multiple languages while preserving the original format and layout. Which Azure service should you recommend to automate this document translation workflow efficiently?

A) Azure Cognitive Services Translator Text
B) Azure Cognitive Services Language Understanding (LUIS)
C) Azure Cognitive Services Text Analytics
D) Azure Cognitive Services Speech Service
E) Azure Cognitive Services Vision Service

QUESTION 29

Your company is developing a custom translation model for a legal firm that frequently deals with contracts and legal documents in multiple languages. Which approach should your team adopt to ensure the accuracy and effectiveness of the custom translation model?

A) Utilize prebuilt translation models from Azure AI Translator service
B) Collect and incorporate domain-specific terminology and phrases
C) Train the model with general-purpose language datasets
D) Use unsupervised learning techniques for model development
E) Implement machine translation without fine-tuning for specific domains

QUESTION 30

You are investigating an issue with an Azure app that utilizes Azure AI Text Analytics for sentiment analysis. Users report inconsistent sentiment scores for similar text inputs. What could be a potential cause of this inconsistency?

A) Variability in text preprocessing techniques applied by the app.
B) Fluctuations in the Azure AI Text Analytics service availability.
C) Inadequate tokenization settings used by the Azure AI Text Analytics service.
D) Outdated version of the Azure AI Text Analytics SDK being used in the app.
E) Insufficient permissions granted to the Azure AI Text Analytics service.

QUESTION 31

You are tasked with training a language understanding model for a customer service chatbot. The model must accurately identify user intents, extract relevant entities, and provide appropriate responses. Which criteria are crucial for successful language model training in this scenario?
Select all answers that apply.

A) Training data diversity and quality
B) Regular model evaluation and iteration
C) Utilizing transfer learning techniques
D) Leveraging pre-trained embeddings
E) Increasing model complexity with more layers

QUESTION 32

You are tasked with optimizing a language understanding model used in a customer support chatbot application. The current model performance is suboptimal, leading to frequent misclassifications of user queries. What techniques should you employ to enhance the model's performance and minimize false positives and negatives in this scenario?
Select all answers that apply.

A) Implement transfer learning to leverage pre-trained models

B) Fine-tune the model on domain-specific data
C) Apply data augmentation techniques to increase training data diversity
D) Introduce regularization methods to prevent overfitting
E) Implement ensemble learning with multiple model architectures

QUESTION 33

You are tasked with implementing a sentiment analysis feature in your Azure app to analyze customer feedback. The app must provide sentiment analysis in real-time and integrate seamlessly with other Azure services. Which Azure service and API combination should you use to meet these requirements effectively?

A) Azure Cognitive Search > Language API
B) Azure Speech Service > Decision API
C) Azure AI Language Service > Text Analytics API
D) Azure Content Moderator > Language API
E) Azure QnA Maker > Vision API

QUESTION 34

What efficient methods can Azure AI engineers employ for importing content sources in a question answering solution?
Select all answers that apply.

A) Manually upload files from local storage
B) Utilize Azure Blob Storage for large-scale data import
C) Integrate with Azure SQL Database for structured data
D) Directly connect to Azure Cosmos DB for real-time data retrieval
E) Ignore source import and rely on manual entry for content management

QUESTION 35

What steps are crucial for publishing and updating knowledge bases in a question answering solution to ensure high availability and reliability?
Select all answers that apply.

A) Implement version control for tracking changes
B) Establish automated deployment pipelines for seamless updates
C) Conduct thorough testing before publishing new content
D) Monitor usage and performance metrics post-publishing
E) Rollback mechanisms for reverting to previous versions when necessary

QUESTION 36

You are tasked with deploying a custom computer vision model in an Azure container environment. Which options should you select to complete the provided bash statement?
Select all answers that apply.

```
A) "mcr.microsoft.com/azure-cognitive-services/vision/customvision"
B) "--memory 183 --cpus 8"
C) "--eula accept"
D) "--billing Hourly"
E) "--api-key {API_KEY}"
```

QUESTION 37

You are tasked with fine-tuning a pre-built language model on Azure to improve its performance in understanding

technical jargon specific to your industry. Which of the following strategies should you consider?
Select all answers that apply.

A) Utilize transfer learning techniques
B) Increase the model's batch size during training
C) Adjust the learning rate schedule
D) Incorporate additional domain-specific training data
E) Reduce the number of training epochs

QUESTION 38

Your company is developing a conversational AI solution using Azure Bot Framework integrated with natural language processing (NLP) models. As part of designing the conversational flows, you need to handle complex user interactions effectively. What approach should you take to achieve this?
Select all answers that apply.

A) Implement multi-turn dialogues for context retention
B) Utilize pre-built Azure Bot Framework templates
C) Use reinforcement learning for dynamic dialogue management
D) Implement rule-based intent recognition for precise interaction handling
E) Integrate sentiment analysis for emotion-aware responses

QUESTION 39

You are tasked with implementing a speech-to-text feature in your Azure application using the Azure Speech service. Complete the provided code snippet to achieve this task effectively:

```
string audioFile = "(audio file path)";
var config = SpeechConfig.FromSubscription("YourSubscriptionKey", "YourServiceRegion");
using var audioInput = AudioConfig.FromWavFileInput(audioFile);
using var recognizer = new SpeechRecognizer(config, audioInput);
var result = await recognizer.RecognizeOnceAsync();
```

Select all answers that apply.

```
A) SpeechRecognizer(config, audioInput)
B) SpeechRecognitionMode.Conversation
C) SpeechRecognitionLanguage.English
D) result.Text
E) SpeechConfig.FromEndpoint(new Uri("YourEndpointURL"))
```

QUESTION 40

Your company is developing a social media monitoring tool that needs to perform advanced sentiment analysis to gauge public opinion accurately. Which Azure AI service would you recommend integrating into the tool to address the challenges of sarcasm, irony, and context in sentiment analysis effectively?

A) Azure Text Analytics
B) Azure Language Understanding (LUIS)
C) Azure Cognitive Search
D) Azure AI Translator service
E) Azure AI Language Service

QUESTION 41

Your company is planning to implement an Azure Cognitive Search solution to enable efficient search capabilities for a large database of academic research papers. As the Azure AI engineer responsible for provisioning the Cognitive Search resource, you need to select the appropriate pricing tier that balances cost and features. Which pricing tier should you choose to meet the requirements?

A) Free Tier
B) Basic Tier
C) Standard Tier
D) Storage Optimized Tier
E) Enterprise Tier

QUESTION 42

You are developing an application that needs to analyze text to detect entities, including Personally Identifiable Information (PII). Which Azure AI service should you use to achieve this?

```
A) CustomVisionPredictionClient
B) TextAnalyticsClient
C) TranslatorTextClient
D) FormRecognizerClient
E) QnAMakerClient
```

QUESTION 43

You are developing a comprehensive Azure Cognitive Search solution for a large e-commerce platform. As part of the solution, you need to enhance the search capabilities by integrating custom skills. The custom skills will involve processing product descriptions to extract relevant features for better search results. Which approach should you use to develop and deploy custom skills in Azure Cognitive Search?

A) Implement custom skills as Azure Functions
B) Develop custom skills using Azure Logic Apps
C) Use Azure Machine Learning to develop custom skills
D) Create custom skills using Azure App Service
E) Develop custom skills using Azure Data Factory

QUESTION 44

Your company is developing an e-commerce platform and plans to implement Azure Cognitive Search for product search functionality. As part of the implementation, you need to craft effective search queries to ensure accurate and relevant search results for users. Which approach should you take to craft effective search queries in Azure Cognitive Search?

A) Utilize fuzzy search to handle spelling variations
B) Apply phonetic matching for sound-alike words
C) Implement synonym maps to expand search results
D) Use regular expressions for advanced pattern matching
E) Leverage proximity search for phrase matching

QUESTION 45

Which method in Azure Text Analytics is used to determine the sentiment of text?

```
A) TextAnalyticsClient
B) SentimentAnalysisClient
```

```
C) LanguageAnalyticsClient
D) TextSentimentClient
E) AnalyzeTextClient
```

QUESTION 46

You are tasked with provisioning an Azure OpenAI Service resource for a machine learning project. Which steps are essential for successfully setting up the service?
Select all answers that apply.

A) Choose the appropriate pricing tier based on project requirements.
B) Specify the region for deployment to optimize latency.
C) Configure security policies to restrict access to authorized users.
D) Define usage quotas to control resource consumption.
E) Enable multi-factor authentication for enhanced security.

QUESTION 47

Your team is implementing an AI-driven content creation system for a marketing campaign using Azure OpenAI Service. To ensure the generated content aligns with brand guidelines, which approach should you prioritize?

A) Enforcing strict character limits on generated text.
B) Incorporating brand-specific keywords in the input prompts.
C) Fine-tuning the language model on historical marketing materials.
D) Using reinforcement learning to optimize content for engagement.
E) Applying sentiment analysis to filter generated content.

QUESTION 48

When using Azure AI services for PM (Personally Identifiable Information) detection, which combination of statements is true?

A) Statement I: You can use Language Studio or REST API for PM detection.
B) Statement II: You can submit data in an unstructured format for PM detection.
C) Statement III: You can retain data for a certain number of hours while using the synchronous feature during PM detection.
D) Statement I, Statement II
E) Statement II, Statement III

QUESTION 49

As part of a project to develop a generative AI model for creating customized travel itineraries, you are responsible for designing prompts to guide the model's decision-making process. To ensure the generated itineraries are comprehensive and tailored to user preferences, which approach should you prioritize when crafting the prompts?
Select all answers that apply.

A) Including destination preferences, travel dates, and activity interests to guide itinerary planning in the prompts.
B) Providing budget constraints and accommodation preferences to optimize the cost and comfort of the generated travel plans.
C) Incorporating transportation options and journey durations to facilitate seamless travel logistics and planning.
D) Leveraging user feedback on previous travel suggestions to refine and adjust the prompt structures for improved model understanding.
E) Experimenting with different prompt formulations to evaluate their impact on the variety and richness of generated travel itineraries.

QUESTION 50

You are designing an AI-driven recommendation system for an e-commerce platform that utilizes generative AI to suggest personalized product bundles to customers. Which architectural consideration should you prioritize to ensure seamless integration of generative AI into the solution while meeting scalability requirements?
Select all answers that apply.

A) Implementing a microservices architecture to modularize generative AI components and enable independent scaling of services.
B) Deploying a serverless architecture using Azure Functions to automatically scale resources based on demand.
C) Leveraging Azure Kubernetes Service (AKS) to orchestrate containerized generative AI models and manage resource allocation dynamically.
D) Utilizing Azure Batch to schedule and execute large-scale generative AI training jobs across distributed computing resources.
E) Implementing Azure Data Factory to orchestrate data pipelines and facilitate seamless data ingestion for generative AI models.

PRACTICE TEST 1 - ANSWERS ONLY

QUESTION 1

Answer - [A, D] Azure Cognitive Services Language Understanding (LUIS), Azure QnA Maker

Option B - Azure Bot Services: While Azure Bot Services can be used for building conversational interfaces, it may not provide the necessary NLP capabilities for understanding and extracting key information from customer queries.
Option C - Azure Cognitive Services Text Analytics: Text Analytics focuses more on sentiment analysis, language detection, and key phrase extraction, rather than understanding user intents in natural language.
Option E - Azure Machine Learning: Azure Machine Learning provides a platform for building, training, and deploying machine learning models, but it may require more customization for NLP tasks.
Option A - Azure Cognitive Services Language Understanding (LUIS): LUIS is specifically designed for language understanding, enabling the application to identify intents and extract entities from user queries, making it suitable for the customer service application scenario.
Option D - Azure QnA Maker: QnA Maker allows you to create question and answer pairs to build a knowledge base, which can be utilized for providing responses to frequently asked questions, complementing the NLP capabilities provided by LUIS.

You should choose LUIS for language understanding and QnA Maker for knowledge-based responses in customer service applications. Keep in mind that Text Analytics and Azure Bot Services may not provide the complete NLP capabilities required for this specific scenario.

Avoid confusing Azure Bot Services with NLP tools like LUIS and QnA Maker. Stay cautioned that Text Analytics focuses more on analyzing text, not intent identification, which is critical for handling customer queries.

QUESTION 2

Answer - [A] Azure AI Metrics Advisor

Option B - Azure AI Content Moderator: Designed for content moderation tasks such as detecting offensive content, not suitable for data monitoring.
Option C - Azure AI Video Indexer: Used for extracting insights from videos, not tailored for continuous data monitoring.
Option D - Azure AI Text Analytics: Primarily for text analysis tasks like sentiment analysis, not suited for data monitoring.
Option E - Azure AI Language Understanding (LUIS): Focused on building conversational AI applications, not intended for data monitoring.

EXAM FOCUS	*Always remember to use Azure AI Metrics Advisor for real-time data monitoring and anomaly detection. Make sure the solution is set up to continuously monitor data streams to detect deviations early.*
CAUTION ALERT	*Stay alert to not mistakenly select services like Video Indexer or Text Analytics for tasks that require continuous data monitoring, as they do not provide the real-time capabilities needed.*

QUESTION 3

Answer - B) az monitor diagnostic-settings show

Option A - Incorrect. This command lists diagnostic settings for monitor resources, not specifically for Azure AI resources. Option C - Incorrect. This command lists log profiles, not diagnostic settings. Option D - Incorrect. This command shows log profiles, not diagnostic settings. Option E - Incorrect. This command lists metrics, not diagnostic settings.

EXAM FOCUS	*You need to use the az monitor diagnostic-settings show command to retrieve diagnostic settings for Azure AI resources. Keep in mind that this command specifically helps monitor logs and performance.*
CAUTION ALERT	*Stay clear of options like az monitor log-profiles list and az monitor metrics list—they do not provide the specific diagnostic information you're looking for.*

QUESTION 4

Answer - B) Subscription key
Answer - E) Azure Active Directory (AAD)

Option A - Incorrect. SAML tokens are not used for authentication to Azure AI Services. Option C - Incorrect. Microsoft Entra ID is a fictitious term and not a valid authentication method. Option D - Incorrect. Kerberos is not used for authentication to Azure AI Services.

EXAM FOCUS	*You should know that Azure AI services typically use a subscription key and Azure Active Directory (AAD) for authentication. Make sure you avoid outdated or incorrect methods like Kerberos.*
CAUTION ALERT	*Avoid confusing SAML token and Kerberos with valid Azure AI authentication methods. Stay alert to false options such as "Microsoft Entra ID," which is not a real service.*

QUESTION 5

Answer - [A, C, D, E]

Option A - Choose an appropriate pricing tier and region for the Azure AI resource: Correct. Selecting the right pricing tier and region ensures cost optimization and scalability of the Azure AI resource.
Option B - Configure network security settings, including virtual network integration and firewall rules: While important for security, this choice does not directly relate to creating the Azure AI resource or ensuring scalability and cost optimization.
Option C - Define resource tags to categorize and track usage and costs: Correct. Resource tagging facilitates cost tracking and management, aligning with cost optimization objectives.
Option D - Specify the required Azure AI services, such as natural language processing and text analytics: Correct. Specifying the necessary services ensures that the Azure AI resource meets the solution requirements while complying with Responsible AI principles.
Option E - Enable encryption at rest and in transit to protect data privacy and security: Correct. Enabling encryption enhances data security and privacy, supporting Responsible AI practices.

EXAM FOCUS	*You need to define resource tags and specify necessary AI services like NLP and Text Analytics to ensure cost-effectiveness. Make sure you select the appropriate pricing tier to match the scale of your application.*
CAUTION ALERT	*Stay cautioned against neglecting encryption requirements. Avoid thinking that configuring network security is the only step; scalability and cost optimization should be part of your planning.*

QUESTION 6

Answer - B) Set up a VPN gateway between the on-premises network and Azure virtual network.

Option A - Incorrect. Azure AD authentication may not provide direct network-level access control between on-premises and Azure networks. Option C - Incorrect. Shared access signatures are typically used for limited-time access to specific resources, not for network-level authentication. Option D - Incorrect. While whitelisting IP ranges can enhance security, it may not provide the necessary secure network connection between on-premises and Azure environments. Option E - Incorrect. OAuth 2.0 authentication with Azure AD may provide user-level authentication but does not establish a secure network connection between on-premises and Azure networks.

EXAM FOCUS	*Always remember to use a VPN gateway for secure access between on-premises networks and Azure AI resources. Keep in mind this minimizes exposure to the public internet while maintaining security.*
CAUTION ALERT	*Stay clear of relying solely on IP whitelisting or Azure AD for network-level security. Avoid overlooking the importance of a secure, direct network connection between environments.*

QUESTION 7

Answer - [A] Enabling Azure Monitor Logs.

Enabling Azure Monitor Logs - Configuring diagnostic logging by enabling Azure Monitor Logs allows for the collection and analysis of logs from Azure AI resources, providing insights for monitoring, troubleshooting, and performance optimization. Options B, C, D, and E are incorrect as they do not align with best practices for setting up diagnostic logging.

EXAM FOCUS	*You should enable Azure Monitor Logs for comprehensive diagnostic logging. Make sure you're collecting logs from all relevant Azure AI services to enhance troubleshooting and performance monitoring.*
CAUTION ALERT	*Stay alert to the fact that third-party logging agents or disabling diagnostic data collection are not best practices. Avoid thinking that Application Insights alone is sufficient for AI-specific diagnostic logging.*

QUESTION 8

Answer - [B] Utilizing Azure Cost Management and Billing.

Utilizing Azure Cost Management and Billing - Azure Cost Management and Billing provides insights into resource usage, cost trends, and recommendations for optimizing Azure AI service costs, enabling informed decision-making and efficient cost management. Options A, C, D, and E lack precision and may lead to inefficient cost optimization.

EXAM FOCUS	*Always remember to use Azure Cost Management and Billing for accurate cost estimation and optimization. Make sure to regularly review the cost trends and make data-driven decisions.*
CAUTION ALERT	*Avoid relying on past invoices or guessing for cost estimation. Stay clear of practices like adjusting resource allocation randomly, which could lead to inefficiencies and increased costs.*

QUESTION 9

Answer - D) Enable Managed Service Identity (MSI) for App2 and assign RBAC permissions to Microsoft Entra ID.

Option A - Incorrect. Azure AD SSO may provide centralized authentication but may not align with the requirement to use Microsoft Entra ID. Option B - Incorrect. While Azure AD authentication is a valid approach, enabling MSI with RBAC permissions directly meets the requirement with minimal administrative overhead. Option C - Incorrect. OAuth 2.0 authentication with Azure AD may not directly support Microsoft Entra ID. Option E - Incorrect. Storing client secrets may introduce additional security risks and administrative overhead.

EXAM FOCUS	*You should enable Managed Service Identity (MSI) for App2 to minimize administrative overhead while ensuring secure authentication. Keep in mind that RBAC permissions can further enhance this setup for Entra ID.*
CAUTION ALERT	*Avoid using client secrets unnecessarily, as this adds administrative complexity. Stay alert that SSO might not fully meet your specific requirements for Microsoft Entra ID.*

QUESTION 10

Answer - [E] Combine Azure Content Moderator with custom text classification models for enhanced accuracy.

Combine Azure Content Moderator with custom text classification models for enhanced accuracy - Integrating Azure Content Moderator with custom text classification models allows for fine-tuning moderation criteria and handling false positives/negatives effectively, unlike options A, C, D, which lack automation or rely on less accurate methods.

EXAM FOCUS	*You can enhance the accuracy of content moderation by combining Azure Content Moderator with custom text classification models. Keep in mind this approach helps reduce false positives and negatives in flagged content.*
CAUTION ALERT	*Stay clear of simplistic keyword filtering, which can result in many false positives or missed inappropriate content. Avoid relying solely on manual content review or user reports for effective moderation.*

QUESTION 11

Answer - [A] Implementing Azure Data Factory pipelines for data ingestion and transformation.

Azure Data Factory provides a managed service for orchestrating and automating data movement and transformation, ensuring seamless integration between the decision support system and existing data sources. Options B, C, D, and E focus on different Azure services but may not provide the same level of integration capabilities required for a decision support system.

EXAM FOCUS	*You should implement Azure Data Factory pipelines when the DSS requires seamless data integration with existing systems. Keep in mind that Azure Data Factory excels at orchestrating and automating ETL processes, providing real-time data ingestion and transformation capabilities for decision support systems.*
CAUTION ALERT	*Stay clear of relying on Azure Event Hubs or Data Lake Storage if your primary requirement is integration and orchestration of data workflows. They are focused on real-time event streaming and scalable storage, respectively, not seamless data integration.*

QUESTION 12

Answer - A) Log Analytics workspace
E) Azure Storage account

Option B - Incorrect. Azure Cosmos DB is not a prerequisite for diagnostic logging. Option C - Incorrect. While Azure Key Vault can be beneficial for managing secrets, it is not a prerequisite for diagnostic logging. Option D - Incorrect. Azure SQL database is not a prerequisite for diagnostic logging.

EXAM FOCUS	*You should always ensure you have both a Log Analytics workspace and an Azure Storage account as prerequisites for diagnostic logging. Keep in mind that Log Analytics is essential for monitoring, while Storage accounts retain the diagnostic data.*
CAUTION ALERT	*Avoid confusing Azure Cosmos DB or SQL Database with services required for diagnostic logging. Stay alert that these are not used for logging configurations but for data storage and processing.*

QUESTION 13

Answer - [A, B, C, E] Options A, B, C, and E address planning for scalability in DSS design.

Option A suggests distributed computing to handle increasing demands, option B recommends serverless computing for automatic scaling, option C proposes microservices for independent scaling, and option E involves caching mechanisms for performance improvement. Option D, monolithic architecture, is not conducive to scalability compared to microservices.

EXAM FOCUS	*You need to plan for scalability using distributed computing and microservices architecture. Always remember that Azure Functions can auto-scale based on workload, making it ideal for fluctuating demands. Caching is critical for performance optimization in a high-traffic environment.*

CAUTION ALERT *Avoid monolithic architectures if scalability is your priority. Stay clear of this approach, as it limits independent scaling of services and makes deployment more complex in large-scale systems.*

QUESTION 14

Answer - [A, B, C] Options A, B, and C are relevant factors to consider when selecting visual features for image analysis in Azure Computer Vision. Color histograms capture color distribution, texture analysis assesses surface patterns, and object detection identifies objects within images, all essential for accurate product recommendation based on visual similarity.

Options D and E are less relevant in this scenario. Shape detection (Option D) focuses on identifying specific geometric shapes, which may not be as crucial for product recommendation. Facial recognition (Option E) is not directly applicable unless the solution requires detecting faces for personalized recommendations.

EXAM FOCUS *Make sure to focus on using color histograms, texture analysis, and object detection for visual feature extraction in Azure Computer Vision when creating product recommendations. You can significantly improve accuracy by selecting the right visual features relevant to the recommendation scenario.*

CAUTION ALERT *Stay cautioned not to prioritize shape detection or facial recognition in scenarios that focus on product similarity. Avoid these as they are less relevant to the core task of product recommendations based on visual features.*

QUESTION 15

Answer - E) Check the network configurations and firewall settings to ensure connectivity to the Azure AI Services resource.

Option A - Incorrect. API key region mismatch usually leads to authentication errors rather than connection errors. Option B - Incorrect. API key resource type mismatch typically results in authorization errors. Option D - Incorrect. Upgrading the resource tier does not directly address connectivity issues. Option C - Incorrect. While verifying the resource's status is important, network configurations and firewall settings are more relevant to resolving connectivity problems.

EXAM FOCUS *You should always start by checking the network configurations and firewall settings when facing connection issues with Azure AI services. Keep in mind that these are common causes of connectivity failures when working with AI service containers.*

CAUTION ALERT *Stay clear of assuming that upgrading the service tier will resolve connection issues. Avoid troubleshooting API key region or type unless authentication errors are the problem, not connectivity.*

QUESTION 16

Answer - [A] Optical Character Recognition (OCR)

A) Optical Character Recognition (OCR) - Correct. OCR is a widely-used method for extracting text from images, particularly in scenarios involving complex backgrounds and layouts. It can accurately identify and convert text within images into machine-readable text, making it suitable for document management systems.
B) Azure AI Form Recognizer - Incorrect. While Azure AI Form Recognizer is designed for extracting structured data from forms and documents, it is not primarily focused on text extraction from images with complex backgrounds.
C) Rule-based parsing - Incorrect. Rule-based parsing involves defining patterns and rules to extract specific information from text, which may not be suitable for handling the complexity of text extraction from images.
D) Semantic analysis - Incorrect. Semantic analysis focuses on understanding the meaning and context of text, rather than extracting text from images.
E) Azure AI Computer Vision API - Incorrect. While Azure AI Computer Vision API offers various image analysis capabilities, including text recognition, it may not provide the level of accuracy needed for text extraction from images

with complex backgrounds.

EXAM FOCUS	*Always remember that OCR is the go-to method for extracting text from images with complex backgrounds and layouts. You can rely on OCR for highly accurate text extraction in document management systems.*
CAUTION ALERT	*Avoid assuming that Azure Form Recognizer is the best solution for text extraction in this scenario. Stay alert to the difference between extracting structured data from forms and raw text from images.*

QUESTION 17

Answer - [A) Utilize transfer learning with a pre-trained model]

Transfer learning with a pre-trained model is an effective approach for image classification tasks, especially when dealing with limited data.
B) Training the model from scratch may require a significant amount of labeled data, which might not be feasible in this scenario.
C) Shallow neural networks may not capture the complex features of clothing items adequately.
D) Unsupervised learning is not suitable for this supervised classification task.
E) Rule-based systems may lack the flexibility to handle diverse clothing items.

EXAM FOCUS	*You should consider using transfer learning with a pre-trained model for image classification, especially when dealing with limited datasets. Keep in mind that this approach saves time and improves accuracy for tasks like classifying clothing items.*
CAUTION ALERT	*Avoid training a model from scratch if data is limited. Stay cautioned against shallow neural networks, which may not capture the complexity of image features adequately.*

QUESTION 18

Answer - [A] Check if the Azure AI Translator service is enabled in the Azure portal.

Option A - Verifying if the Azure AI Translator service is enabled in the Azure portal is crucial as it ensures the availability of the service. Reviewing subscription limits (Option B) is important but may not directly resolve the issue of the service being unavailable. Checking the API endpoint configuration (Option C) is necessary but may not be the root cause of the error. Ensuring the correct region is specified (Option D) is relevant but assumes the service is provisioned. Upgrading the Azure AI Translator service (Option E) may not address the issue if the service is not enabled in the first place.

EXAM FOCUS	*Make sure to verify that the Azure AI Translator service is enabled in the Azure portal when encountering resource availability errors. You should check service status before troubleshooting other aspects like API endpoints or regions.*
CAUTION ALERT	*Stay cautioned not to jump to subscription limits or service tier upgrades when the core issue might be service activation. Avoid over-complicating the troubleshooting process by ignoring service enablement.*

QUESTION 19

Answer - B) Publish the model as a Docker container and deploy it to Azure Kubernetes Service (AKS).

Option A - Exporting and deploying directly to the web server may not provide scalability and flexibility needed for a production environment.
Option C - Hosting a Docker image on a secure registry is relevant but does not address the deployment environment.
Option D - Using Azure Functions for model deployment is suitable but may not leverage containerization benefits for scalability.
Option E - Manual deployment to the web server lacks scalability and maintainability compared to containerization.

EXAM FOCUS	*You should publish custom computer vision models as Docker containers and deploy them to Azure Kubernetes Service (AKS) for scalability and flexibility. Keep in mind that containerization offers an*

CAUTION ALERT	*efficient way to handle model deployment in production environments.* *Avoid directly deploying models to a web server without containerization. Stay alert to the scalability limitations and management issues that come with manual deployment compared to AKS.*

QUESTION 20

Answer - D) Azure AI Vision Spatial Analysis

Option A - Azure AI Video Indexer focuses more on extracting insights and metadata from videos rather than real-time spatial analysis for traffic management.
Option B - While Azure Cognitive Services - Computer Vision offers image analysis capabilities, it may not provide specific features for spatial analysis and traffic optimization.
Option C - Azure Cognitive Services - Video Analyzer is geared towards real-time video processing but may lack the precision required for detailed spatial analysis.
Option E - Azure AI Metrics Advisor is designed for monitoring and analyzing metrics data rather than real-time video analysis for traffic management.

EXAM FOCUS	*Always remember to use Azure AI Vision Spatial Analysis for real-time processing and analysis of video feeds in traffic management systems. Keep in mind that this service is specifically designed for spatial analysis, making it ideal for monitoring vehicle flow and congestion.*
CAUTION ALERT	*Avoid selecting services like Video Indexer or Metrics Advisor for traffic flow analysis. Stay clear of relying on video metadata extraction services when you need real-time spatial analysis capabilities.*

QUESTION 21

Answer - [A] Detecting the language used in the provided text.

Option A - This API request is intended to identify the language used in the input text. It does not perform tasks such as key phrase extraction (Option B), sentiment analysis (Option C), text summarization (Option D), or translation (Option E).

EXAM FOCUS	*You should remember that this API request aims to detect the language of the input text, which is critical in multilingual applications. Keep in mind that this request does not analyze sentiment or extract key phrases.*
CAUTION ALERT	*Stay cautioned not to confuse this API endpoint with others that focus on sentiment analysis or translation. Avoid assuming it performs more complex tasks like key phrase extraction or summarization.*

QUESTION 22

Answer - B) Azure AI Language - Key Phrase Extraction

Option A - While Azure Text Analytics provides key phrase extraction, it may not offer the same level of language support and customization as Azure AI Language.
Option C - Azure Cognitive Search is primarily for indexing and querying structured data, not for text analysis like key phrase extraction.
Option D - While Azure Machine Learning can be used for natural language processing, it requires custom model development, which might not be the most efficient solution for this scenario.
Option E - Azure Translator focuses on translation rather than key phrase extraction, making it less suitable for this specific requirement.

EXAM FOCUS	*You should consider Azure AI Language - Key Phrase Extraction for multilingual support in customer reviews. Keep in mind that this service provides enhanced language support compared to general Text Analytics, especially when working with various dialects.*

CAUTION ALERT	*Avoid using services like Azure Cognitive Search, which is primarily for search functionality, not text analysis. Stay clear of Azure Translator, which focuses on translation, not key phrase extraction.*

QUESTION 23

Answer - [B] Custom sentiment analysis models.

Custom sentiment analysis models can be trained on domain-specific data, allowing for nuanced sentiment analysis across different languages and cultural contexts. Pre-trained models may not capture domain-specific nuances effectively. Rule-based and lexicon-based approaches may lack the flexibility to adapt to varying linguistic nuances and cultural contexts. Frequency-based analysis may oversimplify sentiment detection.

EXAM FOCUS	*You need to train custom sentiment analysis models for domain-specific accuracy across different languages and cultural contexts. Always remember that pre-trained models may not capture nuanced sentiments effectively.*
CAUTION ALERT	*Stay alert to the limitations of rule-based or frequency-based sentiment analysis, which may oversimplify complex linguistic nuances. Avoid relying on lexicon-based methods for comprehensive sentiment analysis.*

QUESTION 24

Answer - [C] Training the anomaly detection model with more historical data.

Option C - Training the anomaly detection model with more historical data can improve its accuracy by providing a richer dataset for learning patterns and anomalies. Increasing the confidence threshold (Option A) might filter out valid anomalies, while adjusting sensitivity parameters (Option B) may not address underlying data quality issues. Enabling real-time detection (Option D) focuses on timing rather than accuracy. Switching algorithms (Option E) is a significant change that may or may not improve accuracy without addressing data adequacy.

EXAM FOCUS	*Make sure to train the anomaly detection model with sufficient historical data to improve accuracy. You can enhance performance by providing more data for the model to learn from.*
CAUTION ALERT	*Avoid solely increasing sensitivity or confidence thresholds without addressing underlying data quality issues. Stay clear of assuming that real-time mode will improve accuracy if the historical data is insufficient.*

QUESTION 25

Answer - B) Utilizing transfer learning with a pre-trained model on a diverse dataset.

Option A - Speaker diarization helps in identifying different speakers but may not directly improve accuracy in transcribing diverse accents.

Option B - Correct. Transfer learning with a pre-trained model on diverse data can enhance accuracy by leveraging knowledge from various accents and dialects.

Option C - While increasing the sampling rate can improve audio quality, it may not specifically address accent variations.

Option D - Post-processing techniques like language modeling can refine transcriptions but may not address accent challenges directly.

Option E - Reinforcement learning can adapt over time but might not be efficient for real-time speech transcription in a call center setting.

EXAM FOCUS	*You should leverage transfer learning with a pre-trained model on diverse datasets to handle various accents in real-time speech-to-text applications. Keep in mind this significantly improves recognition of diverse dialects.*
CAUTION	*Avoid assuming that increasing the audio sampling rate will fully resolve accent challenges. Stay*

ALERT	*cautioned not to rely solely on post-processing techniques, which may not directly address transcription accuracy for different accents.*

QUESTION 26

Answer - [B] Incorporating domain-specific vocabulary and language models.

Option B provides the most appropriate solution by incorporating domain-specific vocabulary and language models, which are crucial for accurate recognition of technical jargon and domain-specific terms. Option A might help in handling accents and dialects but does not address the specific requirement of technical terms. Option C is not recommended as generic models may not perform well for domain-specific applications. Option D is unrelated to improving model accuracy. Option E is incorrect as including non-relevant data could lead to overfitting and reduced performance.

EXAM FOCUS	*You need to incorporate domain-specific vocabulary and language models to accurately recognize technical jargon in speech recognition tasks. Always remember that tailoring the model to your specific use case greatly enhances recognition performance.*
CAUTION ALERT	*Avoid relying on generic pre-trained models, which might not handle specialized terminology well. Stay clear of including non-relevant data in training, as this could degrade model performance.*

QUESTION 27

Answer - [C] Increasing the image resolution for input images.

Option C - Increasing the image resolution for input images can improve the model's ability to detect small objects by providing more detailed visual information. Enabling object tracking (Option A) focuses on dynamic objects and may not directly address the issue of object detection accuracy. Switching algorithms (Option B) is a significant change and might not necessarily solve the problem. Fine-tuning with additional data (Option D) can help but may not be as effective as improving the input quality. Adjusting confidence thresholds (Option E) can filter out detections but does not address the underlying issue of object size.

EXAM FOCUS	*Make sure to increase the image resolution when detecting small objects in images. Keep in mind that higher resolution provides more detail for accurate detection in Azure AI Vision applications.*
CAUTION ALERT	*Avoid switching algorithms prematurely. Stay cautioned that adjusting confidence thresholds will not resolve detection issues caused by low image resolution or insufficient data.*

QUESTION 28

Answer - [A] Azure Cognitive Services Translator Text

Option A is correct because Azure Cognitive Services Translator Text offers automated document translation capabilities while maintaining the original format and layout, making it suitable for large-scale document translation projects. Options B, C, D, and E are not designed specifically for document translation.

EXAM FOCUS	*You should recommend Azure Cognitive Services Translator Text for large-scale document translation projects. Keep in mind that it preserves the original layout and format, which is essential for translating technical documents.*
CAUTION ALERT	*Stay clear of services like LUIS or Text Analytics, which are not designed for document translation. Avoid relying on services focused on language understanding or text analysis when document formatting is critical.*

QUESTION 29

Answer - [B] Collect and incorporate domain-specific terminology and phrases

Explanation: B) Incorporating industry-specific terminology and phrases ensures that the translation model accurately captures the nuances of legal language, enhancing translation accuracy. A) While prebuilt models provide a starting point, they may not capture industry-specific terminology effectively. C) Training with general-purpose datasets may lead to inaccuracies in domain-specific translations. D) Unsupervised learning may not adequately capture the complexity and nuances of legal language. E) Machine translation without fine-tuning lacks the precision required for legal documents.

EXAM FOCUS	*You need to incorporate domain-specific terminology into your custom translation model to ensure accuracy for legal documents. Always remember that industry-specific terms are crucial for specialized translations.*
CAUTION ALERT	*Stay cautioned against using general-purpose language datasets. Avoid unsupervised learning, as it may not capture the complexity and precision required for legal translations.*

QUESTION 30

Answer - [A] Variability in text preprocessing techniques applied by the app.

Option A - Variability in text preprocessing techniques applied by the app can lead to inconsistent sentiment scores, as different preprocessing methods may produce different input representations, affecting the analysis results. Fluctuations in service availability (Option B) might cause intermittent failures but should not directly affect the consistency of sentiment scores. Inadequate tokenization settings (Option C) may affect the accuracy of sentiment analysis but are less likely to cause inconsistency in scores. An outdated SDK version (Option D) may cause compatibility issues but is not the primary cause of inconsistent sentiment scores. Insufficient permissions (Option E) may result in authentication errors but are unlikely to impact sentiment analysis consistency.

EXAM FOCUS	*You should standardize text preprocessing techniques in your application to avoid inconsistent sentiment scores. Keep in mind that variations in preprocessing can lead to inconsistent results, even for similar text inputs.*
CAUTION ALERT	*Stay clear of assuming that service availability or SDK versions are the primary causes of inconsistency in sentiment scores. Avoid overlooking the importance of consistent tokenization and preprocessing methods.*

QUESTION 31

Answer - [A) and B)] - Training data diversity and quality are essential for ensuring that the model captures diverse user intents and entities accurately. Regular model evaluation and iteration are necessary to improve model performance over time.

A) Incorrect - Transfer learning techniques might not be applicable or effective for this specific scenario of training a language understanding model for a chatbot.
D) Incorrect - While pre-trained embeddings can be beneficial, they may not address the specific requirements of this scenario.
E) Incorrect - Increasing model complexity might lead to overfitting and increased computational costs without necessarily improving performance.

EXAM FOCUS	*You should prioritize training data diversity and model evaluation for high-performing chatbots. Always remember that diverse data ensures broader understanding, and regular evaluation allows for continuous improvement.*
CAUTION ALERT	*Avoid increasing model complexity unnecessarily. Stay clear of overfitting by adding too many layers without improving overall performance.*

QUESTION 32

Answer - [A), B), and D)] - Utilizing transfer learning, fine-tuning on domain-specific data, and applying regularization methods are effective techniques for optimizing model performance and minimizing false positives and negatives.

C) Incorrect - While data augmentation can enhance training data diversity, it might not directly address the challenge of minimizing false positives and negatives in model performance optimization.

EXAM FOCUS	*You need to fine-tune the model with domain-specific data and apply regularization to prevent overfitting. Make sure to utilize transfer learning to leverage existing models and enhance performance.*
CAUTION ALERT	*Stay cautioned about over-relying on data augmentation, as it may not directly resolve misclassification issues in language models. Avoid using it as the sole optimization strategy.*

QUESTION 33

Answer - [C] Azure AI Language Service > Text Analytics API

Option C - Utilizing Azure AI Language Service with the Text Analytics API provides real-time sentiment analysis capabilities, aligning with the requirement. Option A is incorrect as Azure Cognitive Search does not offer sentiment analysis functionality. Option B is incorrect as the Speech Service is not typically used for sentiment analysis. Option D is incorrect as the Content Moderator service is more suited for content moderation. Option E is incorrect as QnA Maker is focused on question and answer functionality, not sentiment analysis.

EXAM FOCUS	*Always remember to use Azure AI Language Service with the Text Analytics API for real-time sentiment analysis in your app. Keep in mind that this API is designed for seamless integration with other Azure services.*
CAUTION ALERT	*Stay clear of using services like Cognitive Search or QnA Maker, which do not provide sentiment analysis. Avoid selecting Speech Service, which focuses on audio processing.*

QUESTION 34

Answer - [B) and C)] - Efficient methods for importing content sources include utilizing Azure Blob Storage and integrating with Azure SQL Database.

Option B) - Correct: Azure Blob Storage facilitates large-scale data import efficiently. Option C) - Correct: Azure SQL Database allows structured data integration, enhancing accessibility and organization. Option A) - Incorrect: Manual upload is time-consuming and not suitable for large-scale data. Option D) - Incorrect: Direct connection to Cosmos DB may not be optimal for content import. Option E) - Incorrect: Ignoring source import hinders automation and scalability.

EXAM FOCUS	*You should use Azure Blob Storage for large-scale data imports and SQL Database for structured data. Keep in mind that these methods are scalable and efficient for content source imports.*
CAUTION ALERT	*Avoid relying on manual uploads, which are inefficient for large-scale projects. Stay clear of ignoring content imports, as this limits automation.*

QUESTION 35

Answer - [A), B), C), and D)] - Publishing and updating knowledge bases require implementing version control, automated deployment pipelines, thorough testing, and monitoring post-publishing.

Option A) - Correct: Version control ensures tracking of changes and facilitates rollback if necessary. Option B) - Correct: Automated deployment pipelines streamline the process of updating knowledge bases, reducing manual errors. Option C) - Correct: Thorough testing before publishing ensures the reliability and accuracy of the content. Option D) - Correct: Monitoring usage and performance metrics post-publishing provides insights into the effectiveness and reliability of the knowledge base. Option E) - Incorrect: While rollback mechanisms are essential, they are covered by version control and are not mentioned separately.

EXAM FOCUS	*You need to implement version control and automated pipelines to ensure reliable updates for knowledge bases. Always remember that thorough testing and post-publishing monitoring are crucial for maintaining quality.*
CAUTION ALERT	*Stay cautioned about skipping testing phases. Avoid thinking rollback mechanisms alone will ensure reliability—they should complement version control.*

QUESTION 36

Answer - [A, B, E] "mcr.microsoft.com/azure-cognitive-services/vision/customvision"
"--memory 183 --cpus 8"
"--api-key {API_KEY}"

Option A provides the correct URI for the custom computer vision model. Option B sets memory and CPU limits for the container environment. Option E specifies the API key required for authentication. Option C is incorrect as it does not align with the correct flag to accept the EULA. Option D is incorrect as it is not relevant to container deployment.

EXAM FOCUS	*Make sure to specify the correct URI for custom vision models and allocate appropriate memory and CPU resources. You need to include the API key for authentication.*
CAUTION ALERT	*Avoid selecting options unrelated to container deployment, such as incorrect flags or billing methods. Stay clear of forgetting to include memory and CPU configuration, which impacts performance.*

QUESTION 37

Answer - [A, C, D].

A) Utilizing transfer learning techniques allows the model to leverage knowledge gained from training on a large dataset and adapt it to a smaller, domain-specific dataset. C) Adjusting the learning rate schedule is crucial for fine-tuning to ensure the model converges to the optimal solution effectively. D) Incorporating additional domain-specific training data enhances the model's understanding of industry-specific terminology and nuances. B) Increasing the batch size may lead to memory constraints and slower convergence, while reducing the number of training epochs could limit the model's ability to learn intricate patterns.

EXAM FOCUS	*You should incorporate domain-specific data and adjust learning rates when fine-tuning language models. Always remember that transfer learning accelerates training and enhances performance.*
CAUTION ALERT	*Avoid reducing training epochs prematurely, as this limits the model's learning capacity. Stay alert to the possibility of increasing batch size leading to memory issues.*

QUESTION 38

Answer - [A, C, D].

A) Implementing multi-turn dialogues enables the bot to retain context across interactions, facilitating smoother and more natural conversations. C) Utilizing reinforcement learning for dynamic dialogue management allows the bot to adapt its responses based on user feedback and interaction history, enhancing engagement. D) Implementing rule-based intent recognition ensures precise handling of user interactions based on predefined rules, improving accuracy and user satisfaction. B) While pre-built Azure Bot Framework templates can expedite development, they may not address the complexity of user interactions adequately. Integrating sentiment analysis enhances understanding but may not directly address handling complex interactions.

EXAM FOCUS	*You should implement multi-turn dialogues and use reinforcement learning to handle complex interactions effectively. Keep in mind that rule-based intent recognition improves precision for specific user queries.*

CAUTION ALERT	*Avoid assuming pre-built templates will handle all complexities. Stay clear of relying solely on sentiment analysis for managing complex user flows.*

QUESTION 39

Answer - [A, D] SpeechRecognizer(config, audioInput)
result.Text

Option A is the correct choice as it instantiates the SpeechRecognizer object with the provided configuration and audio input. Option D extracts the recognized text from the result object. Options B, C, and E are irrelevant or incorrect in the context of instantiating the SpeechRecognizer object.

EXAM FOCUS	*You need to use the SpeechRecognizer(config, audioInput) object to initialize speech recognition, and always remember to retrieve the recognized text using result.Text.*
CAUTION ALERT	*Avoid incorrect methods like SpeechRecognitionMode or SpeechConfig.FromEndpoint, which do not apply to basic speech-to-text operations. Stay clear of overcomplicating the process.*

QUESTION 40

Answer - [B] Azure Language Understanding (LUIS).

B) Azure Language Understanding (LUIS) offers advanced natural language processing capabilities, including the ability to understand context, sarcasm, and irony in text, making it suitable for addressing the challenges in sentiment analysis. A) Azure Text Analytics provides basic sentiment analysis features but may struggle with nuanced interpretations like sarcasm and irony. C) Azure Cognitive Search is primarily used for search functionalities and does not specialize in sentiment analysis. D) Azure AI Translator service focuses on translation tasks and does not directly address the challenges of sarcasm, irony, and context in sentiment analysis. E) Azure AI Language Service provides language detection and translation but does not specifically handle the complexities of sentiment analysis like LUIS.

EXAM FOCUS	*You should use Azure Language Understanding (LUIS) for advanced sentiment analysis that addresses sarcasm, irony, and contextual meaning in text. Keep in mind that LUIS specializes in natural language understanding.*
CAUTION ALERT	*Avoid using basic services like Text Analytics, which may struggle with nuanced sentiment. Stay clear of translation-focused services that do not support advanced sentiment analysis.*

QUESTION 41

Answer - [C] Standard Tier.

C) Standard Tier offers a balance of cost-effectiveness and features suitable for implementing search capabilities for academic research papers. A) Free Tier is limited in scale and functionality, not suitable for large databases. B) Basic Tier provides basic search features but may lack scalability for a large database. D) Storage Optimized Tier focuses on storage capacity rather than search capabilities. E) Enterprise Tier is designed for large-scale enterprise solutions with advanced features, potentially overkill for the described scenario.

EXAM FOCUS	*You should choose the Standard Tier for a balance between cost-effectiveness and features when implementing Azure Cognitive Search. Keep in mind that this tier provides enough scalability for a large academic database.*
CAUTION ALERT	*Avoid selecting the Free or Basic Tier, as they may not provide sufficient functionality or scalability for large databases. Stay clear of the Storage Optimized Tier, which is better suited for data-heavy applications rather than search features.*

QUESTION 42

Answer - [B] TextAnalyticsClient

Option A, CustomVisionPredictionClient, is primarily used for image classification tasks, not for text entity detection. Option C, TranslatorTextClient, is used for translating text between languages and does not offer entity detection capabilities. Option D, FormRecognizerClient, is used for extracting information from forms and documents, not for text entity detection. Option E, QnAMakerClient, is used for building question and answer systems and does not include entity detection features. Option B, TextAnalyticsClient, is the correct choice as it provides entity recognition capabilities, including detection of PII, from text data.

EXAM FOCUS	*You should use TextAnalyticsClient for entity detection, especially for identifying PII in text. Keep in mind that this service is designed for entity recognition and works efficiently for PII detection tasks.*
CAUTION ALERT	*Stay clear of using services like CustomVisionPredictionClient or FormRecognizerClient for text analysis—they are focused on image and form data, not PII detection. Avoid selecting TranslatorTextClient, which is not intended for entity detection.*

QUESTION 43

Answer - [A] Implement custom skills as Azure Functions.

A) Implementing custom skills as Azure Functions allows you to leverage serverless computing for scalable and cost-effective execution of processing logic within Azure Cognitive Search. B) Azure Logic Apps are primarily used for workflow automation and may not provide the required flexibility for complex processing tasks. C) While Azure Machine Learning is suitable for model training and deployment, it may not be the best option for developing custom skills directly integrated with Azure Cognitive Search. D) Azure App Service is more suitable for hosting web applications and APIs but may not offer the same level of integration with Azure Cognitive Search for custom skills. E) Azure Data Factory is a data integration service and is not designed for developing custom skills for Azure Cognitive Search.

EXAM FOCUS	*You should implement custom skills in Azure Cognitive Search using Azure Functions for serverless execution and scalability. Always remember that this allows for more flexible processing of product descriptions.*
CAUTION ALERT	*Avoid relying on services like Azure Logic Apps or Azure Machine Learning directly for custom skills—they may not provide the right level of integration and flexibility for Cognitive Search. Stay cautioned about choosing Azure App Service for this task; it's better suited for web apps.*

QUESTION 44

Answer - [C] Implement synonym maps to expand search results.

C) Implementing synonym maps allows for expanding search results by mapping synonymous terms, ensuring comprehensive search coverage and improving the relevance of search results. A) While fuzzy search can handle spelling variations, it may not address synonymous terms and could lead to irrelevant search results. B) Phonetic matching may improve search accuracy for sound-alike words but does not address synonym expansion. D) Using regular expressions for pattern matching is complex and may not be suitable for general search query crafting in Azure Cognitive Search. E) Proximity search is useful for matching terms within a specific distance but does not directly address synonym expansion for comprehensive search coverage.

EXAM FOCUS	*You need to implement synonym maps to enhance search results by expanding query terms in Azure Cognitive Search. Always remember this improves search accuracy and ensures relevant results.*
CAUTION ALERT	*Avoid relying solely on fuzzy search or phonetic matching—they address spelling errors and sound-alike words but won't improve search breadth with synonymous terms. Stay clear of using regular expressions unless there's a specific need for advanced pattern matching.*

QUESTION 45

Answer - D) TextSentimentClient

Option A - TextAnalyticsClient: This is a hypothetical client and not part of the Azure Text Analytics SDK.
Option B - SentimentAnalysisClient: This is a hypothetical client and not part of the Azure Text Analytics SDK.
Option C - LanguageAnalyticsClient: This is a hypothetical client and not part of the Azure Text Analytics SDK.
Option E - AnalyzeTextClient: This is a hypothetical client and not part of the Azure Text Analytics SDK.
Option D is correct because TextSentimentClient is the class used to determine the sentiment of text in Azure Text Analytics.

EXAM FOCUS	*Make sure to use TextSentimentClient for determining the sentiment of text in Azure Text Analytics. Keep in mind this client is designed specifically for analyzing sentiment in text data.*
CAUTION ALERT	*Avoid selecting hypothetical clients like SentimentAnalysisClient or LanguageAnalyticsClient—they are not part of the Azure SDK. Stay clear of incorrect options that don't exist in the Azure Text Analytics SDK.*

QUESTION 46

Answer - [A, B, C] Choose the appropriate pricing tier based on project requirements. Specify the region for deployment to optimize latency. Configure security policies to restrict access to authorized users.

A) Selecting the appropriate pricing tier ensures that the service meets project needs while optimizing costs.
B) Specifying the deployment region strategically reduces latency and improves performance.
C) Configuring security policies helps maintain data integrity and restrict unauthorized access to the service.
D) Defining usage quotas is not a part of the provisioning process but rather a subsequent configuration to manage resource consumption.
E) Enabling multi-factor authentication is a security measure but not directly related to provisioning the service.

EXAM FOCUS	*You need to choose the appropriate pricing tier and region for latency optimization when setting up Azure OpenAI Service. Always remember to configure security policies to restrict unauthorized access.*
CAUTION ALERT	*Avoid skipping the security configuration step—it is crucial for data integrity. Stay clear of assuming that enabling multi-factor authentication is part of provisioning; it's an additional security measure implemented afterward.*

QUESTION 47

Answer - [B] Incorporating brand-specific keywords in the input prompts.

B) Incorporating brand-specific keywords ensures that the generated content aligns with brand identity and messaging.
A) Strict character limits may constrain creativity and relevance.
C) Fine-tuning on historical materials may improve relevance but may not align directly with current brand guidelines.
D) Reinforcement learning optimizes content but may not specifically ensure alignment with brand guidelines.
E) Sentiment analysis filters content based on sentiment, which may not address brand-specific requirements.

EXAM FOCUS	*You should incorporate brand-specific keywords in prompts to ensure content aligns with your brand's messaging in Azure OpenAI Service. Keep in mind that this directs the model to generate content consistent with your brand guidelines.*
CAUTION ALERT	*Avoid focusing solely on character limits or engagement optimization through reinforcement learning. Stay cautioned that fine-tuning historical data may not reflect current branding needs.*

QUESTION 48

Answer - D) Statement I, Statement II

Option C - Statement III: This statement is incorrect because retaining data for a certain number of hours is not related to the synchronous feature during PM (Personally Identifiable Information) detection. Option E - Statement II, Statement III: This statement is incorrect because Statement III is incorrect, as mentioned earlier.
Option A is incorrect because it doesn't include the true statement about unstructured data submission for PM detection (Statement II). Option B is incorrect because it doesn't include the true statement about the use of Language Studio or REST API for PM detection (Statement I). Option D is correct as it includes both true statements: Statement I and Statement II.

EXAM FOCUS	*You can use Language Studio or the REST API for detecting PII. Keep in mind that you can submit unstructured data for PII detection, which makes it versatile for various data formats.*
CAUTION ALERT	*Avoid thinking that data retention for a few hours is related to synchronous detection; it's not relevant for PII detection workflows. Stay clear of misinformation about data retention in the context of PII.*

QUESTION 49

Answer - [A, B]

A) Destination preferences, travel dates, and activity interests provide specific guidance for itinerary planning, ensuring tailored recommendations. B) Budget constraints and accommodation preferences help optimize travel plans for cost-effectiveness and comfort. C) While transportation options are important, they may not directly contribute to itinerary personalization. D) User feedback is valuable but may not directly guide prompt design for initial model training.
E) Experimenting with prompt formulations may be useful but does not guarantee comprehensive and tailored travel itineraries.

EXAM FOCUS	*You should include destination preferences, travel dates, and budget constraints in prompts to guide Azure's generative AI models for personalized itineraries. Keep in mind these key details help the AI generate tailored and relevant travel suggestions.*
CAUTION ALERT	*Avoid relying solely on transportation options or feedback refinement—they may not provide enough guidance for comprehensive itinerary generation. Stay cautioned that prompt experimentation without structure may lead to inconsistent results.*

QUESTION 50

Answer - [A, C] Implementing a microservices architecture to modularize generative AI components and enable independent scaling of services. Leveraging Azure Kubernetes Service (AKS) to orchestrate containerized generative AI models and manage resource allocation dynamically.

A) Microservices architecture enables independent scaling, enhancing flexibility and scalability. C) AKS provides container orchestration, facilitating dynamic resource allocation and scaling for generative AI models.
B) Serverless architecture focuses on event-driven functions rather than orchestration of AI models. D) Azure Batch is primarily used for parallel computing tasks, not for real-time AI model deployment. E) Azure Data Factory is used for data integration and orchestration, not for managing AI model scalability.

EXAM FOCUS	*You need to implement a microservices architecture and leverage Azure Kubernetes Service (AKS) for scalability in your generative AI solution. Always remember that AKS helps manage dynamic resource allocation for containerized models.*
CAUTION ALERT	*Stay clear of using serverless architectures for this task—they are better suited for event-driven processes, not AI model orchestration. Avoid thinking Azure Batch or Data Factory will address real-time scalability—they are more suitable for batch processing and data pipelines.*

PRACTICE TEST 2 - QUESTIONS ONLY

QUESTION 1

Your team is developing a chatbot for a retail company to assist customers with product inquiries and order tracking. The chatbot needs to understand customer queries in natural language, extract relevant information, and provide accurate responses. You need to choose the appropriate Azure AI services for this chatbot. Which services should you select? Select all answers that apply.

A) Azure Cognitive Services Language Understanding (LUIS)
B) Azure Bot Services
C) Azure Cognitive Services Text Analytics
D) Azure QnA Maker
E) Azure Cognitive Services Translator

QUESTION 2

Your company is deploying a decision support solution to analyze images from security cameras in a manufacturing plant. The solution needs to detect objects, analyze spatial patterns, and trigger alerts for potential safety hazards. Which Azure AI service should you choose to fulfill these requirements?

A) Azure AI Computer Vision
B) Azure AI Face API
C) Azure AI Custom Vision
D) Azure AI Video Analyzer
E) Azure AI Form Recognizer

QUESTION 3

When deploying a containerized Azure AI service, which Azure CLI command should be used to specify the container image to be deployed?

```
A) az container create
B) az appservice plan create
C) az aks create
D) az webapp create
E) az cognitiveservices account create
```

QUESTION 4

When integrating Azure AI services into an application, which authentication method provides a secure way to access the service?

```
A) OAuth token
B) Basic authentication
C) API key
D) JWT token
E) Certificate authentication
```

QUESTION 5

Your team is responsible for deploying a new Azure AI solution that leverages machine learning models to analyze sensor data from IoT devices and detect anomalies in real-time. To support the deployment, you need to create an Azure AI resource with the necessary services and configurations. The solution should prioritize reliability, scalability, and efficient resource utilization.

Which actions should you take to create the Azure AI resource while ensuring reliability, scalability, and resource efficiency?
Select all answers that apply.

A) Implement autoscaling to dynamically adjust resources based on workload demands.
B) Choose a high-availability region and configure redundant backups for critical data.
C) Optimize resource utilization by leveraging serverless computing options, such as Azure Functions.
D) Enable logging and monitoring features to track performance metrics and detect potential issues.
E) Deploy services in isolated environments to minimize resource contention and enhance reliability.

QUESTION 6

You are troubleshooting connectivity issues between your Azure AI services and a virtual machine in Azure. Despite having correct permissions, the VM cannot access the services. What should you do to diagnose and resolve the problem?

A) Review Azure AD logs for authentication errors.
B) Check the network security group (NSG) rules associated with the VM.
C) Verify that the virtual machine has the necessary outbound internet connectivity.
D) Examine the Custom Vision service firewall rules and ensure that the VM's IP address is whitelisted.
E) Use Azure Network Watcher to analyze network traffic between the VM and Azure AI services.

QUESTION 7

As part of your AI solution deployment, you need to analyze logs for performance insights and anomaly detection. Which tool should you integrate with Azure AI services to achieve this goal effectively?

A) Azure DevOps
B) Azure Data Lake Storage
C) Azure Monitor
D) Azure Application Insights
E) Azure Log Analytics

QUESTION 8

As part of your Azure AI service monitoring strategy, you need to implement budget controls and alerts. What is a best practice for configuring budget controls and alerts for Azure AI services?

A) Setting up alerts for insignificant cost fluctuations
B) Implementing budget controls only for production environments
C) Defining budgets based on arbitrary estimates
D) Establishing alerts for budget overruns and nearing thresholds
E) Disabling alerts for cost-saving measures

QUESTION 9

You are setting up authentication for an Azure App Services web app named App3. The app must authenticate using Microsoft Entra ID with minimal administrative effort and adhere to the principle of least privilege. What should you do?

A) Implement OAuth 2.0 authentication with Azure AD and grant App3 access to Microsoft Entra ID.
B) Enable Azure Active Directory (Azure AD) authentication and configure App3 to use it.
C) Configure App3 to use Azure AD single sign-on (SSO).
D) Enable Managed Service Identity (MSI) for App3 and assign RBAC permissions to Microsoft Entra ID.
E) Generate a client secret and store it securely for App3 authentication.

QUESTION 10

Your team is developing a news aggregation platform where articles from various sources are displayed. To ensure compliance and user safety, you need to automate moderation workflows efficiently. Which approach should you prioritize for automating text moderation in this scenario?

A) Implement manual content review by human moderators
B) Utilize Azure Content Moderator's built-in text classification capabilities
C) Develop custom text filters based on predefined rules
D) Deploy Azure AI Language service for sentiment analysis
E) Ignore text moderation to streamline development

QUESTION 11

Your organization is customizing a decision support solution to analyze manufacturing data and optimize production processes. What is a critical consideration for ensuring high availability and reliability of the decision support system?

A) Implementing Azure Virtual Machine scale sets for automatic scaling based on demand.
B) Utilizing Azure App Service with redundant instances across multiple regions.
C) Configuring Azure Load Balancer for distributing incoming traffic across backend servers.
D) Deploying Azure Kubernetes Service (AKS) for containerized microservices architecture.
E) Setting up Azure SQL Database with geo-replication for disaster recovery.

QUESTION 12

You are deploying an AI solution in Azure that requires continuous integration and continuous delivery (CI/CD) pipeline integration with Azure AI services. What should you do to achieve this?

A) Implement Azure DevOps pipelines with custom scripts for deploying Azure AI services.
B) Use Azure Logic Apps to automate deployment tasks for Azure AI services.
C) Integrate Azure AI services directly into Azure Kubernetes Service (AKS) for CI/CD.
D) Configure Azure Functions to trigger deployments of Azure AI services based on GitHub commits.
E) Utilize Azure Automation to schedule regular deployments of Azure AI services.

QUESTION 13

Your organization is preparing to deploy an Azure AI solution for decision support on a global scale. What are the best practices for deploying Azure AI solutions in production across different regions?
Select all answers that apply.

A) Utilize Azure Availability Zones to ensure high availability and fault tolerance across geographic regions.
B) Implement Azure Traffic Manager for global load balancing and distribution of user requests.
C) Leverage Azure Front Door for global content delivery and efficient routing based on user location.
D) Configure Azure Traffic Manager with priority routing to direct traffic to the nearest datacenter.
E) Implement Azure CDN to cache content closer to users and reduce latency for global users.

QUESTION 14

Your team is tasked with implementing an AI solution for a retail company to analyze in-store camera footage for customer behavior analysis. The solution aims to optimize store layout and product placement based on visual insights. Which visual feature detection capability should you prioritize to achieve the objectives of this scenario?

A) Object detection
B) Facial recognition
C) Activity recognition

D) Text recognition
E) Emotion detection

QUESTION 15

You are deploying an AI solution that involves natural language processing using Azure AI Language services. During testing, you encounter a performance degradation issue. What steps should you take to optimize the solution's performance?

A) Implement caching mechanisms to reduce redundant API calls.
B) Increase the Azure AI Language service tier for enhanced processing capabilities.
C) Optimize the code by reducing unnecessary data processing and improving algorithm efficiency.
D) Parallelize processing tasks to leverage distributed computing resources effectively.
E) Opt for asynchronous processing to handle concurrent requests efficiently.

QUESTION 16

In a project requiring text extraction from images, you need to ensure high accuracy in recognizing characters and words. Which technique is specifically designed to improve the accuracy of text extraction, especially in scenarios with handwritten text or unusual fonts?

A) Transfer learning
B) Fine-tuning models
C) Azure AI Form Recognizer
D) Preprocessing techniques
E) Ensemble learning

QUESTION 17

Your team is training a custom image classification model using Azure AI Vision. During the training process, you notice that the model's precision is high but its recall is relatively low. What should you do to balance between precision and recall?

A) Increase the training dataset size
B) Adjust the classification threshold
C) Fine-tune the model's hyperparameters
D) Apply data augmentation techniques
E) Decrease the number of training epochs

QUESTION 18

You are developing a custom image classification model using Azure AI Vision. However, during evaluation, you notice a high rate of false positives. What actions could help improve the accuracy of the model?

A) Increase the size of the training dataset to include more diverse samples.
B) Fine-tune the hyperparameters of the image classification model.
C) Implement post-processing techniques to filter out false positives.
D) Adjust the confidence threshold for classification predictions.
E) Upgrade the Azure AI Vision service to a higher tier.

QUESTION 19

Your team has developed a custom computer vision model using Azure AI Vision for detecting defective components in manufacturing. You need to ensure smooth integration of this model into the production environment. Which approach should you take to incorporate version control and rollback strategies effectively?

A) Use Azure DevOps pipelines to manage model versions and deployments, enabling easy rollbacks when needed.
B) Maintain multiple copies of the model code on different servers, enabling quick switching between versions.
C) Keep a log of model training sessions and manually track changes to the model configuration for rollback purposes.
D) Utilize Azure Machine Learning to track model versions and deploy new versions with automated rollback capabilities.
E) Implement a manual process for updating the model, relying on backups to revert to previous versions in case of issues.

QUESTION 20

Your organization is implementing a safety monitoring system for a construction site using video surveillance. The system needs to detect and track workers' movements to ensure compliance with safety protocols and identify potential hazards. You are responsible for selecting the Azure AI service that offers accuracy optimization features in spatial analysis to enhance worker safety. Which Azure AI service should you choose to address this requirement effectively?

A) Azure AI Video Indexer
B) Azure Cognitive Services - Computer Vision
C) Azure Cognitive Services - Video Analyzer
D) Azure AI Vision Spatial Analysis
E) Azure AI Metrics Advisor

QUESTION 21

You are implementing a speech recognition feature using Azure AI Speech service. During configuration, you come across an API request with the command: POST https://<resource-name>.cognitiveservices.azure.com/stt/v1.0/diagnostics/audioQuality. What is the primary purpose of this request?

A) Recognition of speech from audio input.
B) Analysis of audio quality metrics.
C) Generation of synthesized speech from text.
D) Detection of audio sentiment.
E) Translation of speech to text.

QUESTION 22

Your organization is developing a document analysis system to categorize and organize research papers from various sources. As part of this system, you need to extract key phrases from the documents to enable efficient search and retrieval. Additionally, you must ensure compliance with data privacy regulations while processing sensitive information. Which Azure service should you use for extracting key phrases from the research papers, considering the need for compliance and accurate extraction?

A) Azure AI Language - Key Phrase Extraction
B) Azure Cognitive Search
C) Azure Text Analytics
D) Azure Machine Learning - Natural Language Processing
E) Azure Databricks

QUESTION 23

Your organization is deploying an AI-driven feedback analysis system for a multinational retail chain. The system must accurately classify customer feedback as positive, neutral, or negative, considering the context of each message. Which technique would be most appropriate for achieving this goal?

A) Sentiment analysis with context embedding
B) Lexicon-based sentiment analysis
C) Pre-trained sentiment analysis models
D) Rule-based sentiment analysis
E) Frequency-based sentiment analysis

QUESTION 24

You are integrating the Azure AI Text Analytics service into your application to extract key phrases from text data. However, you observe that the service occasionally fails to recognize key phrases accurately. What action should you take to address this issue?

A) Adjusting the language detection threshold for text input.
B) Increasing the maximum text length for key phrase extraction.
C) Preprocessing text data to remove noise and irrelevant content.
D) Enhancing the service's access control settings.
E) Upgrading to a higher-tier service plan.

QUESTION 25

Your organization is deploying a speech-to-text (STT) solution for a mobile application that will be used globally. One of the key requirements is to ensure high accuracy across different languages and audio qualities. Which approach would best address this requirement?

A) Training separate STT models for each target language.
B) Leveraging Azure Speech SDK's multilingual support with customized language models.
C) Using phonetic-based algorithms for language-independent speech recognition.
D) Employing a cloud-based speech recognition service with built-in language detection.
E) Implementing ensemble learning with multiple STT models for improved accuracy.

QUESTION 26

Your company is developing a custom speech recognition solution for a call center application. The solution needs to handle dynamic content generation based on caller interactions. Which technology would be most appropriate for achieving this requirement?

A) Azure Cognitive Services Speech-to-Text API.
B) Python NLTK library for natural language processing.
C) Microsoft Bot Framework for building conversational AI.
D) Azure Speech Synthesis Markup Language (SSML) for text-to-speech conversion.
E) Microsoft Azure OpenAI Service for content generation.

QUESTION 27

You are implementing an Azure AI Vision solution for a document processing application. Your application needs to extract text from images containing handwritten notes. Which feature of Azure AI Vision should you use for this specific task?

A) Face detection
B) Object recognition
C) Optical character recognition (OCR)
D) Image segmentation
E) Text translation

QUESTION 28

Your organization handles confidential documents that require translation, and security is a top priority. Which feature of Azure Cognitive Services Translator Text should you utilize to ensure security and confidentiality in document translation?

A) Role-based access control (RBAC)
B) Encryption at rest
C) Secure end-to-end encryption
D) Data anonymization techniques
E) Integration with Azure Key Vault

QUESTION 29

Your organization is implementing a continuous learning strategy for its custom translation model to ensure ongoing improvement and accuracy. Which approach should you recommend for incorporating new translation data into the model effectively?

A) Periodically retrain the model using all available data
B) Implement an active learning system to prioritize relevant data for model training
C) Fine-tune the model only when significant changes in data distribution occur
D) Manually update the model parameters based on new translation requirements
E) Exclude new data to maintain consistency in translation outputs

QUESTION 30

You are diagnosing an issue with an Azure app that uses Azure AI Form Recognizer for extracting data from scanned documents. Users notice that the app fails to recognize certain fields consistently across different document types. What could be a potential reason for this inconsistency?

A) Insufficient training data provided to the Azure AI Form Recognizer model.
B) Variability in document quality and formatting.
C) Limited language support offered by the Azure AI Form Recognizer service.
D) Outdated version of the Azure AI Form Recognizer SDK being used in the app.
E) Lack of integration between the app's document preprocessing pipeline and Azure AI Form Recognizer.

QUESTION 31

Your team is developing a language understanding model for a legal document review application. You need to evaluate the model's performance to ensure it accurately identifies legal terms and contexts. Which techniques should you employ to evaluate the language understanding model effectively?
Select all answers that apply.

A) Precision, recall, and F1 score calculations
B) Domain-specific evaluation metrics
C) Human-in-the-loop validation
D) Error analysis and confusion matrix examination
E) Model interpretability and explainability assessments

QUESTION 32

Your team is working on optimizing a language understanding model for a legal document analysis application. The model must accurately extract entities and identify relevant clauses within legal documents. How can you incorporate

feedback loops into the optimization process to continuously improve the model's performance and ensure alignment with evolving requirements?
Select all answers that apply.

A) Implement active learning to prioritize labeling uncertain data instances
B) Integrate user feedback mechanisms to capture model performance evaluations
C) Utilize reinforcement learning for real-time model adjustments based on user interactions
D) Establish regular retraining cycles with updated annotated datasets
E) Deploy model versioning for comparison and analysis of performance changes over time

QUESTION 33

Your organization plans to develop an Azure app that requires identifying and extracting key entities from large volumes of text data. Which Azure service and API combination is best suited for this task?

A) Azure AI Language Service > Text Analytics API
B) Azure Content Moderator > Decision API
C) Azure Translator Text > Language API
D) Azure Cognitive Search > Vision API
E) Azure Speech Service > Speech API

QUESTION 34

How can Azure AI engineers handle diverse formats and sources effectively for knowledge mining in a question answering solution?
Select all answers that apply.

A) Convert all sources to a single format before import
B) Utilize Azure Data Factory for format conversion and data integration
C) Implement Azure Functions for real-time data transformation
D) Rely on third-party tools for data preprocessing
E) Limit source types to simplify management

QUESTION 35

How can Azure AI engineers ensure version control and rollback mechanisms for published knowledge bases in a question answering solution?
Select all answers that apply.

A) Utilize Azure DevOps for version control and deployment
B) Implement Azure Git Repos for tracking changes
C) Configure Azure Functions for automated rollback
D) Store backups in Azure Blob Storage for easy retrieval
E) Maintain manual version logs for historical reference

QUESTION 36

Your organization is implementing a chatbot solution that requires natural language understanding capabilities. Which options should you include in the provided bash statement to run the Language Understanding (LUIS) container on Azure? Select all answers that apply.

```
A) "--rm -it"
B) "--memory 256 --cpus 4"
C) "--accept"
```

```
D) "--apply"
E) "--region westus"
```

QUESTION 37

In your AI project, you are tasked with fine-tuning a language model on Azure for sentiment analysis. However, you encounter issues with overfitting during training. Which of the following techniques can help mitigate overfitting?
Select all answers that apply.

A) Increase the model's complexity
B) Reduce the size of the training dataset
C) Apply dropout regularization
D) Decrease the number of layers in the model
E) Use a higher learning rate

QUESTION 38

Your team is developing a conversational AI solution using Azure Bot Framework and integrating it with custom NLP models for analyzing customer inquiries. To ensure the bot's performance over time, which action should you prioritize during development?
Select all answers that apply.

A) Implement continuous training with new data
B) Integrate Azure Monitor for real-time performance monitoring
C) Incorporate user feedback loops for model refinement
D) Apply reinforcement learning for adaptive dialogue management
E) Utilize Azure Application Insights for user behavior analysis

QUESTION 39

Your task is to implement language translation functionality using Azure Translator service in your application. Complete the code snippet below to achieve this:

```
string textToTranslate = "Hello, how are you?";
var translatorClient = new TranslationClient("<YourSubscriptionKey>",
"<YourServiceRegion>");
var translationResult = await translatorClient.TranslateAsync(textToTranslate, "en",
"fr");
```

Select all answers that apply.

```
A) new TranslationClient("<YourSubscriptionKey>", "<YourServiceRegion>")
B) TranslationLanguage.English
C) translationResult.TranslationText
D) await translatorClient.DetectLanguageAsync(textToTranslate)
E) await translatorClient.TranslationResultAsync(textToTranslate, "fr")
```

QUESTION 40

Your team is working on a market research project that involves analyzing sentiment across different demographics to identify trends and preferences. Which Azure AI service would you recommend integrating into your analysis pipeline to perform comparative sentiment analysis effectively?

A) Azure Text Analytics
B) Azure Language Understanding (LUIS)
C) Azure Cognitive Search
D) Azure AI Translator service
E) Azure AI Language Service

QUESTION 41

Your organization is integrating Azure Cognitive Search with an existing Azure data solution to enable full-text search capabilities across various document types. Security is a top priority to ensure sensitive data remains protected. Which security best practice should you implement when configuring Azure Cognitive Search?

A) Enable Azure AD authentication
B) Implement IP firewall rules
C) Use shared access signatures (SAS)
D) Encrypt data at rest
E) Enable role-based access control (RBAC)

QUESTION 42

You need to integrate a feature into your application that identifies and anonymizes Personally Identifiable Information (PII) from text inputs. Which Azure AI service should you leverage to achieve this task?

```
A) ContentModeratorClient
B) FormRecognizerClient
C) TextAnalyticsClient
D) LanguageUnderstandingClient
E) MetricsAdvisorClient
```

QUESTION 43

Your organization is deploying a knowledge management solution using Azure Cognitive Search to index a vast repository of technical documents. To enhance the search capabilities, you decide to integrate external AI services to extract insights from the documents. Which Azure Cognitive Search feature should you utilize to seamlessly integrate custom skills developed with external AI services?

A) Cognitive Skills
B) Custom Analyzers
C) Indexer
D) Skillset
E) Scoring Profiles

QUESTION 44

Your team is developing a knowledge management system using Azure Cognitive Search to allow users to search and filter documents based on various attributes. To enhance user experience, you need to implement faceted search and filters. Which strategy should you adopt to implement faceted search and filters in Azure Cognitive Search?

A) Define facets in the search index schema
B) Implement custom filters using Azure Functions
C) Utilize the built-in faceted search feature
D) Configure query suggestions based on user input
E) Develop custom UI components for filtering

QUESTION 45

Which method in Azure Text Analytics is used to determine the language of text?

```
A) IdentifyLanguage()
B) DetectLanguage()
C) RecognizeLanguage()
D) LanguageDetection()
```

```
E) DetermineLanguage()
```

QUESTION 46

You are setting up an Azure OpenAI Service resource for a natural language generation project. Which factor should you primarily consider when selecting the appropriate Azure OpenAI model?

A) Model accuracy and performance.
B) Model training time.
C) Model interpretability.
D) Model size and resource utilization.
E) Model support for multiple languages.

QUESTION 47

As part of an AI-driven content generation project using Azure OpenAI Service, your team is tasked with optimizing text generation parameters. Which parameter adjustment is most likely to improve the coherence and flow of the generated content while maintaining relevance?

A) Increasing temperature to introduce more randomness in responses.
B) Reducing beam width to focus on fewer response options.
C) Adjusting the nucleus sampling threshold to control response diversity.
D) Decreasing maximum token length to encourage brevity in responses.
E) Fine-tuning the language model on domain-specific data.

QUESTION 48

Which combination of statements accurately describes features of Azure AI Speech service?

A) Statement I: Azure AI Speech service provides speech-to-text conversion.
B) Statement II: Azure AI Speech service supports only synchronous processing.
C) Statement III: Azure AI Speech service includes support for improving text-to-speech using SSML.
D) Statement II, Statement III
E) Statement I, Statement III

QUESTION 49

You are tasked with developing a generative AI model that creates personalized fashion designs based on user preferences. To optimize the model's performance, which step is essential in integrating custom datasets with Azure OpenAI models?

A) Preprocessing the data to standardize features and remove noise.
B) Encrypting the dataset before uploading it to Azure Blob Storage.
C) Assigning unique identifiers to each fashion item in the dataset.
D) Creating a data access policy to restrict unauthorized access to the dataset.
E) Versioning the dataset to track changes and ensure reproducibility in model training.

QUESTION 50

Your team is tasked with integrating a generative AI model into an existing online gaming platform to enhance user experience by generating personalized in-game content. Which challenge is most likely to arise during the integration process, and how should you address it to ensure seamless adoption of the generative AI solution?
Select all answers that apply.

A) Legacy system compatibility: Implement adapters or middleware to bridge the gap between the generative AI model and the legacy gaming platform, ensuring compatibility and data exchange.
B) Scalability constraints: Deploy the generative AI model on Azure Kubernetes Service (AKS) to facilitate dynamic scaling based on user demand and game traffic fluctuations.
C) Data privacy concerns: Implement encryption mechanisms and access controls to safeguard user data processed by the generative AI model, ensuring compliance with regulatory requirements.
D) Performance overhead: Optimize the generative AI model's inference latency by leveraging Azure Machine Learning's model optimization techniques and deploying it on Azure Container Instances for low-latency execution.
E) Integration complexity: Utilize Azure Logic Apps to orchestrate the interaction between the gaming platform's backend services and the generative AI model, simplifying integration and reducing development effort.

PRACTICE TEST 2 - ANSWERS ONLY

QUESTION 1

Answer - [A, B, D] Azure Cognitive Services Language Understanding (LUIS), Azure Bot Services, Azure QnA Maker

Option C - Azure Cognitive Services Text Analytics: While Text Analytics can extract key phrases and perform sentiment analysis, it may not provide the necessary intent recognition and dialogue management required for building a chatbot.
Option E - Azure Cognitive Services Translator: Translator focuses on language translation and may not be directly applicable for understanding and responding to customer queries within a chatbot context.
Option A - Azure Cognitive Services Language Understanding (LUIS): LUIS enables the chatbot to understand user intents and extract entities from natural language queries, facilitating accurate responses.
Option B - Azure Bot Services: Bot Services provides the framework for building and deploying the chatbot, including features for dialogue management and integration with other Azure AI services like LUIS and QnA Maker.
Option D - Azure QnA Maker: QnA Maker allows the chatbot to retrieve answers from a knowledge base, which is essential for responding to common customer inquiries related to products and orders.

EXAM FOCUS	*You should choose Azure Cognitive Services LUIS, Bot Services, and QnA Maker for building a chatbot that can understand queries, manage dialogues, and retrieve answers from a knowledge base. Make sure LUIS is used for intent recognition and QnA Maker for quick response to FAQs.*
CAUTION ALERT	*Avoid selecting services like Text Analytics or Translator as they do not provide dialogue management or intent recognition necessary for chatbot solutions. Stay clear of assuming Translator can manage customer queries.*

QUESTION 2

Answer - [D] Azure AI Video Analyzer

Option A - Azure AI Computer Vision: Suitable for general image analysis tasks but not specifically tailored for video processing and analysis.
Option B - Azure AI Face API: Designed for facial recognition tasks, not ideal for analyzing spatial patterns in security camera footage.
Option C - Azure AI Custom Vision: Primarily used for training custom image classification models, not for video analysis.
Option E - Azure AI Form Recognizer: Intended for extracting structured data from documents, not suitable for video analysis.

EXAM FOCUS	*You should use Azure AI Video Analyzer for analyzing security camera footage and detecting spatial patterns. Keep in mind that this service is designed for video analysis and real-time alerting.*
CAUTION ALERT	*Avoid using services like Face API or Form Recognizer, which are specialized for different use cases such as facial recognition or document analysis. Stay cautioned that Custom Vision is more suited for image classification, not video processing.*

QUESTION 3

Answer - A) az container create

Option B - Incorrect. This command is used for creating an app service plan, not for container deployment. Option C - Incorrect. This command is used for creating AKS clusters, not for container deployment. Option D - Incorrect. This command is used for creating web apps, not for container deployment. Option E - Incorrect. This command is used for creating cognitive services accounts, not for container deployment.

EXAM	*You need to use the az container create command when deploying a containerized Azure AI service. Make*

FOCUS	*sure to provide the correct container image name and other deployment parameters.*
CAUTION ALERT	*Avoid using commands like az appservice plan create or az aks create, which serve different purposes. Stay clear of using az webapp create for container deployment—it's used for creating web apps.*

QUESTION 4

Answer - A) OAuth token
Answer - D) JWT token

Option B - Incorrect. Basic authentication is less secure compared to OAuth or JWT token. Option C - Incorrect. API keys are often used for basic authentication and may be less secure than OAuth or JWT token.

EXAM FOCUS	*You should prioritize OAuth tokens or JWT tokens for secure access to Azure AI services. Always remember that these methods provide stronger security than basic authentication.*
CAUTION ALERT	*Stay cautioned against using API keys for critical services as they are less secure than token-based methods. Avoid relying on basic authentication, which has weaker security measures.*

QUESTION 5

Answer - [A, B, D]

Option A - Implement autoscaling to dynamically adjust resources based on workload demands: Correct. Autoscaling enhances scalability and resource efficiency by adjusting resources based on workload fluctuations.
Option B - Choose a high-availability region and configure redundant backups for critical data: Correct. Selecting a high-availability region and implementing backups improve reliability and data protection.
Option C - Optimize resource utilization by leveraging serverless computing options, such as Azure Functions: While serverless computing can enhance resource efficiency, it may not be the most suitable option for all scenarios, especially those requiring continuous processing of IoT data.
Option D - Enable logging and monitoring features to track performance metrics and detect potential issues: Correct. Logging and monitoring are essential for ensuring reliability and detecting anomalies or performance issues in real-time.
Option E - Deploy services in isolated environments to minimize resource contention and enhance reliability: While isolation can improve reliability, it may not always be necessary and could increase resource overhead.

EXAM FOCUS	*You should implement autoscaling, select high-availability regions, and enable logging to ensure reliability and scalability. Make sure to configure backups for critical data.*
CAUTION ALERT	*Avoid assuming serverless computing is always the best choice for IoT workloads; it may not fit continuous data processing needs. Stay clear of excessive isolation of services unless needed, as it can add overhead.*

QUESTION 6

Answer - E) Use Azure Network Watcher to analyze network traffic between the VM and Azure AI services.

Option A - Incorrect. Reviewing Azure AD logs may not provide insights into network connectivity issues between the VM and Azure AI services. Option B - Incorrect. While NSG rules can affect connectivity, they may not be the root cause of the problem. Option C - Incorrect. Outbound internet connectivity is necessary but does not address potential network configuration issues specific to Azure AI services. Option D - Incorrect. While checking firewall rules is important, it does not address potential network routing or configuration issues affecting connectivity.

EXAM FOCUS	*You should use Azure Network Watcher to analyze network traffic between your VM and Azure AI services. Keep in mind this tool helps you identify network routing and connectivity issues.*
CAUTION	*Avoid assuming that reviewing Azure AD logs will resolve network issues—it's more related to*

ALERT	*authentication. Stay clear of assuming outbound connectivity alone is sufficient to solve the problem.*

QUESTION 7

Answer - [E] Azure Log Analytics.

Azure Log Analytics - Integrating Azure Log Analytics with Azure AI services enables centralized log management, real-time monitoring, and advanced analytics for performance insights and anomaly detection, supporting efficient troubleshooting and optimization. Options A, B, C, and D may be relevant but do not specifically address log analysis for AI services.

EXAM FOCUS	*You need to integrate Azure Log Analytics for centralized log management and performance analysis. Always remember that Log Analytics offers advanced analytics for anomaly detection.*
CAUTION ALERT	*Avoid assuming Azure Monitor alone can provide deep log analysis; it is more suited for real-time monitoring. Stay clear of tools like Azure Data Lake Storage, which are for data storage, not log analysis.*

QUESTION 8

Answer - [D] Establishing alerts for budget overruns and nearing thresholds.

Establishing alerts for budget overruns and nearing thresholds - Configuring alerts for budget overruns and nearing thresholds ensures timely notification of potential cost overruns, allowing proactive measures to be taken to mitigate financial risks. Options A, B, C, and E may result in inadequate budget monitoring and increased likelihood of exceeding allocated funds.

EXAM FOCUS	*You should establish alerts for budget overruns and nearing thresholds to maintain cost control. Always remember to monitor budget alerts regularly to avoid unexpected costs.*
CAUTION ALERT	*Avoid setting alerts for insignificant fluctuations or arbitrary estimates. Stay clear of disabling budget alerts, which can lead to overspending without notice.*

QUESTION 9

Answer - D) Enable Managed Service Identity (MSI) for App3 and assign RBAC permissions to Microsoft Entra ID.

Option A - Incorrect. While OAuth 2.0 authentication with Azure AD is a valid approach, enabling MSI with RBAC permissions directly meets the requirement with minimal administrative overhead. Option B - Incorrect. Azure AD authentication may not directly support Microsoft Entra ID and may introduce unnecessary complexity. Option C - Incorrect. Azure AD SSO may provide centralized authentication but may not align with the requirement to use Microsoft Entra ID. Option E - Incorrect. Storing client secrets may introduce additional security risks and administrative overhead.

EXAM FOCUS	*You need to enable Managed Service Identity (MSI) for App3 and assign RBAC permissions to simplify authentication with Microsoft Entra ID. Always remember this approach minimizes administrative effort.*
CAUTION ALERT	*Avoid relying on OAuth 2.0 or client secrets, which add complexity. Stay clear of Azure AD single sign-on if the goal is least-privileged authentication using Microsoft Entra ID.*

QUESTION 10

Answer - [B] Utilize Azure Content Moderator's built-in text classification capabilities.

Utilize Azure Content Moderator's built-in text classification capabilities - Leveraging Azure Content Moderator's features for text classification enables efficient automation of moderation workflows while ensuring compliance and user safety, unlike options A, C, D, and E, which may lack scalability or accuracy.

EXAM FOCUS	*You should leverage Azure Content Moderator's built-in text classification capabilities for automating moderation workflows. Make sure to configure rules that align with compliance and safety standards.*
CAUTION ALERT	*Avoid manual content review if scalability is important. Stay cautioned against using sentiment analysis for moderation, as it doesn't filter inappropriate content effectively.*

QUESTION 11

Answer - [A] Implementing Azure Virtual Machine scale sets for automatic scaling based on demand.

Azure Virtual Machine scale sets allow for automatic scaling of compute resources based on demand, ensuring high availability and reliability for the decision support system, especially during peak usage periods. Options B, C, D, and E focus on different Azure services but may not provide the same level of scalability and availability as scale sets.

EXAM FOCUS	*You should implement Azure Virtual Machine scale sets to ensure your system scales automatically to meet demand, which is critical for high availability in decision support systems. Keep in mind that this approach ensures reliability during peak usage.*
CAUTION ALERT	*Avoid depending solely on load balancers or geo-replication—they are useful but do not provide dynamic scaling based on real-time demand. Stay clear of assuming that redundant instances alone ensure scalability.*

QUESTION 12

Answer - B) Use Azure Logic Apps to automate deployment tasks for Azure AI services.
D) Configure Azure Functions to trigger deployments of Azure AI services based on GitHub commits.

Option A - Incorrect. While Azure DevOps can be used for CI/CD, it may require additional configuration for Azure AI services integration. Option C - Incorrect. While Azure Kubernetes Service (AKS) can host containerized applications, direct integration with Azure AI services may not be straightforward. Option E - Incorrect. Azure Automation is primarily used for automating repetitive tasks and may not be well-suited for CI/CD integration with Azure AI services.

EXAM FOCUS	*Make sure to configure Azure Logic Apps for automating deployment tasks and Azure Functions for triggering deployments based on code changes. You should combine these with GitHub for continuous integration and delivery.*
CAUTION ALERT	*Avoid using Azure Automation for CI/CD tasks as it's better suited for task scheduling. Stay clear of direct integration with AKS for CI/CD; this is more complex and less straightforward for AI services.*

QUESTION 13

Answer - [A, B, C, E] Options A, B, C, and E provide best practices for deploying Azure AI solutions globally.

Option A ensures high availability, option B enables global load balancing, option C facilitates efficient content delivery, and option E reduces latency through content caching. Option D, priority routing with Traffic Manager, may not be as effective for global deployments compared to other options.

EXAM FOCUS	*You need to utilize Azure Availability Zones, Traffic Manager, and Front Door for global load balancing and content delivery. Always remember to cache content close to users with Azure CDN to reduce latency.*
CAUTION ALERT	*Stay cautioned that priority routing in Traffic Manager may not be sufficient for large-scale global deployments. Avoid overlooking the importance of caching for user experience.*

QUESTION 14

Answer - [A] Option A (Object detection) should be prioritized to identify objects such as customers, products, and their interactions within the store, enabling insights into customer behavior and product placement optimization.

Options B, C, D, and E focus on specific aspects like recognizing faces, activities, text, and emotions, which may be secondary to the primary objective of analyzing customer behavior and optimizing store layout.

EXAM FOCUS	*You should prioritize object detection to capture key visual insights on customer behavior, product interaction, and store layout. Keep in mind that this analysis helps optimize product placement and enhance user experience.*
CAUTION ALERT	*Avoid over-relying on facial recognition or text detection, as these features do not directly help in understanding customer movement or product interaction. Stay clear of focusing on emotion detection unless customer sentiment is being analyzed.*

QUESTION 15

Answer - C) Optimize the code by reducing unnecessary data processing and improving algorithm efficiency.
D) Parallelize processing tasks to leverage distributed computing resources effectively.

Option A - Incorrect. While caching can improve performance, it may not directly address algorithmic inefficiencies. Option B - Incorrect. Scaling up the service tier can increase processing power but may not resolve underlying performance bottlenecks. Option E - Incorrect. Asynchronous processing can enhance scalability but might not directly optimize code efficiency.

EXAM FOCUS	*You need to focus on optimizing your code and parallelizing tasks to improve the performance of natural language processing solutions. Always remember that improving algorithm efficiency can lead to significant gains.*
CAUTION ALERT	*Avoid assuming that increasing service tiers will fix performance issues if the root cause is inefficient code. Stay clear of overusing asynchronous processing—it may help with scalability, not always with performance.*

QUESTION 16

Answer - [B] Fine-tuning models

B) Fine-tuning models - Correct. Fine-tuning models involve adjusting pre-trained models to specialize in specific tasks, such as improving the accuracy of text extraction. By fine-tuning models on handwritten text or unusual fonts, the accuracy of text recognition can be significantly enhanced, ensuring reliable results in scenarios requiring high precision.
A) Transfer learning - Incorrect. While transfer learning can be used to adapt pre-trained models to new tasks, fine-tuning specifically focuses on adjusting model parameters to improve performance on specific tasks, such as text extraction.
C) Azure AI Form Recognizer - Incorrect. Azure AI Form Recognizer is designed for extracting structured data from forms and documents, rather than fine-tuning models for text extraction accuracy.
D) Preprocessing techniques - Incorrect. Preprocessing techniques involve data manipulation and cleaning before model training, but they may not directly address the task of improving text extraction accuracy.
E) Ensemble learning - Incorrect. Ensemble learning combines multiple models to improve performance, but it may not specifically target the task of enhancing text extraction accuracy in scenarios with handwritten text or unusual fonts.

EXAM FOCUS	*You should fine-tune models to improve text extraction accuracy, especially when dealing with handwritten or complex fonts. Always remember that model adjustments tailored to specific tasks often yield better results than generic models.*
CAUTION ALERT	*Avoid assuming that preprocessing techniques alone will solve accuracy issues—they help clean data but don't directly affect model precision. Stay clear of expecting Azure Form Recognizer to handle fine-tuning—it's primarily for structured document extraction.*

QUESTION 17

Answer - [B) Adjust the classification threshold, C) Fine-tune the model's hyperparameters]

Adjusting the classification threshold and fine-tuning the model's hyperparameters are common strategies to balance between precision and recall.
A) Increasing the training dataset size may not directly address the imbalance between precision and recall.
D) Data augmentation techniques can enhance model generalization but may not directly affect precision-recall balance.
E) Decreasing the number of training epochs might not solve the precision-recall imbalance issue.

EXAM FOCUS	*You should adjust the classification threshold and fine-tune hyperparameters to balance precision and recall in image classification tasks. Keep in mind that these adjustments can help mitigate overfitting and improve overall model performance.*
CAUTION ALERT	*Avoid assuming that increasing the dataset size or decreasing training epochs will solve precision-recall imbalances. Stay clear of expecting data augmentation to directly fix precision-recall issues—it primarily improves model generalization.*

QUESTION 18

Answer - [D] Adjust the confidence threshold for classification predictions.

Option D - Increasing the size of the training dataset (Option A) may improve generalization but might not specifically address false positives. Fine-tuning hyperparameters (Option B) can enhance model performance but may not directly reduce false positives. Implementing post-processing techniques (Option C) could help filter out false positives but might not address the root cause within the model. Upgrading the Azure AI Vision service (Option E) is not necessary initially. Adjusting the confidence threshold (Option D) allows for more stringent classification, potentially reducing false positives.

EXAM FOCUS	*You need to adjust the confidence threshold to reduce false positives in your classification model. Keep in mind this helps the model become more conservative in its predictions.*
CAUTION ALERT	*Avoid upgrading the service tier immediately—it's not necessary for addressing false positives. Stay clear of increasing dataset size without addressing threshold tuning—it may not solve the issue directly.*

QUESTION 19

Answer - A) Use Azure DevOps pipelines to manage model versions and deployments, enabling easy rollbacks when needed.

Option B - Maintaining copies of the model code on different servers lacks efficiency and consistency in managing versions.
Option C - Manually tracking changes and rolling back is error-prone and lacks automation.
Option D - While Azure ML tracks versions, it may not provide direct rollback capabilities like DevOps pipelines.
Option E - Manual processes for updates and rollbacks are inefficient and prone to errors, especially in production environments.

EXAM FOCUS	*You should use Azure DevOps pipelines for managing model versions and enabling automated rollbacks. Always remember that automated pipelines streamline deployment and ensure consistency across environments.*
CAUTION ALERT	*Avoid manual version control and rollback processes, which are prone to errors. Stay clear of relying on multiple server copies for version management—it's inefficient and difficult to scale.*

QUESTION 20

Answer - D) Azure AI Vision Spatial Analysis

Option A - Azure AI Video Indexer focuses more on extracting insights and metadata from videos rather than real-time spatial analysis for safety monitoring.
Option B - While Azure Cognitive Services - Computer Vision offers image analysis capabilities, it may not provide specific features for accuracy optimization in spatial analysis for safety monitoring.
Option C - Azure Cognitive Services - Video Analyzer is geared towards real-time video processing but may not offer the precision required for detailed spatial analysis.
Option E - Azure AI Metrics Advisor is designed for monitoring and analyzing metrics data rather than real-time video analysis for safety monitoring.

EXAM FOCUS	*Make sure to use Azure AI Vision Spatial Analysis for detecting and tracking worker movements. You should ensure accuracy optimization in spatial analysis to enhance worker safety on construction sites.*
CAUTION ALERT	*Avoid using Azure AI Video Indexer, which is better suited for extracting metadata rather than real-time spatial analysis. Stay clear of focusing on general image analysis with Cognitive Services if spatial safety analysis is required.*

QUESTION 21

Answer - [B] Analysis of audio quality metrics.

Option B - This API request is used to assess and analyze the quality of audio inputs, focusing on metrics related to the clarity, accuracy, and overall quality of the audio signal. It is not involved in speech recognition (Option A), synthesis of speech from text (Option C), detection of audio sentiment (Option D), or translation of speech to text (Option E).

EXAM FOCUS	*You should use this API to analyze the quality of audio inputs before proceeding with speech recognition tasks. Make sure you assess audio quality to ensure better transcription results in Azure AI Speech service.*
CAUTION ALERT	*Avoid confusing this API with speech recognition or sentiment detection APIs. Stay clear of using this for generating synthesized speech—it's purely for audio quality analysis.*

QUESTION 22

Answer - A) Azure AI Language - Key Phrase Extraction

Option B - While Azure Cognitive Search can index and search documents, it may not provide the same level of text analysis and accuracy as Azure AI Language for key phrase extraction.
Option C - Azure Text Analytics offers key phrase extraction, but Azure AI Language may provide more customization options and better accuracy.
Option D - Azure Machine Learning requires custom model development and might not be the most efficient solution for this scenario.
Option E - Azure Databricks is more focused on big data processing and analytics rather than text analysis and key phrase extraction.

EXAM FOCUS	*You should use Azure AI Language - Key Phrase Extraction for accurate phrase identification while ensuring compliance with data privacy regulations. Make sure this service is configured correctly for sensitive data handling.*
CAUTION ALERT	*Avoid using services like Azure Cognitive Search or Azure Databricks for key phrase extraction as they do not provide the same level of customization or compliance features. Stay clear of using complex ML solutions unless necessary.*

QUESTION 23

Answer - [A] Sentiment analysis with context embedding.

Sentiment analysis with context embedding allows the model to consider the surrounding context of each message, enabling more accurate classification of feedback as positive, neutral, or negative, especially in cases where the sentiment might be influenced by context. Lexicon-based, pre-trained, rule-based, and frequency-based approaches may not adequately capture contextual nuances in sentiment analysis.

EXAM FOCUS	*You should use sentiment analysis with context embedding to classify customer feedback accurately, as it considers the surrounding text for more nuanced sentiment detection. Make sure to use this technique for multilingual and culturally diverse feedback.*
CAUTION ALERT	*Avoid rule-based or lexicon-based methods, which may fail to capture the context of messages. Stay clear of frequency-based analysis for sentiment detection in customer feedback.*

QUESTION 24

Answer - [C] Preprocessing text data to remove noise and irrelevant content.

Option C - Preprocessing text data to remove noise and irrelevant content can improve the accuracy of key phrase extraction by providing cleaner input for the AI service. Adjusting language detection thresholds (Option A) focuses on language identification rather than phrase extraction. Increasing text length limits (Option B) may not directly address accuracy issues. Enhancing access control (Option D) and upgrading service plans (Option E) do not typically affect accuracy related to data quality.

EXAM FOCUS	*You need to preprocess text data to remove noise and irrelevant content to improve key phrase extraction accuracy. Always remember that clean data improves the performance of any AI service.*
CAUTION ALERT	*Avoid assuming that increasing the maximum text length or adjusting access control will solve accuracy issues. Stay clear of thinking that upgrading the service plan will directly improve extraction accuracy.*

QUESTION 25

Answer - B) Leveraging Azure Speech SDK's multilingual support with customized language models.

Option A - Training separate models for each language might be resource-intensive and less efficient.
Option B - Correct. Leveraging Azure Speech SDK's multilingual support allows for customized language models, ensuring high accuracy across different languages and audio qualities.
Option C - Phonetic-based algorithms may not adequately address the nuances of different languages and accents.
Option D - While cloud-based services may offer language detection, they may not provide customized models for each language.
Option E - Ensemble learning could be complex to implement and may not guarantee better accuracy across languages.

EXAM FOCUS	*You should leverage Azure Speech SDK's multilingual support with customized language models to ensure high accuracy across different languages and audio qualities. Make sure you customize models based on specific language requirements.*
CAUTION ALERT	*Avoid training separate models for each language—it can be resource-intensive. Stay clear of relying on phonetic algorithms or generic cloud services without customization for accurate multilingual support.*

QUESTION 26

Answer - [C] Microsoft Bot Framework for building conversational AI.

Option C is the most suitable choice as the Microsoft Bot Framework enables the development of conversational AI solutions, allowing for dynamic content generation based on caller interactions in a call center application. Options A, D, and E are related to speech recognition or synthesis but do not address the dynamic content generation requirement. Option B is primarily for natural language processing tasks and may not be well-suited for real-time interaction in a call center setting.

EXAM FOCUS	*You should use Microsoft Bot Framework to build conversational AI for generating dynamic content based on caller interactions. Always remember that the framework is designed to handle real-time user interactions effectively.*
CAUTION ALERT	*Avoid using Azure Speech-to-Text API or Azure OpenAI Service for dynamic content generation—they are more suited for recognition or generative tasks, not real-time interactions. Stay clear of using NLP libraries like NLTK for real-time conversational AI.*

QUESTION 27

Answer - [C] Optical character recognition (OCR)

Option C - Optical character recognition (OCR) is specifically designed to extract text from images, including handwritten notes, making it the most suitable choice for this task. Face detection (Option A) focuses on identifying faces, not text. Object recognition (Option B) identifies objects but not textual content. Image segmentation (Option D) divides images into segments but does not extract text. Text translation (Option E) translates text from one language to another, which is not relevant to text extraction from images.

EXAM FOCUS	*You should use Optical Character Recognition (OCR) in Azure AI Vision to extract text, especially handwritten notes, from images. Keep in mind OCR is specifically designed for text extraction, even from challenging backgrounds.*
CAUTION ALERT	*Avoid using face detection, object recognition, or segmentation—they are not designed for extracting text. Stay clear of using text translation if your goal is to extract text, not translate it.*

QUESTION 28

Answer - [E] Integration with Azure Key Vault

Option E is the correct choice because integrating with Azure Key Vault allows for securely storing and managing sensitive information such as encryption keys, enhancing security and confidentiality in document translation. Options A, B, C, and D are less relevant or unrelated to ensuring security in document translation.

EXAM FOCUS	*You should integrate Azure Cognitive Services Translator Text with Azure Key Vault to ensure encryption and secure management of sensitive information during document translation. Always remember that security is critical when handling confidential documents.*
CAUTION ALERT	*Avoid relying solely on RBAC or encryption at rest for security—Azure Key Vault ensures higher security for sensitive keys. Stay cautioned against neglecting the need for end-to-end encryption.*

QUESTION 29

Answer - [B] Implement an active learning system to prioritize relevant data for model training

Explanation: B) An active learning system prioritizes relevant data, ensuring efficient use of resources and continual improvement of the model. A) Periodically retraining the model with all data may be resource-intensive and less effective for incremental learning. C) Waiting for significant data distribution changes may lead to missed opportunities for model improvement. D) Manual updates may not scale well and may introduce biases. E) Excluding new data hinders the model's ability to adapt and improve over time.

EXAM FOCUS	*You need to implement an active learning system that prioritizes relevant data for continuous improvement of your custom translation model. Always remember that active learning is more efficient than retraining*

CAUTION ALERT	*on all data.* *Avoid manually updating model parameters or retraining periodically on all data—it's resource-intensive and inefficient. Stay clear of excluding new data, as it hinders the model's ability to adapt.*

QUESTION 30

Answer - [B] Variability in document quality and formatting.

Option B - Variability in document quality and formatting can lead to inconsistencies in field recognition, as the Azure AI Form Recognizer model may struggle to extract data accurately from documents with diverse layouts or poor quality scans. Insufficient training data (Option A) may affect overall performance but is less likely to cause inconsistency across different document types. Limited language support (Option C) may impact recognition accuracy but should not directly cause inconsistency. An outdated SDK version (Option D) may lead to compatibility issues but is not the primary cause of recognition inconsistency. Lack of integration (Option E) between the preprocessing pipeline and Form Recognizer might affect data flow but is not directly related to recognition inconsistency.

EXAM FOCUS	*You should consider variability in document quality and formatting as a common cause of inconsistent field recognition in Azure AI Form Recognizer. Always remember that better document quality yields more reliable results.*
CAUTION ALERT	*Avoid assuming that an outdated SDK or insufficient training data is the root cause—it's often the inconsistency in the document quality. Stay clear of ignoring preprocessing before feeding documents to Form Recognizer.*

QUESTION 31

Answer - [A), B), and D)] - Precision, recall, and F1 score calculations provide a comprehensive evaluation of model performance. Domain-specific evaluation metrics ensure the model meets the specific requirements of legal document review. Error analysis and confusion matrix examination help identify areas for improvement.

C) Incorrect - While human-in-the-loop validation can be valuable, it might not provide quantifiable metrics necessary for comprehensive evaluation.
E) Incorrect - While model interpretability is essential, it might not directly address the need for evaluating model performance in this scenario.

EXAM FOCUS	*You should use precision, recall, and F1 score to evaluate the model comprehensively. Make sure to focus on domain-specific evaluation metrics for legal terms, and analyze confusion matrices to identify problem areas.*
CAUTION ALERT	*Avoid relying solely on basic metrics like accuracy without considering domain-specific needs. Stay clear of skipping error analysis, as it provides key insights for improvement.*

QUESTION 32

Answer - [B), D), and E)] - Integrating user feedback mechanisms, establishing regular retraining cycles, and deploying model versioning enable continuous improvement of model performance and alignment with evolving requirements.

A) Incorrect - While active learning can prioritize labeling uncertain data instances, it might not directly address the challenge of incorporating feedback loops for continuous optimization and performance improvement.

EXAM FOCUS	*You should establish regular retraining cycles with updated datasets and integrate user feedback to ensure ongoing optimization. Always remember to use model versioning to track performance changes effectively.*
CAUTION ALERT	*Avoid delaying retraining until major issues arise. Stay alert to the risk of model drift if regular feedback loops are not implemented.*

QUESTION 33

Answer - [A] Azure AI Language Service > Text Analytics API

Option A - Azure AI Language Service with the Text Analytics API is designed for extracting key entities from text data, making it the most suitable choice. Option B is incorrect as the Content Moderator service is more focused on content moderation. Option C is incorrect as Translator Text is used for translation, not entity extraction. Option D is incorrect as Cognitive Search is more oriented towards indexing and searching content. Option E is incorrect as the Speech Service is for speech-to-text and text-to-speech conversion.

EXAM FOCUS	*You need to use Azure AI Language Service with Text Analytics API to extract entities efficiently from large text data. Always remember this is the most efficient API for such tasks.*
CAUTION ALERT	*Avoid using services like Azure Cognitive Search or Translator Text for entity extraction—they are focused on search and translation, not entity identification.*

QUESTION 34

Answer - [B) and C)] - Handling diverse formats and sources involves utilizing Azure Data Factory for format conversion and Azure Functions for real-time data transformation.

Option B) - Correct: Azure Data Factory facilitates format conversion and data integration seamlessly. Option C) - Correct: Azure Functions enable real-time data transformation, enhancing adaptability. Option A) - Incorrect: Converting all sources to a single format may lead to data loss and inefficiency. Option D) - Incorrect: Third-party tools may introduce complexity and compatibility issues. Option E) - Incorrect: Limiting source types restricts flexibility and coverage.

EXAM FOCUS	*You should utilize Azure Data Factory for data integration and format conversion, and Azure Functions for real-time transformation. Make sure to handle data from diverse formats efficiently.*
CAUTION ALERT	*Avoid limiting source types to simplify management—it will reduce the coverage of your solution. Stay clear of third-party tools when native Azure tools offer seamless integration and better compatibility.*

QUESTION 35

Answer - [A), B), and D)] - Ensuring version control and rollback mechanisms involve utilizing Azure DevOps, Azure Git Repos, and storing backups in Azure Blob Storage.

Option A) - Correct: Azure DevOps provides comprehensive version control and deployment capabilities. Option B) - Correct: Azure Git Repos enables tracking changes and maintaining version history. Option C) - Incorrect: While Azure Functions can automate processes, they are not typically used for rollback mechanisms. Option D) - Correct: Storing backups in Azure Blob Storage facilitates easy retrieval and restoration of previous versions. Option E) - Incorrect: Manual version logs are prone to errors and may not offer efficient rollback mechanisms compared to automated solutions.

EXAM FOCUS	*You need to leverage Azure DevOps and Azure Git Repos for version control, and back up knowledge bases in Azure Blob Storage for easy rollback. Always remember to automate deployment processes for efficiency.*
CAUTION ALERT	*Avoid relying on manual version logs—they are prone to error and inefficiency. Stay clear of overlooking backup storage as it ensures quick retrieval during rollbacks.*

QUESTION 36

Answer - [A, B, E] "--rm -it"
"--memory 256 --cpus 4"
"--region westus"

Option A is essential for running the container interactively and removing it after execution. Option B specifies memory and CPU limits for the container. Option E specifies the region for deployment. Option C is incorrect as it does not align with the purpose of the container deployment. Option D is not relevant to running containers.

EXAM FOCUS	*You should include "--rm -it" for container management, specify "--memory 256 --cpus 4" for resource allocation, and set the correct region with "--region westus". Always remember to allocate sufficient resources for smooth operation.*
CAUTION ALERT	*Avoid omitting region or resource specifications in container configurations. Stay clear of irrelevant parameters like "--apply" or incomplete configurations.*

QUESTION 37

Answer - [C, D].

C) Applying dropout regularization helps prevent overfitting by randomly dropping neurons during training, forcing the model to learn more robust features. D) Decreasing the number of layers in the model reduces its complexity, thereby reducing the risk of overfitting. A) Increasing the model's complexity exacerbates overfitting, while reducing the size of the training dataset may lead to underfitting. Using a higher learning rate can destabilize training and hinder convergence.

EXAM FOCUS	*You should apply dropout regularization and reduce model layers to mitigate overfitting. Keep in mind that these techniques reduce the model's complexity and improve generalization.*
CAUTION ALERT	*Avoid increasing the model's complexity or reducing the dataset size, as this can worsen overfitting or lead to underfitting. Stay clear of high learning rates, which can destabilize training.*

QUESTION 38

Answer - [A, C].

A) Implementing continuous training with new data ensures that the bot remains up-to-date and responsive to evolving user queries, enhancing long-term performance. C) Incorporating user feedback loops allows for iterative model refinement based on real-world interactions, improving accuracy and relevance over time. B) While Azure Monitor provides valuable insights, it primarily focuses on real-time monitoring and may not directly contribute to long-term performance improvement. D) Reinforcement learning enhances adaptive dialogue management but may not be the primary focus for ensuring performance over time. E) Azure Application Insights is useful for user behavior analysis but may not directly contribute to improving the bot's performance over time.

EXAM FOCUS	*You should implement continuous training with new data and integrate feedback loops for improving model performance over time. Keep in mind that user feedback is critical for maintaining relevance and accuracy.*
CAUTION ALERT	*Avoid neglecting regular updates—this can lead to stale performance in dynamic environments. Stay cautioned against relying solely on real-time monitoring without refining models based on actual user interactions.*

QUESTION 39

Answer - [A, C] new TranslationClient("<YourSubscriptionKey>", "<YourServiceRegion>")
translationResult.TranslationText

Option A initializes the TranslationClient object with the provided subscription key and service region. Option C retrieves the translated text from the translation result. Options B, D, and E are incorrect or irrelevant for translation initialization or retrieval.

EXAM FOCUS	*You should correctly initialize the TranslationClient with "<YourSubscriptionKey>" and "<YourServiceRegion>" and retrieve the translated text using translationResult.TranslationText. Always remember that correct API initialization is essential for proper functionality.*
CAUTION ALERT	*Avoid incorrect API calls like TranslationLanguage.English or DetectLanguageAsync in translation tasks—they are not relevant to this operation.*

QUESTION 40

Answer - [A] Azure Text Analytics.

A) Azure Text Analytics offers sentiment analysis capabilities that can be applied across different demographics, allowing for comparative analysis of sentiment trends and preferences. B) Azure Language Understanding (LUIS) focuses on understanding user intents and entities within a single language and is not specialized for comparative sentiment analysis. C) Azure Cognitive Search is primarily used for search functionalities and does not specialize in sentiment analysis. D) Azure AI Translator service focuses on translation tasks and does not provide sentiment analysis capabilities. E) Azure AI Language Service provides language detection and translation but does not specifically handle sentiment analysis like Azure Text Analytics.

EXAM FOCUS	*You should integrate Azure Text Analytics for effective sentiment analysis across different demographics. Always remember to leverage its capabilities for comparative analysis.*
CAUTION ALERT	*Avoid using services like LUIS or Translator for sentiment analysis—they are not specialized for this purpose. Stay clear of tools that don't offer direct sentiment analysis functionalities.*

QUESTION 41

Answer - [A] Enable Azure AD authentication.

A) Enabling Azure AD authentication ensures secure access control to the Cognitive Search service, allowing only authorized users to interact with the search functionality. B) IP firewall rules restrict access based on IP addresses but may not provide granular user authentication. C) Shared access signatures (SAS) are primarily used for granting limited access to storage resources, not Cognitive Search. D) Encrypting data at rest adds an additional layer of security but may not directly address authentication concerns. E) Role-based access control (RBAC) is more applicable to managing access to Azure resources rather than securing Cognitive Search queries.

EXAM FOCUS	*You should enable Azure AD authentication to ensure secure access control for Azure Cognitive Search. Keep in mind that this helps manage user access effectively and reduces unauthorized access.*
CAUTION ALERT	*Avoid relying solely on IP firewall rules, as they are not sufficient for managing user-level access. Stay clear of shared access signatures (SAS) for Cognitive Search security.*

QUESTION 42

Answer - [A] ContentModeratorClient

Option B, FormRecognizerClient, is used for extracting information from forms and documents, not for PII identification and anonymization in text inputs. Option C, TextAnalyticsClient, is used for text analytics tasks like sentiment analysis and key phrase extraction, not specifically for PII anonymization. Option D, LanguageUnderstandingClient, is used for understanding user intents from natural language inputs and does not include PII anonymization features. Option E, MetricsAdvisorClient, is used for monitoring and analyzing metrics data and is unrelated to PII identification and anonymization. Option A, ContentModeratorClient, is the correct choice as it provides capabilities for identifying and anonymizing PII data from text inputs.

EXAM FOCUS	*Make sure to use the ContentModeratorClient for identifying and anonymizing PII data from text inputs. Keep in mind that it provides built-in tools for text moderation, including PII detection.*
CAUTION ALERT	*Stay alert to confusing PII anonymization with text analytics tasks like sentiment analysis, which do not include PII management. Avoid using Form Recognizer or Text Analytics for this task.*

QUESTION 43

Answer - [D] Skillset.

D) Skillsets in Azure Cognitive Search allow you to define processing pipelines that include custom skills developed using external AI services, enabling seamless integration for extracting insights from documents. A) Cognitive Skills is not a specific feature in Azure Cognitive Search; rather, it refers to the broader capability of the service to process and extract insights from content. B) Custom Analyzers are used to define how text is processed and indexed but do not directly integrate external AI services for document processing. C) Indexers are used to populate the search index but do not directly handle custom processing logic with external AI services. E) Scoring Profiles are used to define ranking rules for search results but do not relate to integrating custom skills developed with external AI services.

EXAM FOCUS	*You should use skillsets in Azure Cognitive Search to integrate external AI services for document processing. Always remember that skillsets allow custom processing pipelines to extract insights effectively.*
CAUTION ALERT	*Stay clear of using custom analyzers or indexers to perform AI integrations—they are not designed for handling external AI services. Avoid relying solely on scoring profiles for enhancing search capabilities.*

QUESTION 44

Answer - [A] Define facets in the search index schema.

A) Defining facets in the search index schema allows for implementing faceted search and filters directly within Azure Cognitive Search, enabling users to refine search results based on predefined attributes. B) Implementing custom filters using Azure Functions adds unnecessary complexity and may not provide seamless integration with search results. C) While Azure Cognitive Search offers built-in support for faceted search, defining facets in the index schema provides more flexibility and control over the filtering process. D) Query suggestions based on user input are unrelated to faceted search and do not directly address the requirement for filtering search results. E) Developing custom UI components for filtering may enhance user experience but does not address the backend implementation of faceted search and filters in Azure Cognitive Search.

EXAM FOCUS	*Make sure to define facets in the search index schema to enable faceted search and filtering. Always remember that this is the most straightforward way to implement user-friendly search filtering.*
CAUTION ALERT	*Avoid complicating the solution with custom filters in Azure Functions—they add unnecessary complexity. Stay clear of ignoring the built-in faceted search capabilities in Azure Cognitive Search.*

QUESTION 45

Answer - B) DetectLanguage()

Option A - IdentifyLanguage(): This is a hypothetical method and not part of the Azure Text Analytics SDK.
Option C - RecognizeLanguage(): This is a hypothetical method and not part of the Azure Text Analytics SDK.
Option D - LanguageDetection(): This is a hypothetical method and not part of the Azure Text Analytics SDK.
Option E - DetermineLanguage(): This is a hypothetical method and not part of the Azure Text Analytics SDK.
Option B is correct because DetectLanguage() is the method used to determine the language of text in Azure Text Analytics.

EXAM FOCUS	*You need to use the DetectLanguage() method in Azure Text Analytics for determining the language of text. Keep in mind that this is the correct and efficient method for language detection.*
CAUTION ALERT	*Avoid using hypothetical methods like IdentifyLanguage() or RecognizeLanguage()—they do not exist in the Azure SDK. Stay alert to avoiding confusion with incorrect method names.*

QUESTION 46

Answer - [A] Model accuracy and performance.

A) The primary concern when selecting an Azure OpenAI model should be its accuracy and performance to ensure it meets project requirements effectively.
B) Model training time is a consideration during the training phase but does not impact the selection of the pre-trained model.
C) Model interpretability is important for understanding model behavior but may not be the primary factor in model selection.
D) Model size and resource utilization are relevant for deployment but may vary based on the project's infrastructure capabilities.
E) Model support for multiple languages is valuable but may not be the primary consideration depending on the project's language requirements.

Always remember to prioritize model accuracy and performance when selecting an Azure OpenAI model. You should ensure the model meets the specific project requirements effectively.

Avoid focusing solely on factors like model training time or resource utilization—accuracy is key for optimal project results. Stay clear of overemphasizing secondary considerations like model interpretability unless critical for your use case.

QUESTION 47

Answer - [C] Adjusting the nucleus sampling threshold to control response diversity.

C) Nucleus sampling threshold allows for more dynamic control over response diversity, ensuring coherence while maintaining relevance.
A) Increasing temperature introduces randomness but may decrease coherence.
B) Reducing beam width may limit the scope of responses, potentially affecting relevance.
D) Decreasing maximum token length may lead to truncated responses, impacting coherence.
E) Fine-tuning the language model enhances relevance but may not directly address coherence concerns.

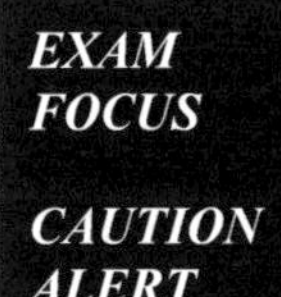

You should adjust the nucleus sampling threshold to improve the coherence and flow of generated content while maintaining relevance. Keep in mind that controlling response diversity is essential for balanced content generation.

Avoid increasing the temperature too much, as it can reduce content coherence. Stay clear of excessively reducing the maximum token length, which may lead to incomplete responses.

QUESTION 48

Answer - E) Statement I, Statement III

Option B - Statement II: This statement is incorrect because Azure AI Speech service supports both synchronous and asynchronous processing.
Option D - Statement II, Statement III: This statement is incorrect because Statement II is incorrect, as mentioned earlier.
Option A is correct because Azure AI Speech service provides speech-to-text conversion, making Statement I true.
Option C is correct because Azure AI Speech service includes support for improving text-to-speech using SSML, making

Statement III true.
Option E is correct as it includes both true statements: Statement I and Statement III.

EXAM FOCUS	*You should remember that Azure AI Speech service supports both speech-to-text conversion and text-to-speech with SSML. Make sure to utilize both capabilities effectively in your project.*
CAUTION ALERT	*Stay clear of assuming that the service only supports synchronous processing—it also offers asynchronous options. Avoid missing out on SSML features for text-to-speech improvements.*

QUESTION 49

Answer - [A, E] Preprocessing the data to standardize features and remove noise. Versioning the dataset to track changes and ensure reproducibility in model training.

A) Preprocessing the data helps standardize features and improve the quality of training.
E) Versioning the dataset is crucial for tracking changes and ensuring reproducibility in model training.
B) Encryption of the dataset may enhance security but is not directly related to integration with Azure OpenAI models.
C) Assigning unique identifiers can be beneficial but is not specifically required for dataset integration.
D) While creating access policies is important for security, it does not directly address the integration of custom datasets.

EXAM FOCUS	*Make sure to preprocess data for noise removal and standardization when integrating custom datasets into Azure OpenAI models. Always remember to version datasets for reproducibility and accurate model training.*
CAUTION ALERT	*Avoid skipping preprocessing steps, as this can reduce model performance. Stay cautioned against relying on unversioned datasets, as it complicates tracking and improvements.*

QUESTION 50

Answer - [A, C] Legacy system compatibility: Implement adapters or middleware to bridge the gap between the generative AI model and the legacy gaming platform, ensuring compatibility and data exchange. Data privacy concerns: Implement encryption mechanisms and access controls to safeguard user data processed by the generative AI model, ensuring compliance with regulatory requirements.

A) Legacy system compatibility often poses challenges when integrating new technologies, requiring adapters or middleware for seamless integration.
C) Data privacy is crucial, and encryption mechanisms and access controls are essential to protect user data processed by AI models.
B) While scalability is important, it may not be the most immediate challenge during integration.
D) Performance optimization is vital but may not be the primary challenge during integration.
E) Integration complexity can be addressed using various Azure services, but legacy system compatibility and data privacy are more immediate concerns.

EXAM FOCUS	*You should address legacy system compatibility by implementing adapters or middleware for seamless integration of generative AI models with older systems. Keep in mind that encryption and access controls are critical for data privacy.*
CAUTION ALERT	*Avoid overlooking legacy system constraints, which can impede AI model integration. Stay alert to data privacy regulations when handling user data in generative AI projects.*

PRACTICE TEST 3 - QUESTIONS ONLY

QUESTION 1

Your organization is developing a social media monitoring tool that analyzes user comments and posts to gauge public sentiment and identify emerging trends. You need to select the appropriate Azure AI service for sentiment analysis and trend detection. Which service should you choose? Select all answers that apply.

A) Azure Cognitive Services Language Understanding (LUIS)
B) Azure Bot Services
C) Azure Cognitive Services Text Analytics
D) Azure QnA Maker
E) Azure Cognitive Services Personalizer

QUESTION 2

You are tasked with implementing a decision support solution for a financial institution to analyze customer feedback from emails and social media posts. The solution needs to extract key phrases, determine sentiment, and identify personally identifiable information (PII) for compliance purposes.
Which Azure AI service or combination of services should you select to meet these requirements effectively?
Select all answers that apply.

A) Azure AI Metrics Advisor
B) Azure AI Text Analytics
C) Azure AI Language Understanding (LUIS)
D) Azure AI Content Moderator
E) Azure AI Translator Text

QUESTION 3

To monitor the usage and performance of an Azure AI service, which Azure CLI command can be used to retrieve the resource's metrics?

```
A) az monitor metrics list
B) az monitor diagnostic-settings show
C) az monitor log-profiles list
D) az monitor log-profiles show
E) az monitor diagnostic-settings list
```

QUESTION 4

In a scenario where multiple users need access to Azure AI services, what authentication method can provide individualized access control and tracking of usage?

A) Shared access signature
B) OAuth 2.0
C) Role-based access control (RBAC)
D) Certificate authentication
E) Multi-factor authentication (MFA)

QUESTION 5

Your organization is deploying a new Azure AI solution to automate the processing of medical imaging data for diagnosing various health conditions. As part of the deployment process, you need to create an Azure AI resource to

host the required services, ensuring compliance with healthcare regulations and data privacy standards.
Which steps should you follow to create the Azure AI resource while addressing compliance requirements and ensuring data privacy and security?
Select all answers that apply.

A) Implement role-based access control (RBAC) to restrict access to sensitive data and services.
B) Enable data encryption using Azure Key Vault to protect sensitive information at rest and in transit.
C) Choose Azure regions that comply with relevant healthcare regulations and certifications.
D) Deploy services in a HIPAA-compliant environment to ensure adherence to healthcare data privacy standards.
E) Implement data anonymization techniques to protect patient privacy and comply with data protection laws.

QUESTION 6

You are tasked with ensuring that an application running on an Azure virtual machine can securely access Azure AI services without exposing unnecessary endpoints to the public internet. Which action should you take to achieve this goal?

A) Configure Azure Private Link for the Azure AI services.
B) Implement network security group (NSG) rules to restrict inbound traffic to the virtual machine.
C) Enable Azure AD authentication for the Azure AI services.
D) Use a VPN gateway to establish a secure connection between the virtual machine and Azure AI services.
E) Whitelist the virtual machine's IP address in the Azure AI services firewall settings.

QUESTION 7

Your organization needs to define log retention policies for Azure AI services to ensure compliance with regulatory requirements. Which consideration should influence your decision regarding log retention policies?
Select all answers that apply.

A) Minimizing storage costs
B) Retaining logs indefinitely
C) Aligning with data privacy regulations
D) Optimizing log query performance
E) Storing logs on local servers

QUESTION 8

Your organization is implementing cost-saving strategies for Azure AI services across development, testing, and production environments. Which practice can help optimize costs effectively while maintaining service quality?

A) Using the highest-tier service plans for all environments
B) Minimizing resource utilization to zero during off-hours
C) Utilizing cost-effective service tiers based on workload requirements
D) Conducting cost reviews once a year
E) Disabling cost tracking to avoid overhead

QUESTION 9

You are configuring authentication for an Azure App Services web app named App4. The app needs to authenticate using Microsoft Entra ID while minimizing administrative effort and adhering to the principle of least privilege. What is the best course of action?

A) Use Azure Active Directory (Azure AD) authentication and configure App4 to use it.
B) Enable Managed Service Identity (MSI) for App4 and assign RBAC permissions to Microsoft Entra ID.
C) Implement OAuth 2.0 authentication with Azure AD and grant App4 access to Microsoft Entra ID.

D) Configure App4 to use Azure AD single sign-on (SSO).
E) Generate a client secret and store it securely for App4 authentication.

QUESTION 10

Your organization is implementing Azure AI Content Safety for text moderation in a large-scale chat application. However, you're encountering challenges with false positives and negatives in the moderation process. What strategy should you employ to address this issue effectively?

A) Increase the sensitivity of text filters to reduce false negatives
B) Adjust moderation criteria based on user feedback and historical data
C) Ignore false positives and focus solely on eliminating harmful content
D) Manually review all flagged content to minimize errors
E) Disable text moderation temporarily until a better solution is found

QUESTION 11

Your team is leveraging Azure AI for predictive analytics and insights in a decision support system for financial forecasting. Which Azure service is most suitable for implementing predictive analytics models and generating insights from historical financial data?

A) Azure Machine Learning service for building, training, and deploying machine learning models.
B) Azure Databricks for collaborative Apache Spark-based analytics and machine learning.
C) Azure Synapse Analytics for data warehousing and big data analytics at scale.
D) Azure Cognitive Services for adding AI capabilities like sentiment analysis to applications.
E) Azure Functions for serverless event-driven compute.

QUESTION 12

You are tasked with optimizing a generative AI model deployed on Azure OpenAI Service. Which actions can you take to improve the model's performance and response quality?

A) Adjust the model's parameters to fine-tune its generative behavior.
B) Implement prompt engineering techniques to refine the quality of generated responses.
C) Use custom data sets to train the model and enhance its understanding.
D) Explore different Azure OpenAI models and select the most suitable one for the desired output.
E) Apply reinforcement learning algorithms to optimize the model's decision-making process.

QUESTION 13

Your team is responsible for managing resource allocation and autoscaling for an Azure AI solution deployed in a production environment. What strategies should you employ to optimize resource utilization and ensure performance under varying workloads?
Select all answers that apply.

A) Implement Azure Monitor to collect performance metrics and trigger autoscaling based on predefined thresholds.
B) Utilize Azure Logic Apps to automate resource provisioning and deallocation based on schedule and demand.
C) Configure Azure Load Balancer to distribute incoming traffic evenly across multiple instances of the AI solution.
D) Use Azure Application Gateway to optimize traffic routing and improve application performance for end users.
E) Employ Azure Virtual Machine Scale Sets to automatically adjust the number of VM instances based on workload changes.

QUESTION 14

You are designing an AI solution for a manufacturing plant to monitor equipment condition and detect potential defects

in real-time using image analysis. The solution requires robust visual feature detection capabilities to ensure accurate detection of anomalies. Which limitation should you consider when selecting visual features for defect detection in Azure Computer Vision?
Select all answers that apply.

A) Sensitivity to lighting conditions
B) Limited vocabulary of predefined objects
C) Inability to detect fine texture details
D) Difficulty in recognizing irregular shapes
E) Lack of support for custom object classes

QUESTION 15

While integrating a computer vision solution into your application, you encounter an issue where the image analysis responses are inconsistent, sometimes failing to detect objects accurately. What actions should you take to address this problem?

A) Review and refine the image processing request parameters to ensure they align with the characteristics of the input images.
B) Increase the resource allocation for the Azure AI Vision service to handle complex image analysis tasks more effectively.
C) Implement error handling mechanisms to retry failed image analysis requests automatically.
D) Train a custom computer vision model using labeled data to improve object detection accuracy for specific scenarios.
E) Adjust the confidence threshold settings for object detection to balance precision and recall rates.

QUESTION 16

You are tasked with implementing text extraction from images in an AI solution. The project requires distinguishing between different languages present in the images. Which Azure service provides language detection capabilities, allowing for accurate extraction of multilingual text from images?

A) Azure AI Computer Vision API
B) Azure AI Text Analytics
C) Azure AI Translator
D) Azure AI Form Recognizer
E) Azure AI Language Understanding

QUESTION 17

You are tasked with implementing an image classification solution for a manufacturing company to identify defects in product components. Which industry scenario does this image classification solution address?

A) Retail inventory management
B) Medical diagnosis
C) Autonomous vehicles
D) Quality control in manufacturing
E) Wildlife conservation monitoring

QUESTION 18

During the integration of Azure AI Speech service into your application, you encounter an error indicating "Invalid API key." How should you proceed to resolve this issue?

A) Generate a new API key for the Azure AI Speech service.

B) Check if the API key has been properly configured in the application settings.
C) Verify if the Azure AI Speech service resource is active and accessible.
D) Ensure that the correct API version is being used in the application.
E) Upgrade the Azure AI Speech service to a higher tier.

QUESTION 19

As part of deploying a computer vision model for detecting objects in images using Azure AI Vision, you want to ensure effective monitoring of the model's performance in the production environment. Which strategy should you employ to achieve this goal efficiently?

A) Implement Azure Monitor to track model inference latency and error rates, setting up alerts for deviations from baseline performance.
B) Periodically run batch inference jobs on a separate server and compare the results with ground truth labels to measure model accuracy.
C) Use Azure Application Insights to monitor server-side performance metrics, such as CPU and memory usage, to indirectly assess model performance.
D) Conduct manual testing of the model's performance on a regular basis by presenting it with a variety of test images and evaluating its accuracy.
E) Deploy a separate monitoring application that periodically queries the model endpoint and logs its responses for later analysis.

QUESTION 20

Your team is developing an AI-driven retail analytics platform that analyzes in-store customer behavior using video feeds from surveillance cameras. The platform aims to optimize store layout and product placement based on customer movement patterns. As part of the solution, you need to address privacy considerations in video spatial analysis to ensure compliance with data protection regulations. Which Azure AI service provides features for handling privacy concerns and ensuring data anonymization in spatial analysis for retail analytics?

A) Azure AI Video Indexer
B) Azure Cognitive Services - Computer Vision
C) Azure Cognitive Services - Video Analyzer
D) Azure AI Vision Spatial Analysis
E) Azure AI Content Moderator

QUESTION 21

In your application, you are utilizing Azure Cognitive Search for indexing and searching documents. While configuring the service, you encounter an API request with the command: GET https://<resource-name>.search.windows.net/indexes/<index-name>/docs/autocomplete. What does this request facilitate?

A) Indexing documents in the search service.
B) Retrieving autocomplete suggestions based on user input.
C) Analyzing search performance metrics.
D) Translation of search queries to multiple languages.
E) Synthesis of search results into a structured format.

QUESTION 22

Your team is developing a chatbot for a customer service application, which needs to extract key information from user inquiries to provide relevant responses. The chatbot should be able to handle queries in multiple languages and adapt to new languages easily. Additionally, you need to ensure the security and privacy of user data during key phrase extraction. Which Azure service should you use for implementing key phrase extraction in the chatbot, considering the need for multilingual support and data privacy?

A) Azure Text Analytics
B) Azure AI Language - Key Phrase Extraction
C) Azure Machine Learning - Natural Language Processing
D) Azure Cognitive Search
E) Azure Translator

QUESTION 23

You are designing an AI solution for a news aggregator platform to categorize articles based on sentiment for personalized recommendations. The system must handle a large volume of real-time news articles from various sources. Which technique would best suit this scenario, considering both accuracy and scalability?

A) Custom sentiment analysis models
B) Pre-trained sentiment analysis models
C) Rule-based sentiment analysis
D) Frequency-based sentiment analysis
E) Lexicon-based sentiment analysis

QUESTION 24

You are utilizing the Azure AI Custom Vision service to train a custom image classification model for your application. However, you encounter difficulties in achieving satisfactory model performance. What step should you prioritize to enhance the model's accuracy?

A) Augmenting the training dataset with additional diverse images.
B) Adjusting the learning rate of the training algorithm.
C) Increasing the number of training epochs.
D) Utilizing transfer learning from a pre-trained model.
E) Decreasing the batch size for training iterations.

QUESTION 25

Your team is developing a real-time speech recognition system for use in noisy environments such as manufacturing plants. It's crucial to maintain accurate transcriptions despite background noise. Which technique would be most effective for noise reduction in this scenario?

A) Implementing beamforming microphones to focus on the speaker's voice.
B) Using convolutional neural networks (CNNs) for noise cancellation.
C) Employing Azure Cognitive Services' noise suppression feature.
D) Adding a noise reduction layer to the acoustic model training process.
E) Applying dynamic time warping (DTW) to align speech signals with noise patterns.

QUESTION 26

You are tasked with deploying a custom speech recognition solution for an e-learning platform. The platform requires recognition of spoken commands from users to navigate through course content. What strategy should you employ to ensure the accuracy of the speech recognition system?

A) Implement a single generic speech model for all users.
B) Train separate models for different user demographics.
C) Use background noise reduction techniques during model training.
D) Regularly update the speech model with new vocabulary and commands.
E) Limit the variety of speech patterns in the training dataset.

QUESTION 27

You are developing an application that utilizes Azure AI Vision for analyzing satellite images to identify specific geographic features. However, the current implementation struggles with accurately distinguishing between forests and water bodies. What approach should you consider to improve the accuracy of feature detection?

A) Increasing the number of training epochs for the model.
B) Enhancing the contrast and brightness of input satellite images.
C) Adding additional spectral bands to the input image data.
D) Implementing transfer learning from a pre-trained feature detection model.
E) Fine-tuning the model with ground truth labels for forests and water bodies.

QUESTION 28

Your team is tasked with translating technical documents containing specialized terminology and jargon. Which Azure service should you recommend to address translation challenges in domain-specific documents effectively?

A) Azure Cognitive Services Language Understanding (LUIS)
B) Azure Cognitive Services Text Analytics
C) Azure Cognitive Services Translator Text
D) Azure Cognitive Services Speech Service
E) Azure Cognitive Services Vision Service

QUESTION 29

Your team is developing a custom translation model for a manufacturing company that requires accurate translation of technical documentation and specifications. What should be a primary consideration when selecting data sources for training the model?

A) Use publicly available general-purpose language datasets
B) Incorporate internal technical documents and industry-specific glossaries
C) Gather data from diverse sources without focusing on relevance
D) Include non-technical documents to enhance model versatility
E) Rely solely on machine-generated translations for training

QUESTION 30

You are troubleshooting an issue with an Azure app that integrates Azure AI Text Analytics for named entity recognition (NER). Users report that the app fails to identify certain entities correctly, leading to inaccurate analysis results. What could be a potential reason for this failure?

A) Insufficient domain-specific training data used by the Azure AI Text Analytics service.
B) Lack of language detection capability in the Azure AI Text Analytics service.
C) Inadequate tokenization settings configured for the Azure AI Text Analytics service.
D) Outdated version of the Azure AI Text Analytics SDK being used in the app.
E) Limited access to external knowledge bases for entity resolution.

QUESTION 31

During the training phase of a language understanding model for a customer feedback analysis system, your team encounters challenges with overfitting and data bias. What strategies should you implement to address these challenges effectively?
Select all answers that apply.

A) Regularization techniques such as dropout and L2 regularization
B) Data augmentation and balanced sampling

C) Ensemble learning with diverse model architectures
D) Hyperparameter tuning and cross-validation
E) Incorporating fairness-aware algorithms into the training pipeline

QUESTION 32

You are working on optimizing a language understanding model for a customer feedback analysis application. The model must accurately classify customer sentiments and identify key issues mentioned in feedback. How can you leverage A/B testing as a strategy to validate model enhancements and ensure seamless integration into the production environment while minimizing disruptions?
Select all answers that apply.

A) Deploy two versions of the model and compare their performance metrics in a controlled environment
B) Randomly assign users to different model versions and measure user satisfaction
C) Utilize feature flags to gradually enable new model features for selected user groups
D) Conduct offline evaluations of model versions using historical data
E) Implement canary deployments with staged rollout of model updates based on user segmentation

QUESTION 33

You are developing an Azure app that requires identifying objects in images uploaded by users. Which Azure service and API combination should you use to achieve this functionality?

A) Azure Cognitive Search > Vision API
B) Azure Content Moderator > Language API
C) Azure AI Language Service > Text Analytics API
D) Azure Computer Vision > Vision API
E) Azure QnA Maker > Decision API

QUESTION 34

What strategies should Azure AI engineers adopt for content update and synchronization in a question answering solution?
Select all answers that apply.

A) Implement manual updates on a fixed schedule
B) Utilize Azure Logic Apps for automated content synchronization
C) Assign a dedicated team for ad-hoc content management
D) Ignore updates as long as core content remains relevant
E) Rely on user feedback alone for content improvement

QUESTION 35

What best practices should Azure AI engineers follow for monitoring usage and performance metrics post-publishing of knowledge bases?
Select all answers that apply.

A) Set up alerts for significant deviations in usage patterns
B) Implement Azure Application Insights for real-time monitoring
C) Monitor latency and response times for user queries
D) Track user feedback and sentiment analysis
E) Schedule regular backups for data redundancy

QUESTION 36

You are deploying an Azure app that utilizes Azure AI services for sentiment analysis of customer feedback. Which options should you include in the bash statement to deploy the Sentiment Analysis container?
Select all answers that apply.

```
A) "mcr.microsoft.com/azure-ai/sentimentanalysis"
B) "--memory 512 --cpus 2"
C) "--accept"
D) "--endpoint {ENDPOINT_URI}"
E) "--api-key {API_KEY}"
```

QUESTION 37

You are fine-tuning a language model on Azure for text generation in a customer service chatbot. Your goal is to maintain fluency while ensuring the generated responses are contextually relevant. Which approach would be most suitable for achieving this?
Select all answers that apply.

A) Increase the model's temperature parameter
B) Incorporate beam search decoding
C) Implement greedy decoding
D) Apply top-k sampling
E) Adjust the model's layer normalization

QUESTION 38

Your organization is deploying a conversational AI solution using Azure Bot Framework for customer support inquiries. As part of best practices for developing engaging conversational AI, what approach should you consider?
Select all answers that apply.

A) Implement personalized responses based on user profiles
B) Utilize proactive messaging for timely notifications
C) Incorporate multimedia content for interactive experiences
D) Integrate sentiment analysis for empathetic responses
E) Enable natural language understanding for flexible user inputs

QUESTION 39

You are developing an image classification application using Azure Custom Vision service. Complete the code snippet below to instantiate the CustomVisionClient object with the appropriate parameters:

```
var trainingEndpoint = new Uri("<YourTrainingEndpoint>");
var trainingKey = "<YourTrainingKey>";
var predictionEndpoint = new Uri("<YourPredictionEndpoint>");
var predictionKey = "<YourPredictionKey>";
var client = new CustomVisionClient(trainingKey, trainingEndpoint, predictionKey,
predictionEndpoint);
```

Select all answers that apply.

```
A) new Uri("<YourTrainingEndpoint>")
B) new Uri("<YourPredictionEndpoint>")
C) "<YourTrainingKey>"
D) "<YourPredictionKey>"
E) new CustomVisionClient(trainingKey, predictionKey)
```

QUESTION 40

Your organization is developing a sentiment analysis tool for monitoring online reviews and customer feedback. One of the key requirements is to identify sentiment trends over time and correlate them with business events. Which Azure AI service would you recommend integrating into the tool to meet this requirement effectively?

A) Azure Text Analytics
B) Azure Language Understanding (LUIS)
C) Azure Cognitive Search
D) Azure AI Translator service
E) Azure AI Language Service

QUESTION 41

Your team is tasked with provisioning an Azure Cognitive Search resource to implement a search solution for a large e-commerce platform. Performance and scalability are critical factors in ensuring responsive search results, especially during peak usage periods. Which configuration setting should you adjust to optimize performance and scale for the search solution?

A) Indexer Batch Size
B) Replica Count
C) Partition Count
D) Search Mode
E) Scoring Profile

QUESTION 42

You are tasked with implementing a feature in your application that detects and redacts Personally Identifiable Information (PII) from user-generated content. Which Azure AI service should you use for this purpose?

```
A) LanguageUnderstandingClient
B) ContentModeratorClient
C) TextAnalyticsClient
D) TranslatorTextClient
E) MetricsAdvisorClient
```

QUESTION 43

Your team is developing a custom skill for Azure Cognitive Search that involves processing large volumes of textual data. As part of the development process, you need to consider performance considerations to ensure efficient execution of the skill. Which factor should you prioritize to optimize the performance of the custom skill?

A) Minimize data transformation steps
B) Optimize network bandwidth usage
C) Utilize in-memory caching
D) Parallelize processing tasks
E) Increase server resources

QUESTION 44

Your organization is deploying Azure Cognitive Search to power a real-time analytics dashboard that displays customer insights based on user interactions with an e-commerce platform. To ensure optimal query performance for the analytics dashboard, you need to implement query optimizations in Azure Cognitive Search. What should you prioritize to optimize query performance effectively?

A) Implement caching for frequently accessed queries

B) Enable query logging for performance analysis
C) Utilize caching for search index data
D) Configure automatic query throttling
E) Optimize search index schema for query efficiency

QUESTION 45

Which method in Azure Text Analytics is used to extract entities from text?

```
A) IdentifyEntities()
B) ExtractEntities()
C) RecognizeEntities()
D) EntityRecognition()
E) ExtractPII()
```

QUESTION 46

When provisioning an Azure OpenAI Service resource, which configuration setting is crucial for optimal service utilization and management?

A) Setting up billing alerts to monitor usage and costs.
B) Enabling automatic scaling based on resource demand.
C) Configuring role-based access control (RBAC) for resource management.
D) Defining service-level agreements (SLAs) for performance metrics.
E) Establishing network security groups (NSGs) to control inbound and outbound traffic.

QUESTION 47

Your organization is developing an AI-powered virtual assistant using Azure OpenAI Service to handle customer inquiries. To ensure the generated responses are accurate and contextually relevant, which strategy should you prioritize during model training and deployment?
Select all answers that apply.

A) Collecting and curating a diverse dataset of customer inquiries.
B) Fine-tuning the language model on historical chat logs.
C) Implementing reinforcement learning to optimize response generation.
D) Adjusting the model's temperature parameter for controlled randomness.
E) Incorporating real-time customer feedback into model updates.

QUESTION 48

Which combination of statements accurately describes features of Azure AI Translator service?

A) Statement I: Azure AI Translator service supports translation between text and documents.
B) Statement II: Azure AI Translator service allows custom translation models to be trained and published.
C) Statement III: Azure AI Translator service supports real-time translation of speech-to-speech.
D) Statement I, Statement II
E) Statement II, Statement III

QUESTION 49

In a project aimed at generating personalized meal plans using generative AI, you need to measure the impact of different dietary datasets on the quality of the generated plans. Which approach should you take to evaluate the influence of custom data on the generative outcomes?
Select all answers that apply.

A) Randomly selecting samples from each dataset to compare the diversity of generated meal plans.
B) Implementing A/B testing with different datasets to assess the effectiveness of each.
C) Analyzing the sentiment of user feedback on the meal plans generated from different datasets.
D) Tracking the computational resources utilized during model training with each dataset.
E) Conducting user surveys to gather subjective preferences on the meal plans generated from different datasets.

QUESTION 50

You are tasked with fine-tuning an Azure OpenAI model to improve its performance in generating natural language responses for a customer service chatbot application. Which of the following processes and tools would be most suitable for this task?

A) Hyperparameter tuning using Azure Machine Learning
B) Fine-tuning with reinforcement learning techniques
C) Training with additional data samples
D) Leveraging Azure OpenAI's built-in optimization algorithms
E) Customizing prompt engineering techniques for specific dialogue contexts

PRACTICE TEST 3 - ANSWERS ONLY

QUESTION 1

Answer - [C, E] Azure Cognitive Services Text Analytics, Azure Cognitive Services Personalizer

Option A - Azure Cognitive Services Language Understanding (LUIS): LUIS focuses on intent recognition and entity extraction rather than sentiment analysis and trend detection.
Option B - Azure Bot Services: Bot Services is used for building conversational interfaces and managing dialogue flow, which is not relevant for sentiment analysis and trend detection in social media content.
Option D - Azure QnA Maker: QnA Maker is designed for creating question and answer pairs, not for sentiment analysis or trend detection.
Option C - Azure Cognitive Services Text Analytics: Text Analytics offers sentiment analysis capabilities, allowing the social media monitoring tool to assess the sentiment (positive, negative, or neutral) of user comments and posts.
Option E - Azure Cognitive Services Personalizer: Personalizer enables personalized content recommendations and can be used to identify emerging trends based on user interactions and preferences, complementing the sentiment analysis provided by Text Analytics.

Make sure to use Azure Cognitive Services Text Analytics for sentiment analysis and Azure Personalizer for trend detection, ensuring comprehensive analysis of social media content. Keep in mind that Personalizer can recommend personalized content based on user behavior trends.

Stay alert to not using services like LUIS or QnA Maker, which focus on intent recognition and question-answering, not sentiment analysis. Avoid assuming bot-related services will handle social media analysis efficiently.

QUESTION 2

Answer - [B, D] Azure AI Text Analytics, Azure AI Content Moderator

Option A - Azure AI Metrics Advisor: Used for monitoring and analyzing metrics, not suitable for text analysis tasks.
Option C - Azure AI Language Understanding (LUIS): Designed for building conversational AI applications, not suited for text analysis.
Option E - Azure AI Translator Text: Used for language translation, not tailored for text analysis tasks.

You should leverage Azure AI Text Analytics for sentiment analysis and key phrase extraction, and always remember to use Azure Content Moderator to identify and anonymize PII data. This combination ensures compliance and covers all analysis needs.

Stay clear of using LUIS, which is not designed for text analysis or PII identification. Avoid using metrics or translator services, as they are not relevant for this task.

QUESTION 3

Answer - A) az monitor metrics list

Option B - Incorrect. This command is used to show diagnostic settings, not metrics. Option C - Incorrect. This command lists log profiles, not metrics. Option D - Incorrect. This command shows log profiles, not metrics. Option E - Incorrect. This command lists diagnostic settings, not metrics.

EXAM FOCUS	*Make sure to use the az monitor metrics list command to retrieve metrics for monitoring Azure AI services. Keep in mind that this command provides access to performance and usage data in real time.*
CAUTION ALERT	*Avoid using commands like az monitor diagnostic-settings show, which focus on diagnostic settings and are not relevant to retrieving metrics. Stay clear of confusing log profiles with metrics-related commands.*

QUESTION 4

Answer - C) Role-based access control (RBAC)

Option A - Incorrect. Shared access signatures are used for providing limited permissions to resources, but they may not offer individualized access control for users. Option B - Incorrect. OAuth 2.0 is a protocol for authorization, not specifically for individualized access control. Option D - Incorrect. Certificate authentication is a method for validating the authenticity of a user or service, but it may not provide individualized access control. Option E - Incorrect. While multi-factor authentication enhances security, it does not inherently provide individualized access control or tracking of usage.

EXAM FOCUS	*You need to implement role-based access control (RBAC) to ensure individualized access to Azure AI services while tracking usage. Keep in mind that this method provides granular access control for different user roles.*
CAUTION ALERT	*Stay clear of using shared access signatures (SAS) for individualized access, as they do not provide sufficient control. Avoid relying on OAuth 2.0 alone, which is a protocol but does not handle access control directly.*

QUESTION 5

Answer - [A, B, C, D]

Option A - Implement role-based access control (RBAC) to restrict access to sensitive data and services: Correct. RBAC helps enforce access controls and limit exposure to sensitive healthcare data, supporting compliance with data privacy regulations.

Option B - Enable data encryption using Azure Key Vault to protect sensitive information at rest and in transit: Correct. Encryption enhances data security and privacy, aligning with compliance requirements.

Option C - Choose Azure regions that comply with relevant healthcare regulations and certifications: Correct. Selecting compliant regions ensures that the Azure AI resource meets regulatory standards for healthcare data processing.

Option D - Deploy services in a HIPAA-compliant environment to ensure adherence to healthcare data privacy standards: Correct. Deploying in a HIPAA-compliant environment is crucial for handling healthcare data in compliance with industry regulations.

Option E - Implement data anonymization techniques to protect patient privacy and comply with data protection laws: While data anonymization is important, it may not address all compliance requirements, especially those specific to healthcare regulations like HIPAA.

EXAM FOCUS	*You should enable RBAC, encryption, and select HIPAA-compliant regions to ensure your deployment adheres to healthcare regulations. Always remember to deploy services in HIPAA-compliant environments for privacy and security.*
CAUTION ALERT	*Stay cautioned about missing HIPAA compliance for sensitive healthcare data. Avoid relying only on data anonymization as it may not cover all regulatory requirements for healthcare.*

QUESTION 6

Answer - A) Configure Azure Private Link for the Azure AI services.

Option B - Incorrect. While NSG rules can restrict inbound traffic, they do not provide the same level of secure access as Azure Private Link. Option C - Incorrect. Azure AD authentication is more about user identity than securing network connections between resources. Option D - Incorrect. While VPN gateway provides a secure connection, Azure Private Link is specifically designed for secure access to Azure services. Option E - Incorrect. Whitelisting the VM's IP address may not provide the level of security and control offered by Azure Private Link.

EXAM FOCUS	*Make sure to configure Azure Private Link for secure access to Azure AI services without exposing endpoints to the public internet. Keep in mind that Private Link ensures private, secure connections.*

Avoid depending on IP whitelisting or NSG rules alone; they do not provide the same level of security as Private Link. Stay alert to VPN or AD authentication misconfigurations, which may not fully secure service access.

QUESTION 7

Answer - [C, D] Aligning with data privacy regulations; Optimizing log query performance.

Aligning with data privacy regulations - Defining log retention policies that align with data privacy regulations ensures compliance and protects sensitive information contained within logs. Optimizing log query performance - Balancing log retention periods with query performance considerations helps maintain efficient log analysis and troubleshooting capabilities. Options A, B, and E may have relevance but do not directly address compliance or performance considerations.

EXAM FOCUS *Always remember to align log retention policies with data privacy regulations and optimize log query performance to ensure regulatory compliance and efficient troubleshooting.*

CAUTION ALERT *Stay clear of retaining logs indefinitely, as it can increase storage costs and violate privacy regulations. Avoid storing logs on local servers, which might not offer sufficient security.*

QUESTION 8

Answer - [C] Utilizing cost-effective service tiers based on workload requirements.

Utilizing cost-effective service tiers based on workload requirements - Choosing service tiers that align with workload requirements enables cost optimization without compromising service quality, ensuring efficient resource utilization and budget management across development, testing, and production environments. Options A, B, D, and E may lead to either underutilization or overspending on resources.

EXAM FOCUS *You should utilize cost-effective service tiers based on workload requirements to optimize costs while maintaining service quality. Always remember to evaluate resource needs across environments (development, testing, production).*

CAUTION ALERT *Avoid using high-tier service plans for all environments—it leads to unnecessary costs. Stay clear of infrequent cost reviews, which might overlook opportunities for cost savings.*

QUESTION 9

Answer - B) Enable Managed Service Identity (MSI) for App4 and assign RBAC permissions to Microsoft Entra ID.

Option A - Incorrect. While Azure AD authentication is a valid approach, enabling MSI with RBAC permissions directly meets the requirement with minimal administrative overhead. Option C - Incorrect. OAuth 2.0 authentication with Azure AD may not directly support Microsoft Entra ID and may introduce unnecessary complexity. Option D - Incorrect. Azure AD SSO may provide centralized authentication but may not align with the requirement to use Microsoft Entra ID. Option E - Incorrect. Storing client secrets may introduce additional security risks and administrative overhead.

EXAM FOCUS *Make sure to enable Managed Service Identity (MSI) for App4 and assign RBAC permissions to ensure secure, least-privilege access. Keep in mind that MSI reduces administrative overhead while maintaining security.*

CAUTION ALERT *Avoid manual client secret storage—it introduces security risks. Stay alert to OAuth or SSO complexities that may add unnecessary configuration steps.*

QUESTION 10

Answer - [B] Adjust moderation criteria based on user feedback and historical data.

Adjust moderation criteria based on user feedback and historical data - Incorporating user feedback and historical data allows for fine-tuning moderation criteria, reducing false positives and negatives over time, unlike options A, C, D, and E, which may not effectively address the underlying issues.

EXAM FOCUS	*You should adjust text moderation criteria based on user feedback and historical data to fine-tune the accuracy of Azure AI Content Safety. Always remember to continuously refine the system for improved results.*
CAUTION ALERT	*Avoid increasing filter sensitivity excessively—it may lead to an increase in false positives. Stay cautioned against manual reviews of all flagged content, which is impractical at scale.*

QUESTION 11

Answer - [A] Azure Machine Learning service for building, training, and deploying machine learning models.

Azure Machine Learning service provides a comprehensive platform for developing and operationalizing machine learning models, making it ideal for implementing predictive analytics and generating insights from financial data. Options B, C, D, and E focus on different Azure services but may not provide the same level of functionality required for building predictive models.

EXAM FOCUS	*You should choose Azure Machine Learning service for building, training, and deploying predictive models, especially when working with financial data, to ensure a scalable and manageable machine learning workflow. Keep in mind that Azure ML supports integration with other services for advanced analytics.*
CAUTION ALERT	*Avoid using services like Azure Databricks, which focuses on collaborative data analytics, or Synapse Analytics, which is more suited for data warehousing, not predictive model building.*

QUESTION 12

Answer - A) Adjust the model's parameters to fine-tune its generative behavior.
B) Implement prompt engineering techniques to refine the quality of generated responses.

Option C - Incorrect. While using custom data sets can improve model understanding, it may not directly optimize generative behavior. Option D - Incorrect. Exploring different Azure OpenAI models may help select the most appropriate model but may not directly optimize the performance of a specific model. Option E - Incorrect. While reinforcement learning can enhance decision-making, it may not be applicable for all types of generative AI models.

EXAM FOCUS	*Make sure to refine your model's behavior by adjusting parameters and employing prompt engineering techniques. Always remember that fine-tuning your prompts can significantly improve the quality and coherence of generated responses.*
CAUTION ALERT	*Stay cautioned against assuming custom datasets or different model selections will automatically improve response quality. Avoid using reinforcement learning unless your application specifically requires continuous decision-making optimization.*

QUESTION 13

Answer - [A, C, E] Options A, C, and E are relevant strategies for optimizing resource allocation and autoscaling.

Option A involves using Azure Monitor for performance metrics and autoscaling triggers, option C distributes traffic evenly across instances, and option E adjusts VM instances based on workload changes. Options B and D are not directly related to resource allocation and autoscaling.

EXAM FOCUS	*You need to implement Azure Monitor to track performance metrics and set autoscaling triggers based on demand. Always remember to distribute incoming traffic with Azure Load Balancer and adjust VM instances using Scale Sets for effective resource management.*
CAUTION ALERT	*Stay clear of relying on Azure Logic Apps for resource provisioning, as it is not designed for performance-based autoscaling. Avoid assuming Application Gateway will handle autoscaling—it optimizes traffic but is not a replacement for scaling strategies.*

QUESTION 14

Answer - [A, D] Options A and D highlight limitations that should be considered when selecting visual features for defect detection in Azure Computer Vision. Sensitivity to lighting conditions (Option A) can affect the accuracy of anomaly detection, while difficulty in recognizing irregular shapes (Option D) may lead to false positives or negatives.

Options B, C, and E are less relevant in the context of defect detection. Limited vocabulary of predefined objects (Option B) and inability to detect fine texture details (Option C) may be less critical compared to overall shape and anomaly recognition. Lack of support for custom object classes (Option E) may not be as crucial if the predefined classes cover common defect types.

EXAM FOCUS	*Keep in mind that sensitivity to lighting conditions and difficulty with irregular shapes are key limitations when using Azure Computer Vision for anomaly detection. You should factor in environmental conditions to avoid detection inaccuracies.*
CAUTION ALERT	*Avoid relying solely on Azure's predefined object classes, as they may not be sufficient for specialized defect detection in industrial environments. Stay alert to lighting inconsistencies that could skew the model's accuracy.*

QUESTION 15

Answer - A) Review and refine the image processing request parameters to ensure they align with the characteristics of the input images.
D) Train a custom computer vision model using labeled data to improve object detection accuracy for specific scenarios.

Option B - Incorrect. Increasing resource allocation might improve overall performance but may not specifically address inconsistent object detection. Option C - Incorrect. While error handling is essential, it does not directly tackle the root cause of inconsistent object detection. Option E - Incorrect. Adjusting confidence thresholds can fine-tune detection, but refining request parameters and training custom models address the core issue more effectively.

EXAM FOCUS	*You should refine your image processing parameters to better align with the input images and consider training a custom model for more accurate object detection. This will improve the model's precision in specific scenarios.*
CAUTION ALERT	*Avoid simply increasing resource allocation without addressing underlying detection issues. Stay cautioned against assuming that adjusting confidence thresholds alone will resolve detection inconsistencies.*

QUESTION 16

Answer - [B] Azure AI Text Analytics

B) Azure AI Text Analytics - Correct. Azure AI Text Analytics offers language detection capabilities, enabling accurate extraction of multilingual text from images. By detecting the language of the text within images, this service facilitates the processing of diverse linguistic content, ensuring precise extraction and analysis of text regardless of the language used.
A) Azure AI Computer Vision API - Incorrect. While Azure AI Computer Vision API includes text recognition features, it

may not provide language detection capabilities needed for distinguishing between different languages present in images.
C) Azure AI Translator - Incorrect. Azure AI Translator focuses on translating text between different languages, rather than detecting the language of text within images for extraction purposes.
D) Azure AI Form Recognizer - Incorrect. Azure AI Form Recognizer is designed for extracting structured data from forms and documents, rather than language detection within images.
E) Azure AI Language Understanding - Incorrect. Azure AI Language Understanding is used for building language models and understanding user intents, but it does not provide language detection capabilities for text extraction from images.

EXAM FOCUS	*Always remember that Azure AI Text Analytics provides language detection, making it an ideal choice for extracting multilingual text from images. You should leverage this service for diverse language extraction needs.*
CAUTION ALERT	*Stay clear of using services like Azure AI Translator or Azure Form Recognizer, as they focus on translation and form data extraction, not language detection. Avoid assuming Azure Computer Vision can handle detailed language detection.*

QUESTION 17

Answer - [D) Quality control in manufacturing]

Implementing an image classification solution to identify defects in product components aligns with quality control practices in manufacturing.
A) Retail inventory management typically involves categorizing products based on attributes rather than identifying defects.
B) Medical diagnosis often requires more specialized image analysis techniques tailored to medical imaging data.
C) Autonomous vehicles rely on different types of sensors and perception algorithms.
E) Wildlife conservation monitoring may involve image analysis but for different purposes.

EXAM FOCUS	*You should recognize that this image classification solution addresses quality control in manufacturing, where accurate defect detection is key. Keep in mind that this use case focuses on identifying specific flaws in product components.*
CAUTION ALERT	*Avoid confusing this scenario with retail inventory management or medical diagnosis, where classification goals differ significantly. Stay alert to the need for highly tailored models to meet manufacturing accuracy standards.*

QUESTION 18

Answer - [B] Check if the API key has been properly configured in the application settings.

Option B - Verifying if the API key has been properly configured in the application settings is essential as it ensures correct authentication. Generating a new API key (Option A) might not resolve the issue if the problem lies with the configuration. Checking the availability and accessibility of the Azure AI Speech service resource (Option C) is important but assumes the API key is correctly configured. Ensuring the correct API version (Option D) is being used is relevant but may not directly address the invalid API key error. Upgrading the Azure AI Speech service (Option E) is not necessary for resolving an authentication issue.

EXAM FOCUS	*Make sure to verify that the API key has been properly configured in the application settings before generating a new key. Always remember to check your key configuration to avoid unnecessary troubleshooting steps.*
CAUTION ALERT	*Avoid jumping to the conclusion that the API key is invalid without checking its configuration first. Stay alert to potential API version mismatches that could cause key-related errors.*

QUESTION 19

Answer - A) Implement Azure Monitor to track model inference latency and error rates, setting up alerts for deviations from baseline performance.

Option B - Periodic batch inference jobs are resource-intensive and may not provide real-time insights into model performance.
Option C - Server-side metrics may not reflect model-specific performance accurately and may miss issues specific to the model.
Option D - Manual testing is time-consuming and impractical for continuous monitoring in a production environment.
Option E - Deploying a separate monitoring application adds complexity and maintenance overhead compared to leveraging Azure Monitor.

EXAM FOCUS	*You need to implement Azure Monitor to track inference latency and error rates in real time, allowing you to proactively address performance issues. Keep in mind that setting up alerts will help detect performance deviations.*
CAUTION ALERT	*Avoid relying on manual testing or batch inference jobs, which are impractical for continuous production monitoring. Stay clear of monitoring server-side metrics alone; they may not accurately reflect the model's performance.*

QUESTION 20

Answer - E) Azure AI Content Moderator

Option A - Azure AI Video Indexer focuses more on extracting insights and metadata from videos rather than addressing privacy concerns in spatial analysis.
Option B - While Azure Cognitive Services - Computer Vision offers image analysis capabilities, it may not provide specific features for privacy protection in spatial analysis.
Option C - Azure Cognitive Services - Video Analyzer is geared towards real-time video processing but may not offer comprehensive privacy features for spatial analysis.
Option D - Azure AI Vision Spatial Analysis focuses on spatial analysis but may lack specific tools for privacy protection and data anonymization.
Option E - Azure AI Content Moderator offers features for content moderation and data anonymization, making it suitable for addressing privacy concerns in spatial analysis for retail analytics.

EXAM FOCUS	*You should use Azure AI Content Moderator for handling privacy concerns and data anonymization in spatial analysis. Always remember to prioritize privacy and data protection in customer behavior analysis solutions.*
CAUTION ALERT	*Avoid using services like Azure Video Indexer or Video Analyzer for privacy needs, as they focus on different aspects of video processing. Stay alert to the importance of meeting data protection regulations in customer-facing analytics solutions.*

QUESTION 21

Answer - [B] Retrieving autocomplete suggestions based on user input.

Option B - This API request is designed to provide autocomplete suggestions based on user input within the specified search index. It does not involve indexing documents (Option A), analyzing search performance metrics (Option C), translation of search queries (Option D), or synthesis of search results (Option E).

EXAM FOCUS	*Always remember that API requests like autocomplete are used for enhancing user search experiences by providing suggestions. You should integrate this feature to improve the interactivity of your application and help users navigate large datasets efficiently.*
CAUTION	*Stay alert to not confuse autocomplete with document indexing or search translation. These are separate*

ALERT	*functionalities that serve different purposes in Azure Cognitive Search.*

QUESTION 22

Answer - B) Azure AI Language - Key Phrase Extraction

Option A - While Azure Text Analytics offers key phrase extraction, Azure AI Language may provide more flexibility for customization and better support for multiple languages.
Option C - Azure Machine Learning requires custom model development, which might not be the most efficient solution for this scenario.
Option D - Azure Cognitive Search focuses on indexing and searching structured data, not on key phrase extraction from unstructured text.
Option E - Azure Translator is more suitable for translation tasks rather than key phrase extraction, making it less ideal for this specific requirement.

EXAM FOCUS	*Make sure to choose Azure AI Language - Key Phrase Extraction for handling multilingual queries and secure data processing. You should prioritize Azure AI Language because it supports multiple languages and robust security features for key phrase extraction in real-time chatbot applications.*
CAUTION ALERT	*Avoid confusing Azure AI Language with Translator or Cognitive Search, which focus on different capabilities like translation and indexing, not key phrase extraction with multilingual support.*

QUESTION 23

Answer - [B] Pre-trained sentiment analysis models.

Pre-trained sentiment analysis models offer a balance between accuracy and scalability, as they are trained on diverse datasets and can handle real-time articles effectively. Custom models may require extensive training data and resources. Rule-based, frequency-based, and lexicon-based approaches may struggle with the dynamic nature of news articles and may not provide accurate sentiment analysis at scale.

EXAM FOCUS	*Keep in mind that pre-trained sentiment models offer scalability and accuracy without the need for extensive retraining. You should leverage them for handling dynamic and large-scale datasets like real-time news articles.*
CAUTION ALERT	*Stay clear of rule-based and lexicon-based models as they may not capture the nuances and dynamism of real-time news content, leading to less accurate sentiment classification.*

QUESTION 24

Answer - [A] Augmenting the training dataset with additional diverse images.

Option A - Augmenting the training dataset with additional diverse images can enhance the model's ability to generalize and recognize patterns effectively, thereby improving accuracy. Adjusting learning rates (Option B) and training epochs (Option C) may optimize training but may not address dataset adequacy. Utilizing transfer learning (Option D) is beneficial but might not fully compensate for insufficient data diversity. Decreasing batch size (Option E) could impact training stability but is less impactful than dataset augmentation for improving accuracy.

EXAM FOCUS	*You need to augment the training dataset with diverse images to improve the generalization capability of your model. Always remember that a more varied dataset allows the model to perform better across different image classifications.*
CAUTION ALERT	*Avoid over-relying on adjusting parameters like learning rate or epochs without addressing the fundamental issue of dataset diversity. Stay alert to the importance of the training data's quality and diversity.*

QUESTION 25

Answer - D) Adding a noise reduction layer to the acoustic model training process.

Option A - Beamforming microphones can help isolate the speaker's voice but may not directly reduce noise in the transcription process.
Option B - While CNNs can be effective for noise cancellation, adding noise reduction during acoustic model training might be more efficient.
Option C - Azure Cognitive Services' noise suppression feature may not be sufficient for complex industrial noise environments.
Option D - Correct. Adding a noise reduction layer to the acoustic model training process allows the model to learn to filter out noise during transcription.
Option E - DTW is primarily used for aligning sequences and may not directly address noise reduction in speech recognition.

EXAM FOCUS	*You should add a noise reduction layer during acoustic model training to effectively handle transcription in noisy environments. Keep in mind that this approach helps the model filter out background noise, improving transcription accuracy.*
CAUTION ALERT	*Avoid assuming that external hardware like beamforming microphones will solve noise-related transcription issues. Stay cautioned against using noise reduction techniques that do not directly enhance the model's performance in noisy conditions.*

QUESTION 26

Answer - [D] Regularly update the speech model with new vocabulary and commands.

Option D is the most appropriate strategy as regularly updating the speech model with new vocabulary and commands ensures that the system remains accurate and up-to-date with evolving user needs. Options A and B are not ideal as they may not account for individual user preferences or variations. Option C addresses background noise but does not directly relate to accuracy improvement. Option E is incorrect as limiting the variety of speech patterns could lead to a less robust model.

EXAM FOCUS	*Make sure to regularly update the speech model with new vocabulary and commands to keep it aligned with user needs. You should prioritize continuous updates to ensure accurate recognition of evolving user commands.*
CAUTION ALERT	*Avoid training separate models for different demographics, as this can lead to unnecessary complexity. Stay clear of limiting speech patterns in your dataset, as it could reduce the model's robustness.*

QUESTION 27

Answer - [C] Adding additional spectral bands to the input image data.

Option C - Adding additional spectral bands to the input image data can provide more diverse and detailed information about the geographic features, which can help improve the model's ability to distinguish between forests and water bodies. Increasing epochs (Option A) may improve training but might not address feature detection accuracy directly. Enhancing contrast and brightness (Option B) may enhance visual quality but may not affect feature detection. Transfer learning (Option D) can be beneficial but may not fully address the specificity of the problem. Fine-tuning with ground truth labels (Option E) helps but may not be as effective as enriching the input data.

EXAM FOCUS	*You should consider adding spectral bands to satellite images to improve feature detection. Keep in mind that enriched image data can significantly enhance the model's ability to distinguish between different geographic features like forests and water bodies.*
CAUTION ALERT	*Stay cautioned against simply increasing training epochs or enhancing image quality through contrast adjustments, as these may not improve the model's performance in detecting specific features.*

QUESTION 28

Answer - [C] Azure Cognitive Services Translator Text

Option C is the correct choice because Azure Cognitive Services Translator Text offers customizable translation models, allowing for effective translation of domain-specific documents with specialized terminology and jargon. Options A, B, D, and E are less suitable for addressing translation challenges in domain-specific documents.

EXAM FOCUS	*Always remember that Azure Cognitive Services Translator Text is designed to handle specialized terminology effectively. You should customize models for translating domain-specific documents to ensure accurate translations.*
CAUTION ALERT	*Avoid using services like LUIS or Text Analytics for translation tasks, as they are designed for language understanding and text analysis, not translation of technical documents.*

QUESTION 29

Answer - [B] Incorporate internal technical documents and industry-specific glossaries

Explanation: B) Internal technical documents and industry-specific glossaries provide domain-specific terminology and context crucial for accurate translation of technical content. A) Publicly available datasets may lack industry-specific terminology and context. C) Gathering data from diverse sources without relevance may introduce noise and decrease model performance. D) Including non-technical documents may dilute the focus on technical terminology. E) Relying solely on machine-generated translations may not capture the specific requirements of the manufacturing domain.

EXAM FOCUS	*Make sure to use internal technical documents and industry-specific glossaries when training your translation model. You should prioritize data sources that reflect the exact terminology and context needed for accurate domain-specific translations.*
CAUTION ALERT	*Avoid using general-purpose datasets that lack the depth of industry-specific terminology. Stay alert to the importance of using relevant and accurate data for training technical translation models.*

QUESTION 30

Answer - [A] Insufficient domain-specific training data used by the Azure AI Text Analytics service.

Option A - Insufficient domain-specific training data can lead to failures in identifying certain entities correctly, as the Azure AI Text Analytics model may not have learned the necessary patterns and contexts for accurate recognition within specific domains. Lack of language detection (Option B) might impact multilingual analysis but is not directly related to entity recognition failure. Inadequate tokenization settings (Option C) may affect analysis accuracy but are less likely to cause failure in entity recognition. An outdated SDK version (Option D) may cause compatibility issues but is not the primary cause of recognition failure. Limited access to external knowledge bases (Option E) may affect entity resolution but is not the primary cause of recognition failure.

EXAM FOCUS	*You should ensure that your Azure AI Text Analytics service is trained with sufficient domain-specific data to improve entity recognition accuracy. Keep in mind that generic models may struggle with domain-specific language.*
CAUTION ALERT	*Avoid overlooking the importance of domain-specific training data, as it is crucial for accurate entity recognition. Stay cautioned against assuming that tokenization or SDK versions alone will resolve recognition failures in specialized domains.*

QUESTION 31

Answer - [A) and B)] - Regularization techniques like dropout and L2 regularization can help prevent overfitting, while data augmentation and balanced sampling can mitigate data bias issues.

C) Incorrect - Ensemble learning might not directly address overfitting or data bias issues and could introduce unnecessary complexity.
D) Incorrect - Hyperparameter tuning and cross-validation are essential but may not directly solve the specific challenges mentioned in the scenario.
E) Incorrect - While fairness-aware algorithms are crucial for mitigating bias, they may not directly address overfitting or data bias during training.

EXAM FOCUS	*You need to apply regularization techniques like dropout or L2 regularization to mitigate overfitting in models, and make sure to use data augmentation and balanced sampling to address data bias effectively in language understanding models.*
CAUTION ALERT	*Avoid assuming that ensemble learning alone will fix overfitting or data bias. Stay clear of tuning hyperparameters without tackling data augmentation or bias directly.*

QUESTION 32

Answer - [A), C), and E)] - Deploying two versions for comparison, utilizing feature flags, and implementing canary deployments enable validation of model enhancements and seamless integration while minimizing disruptions.

B) Incorrect - While randomly assigning users to different model versions can provide insights, it might not ensure controlled testing and validation of enhancements as effectively as A/B testing methodologies.

EXAM FOCUS	*Always remember to use A/B testing with feature flags and canary deployments to ensure model enhancements are validated without disrupting production. Make sure you monitor real user feedback to fine-tune the deployment.*
CAUTION ALERT	*Stay cautioned not to rely solely on user satisfaction metrics during testing without considering controlled A/B testing for performance evaluation.*

QUESTION 33

Answer - [D] Azure Computer Vision > Vision API

Option D - Azure Computer Vision service provides advanced image processing capabilities, including object detection, making it the best choice for identifying objects in images. Option A is incorrect as Cognitive Search is not designed for image processing. Option B is incorrect as Content Moderator is more focused on text and content moderation. Option C is incorrect as the Text Analytics API does not include image processing features. Option E is incorrect as QnA Maker is used for question and answer functionality.

EXAM FOCUS	*You should use Azure Computer Vision and the Vision API for object detection tasks. Keep in mind that this service offers robust object identification capabilities suited for user-uploaded images.*
CAUTION ALERT	*Avoid confusing Azure Cognitive Search with Vision API, as Cognitive Search does not process images. Stay alert to select the right API for object detection scenarios.*

QUESTION 34

Answer - [B) and D)] - Strategies for content update and synchronization include utilizing Azure Logic Apps for automation and ignoring updates only when core content remains relevant.

Option B) - Correct: Azure Logic Apps enable automated content synchronization, ensuring timely updates. Option D) - Correct: Ignoring updates when core content remains relevant reduces unnecessary overhead. Option A) - Incorrect: Manual updates are time-consuming and prone to errors. Option C) - Incorrect: Assigning a dedicated team may not be scalable or cost-effective. Option E) - Incorrect: Sole reliance on user feedback may overlook important updates and trends.

EXAM FOCUS	*Make sure to use Azure Logic Apps for automated content updates in a question answering solution. You need to focus on automating content management to maintain relevance and reduce overhead.*
CAUTION ALERT	*Avoid relying on manual updates, which can be time-consuming and prone to errors. Stay clear of ignoring content updates when they are critical to maintaining accuracy.*

QUESTION 35

Answer - [A), B), C), and D)] - Monitoring usage and performance metrics post-publishing involves setting up alerts, implementing monitoring tools, tracking latency, and analyzing user feedback.

Option A) - Correct: Setting up alerts helps identify significant deviations in usage patterns, allowing prompt action. Option B) - Correct: Azure Application Insights provides real-time monitoring capabilities, enabling proactive management. Option C) - Correct: Monitoring latency and response times ensures the responsiveness and reliability of the knowledge base. Option D) - Correct: Tracking user feedback and sentiment analysis offers insights into user satisfaction and areas for improvement. Option E) - Incorrect: While regular backups are essential, they are not directly related to monitoring usage and performance metrics post-publishing.

EXAM FOCUS	*Always remember to set up real-time monitoring with Azure Application Insights and configure alerts for unusual usage patterns. You should regularly monitor query response times and user satisfaction metrics for continuous optimization.*
CAUTION ALERT	*Avoid overlooking performance indicators like latency or feedback. Stay alert to changes in query performance that could signal potential issues with your knowledge base.*

QUESTION 36

Answer - [A, B, E] "mcr.microsoft.com/azure-ai/sentimentanalysis"
"--memory 512 --cpus 2"
"--api-key {API_KEY}"

Option A provides the correct URI for the Sentiment Analysis container. Option B sets memory and CPU limits for the container. Option E specifies the API key required for authentication. Option C and D are irrelevant for container deployment.

EXAM FOCUS	*You need to include the correct container image, memory, and CPU limits, as well as an API key when deploying the Sentiment Analysis container. Make sure to define resources properly for optimal performance.*
CAUTION ALERT	*Avoid omitting essential parameters like API keys and endpoint URIs. Stay clear of deploying containers without defining resource limits, which can lead to inefficiencies.*

QUESTION 37

Answer - [B, D].

B) Incorporating beam search decoding improves the relevance of generated responses by exploring multiple paths and selecting the most likely sequence of tokens. D) Applying top-k sampling helps control the diversity of generated responses while maintaining relevance to the context. A) Increasing the model's temperature parameter can lead to more diverse but potentially less coherent outputs. Greedy decoding and adjusting layer normalization are less effective for maintaining relevance and fluency.

EXAM FOCUS	*Keep in mind that using beam search decoding and top-k sampling ensures more contextually relevant and coherent responses in text generation models. You should prioritize these methods over simpler decoding techniques.*
CAUTION	*Avoid increasing temperature excessively, as it can introduce randomness and degrade response fluency.*

ALERT *Stay alert to avoid using greedy decoding, which may result in repetitive or less meaningful outputs.*

QUESTION 38

Answer - [A, B, D].

A) Implementing personalized responses based on user profiles enhances engagement by catering to individual preferences and history. B) Utilizing proactive messaging ensures timely communication and engagement with users, improving overall satisfaction. D) Integrating sentiment analysis allows the bot to respond empathetically to user emotions, enhancing the conversational experience. C) While multimedia content can enhance interactivity, it may not be suitable for all scenarios and could introduce complexity. E) Enabling natural language understanding is essential but may not directly address engagement aspects.

EXAM FOCUS *You should implement personalized responses, proactive messaging, and sentiment analysis to enhance the conversational experience in customer service bots. Make sure your bot can empathize with users through intelligent responses.*

CAUTION ALERT *Stay cautioned not to overcomplicate the bot with unnecessary multimedia elements. Avoid solely focusing on predefined responses—natural language understanding should also be prioritized.*

QUESTION 39

Answer - [A, C, B, D] new Uri("<YourTrainingEndpoint>")
"<YourTrainingKey>"
new Uri("<YourPredictionEndpoint>")
"<YourPredictionKey>"

Options A and B correctly initialize Uri objects with the training and prediction endpoints. Options C and D provide the training and prediction keys, respectively. Option E is incorrect as it does not include both endpoints and keys.

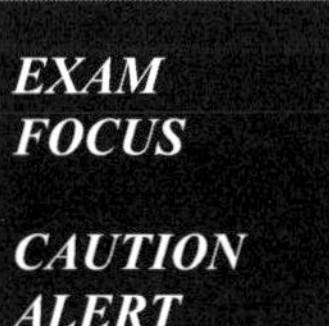

You need to ensure the correct initialization of Uri objects and use training and prediction keys when creating a CustomVisionClient. Always remember that proper instantiation is critical for the client's functionality.

Avoid omitting any of the required parameters like the endpoint or API key when initializing the CustomVisionClient. Stay clear of shortcuts that do not involve full URI and key usage.

QUESTION 40

Answer - [C] Azure Cognitive Search.

C) Azure Cognitive Search can index and analyze large volumes of text data, making it suitable for monitoring sentiment trends over time and correlating them with business events. A) Azure Text Analytics provides sentiment analysis but may not be optimized for handling large-scale data indexing and correlation tasks. B) Azure Language Understanding (LUIS) focuses on understanding user intents and entities within a single language and is not specialized for sentiment trend analysis. D) Azure AI Translator service focuses on translation tasks and does not provide sentiment analysis or data correlation capabilities. E) Azure AI Language Service provides language detection and translation but does not specifically handle sentiment trend analysis like Azure Cognitive Search.

EXAM FOCUS *Always remember that Azure Cognitive Search is ideal for indexing and analyzing large datasets, helping you identify trends and correlate sentiment with business events. You should leverage its scalability for sentiment trend analysis over time.*

CAUTION ALERT *Avoid using services like Azure Text Analytics or LUIS alone for sentiment trend analysis. Stay clear of choosing services that are not optimized for large-scale data indexing and correlation.*

QUESTION 41

Answer - [C] Partition Count.

C) Adjusting the Partition Count allows for horizontal scaling of the search service, improving performance and scalability by distributing the workload across multiple partitions. A) Indexer Batch Size determines the number of documents processed in each batch but may not directly impact performance and scale. B) Replica Count controls the number of replicas for fault tolerance but does not directly impact performance. D) Search Mode determines the search behavior but does not directly address performance optimization. E) Scoring Profile is used to customize relevance scoring but is not related to performance and scale optimization.

EXAM FOCUS	*You should prioritize adjusting the Partition Count in Azure Cognitive Search to enhance scalability and distribute workloads, especially during peak usage. This ensures smooth handling of high search query volumes.*
CAUTION ALERT	*Avoid focusing on Replica Count or Indexer Batch Size for scalability improvements—they primarily impact fault tolerance and document processing, not query scalability.*

QUESTION 42

Answer - [B] ContentModeratorClient

Option A, LanguageUnderstandingClient, is used for understanding user intents from natural language inputs and does not include PII detection and redaction features. Option C, TextAnalyticsClient, is used for text analytics tasks like sentiment analysis and key phrase extraction, not for PII redaction. Option D, TranslatorTextClient, is used for translating text between languages and does not offer PII detection and redaction capabilities. Option E, MetricsAdvisorClient, is used for monitoring and analyzing metrics data and is unrelated to PII detection and redaction. Option B, ContentModeratorClient, is the correct choice as it provides capabilities for detecting and redacting PII data from user-generated content.

EXAM FOCUS	*Make sure to leverage ContentModeratorClient for detecting and redacting Personally Identifiable Information (PII) from user-generated content, as it is purpose-built for content moderation, including PII handling.*
CAUTION ALERT	*Don't confuse ContentModeratorClient with TextAnalyticsClient, which is not designed specifically for PII redaction. Stay alert for ensuring compliance when handling sensitive data.*

QUESTION 43

Answer - [D] Parallelize processing tasks.

D) Prioritizing parallelizing processing tasks enables efficient utilization of resources and can significantly improve the performance of custom skills by distributing workloads across multiple threads or processes. A) While minimizing data transformation steps can improve performance, it may not be as impactful as parallelizing processing tasks. B) Optimizing network bandwidth usage is essential but may not directly influence the performance of custom skills within Azure Cognitive Search. C) Utilizing in-memory caching can improve performance for certain types of operations but may not be directly applicable to custom skill execution. E) Increasing server resources can improve performance but may not address scalability or efficiency concerns as effectively as parallel processing.

EXAM FOCUS	*You should prioritize parallelizing processing tasks when developing custom skills for Azure Cognitive Search, as it significantly improves performance for large-scale text processing.*
CAUTION ALERT	*Stay clear of relying solely on in-memory caching or data transformation optimization for large volumes. Avoid overlooking the benefits of parallel processing for scaling performance.*

QUESTION 44

Answer - [E] Optimize search index schema for query efficiency.

E) Optimizing the search index schema for query efficiency involves designing the schema to minimize unnecessary fields, reducing index size, and optimizing data types for faster query execution, thereby improving overall query performance. A) Implementing caching for frequently accessed queries may improve response times but does not directly address query optimization within Azure Cognitive Search. B) Enabling query logging for performance analysis is valuable for monitoring but does not directly optimize query performance. C) Utilizing caching for search index data may improve overall system performance but does not specifically target query optimization. D) Configuring automatic query throttling helps manage resource utilization but does not directly optimize query performance in Azure Cognitive Search.

EXAM FOCUS	*Always remember to optimize your search index schema to ensure efficient query execution. This includes trimming unnecessary fields and using the correct data types for quicker search results.*
CAUTION ALERT	*Stay cautioned not to overlook the search index schema—relying solely on query caching or query logging will not solve core performance issues in high-demand systems.*

QUESTION 45

Answer - C) RecognizeEntities()

Option A - IdentifyEntities(): This is a hypothetical method and not part of the Azure Text Analytics SDK.
Option B - ExtractEntities(): This is a hypothetical method and not part of the Azure Text Analytics SDK.
Option D - EntityRecognition(): This is a hypothetical method and not part of the Azure Text Analytics SDK.
Option E - ExtractPII(): This is a hypothetical method and not part of the Azure Text Analytics SDK.
Option C is correct because RecognizeEntities() is the method used to extract entities from text in Azure Text Analytics.

EXAM FOCUS	*You need to use the RecognizeEntities() method in Azure Text Analytics for extracting entities from text. Keep in mind that this method is optimized for recognizing entities such as names, dates, and locations.*
CAUTION ALERT	*Avoid using non-existent methods like IdentifyEntities() or EntityRecognition(). Stay clear of hypothetical methods not supported by the Azure SDK.*

QUESTION 46

Answer - [B] Enabling automatic scaling based on resource demand.

A) Enabling automatic scaling ensures that the service can dynamically adjust resources based on demand, optimizing performance and resource utilization.
B) Setting up billing alerts helps monitor costs but does not directly impact service utilization.
C) Configuring RBAC is essential for access control but not directly related to service utilization.
D) Defining SLAs is important for performance expectations but does not directly affect service utilization.
E) Establishing NSGs is crucial for network security but does not directly impact service utilization and management.

EXAM FOCUS	*Make sure to enable automatic scaling when provisioning Azure OpenAI Service to dynamically handle fluctuating resource demands, ensuring optimal performance during peak periods.*
CAUTION ALERT	*Stay alert to service demand and ensure scaling configurations are in place—don't confuse setting billing alerts with ensuring performance scaling.*

QUESTION 47

Answer - [A, B] Collecting and curating a diverse dataset of customer inquiries. Fine-tuning the language model on historical chat logs.

A) Collecting diverse data ensures the model encounters various scenarios, improving accuracy and relevance.
B) Fine-tuning on historical logs captures domain-specific nuances, enhancing contextual understanding.
C) Reinforcement learning may optimize responses but requires extensive training data and evaluation.
D) Adjusting temperature parameter influences randomness but may not guarantee accuracy.
E) Real-time feedback is valuable but may not directly improve model accuracy without proper integration into the training pipeline.

EXAM FOCUS	*You should fine-tune your OpenAI model using a diverse dataset of customer inquiries and historical chat logs to ensure responses are both accurate and contextually relevant.*
CAUTION ALERT	*Avoid relying solely on temperature adjustments to control response randomness. Stay cautioned when using reinforcement learning without adequate data and evaluation.*

QUESTION 48

Answer - B) Statement II: Azure AI Translator service allows custom translation models to be trained and published.

Option D - Statement I, Statement II: This statement is incorrect because Statement I is incorrect. Azure AI Translator service supports translation between text and documents, not between text and documents.
Option E - Statement II, Statement III: This statement is incorrect because it doesn't include the true statement about real-time speech-to-speech translation (Statement III).
Option A is incorrect because it includes an incorrect statement about the translation capabilities of Azure AI Translator service.
Option C is incorrect because it includes an incorrect statement about real-time speech-to-speech translation.
Option B is correct because it includes the true statement about training and publishing custom translation models in Azure AI Translator service.

EXAM FOCUS	*You need to recognize that Azure AI Translator supports the training and publishing of custom translation models, which is crucial for handling domain-specific terminologies.*
CAUTION ALERT	*Stay clear of misinterpreting Azure AI Translator's capabilities—it does not support real-time speech-to-speech translation. Avoid assuming incorrect functionalities based on hypothetical statements.*

QUESTION 49

Answer - [B, E] Implementing A/B testing with different datasets to assess the effectiveness of each. Conducting user surveys to gather subjective preferences on the meal plans generated from different datasets.

B) A/B testing allows for direct comparison of different datasets' effectiveness in generating meal plans.
E) User surveys provide subjective feedback on meal plans generated from different datasets, aiding in understanding user preferences.
A) Randomly selecting samples may not systematically evaluate the impact of datasets on generative outcomes.
C) Sentiment analysis of user feedback may not capture the nuances of dataset influence on generative quality.
D) Tracking computational resources does not directly assess the impact of datasets on generative outcomes.

EXAM FOCUS	*Make sure to implement A/B testing and gather subjective feedback through user surveys to effectively measure the impact of different datasets on generative outcomes.*
CAUTION ALERT	*Don't confuse random sampling or resource tracking with true generative performance evaluation. Stay clear of relying solely on computational resources as a metric for dataset quality.*

QUESTION 50

Answer - [C] Training with additional data samples.

A) Hyperparameter tuning is not typically used for fine-tuning pre-trained models like Azure OpenAI. B) Fine-tuning with reinforcement learning might be too complex and computationally expensive for this task. D) Azure OpenAI may not provide built-in optimization algorithms specifically for fine-tuning. E) While prompt engineering is important, it's not the primary focus when fine-tuning for performance.

EXAM FOCUS	*You should focus on training your Azure OpenAI model with additional data samples to improve performance in generating natural language responses. Always remember that additional, diverse data can enhance model adaptability.*
CAUTION ALERT	*Avoid relying on hyperparameter tuning or reinforcement learning for fine-tuning purposes in Azure OpenAI. Stay alert for over-complicating the fine-tuning process with unnecessary tools or techniques.*

PRACTICE TEST 4 - QUESTIONS ONLY

QUESTION 1

Your team is developing a multilingual chatbot that needs to support conversations in multiple languages. The chatbot should be able to understand and respond to user queries in different languages seamlessly. You need to select the Azure AI service that can address the multilingual requirements of the chatbot. Which service should you choose?
Select all answers that apply.

A) Azure Cognitive Services Translator
B) Azure Bot Services
C) Azure Cognitive Services Language Understanding (LUIS)
D) Azure QnA Maker
E) Azure Cognitive Services Text Analytics

QUESTION 2

Your team is developing a decision support solution for a retail company to analyze customer reviews and feedback. The solution needs to extract key phrases, determine sentiment, and categorize reviews based on product attributes.
Which Azure AI service or combination of services should you choose to fulfill these requirements effectively?
Select all answers that apply.

A) Azure AI Text Analytics
B) Azure AI Language Understanding (LUIS)
C) Azure AI Content Moderator
D) Azure AI Form Recognizer
E) Azure AI Translator Text

QUESTION 3

Which Azure CLI command should be used to manage account keys for an Azure AI service resource?

```
A) az account keys list
B) az cognitiveservices account keys list
C) az keyvault key list
D) az keyvault secret list
E) az storage account keys list
```

QUESTION 4

When considering security measures for accessing Azure AI services, which authentication method provides a unique identifier tied to an individual or organization?

A) Azure Active Directory (AAD)
B) Shared access signature (SAS)
C) API key
D) Client secret
E) Azure Key Vault

QUESTION 5

Your team is tasked with deploying a new Azure AI solution to analyze customer feedback data and extract actionable insights to improve product offerings and customer satisfaction. To support the deployment, you need to create an Azure AI resource with the necessary services and configurations. The solution should prioritize efficiency, cost-

effectiveness, and scalability.
Which actions should you take to create the Azure AI resource while ensuring efficiency, cost-effectiveness, and scalability?
Select all answers that apply.

A) Utilize Azure Cognitive Services to leverage pre-built AI models and reduce development time and costs.
B) Choose Azure regions with low-latency connectivity to minimize data transfer costs and improve performance.
C) Implement serverless computing options, such as Azure Functions, to optimize resource utilization and reduce operational overhead.
D) Use Azure Cost Management tools to analyze spending patterns and identify opportunities for optimization and cost savings.
E) Configure auto-shutdown policies for development and testing environments to prevent unnecessary resource usage and reduce costs.

QUESTION 6

You are deploying a web application on an Azure virtual machine that needs to communicate with Azure AI services securely. However, the application should not have direct access to the public internet. What should you do to ensure secure communication between the VM and Azure AI services while adhering to the security requirements?

A) Use a reverse proxy server to relay requests to Azure AI services.
B) Implement Azure AD authentication for the web application.
C) Configure Azure Private Endpoint for the Azure AI services.
D) Restrict outbound traffic from the VM to the public internet using network security group (NSG) rules.
E) Install a firewall on the VM to block unauthorized access to Azure AI services.

QUESTION 7

You encounter a common issue while troubleshooting an Azure AI service deployment and decide to analyze diagnostic logs. Which action should you take to effectively troubleshoot the issue using diagnostic logs?

A) Reviewing log data manually in a text editor
B) Filtering logs based on severity levels
C) Ignoring log entries related to errors
D) Disabling diagnostic logging temporarily
E) Deleting old log entries to free up storage space

QUESTION 8

Your team is tasked with monitoring Azure AI resource consumption to identify potential cost-saving opportunities. Which tool should you leverage for comprehensive monitoring of Azure AI service usage and costs?

A) Azure DevOps
B) Azure Resource Manager
C) Azure Monitor
D) Azure IoT Hub
E) Azure Data Lake Storage

QUESTION 9

You need to set up authentication for an Azure App Services web app named App5. The app must authenticate using Microsoft Entra ID with minimal administrative effort and adhere to the principle of least privilege. What should you do?

A) Configure App5 to use Azure AD single sign-on (SSO).

B) Enable Managed Service Identity (MSI) for App5 and assign RBAC permissions to Microsoft Entra ID.
C) Implement OAuth 2.0 authentication with Azure AD and grant App5 access to Microsoft Entra ID.
D) Enable Azure Active Directory (Azure AD) authentication and configure App5 to use it.
E) Generate a client secret and store it securely for App5 authentication.

QUESTION 10

Your team is integrating text moderation with Azure Cognitive Services to create a comprehensive solution for content management. Which best practice should you prioritize when integrating text moderation with other Azure services?

A) Maintain separate moderation workflows for each service to avoid complexity
B) Ensure seamless communication between text moderation and content storage services
C) Ignore integration with other Azure services to minimize dependencies
D) Use third-party APIs instead of Azure services for text moderation
E) Implement manual synchronization between text moderation and data storage

QUESTION 11

Your company is integrating Azure AI capabilities into an existing healthcare system to improve patient care and medical diagnosis. What compliance consideration is paramount when customizing decision support solutions for the healthcare industry?

A) Ensuring compliance with GDPR regulations for protecting patient data privacy.
B) Implementing HIPAA-compliant security measures for handling sensitive medical information.
C) Adhering to SOC 2 standards for ensuring the security, availability, and confidentiality of data.
D) Following ISO 27001 guidelines for establishing an information security management system (ISMS).
E) Obtaining FDA approval for deploying AI-driven medical diagnosis algorithms.

QUESTION 12

You are building a natural language processing (NLP) solution on Azure AI Language. Which actions are necessary for managing and deploying the language understanding model effectively?

A) Train and evaluate the language understanding model using Azure AI Language.
B) Optimize the language understanding model by fine-tuning its parameters.
C) Integrate the language understanding model into client applications for consumption.
D) Backup and recover language understanding models regularly to prevent data loss.
E) Utilize Azure OpenAI Service to enhance the language understanding model's capabilities.

QUESTION 13

Your organization is planning to deploy a decision support system (DSS) across multiple regions to support localized decision-making processes. How can you ensure effective global deployment and localization of the DSS?
Select all answers that apply.

A) Utilize Azure Traffic Manager with geographic routing to direct users to the nearest datacenter based on their location.
B) Implement Azure CDN to cache content and optimize delivery based on user proximity to edge servers.
C) Configure Azure Cosmos DB with multi-region writes to ensure data consistency and availability across regions.
D) Employ Azure Kubernetes Service (AKS) to orchestrate containerized DSS components and deploy them across multiple regions.
E) Leverage Azure ExpressRoute to establish private connections between on-premises datacenters and Azure regions for secure and reliable communication.

QUESTION 14

Your team is developing an AI solution for a security company to analyze surveillance footage for threat detection. The solution requires identifying specific objects and activities indicative of security threats. Which Azure Computer Vision feature should you leverage to detect potential threats accurately?
Select all answers that apply.

A) Object detection
B) Facial recognition
C) Scene understanding
D) Emotion detection
E) Text recognition

QUESTION 15

You are developing a speech-to-text solution using Azure AI Speech services. However, you encounter an error indicating "Input Format Mismatch" during the processing of audio files. How can you rectify this issue?

A) Validate and ensure that the audio files conform to the supported input formats specified by the Azure AI Speech service.
B) Convert the audio files to a compatible format using appropriate conversion tools or libraries before processing.
C) Upgrade the Azure AI Speech service to a higher tier with broader support for audio file formats.
D) Implement error handling to skip processing for incompatible audio files and log the details for manual review.
E) Consult the Azure AI Speech service documentation to identify any recent updates or changes impacting supported input formats.

QUESTION 16

In a project focusing on extracting text from images for data analysis, you need to compare different approaches for text extraction, including Optical Character Recognition (OCR) and advanced techniques. Which statement accurately contrasts OCR with advanced text extraction methods?

A) OCR provides higher accuracy in extracting handwritten text.
B) Advanced techniques offer better performance in extracting text from complex backgrounds.
C) OCR supports multilingual text extraction with high precision.
D) Advanced techniques are more suitable for simple document layouts.
E) OCR requires less computational resources compared to advanced methods.

QUESTION 17

Your team is evaluating the performance of a custom image classification model trained on Azure AI Vision. Which metric should you prioritize to assess the model's effectiveness in correctly identifying objects in images?

A) Precision
B) Recall
C) F1 score
D) Accuracy
E) Mean Average Precision (mAP)

QUESTION 18

While developing a custom language understanding model with Azure AI Language, you encounter a challenge with low accuracy in intent recognition. What steps should you take to address this issue?

A) Expand the training data with additional examples for each intent.
B) Fine-tune the language model using transfer learning techniques.

C) Implement context-aware features to improve intent disambiguation.
D) Adjust the confidence threshold for intent recognition.
E) Upgrade the Azure AI Language service to a higher tier.

QUESTION 19

You have deployed a custom computer vision model for analyzing satellite images to identify environmental changes using Azure AI Vision. Now, you need to ensure efficient updates and maintenance of the deployed model to adapt to changing conditions. What is a recommended best practice for managing updates to the model while minimizing disruption to the production environment?

A) Use Azure DevOps pipelines to automate the deployment of updated model versions, incorporating canary deployments for gradual rollout.
B) Schedule regular downtime for the application to manually update the model files and configurations on the production server.
C) Maintain multiple versions of the model in parallel, allowing users to switch between versions based on performance feedback.
D) Implement a manual process where developers directly upload updated model files to the production server and restart the application.
E) Create a staging environment where updated model versions are tested before deployment to the production environment, ensuring minimal impact on live operations.

QUESTION 20

Your organization is deploying a video analytics solution for crowd management at a large-scale event venue. The solution needs to analyze video feeds from multiple cameras to detect crowd density and movement patterns in real-time. You are tasked with selecting the Azure AI service that offers real-world applications of spatial analysis for crowd management. Which Azure AI service should you choose based on its ability to provide insights into crowd behavior and facilitate crowd control measures effectively?

A) Azure AI Video Indexer
B) Azure Cognitive Services - Computer Vision
C) Azure Cognitive Services - Video Analyzer
D) Azure AI Vision Spatial Analysis
E) Azure AI Metrics Advisor

QUESTION 21

While developing a conversational AI solution using Azure AI Language, you encounter an API request with the command: `GET https://<resource-name>.cognitiveservices.azure.com/luis/prediction/v3.0/apps/<app-id>/slots/production/predict.` What is the purpose of this request?

A) Training the language understanding model.
B) Evaluating the language understanding model.
C) Predicting intents and entities from user input.
D) Importing data into the language understanding model.
E) Exporting the language understanding model.

QUESTION 22

Your organization is building a content recommendation system for an e-learning platform. The system needs to analyze course descriptions and user feedback to suggest relevant courses to learners. As part of the recommendation engine, you want to extract key concepts and topics from the course materials to improve the accuracy of recommendations. Which Azure service should you integrate into the recommendation system for extracting key phrases from course descriptions, considering the need for accuracy and relevance in recommendations?

A) Azure AI Language - Key Phrase Extraction
B) Azure Text Analytics
C) Azure Machine Learning - Natural Language Processing
D) Azure Cognitive Search
E) Azure Databricks

QUESTION 23

Your team is developing an AI-powered customer feedback analysis tool for a global hospitality chain. The tool must accurately identify the sentiment expressed in customer reviews across multiple languages. Which Azure AI service would be most suitable for implementing sentiment analysis in this scenario?

A) Azure Text Analytics
B) Azure Cognitive Search
C) Azure Language Understanding (LUIS)
D) Azure Translator
E) Azure Speech to Text

QUESTION 24

You are integrating the Azure AI Language Understanding service into your chatbot application to interpret user queries and intents. However, you notice that the service struggles to accurately recognize and classify certain user intents. What action should you take to address this issue?

A) Increasing the confidence threshold for intent classification.
B) Retraining the language model with additional labeled examples.
C) Adjusting the language detection settings for user inputs.
D) Enabling multi-language support for the language understanding model.
E) Fine-tuning the response generation mechanism of the chatbot.

QUESTION 25

Your organization is developing a speech-to-text (STT) system for a virtual assistant application. The application must respond to user commands in real-time with high accuracy. Which Azure service would be most suitable for implementing real-time STT with low latency?

A) Azure Cognitive Services Speech Service
B) Azure Machine Learning
C) Azure Kubernetes Service (AKS)
D) Azure IoT Edge

QUESTION 26

Your team is developing a custom speech recognition solution for an automotive application. The system needs to accurately recognize spoken commands from drivers in different driving conditions, including noisy environments. What technique should you employ to enhance the robustness of the speech recognition model?

A) Implementing speaker adaptation algorithms to account for individual voice characteristics.
B) Using data augmentation to simulate various driving conditions during model training.
C) Applying transfer learning from pre-trained speech models to fine-tune the custom model.
D) Utilizing beamforming microphones to capture clear audio signals in noisy environments.
E) Incorporating complex neural network architectures for speech feature extraction.

QUESTION 27

You are developing an application that utilizes Azure AI Vision for quality control in manufacturing. The application needs to detect defects in product images captured on the production line. Which feature of Azure AI Vision should you use for this specific task?

A) Face detection
B) Object recognition
C) Optical character recognition (OCR)
D) Image classification
E) Anomaly detection

QUESTION 28

Your company is involved in a large-scale document translation project and requires an Azure service that can handle translating multiple document formats seamlessly. Which Azure service should you recommend to maintain format and layout in translated documents effectively?

A) Azure Cognitive Services Translator Text
B) Azure Cognitive Services Language Understanding (LUIS)
C) Azure Cognitive Services Text Analytics
D) Azure Cognitive Services Speech Service
E) Azure Cognitive Services Vision Service

QUESTION 29

Your organization is deploying a custom translation model for a multinational e-commerce platform to facilitate international transactions. What is a key consideration for ensuring compliance with privacy regulations while using customer transaction data for model training?

A) Anonymize customer transaction data before incorporating it into the training dataset
B) Obtain explicit consent from customers to use their transaction data for model training
C) Limit the scope of data used for training to minimize privacy risks
D) Store customer transaction data in an encrypted format to prevent unauthorized access
E) Exclude customer transaction data from the training dataset to avoid privacy concerns

QUESTION 30

You are diagnosing an issue with an Azure app that utilizes Azure AI Optical Character Recognition (OCR) for extracting text from images. Users report that the app fails to recognize certain characters accurately, especially in images with low resolution. What could be a potential reason for this inaccuracy?

A) Insufficient contrast between text and background in the images.
B) Variability in font types used across different images.
C) Limited language support offered by the Azure AI OCR service.
D) Outdated version of the Azure AI OCR SDK being used in the app.
E) Lack of integration between the app's image preprocessing pipeline and Azure AI OCR.

QUESTION 31

Your team is deploying a sentiment analysis model for a social media monitoring platform. After deployment, you aim to continuously improve the model's accuracy and adaptability to evolving user language patterns. Which strategies should you employ for model retraining and enhancement?
Select all answers that apply.

A) Implementing active learning to collect labeled data iteratively

B) Monitoring model performance metrics in production
C) Incorporating user feedback into model updates
D) Periodically retraining the model with updated data
E) Employing transfer learning from related domains

QUESTION 32

Your team is optimizing a language understanding model for a social media sentiment analysis platform. The model must accurately classify diverse user sentiments expressed in social media posts. What considerations should you account for when fine-tuning the model to achieve optimal performance in handling sentiment variations across different demographic groups and languages?
Select all answers that apply.

A) Collect representative training data reflecting the diversity of user demographics and languages
B) Implement fairness-aware algorithms to mitigate biases in model predictions
C) Conduct sensitivity analysis to evaluate model performance across various demographic segments
D) Employ transfer learning from models trained on multilingual datasets
E) Utilize domain adaptation techniques to align model behavior with specific user contexts

QUESTION 33

Your team is working on an Azure app that requires detecting the sentiment of live conversations in a chat interface. Which Azure service and API combination should you implement to achieve this requirement?

A) Azure Cognitive Search > Language API
B) Azure Speech Service > Speech API
C) Azure AI Language Service > Text Analytics API
D) Azure Computer Vision > Vision API
E) Azure Content Moderator > Decision API

QUESTION 34

What are the best practices for ensuring content security and access control in a question answering solution?
Select all answers that apply.

A) Implement role-based access control (RBAC) for content moderation
B) Encrypt all content using Azure Key Vault for data protection
C) Restrict access to authorized users through Azure Active Directory
D) Share content publicly to maximize accessibility
E) Ignore security measures for streamlined access

QUESTION 35

How can Azure AI engineers ensure high availability and reliability of published content in a question answering solution?
Select all answers that apply.

A) Deploy content across multiple Azure regions for redundancy
B) Implement Azure CDN for global content delivery
C) Configure auto-scaling for dynamic resource allocation
D) Utilize Azure Traffic Manager for load balancing
E) Optimize cache settings for improved performance

QUESTION 36

Your task is to deploy a custom speech recognition model in an Azure container. Which options should you include in the bash statement to accomplish this task?
Select all answers that apply.

```
A) "mcr.microsoft.com/azure-cognitive-services/speech/recognition"
B) "--memory 384 --cpus 6"
C) "--eula accept"
D) "--region eastus"
E) "--api-key {API_KEY}"
```

QUESTION 37

As part of your AI project, you need to fine-tune a pre-trained language model on Azure to generate product descriptions in multiple languages for an e-commerce platform. What is a crucial consideration when fine-tuning the model for multi-language support?
Select all answers that apply.

A) Use separate models for each language
B) Normalize text input across languages
C) Train the model with language-specific tokens
D) Limit the vocabulary size for each language
E) Apply language-specific data augmentation techniques

QUESTION 38

Your team is developing a conversational AI solution using Azure Bot Framework integrated with custom NLP models for a healthcare application. To ensure compliance with regulations, what action should you take during development?
Select all answers that apply.

A) Implement encryption for data security
B) Use Azure Key Vault for managing sensitive information
C) Incorporate role-based access control (RBAC) for data access
D) Ensure data anonymization for protecting user privacy
E) Conduct regular security audits and vulnerability assessments

QUESTION 39

Your task is to implement sentiment analysis functionality in your Azure application using Azure Text Analytics service. Complete the code snippet below to accomplish this:

```
string textToAnalyze = "This movie is fantastic!";
var client = new TextAnalyticsClient("<YourSubscriptionKey>", "<YourServiceRegion>");
var sentimentResult = await client.AnalyzeSentimentAsync(textToAnalyze);
```

Select all answers that apply.

```
A) TextAnalyticsClient("<YourSubscriptionKey>", "<YourServiceRegion>")
B) textToAnalyze
C) sentimentResult.Sentiment
D) await client.GetSentimentAsync(textToAnalyze)
E) TextAnalyticsClient.GetSentiment(textToAnalyze)
```

QUESTION 40

Your team is tasked with developing a sentiment analysis model that can accurately detect sentiment from customer feedback in multiple languages. Which Azure AI service would you recommend integrating into the model to achieve this requirement efficiently?

A) Azure Text Analytics
B) Azure Language Understanding (LUIS)
C) Azure Cognitive Search
D) Azure AI Translator service
E) Azure AI Language Service

QUESTION 41

Your organization is planning to deploy an Azure Cognitive Search solution to index and search a large volume of documents stored in Azure Blob Storage. As the Azure AI engineer responsible for provisioning the search service, you need to ensure seamless integration with the existing Azure infrastructure. Which Azure service should you configure to enable the Cognitive Search service to access documents stored in Azure Blob Storage securely?

A) Azure Key Vault
B) Azure Storage Account
C) Azure Active Directory
D) Azure Virtual Network
E) Azure API Management

QUESTION 42

You are developing an application that needs to translate text from one language to another while ensuring that any Personally Identifiable Information (PII) is preserved. Which Azure AI service should you use for this task?

```
A) TranslatorTextClient
B) ContentModeratorClient
C) TextAnalyticsClient
D) FormRecognizerClient
E) LanguageUnderstandingClient
```

QUESTION 43

Your organization is developing a custom skill for Azure Cognitive Search to extract entity information from documents. During testing, you encounter errors related to skill execution, and you need to troubleshoot the issues effectively. Which approach should you take to debug and troubleshoot custom skill processing errors in Azure Cognitive Search?

A) Analyze skill execution logs
B) Increase the timeout duration for the skill
C) Check network connectivity to external services
D) Review document format compatibility
E) Restart the Azure Cognitive Search service

QUESTION 44

Your team is tasked with personalizing search results in an e-commerce platform powered by Azure Cognitive Search. You need to implement a mechanism to adjust search rankings based on user preferences and behavior. What should you utilize to influence search rankings and personalize search results effectively?

A) Implement user-specific scoring profiles
B) Configure query pipelines for personalized ranking
C) Utilize Azure Machine Learning models for ranking adjustments
D) Apply custom boosting functions based on user interactions
E) Develop custom relevance models for search ranking

QUESTION 45

Which method in Azure Text Analytics is used to determine the sentiment of text?

```
A) TextAnalyticsClient.detectSentiment()
B) SentimentAnalysisClient.analyzeSentiment()
C) TextSentimentClient.analyze()
D) AnalyzeTextClient.detectSentiment()
E) SentimentDetectionClient.analyze()
```

QUESTION 46

You are tasked with provisioning an Azure OpenAI Service resource for a project with strict compliance requirements. What should you consider regarding pricing and cost management during the setup?

A) Selecting the highest pricing tier for enhanced service features.
B) Opting for a pay-as-you-go pricing model for flexibility.
C) Understanding pricing models to estimate long-term costs accurately.
D) Utilizing promotional credits to reduce initial expenses.
E) Negotiating custom pricing plans with Microsoft sales representatives.

QUESTION 47

Your team is developing a software solution that requires automated code generation for specific tasks using Azure OpenAI Service. What best practice should you follow to ensure the generated code meets quality standards and integrates seamlessly into the existing codebase?

A) Providing comprehensive input prompts with detailed task descriptions.
B) Using pre-trained models without customization for faster code generation.
C) Reviewing and refining generated code iteratively based on developer feedback.
D) Ignoring generated code quality as long as it fulfills the functional requirements.
E) Including code generation as a separate phase after development completion.

QUESTION 48

When working with Azure AI Language service, which combination of statements is true?

A) Statement I: Azure AI Language service can detect the language used in text.
B) Statement II: Azure AI Language service can extract key phrases from text.
C) Statement III: Azure AI Language service provides support for sentiment analysis.
D) Statement I, Statement II
E) Statement II, Statement III

QUESTION 49

As part of a project to develop a generative AI model for creating personalized workout routines, you are tasked with ensuring data privacy and security when using custom fitness datasets. Which measure is essential to maintain data privacy and security in this scenario?
Select all answers that apply.

A) Implementing role-based access control (RBAC) to restrict access to sensitive fitness data.
B) Using homomorphic encryption to perform computations on encrypted fitness data.
C) Regularly auditing access logs to identify unauthorized attempts to access fitness datasets.
D) Hashing user identifiers before storing them in the dataset to anonymize personal information.
E) Employing differential privacy techniques to protect individual workout details while preserving overall dataset utility.

QUESTION 50

Your company has implemented an Azure OpenAI model for generating code snippets based on natural language prompts. After fine-tuning the model, you need to evaluate its performance to ensure it meets the project requirements. Which metrics or techniques would be most appropriate for this evaluation?

A) F1 Score
B) BLEU Score
C) Precision-Recall Curve analysis
D) Mean Squared Error
E) Semantic Similarity measurement

PRACTICE TEST 4 - ANSWERS ONLY

QUESTION 1

Answer - [A, C] Azure Cognitive Services Translator, Azure Cognitive Services Language Understanding (LUIS)

Option B - Azure Bot Services: While Bot Services provides the framework for building chatbots, it does not inherently support multilingual capabilities.
Option D - Azure QnA Maker: QnA Maker is used for creating question and answer pairs and does not directly address multilingual requirements.
Option E - Azure Cognitive Services Text Analytics: Text Analytics focuses on sentiment analysis and key phrase extraction, but it does not specialize in multilingual language understanding.
Option A - Azure Cognitive Services Translator: Translator is specifically designed for language translation and can be integrated into the chatbot to support conversations in multiple languages, ensuring seamless communication with users.
Option C - Azure Cognitive Services Language Understanding (LUIS): LUIS provides intent recognition and entity extraction capabilities, which are essential for understanding user queries across different languages, making it suitable for multilingual chatbots.

EXAM FOCUS	*You need to use Azure Cognitive Services Translator and LUIS to support multilingual conversations in chatbots. This combination enables both translation and intent recognition across languages.*
CAUTION ALERT	*Don't confuse Bot Services or QnA Maker with services designed for multilingual capabilities. These are more focused on the structure of conversations, not multilingual processing.*

QUESTION 2

Answer - [A, D] Azure AI Text Analytics, Azure AI Form Recognizer

Option B - Azure AI Language Understanding (LUIS): Designed for intent recognition in conversational AI applications, not suited for text analysis.
Option C - Azure AI Content Moderator: Primarily used for content moderation tasks such as detecting offensive content, not suitable for text analysis.
Option E - Azure AI Translator Text: Used for language translation, not tailored for text analysis tasks.

EXAM FOCUS	*Make sure to combine Azure Text Analytics with Form Recognizer to extract insights from customer reviews. Text Analytics handles sentiment and key phrases, while Form Recognizer handles structured data extraction from forms.*
CAUTION ALERT	*Stay clear of relying on LUIS or Content Moderator for this task—they are designed for conversational AI and content moderation, not detailed text analysis.*

QUESTION 3

Answer - B) az cognitiveservices account keys list

Option A - Incorrect. This command lists account keys for Azure accounts, not specifically for Azure AI service resources. Option C - Incorrect. This command lists keys in a key vault, not for Azure AI service resources. Option D - Incorrect. This command lists secrets in a key vault, not for Azure AI service resources. Option E - Incorrect. This command lists keys for storage accounts, not for Azure AI service resources.

EXAM FOCUS	*Keep in mind that to manage account keys for Azure Cognitive Services, you should use the command az cognitiveservices account keys list. This specifically handles Cognitive Services resource keys.*
CAUTION	*Avoid using commands like az keyvault or az storage, as they are designed for different resources and*

ALERT	*won't give you the required access to Azure AI service keys.*

QUESTION 4

Answer - A) Azure Active Directory (AAD)

Option B - Incorrect. Shared access signatures provide access to resources but may not tie directly to an individual or organization. Option C - Incorrect. API keys are often shared and may not uniquely identify an individual or organization. Option D - Incorrect. Client secrets are used in OAuth 2.0 flow for client authentication but may not directly tie to an individual or organization. Option E - Incorrect. Azure Key Vault is used for storing secrets securely but does not directly tie to an individual or organization.

EXAM FOCUS	*Always remember that Azure Active Directory (AAD) offers identity-based access management tied to individuals or organizations, making it the most secure and scalable solution for authenticating users.*
CAUTION ALERT	*Stay alert for using Shared Access Signatures (SAS) or API keys, as these are not tied to individuals and may lead to weaker security.*

QUESTION 5

Answer - [A, B, D, E]

Option A - Utilize Azure Cognitive Services to leverage pre-built AI models and reduce development time and costs: Correct. Leveraging pre-built AI models from Azure Cognitive Services can expedite development and reduce overall costs.

Option B - Choose Azure regions with low-latency connectivity to minimize data transfer costs and improve performance: Correct. Selecting regions with low latency helps optimize costs and enhance user experience.

Option C - Implement serverless computing options, such as Azure Functions, to optimize resource utilization and reduce operational overhead: While serverless computing can improve resource efficiency, it may not always be the most cost-effective option for all scenarios, especially those with consistent workloads.

Option D - Use Azure Cost Management tools to analyze spending patterns and identify opportunities for optimization and cost savings: Correct. Cost management tools are essential for ensuring cost-effectiveness and identifying areas for optimization.

Option E - Configure auto-shutdown policies for development and testing environments to prevent unnecessary resource usage and reduce costs: Correct. Auto-shutdown policies help minimize resource waste and control costs in non-production environments.

EXAM FOCUS	*You should leverage pre-built AI models in Cognitive Services to reduce development time and costs, while using Azure Cost Management tools to keep costs optimized. Auto-shutdown for non-production environments is a great way to minimize unnecessary expenses.*
CAUTION ALERT	*Stay clear of overlooking Azure regions with low latency, as data transfer costs and performance can be affected. Additionally, avoid over-provisioning serverless options for consistent workloads.*

QUESTION 6

Answer - C) Configure Azure Private Endpoint for the Azure AI services.

Option A - Incorrect. While a reverse proxy can provide additional security layers, it may not address the requirement to avoid direct internet access. Option B - Incorrect. Azure AD authentication is more about user identity than securing network connections between resources. Option D - Incorrect. While NSG rules can restrict outbound traffic, they do not provide the same level of secure connectivity as Azure Private Endpoint. Option E - Incorrect. Installing a firewall on the VM may not address the requirement to avoid direct internet access and secure communication with Azure AI services.

EXAM FOCUS	*Make sure to configure Azure Private Endpoint for secure communication between your virtual machine and Azure AI services. This will keep traffic secure without needing direct public internet access.*
CAUTION ALERT	*Avoid relying on firewalls or NSG rules alone. While they provide some security, they do not ensure private network connections like Azure Private Endpoint does.*

QUESTION 7

Answer - [B] Filtering logs based on severity levels.

Filtering logs based on severity levels - Focusing on logs relevant to the severity of the issue allows for efficient troubleshooting and prioritization of corrective actions, facilitating timely resolution. Options A, C, D, and E are counterproductive or incorrect actions for effective troubleshooting using diagnostic logs.

EXAM FOCUS	*You should filter diagnostic logs based on severity levels to quickly find and address critical issues during deployment. Focus on error-level logs for efficient troubleshooting.*
CAUTION ALERT	*Don't confuse this with reviewing logs manually or ignoring logs related to errors. Filtering helps prioritize your analysis and saves time.*

QUESTION 8

Answer - [C] Azure Monitor.

Azure Monitor - Leveraging Azure Monitor enables comprehensive monitoring of Azure AI service usage and costs, providing insights into resource consumption patterns and opportunities for cost optimization, thereby supporting effective budget management and control. Options A, B, D, and E are relevant but do not specifically focus on monitoring Azure AI service usage and costs.

EXAM FOCUS	*Make sure to use Azure Monitor for a comprehensive view of your AI service usage and costs. This tool provides insights into resource consumption patterns and supports cost-saving measures.*
CAUTION ALERT	*Avoid using tools like Azure DevOps or IoT Hub, which are designed for different purposes and won't offer the detailed cost insights needed for AI service optimization.*

QUESTION 9

Answer - B) Enable Managed Service Identity (MSI) for App5 and assign RBAC permissions to Microsoft Entra ID.

Option A - Incorrect. Azure AD SSO may provide centralized authentication but may not align with the requirement to use Microsoft Entra ID. Option C - Incorrect. OAuth 2.0 authentication with Azure AD may not directly support Microsoft Entra ID and may introduce unnecessary complexity. Option D - Incorrect. Azure AD authentication may not directly support Microsoft Entra ID and may introduce additional configuration overhead. Option E - Incorrect. Storing client secrets may introduce additional security risks and administrative overhead.

EXAM FOCUS	*Always consider enabling Managed Service Identity (MSI) for your Azure app and assigning RBAC permissions to ensure a secure, automated authentication process with least privilege access.*
CAUTION ALERT	*Stay clear of using client secrets or OAuth 2.0 flows when MSI can simplify authentication securely. These alternatives add more complexity and potential security risks.*

QUESTION 10

Answer - [B] Ensure seamless communication between text moderation and content storage services.

Ensure seamless communication between text moderation and content storage services - Seamless integration facilitates efficient moderation workflows and ensures consistency between text moderation and content management processes, unlike options A, C, D, and E, which may lead to fragmented systems or increased complexity.

EXAM FOCUS	*You need to ensure seamless communication between your text moderation workflows and content storage services for smooth integration. This practice ensures consistent moderation and content management.*
CAUTION ALERT	*Avoid maintaining separate workflows or ignoring integration with other Azure services, as this could lead to inefficiencies and fragmented content management processes.*

QUESTION 11

Answer - [B] Implementing HIPAA-compliant security measures for handling sensitive medical information.

Compliance with HIPAA regulations is critical for protecting the privacy and security of patient data in healthcare environments, ensuring that decision support solutions meet industry-specific requirements. Options A, C, D, and E focus on different compliance standards but may not be directly applicable to healthcare data privacy regulations.

EXAM FOCUS	*You need to ensure compliance with HIPAA regulations when implementing decision support solutions in healthcare. Prioritizing HIPAA safeguards sensitive patient data, maintaining industry standards for security and privacy.*
CAUTION ALERT	*Don't confuse GDPR, SOC 2, or ISO 27001 with HIPAA. While they are important, HIPAA is specifically critical for medical information protection in the U.S. healthcare context.*

QUESTION 12

Answer - A) Train and evaluate the language understanding model using Azure AI Language.
C) Integrate the language understanding model into client applications for consumption.

Option B - Incorrect. While fine-tuning parameters can improve model performance, it may not be categorized as necessary for managing and deploying the model. Option D - Incorrect. While backup and recovery are important, they may not directly relate to managing and deploying the model. Option E - Incorrect. Azure OpenAI Service is not directly related to managing and deploying language understanding models on Azure AI Language.

EXAM FOCUS	*Make sure to train and evaluate the language understanding model before integrating it into client applications. Efficient model training ensures that your NLP solution functions accurately within real-world use cases.*
CAUTION ALERT	*Avoid using Azure OpenAI Service for managing Azure AI Language models—they are separate services with different focuses. Azure AI Language is built for language understanding.*

QUESTION 13

Answer - [A, B, C, D] Options A, B, C, and D contribute to effective global deployment and localization of the DSS.

Option A directs users to the nearest datacenter, option B optimizes content delivery, option C ensures data consistency across regions, and option D facilitates deployment across multiple regions using Kubernetes. Option E, Azure ExpressRoute, is not directly related to global deployment and localization of applications.

EXAM FOCUS	*Always remember to use Azure Traffic Manager and Azure Cosmos DB for effective global deployment and localization. Traffic Manager ensures geographic routing, while Cosmos DB supports multi-region writes for consistency.*
CAUTION ALERT	*Don't confuse Azure ExpressRoute with a solution for global deployment; it's used for private connections, not application localization.*

QUESTION 14

Answer - [A, C] Options A and C are essential for accurately detecting potential threats in surveillance footage. Object detection (Option A) helps identify suspicious objects or individuals, while scene understanding (Option C) provides context to detect abnormal activities or situations indicative of security threats.

Options B, D, and E are less relevant for threat detection. Facial recognition (Option B) focuses on identifying individuals, emotion detection (Option D) assesses emotional states, and text recognition (Option E) extracts textual information, which may not directly contribute to threat detection in surveillance footage analysis.

EXAM FOCUS	*You should leverage Object Detection and Scene Understanding in Azure Computer Vision to detect threats in security footage. These features help analyze surveillance footage for suspicious objects and situations.*
CAUTION ALERT	*Stay clear of relying on emotion detection or text recognition for threat analysis. These features are not designed for detecting physical security threats in surveillance environments.*

QUESTION 15

Answer - A) Validate and ensure that the audio files conform to the supported input formats specified by the Azure AI Speech service.
B) Convert the audio files to a compatible format using appropriate conversion tools or libraries before processing.

Option C - Incorrect. Upgrading the service tier does not address input format compatibility issues. Option D - Incorrect. While error handling is important, ensuring input format compatibility is crucial for successful processing. Option E - Incorrect. Checking documentation is a good practice, but immediate resolution requires addressing input format mismatches directly.

EXAM FOCUS	*Keep in mind to validate audio file formats before processing them with Azure AI Speech services. Correct input formats are critical to avoiding errors like "Input Format Mismatch."*
CAUTION ALERT	*Don't confuse upgrading the service tier with solving format issues. Service tier upgrades don't change input format compatibility; conversion or validation of formats is required.*

QUESTION 16

Answer - [B] Advanced techniques offer better performance in extracting text from complex backgrounds.

B) Advanced techniques offer better performance in extracting text from complex backgrounds. - Correct. Advanced text extraction methods excel in scenarios involving complex backgrounds, where OCR may struggle to accurately extract text due to noise or clutter. These advanced techniques utilize sophisticated algorithms and deep learning models to achieve superior performance in handling challenging image environments, ensuring reliable text extraction even in complex situations.
A) OCR provides higher accuracy in extracting handwritten text. - Incorrect. While OCR can be effective in recognizing handwritten text, advanced techniques may offer better accuracy, especially in challenging environments.
C) OCR supports multilingual text extraction with high precision. - Incorrect. OCR may have limitations in handling multilingual text or complex layouts compared to advanced methods.
D) Advanced techniques are more suitable for simple document layouts. - Incorrect. Advanced techniques are often preferred for handling complex layouts, while OCR may suffice for simpler document structures.
E) OCR requires less computational resources compared to advanced methods. - Incorrect. The computational requirements of OCR and advanced methods can vary depending on factors such as model complexity and dataset size.

EXAM FOCUS	*You should consider advanced text extraction techniques when dealing with complex backgrounds in images. They perform better than traditional OCR in challenging environments.*
CAUTION ALERT	*Stay alert that OCR alone may struggle with noise or clutter in complex images. Advanced techniques are better for such scenarios, especially when extracting text from difficult visual contexts.*

QUESTION 17

Answer - [B) Recall, E) Mean Average Precision (mAP)]

Prioritizing recall ensures that the model effectively identifies all relevant objects in images. Additionally, Mean Average Precision (mAP) provides a comprehensive measure of object detection performance.
A) Precision focuses on the proportion of correctly identified objects among all objects predicted.
C) F1 score combines precision and recall but may not be the most suitable metric for this scenario.
D) Accuracy measures the overall correctness of the model's predictions but may not capture object detection performance comprehensively.

EXAM FOCUS	*Always prioritize using Recall and Mean Average Precision (mAP) when evaluating an image classification model. These metrics provide a comprehensive view of the model's performance in detecting all relevant objects.*
CAUTION ALERT	*Avoid over-relying on accuracy alone. Accuracy might not fully represent the effectiveness of object detection, especially in cases where recall and precision are more important.*

QUESTION 18

Answer - [C] Implement context-aware features to improve intent disambiguation.

Option C - Expanding the training data (Option A) can help but might not specifically address intent recognition accuracy. Fine-tuning the language model (Option B) is valuable but may not directly improve intent recognition if the issue lies with disambiguation. Adjusting the confidence threshold (Option D) can be helpful but may not solve underlying ambiguity problems. Upgrading the Azure AI Language service (Option E) is not the initial solution. Implementing context-aware features (Option C) can improve intent disambiguation, thereby enhancing accuracy.

EXAM FOCUS	*Make sure to implement context-aware features to improve intent recognition accuracy in NLP models. Contextual features help disambiguate intents, especially when users provide ambiguous inputs.*
CAUTION ALERT	*Avoid relying solely on expanding training data or adjusting thresholds without addressing the core issue of intent disambiguation through context awareness.*

QUESTION 19

Answer - A) Use Azure DevOps pipelines to automate the deployment of updated model versions, incorporating canary deployments for gradual rollout.

Option B - Regular downtime for manual updates disrupts operations and may not support continuous deployment practices.
Option C - Maintaining multiple versions increases complexity and may lead to inconsistencies in model usage.
Option D - Manual uploads and restarts lack automation and may cause service interruptions.
Option E - While staging environments are useful, they may not prevent all production disruptions without automation like DevOps pipelines provide.

EXAM FOCUS	*You should use Azure DevOps pipelines with canary deployments to automate updates to models, minimizing production disruptions. Canary deployments ensure gradual rollouts while monitoring for issues.*
CAUTION ALERT	*Stay clear of manual updates or scheduling downtime, which can interrupt operations and are less efficient than automated DevOps approaches.*

QUESTION 20

Answer - D) Azure AI Vision Spatial Analysis

Option A - Azure AI Video Indexer focuses more on extracting insights and metadata from videos rather than real-time spatial analysis for crowd management.
Option B - While Azure Cognitive Services - Computer Vision offers image analysis capabilities, it may not provide specific features for crowd behavior analysis and spatial analysis.
Option C - Azure Cognitive Services - Video Analyzer is geared towards real-time video processing but may lack the precision required for detailed spatial analysis.
Option E - Azure AI Metrics Advisor is designed for monitoring and analyzing metrics data rather than real-time video analysis for crowd management.

EXAM FOCUS	*You need to choose Azure AI Vision Spatial Analysis for real-time crowd behavior insights. This service is tailored for detecting movement patterns and managing crowd density in large venues.*
CAUTION ALERT	*Don't confuse Video Indexer or Computer Vision with Spatial Analysis. These services focus on video metadata and image analysis, but Spatial Analysis is designed for real-time crowd behavior monitoring.*

QUESTION 21

Answer - [C] Predicting intents and entities from user input.

Option C - This API request is used to predict intents and entities from user input using the language understanding model associated with the specified application and production slot. Training the model (Option A), evaluating the model (Option B), importing data (Option D), and exporting the model (Option E) are unrelated operations.

EXAM FOCUS	*You need to understand that the API request used with the Azure Language service is for predicting intents and entities. This is essential for interpreting user inputs accurately within a production environment.*
CAUTION ALERT	*Stay clear of confusing this request with training or evaluating the model, as it's specifically used for prediction. The API request is geared toward identifying intents and entities, not training or importing data.*

QUESTION 22

Answer - A) Azure AI Language - Key Phrase Extraction

Option B - While Azure Text Analytics offers key phrase extraction, Azure AI Language may provide more customization options and better accuracy for this specific scenario.
Option C - Azure Machine Learning requires custom model development, which might not be the most efficient solution for this scenario.
Option D - Azure Cognitive Search focuses on indexing and searching structured data, not on key phrase extraction from unstructured text.
Option E - Azure Databricks is more focused on big data processing and analytics rather than text analysis and key phrase extraction.

EXAM FOCUS	*Always remember that Azure AI Language - Key Phrase Extraction offers higher accuracy and relevance for content analysis. It improves the ability to recommend relevant courses based on extracted key concepts.*
CAUTION ALERT	*Don't confuse Azure Cognitive Search with key phrase extraction. It focuses on searching and indexing structured data, whereas key phrase extraction is about identifying critical terms from unstructured content.*

QUESTION 23

Answer - [A] Azure Text Analytics.

Azure Text Analytics provides pre-built sentiment analysis capabilities that can accurately identify sentiment in customer reviews across multiple languages. Azure Cognitive Search focuses on indexing and searching text data, not sentiment analysis. Azure Language Understanding (LUIS) is designed for intent classification and entity recognition, not sentiment analysis. Azure Translator and Azure Speech to Text are not specifically tailored for sentiment analysis.

EXAM FOCUS	*Make sure to use Azure Text Analytics for multilingual sentiment analysis. It provides built-in support for detecting sentiment across multiple languages, which is crucial for global customer feedback analysis.*
CAUTION ALERT	*Avoid using Azure Language Understanding (LUIS) or Azure Cognitive Search for sentiment analysis. They focus on intent recognition and text search rather than sentiment analysis.*

QUESTION 24

Answer - [B] Retraining the language model with additional labeled examples.

Option B - Retraining the language model with additional labeled examples can improve the model's ability to recognize and classify user intents accurately by providing more diverse and representative training data. Increasing confidence thresholds (Option A) may filter out valid intents, while adjusting language detection settings (Option C) is more relevant for multilingual applications. Enabling multi-language support (Option D) addresses a different aspect of language processing. Fine-tuning response generation (Option E) focuses on chatbot behavior rather than intent recognition.

EXAM FOCUS	*You should retrain the model with additional labeled examples to improve accuracy in classifying intents. Expanding the training set helps the model better generalize and handle a variety of inputs.*
CAUTION ALERT	*Stay cautioned that simply adjusting thresholds or enabling multilingual support won't improve intent recognition if the training data is insufficient. Focus on retraining with relevant examples.*

QUESTION 25

Answer - A) Azure Cognitive Services Speech Service

Option A - Correct. Azure Cognitive Services Speech Service provides real-time speech recognition capabilities with low latency, making it suitable for virtual assistant applications.

Option B - Azure Machine Learning is more focused on training and deploying machine learning models rather than real-time STT.

Option C - Azure Kubernetes Service (AKS) is a container orchestration service and may not be optimized for real-time STT.

Option D - Azure IoT Edge is designed for deploying cloud intelligence to edge devices and is not specifically tailored for real-time speech recognition.

EXAM FOCUS	*You need to use Azure Cognitive Services Speech Service for real-time speech-to-text (STT) with low latency. This service is optimized for real-time applications like virtual assistants where response time is critical.*
CAUTION ALERT	*Don't confuse Azure Machine Learning or AKS with real-time speech recognition needs. These are more suitable for model training and orchestration, not optimized for real-time STT.*

QUESTION 26

Answer - [B] Using data augmentation to simulate various driving conditions during model training.

Option B is the most appropriate technique as data augmentation can help simulate diverse driving conditions during model training, making the system more robust to different environments. Option A is relevant for adapting to individual voices but does not address environmental variability. Option C could be beneficial but may not specifically enhance robustness to different driving conditions. Option D addresses noise capture but may not fully simulate various driving conditions. Option E focuses on architecture complexity but does not directly address environmental robustness.

EXAM FOCUS	*You should consider data augmentation during model training to simulate noisy environments and driving conditions. This will improve the model's robustness and adaptability to real-world scenarios.*
CAUTION ALERT	*Stay alert that speaker adaptation or complex neural architectures alone won't address variability in environmental noise. Focus on augmenting the training data with different driving conditions.*

QUESTION 27

Answer - [B] Object recognition

Option B - Object recognition is suitable for identifying and classifying objects within images, making it the most appropriate choice for detecting defects in product images during quality control. Face detection (Option A) focuses on identifying human faces. Optical character recognition (OCR) (Option C) extracts text from images. Image classification (Option D) categorizes entire images rather than detecting specific defects. Anomaly detection (Option E) identifies outliers or irregularities in data, which is not specific to defect detection in images.

EXAM FOCUS	*Always use Object Recognition for detecting defects in product images during manufacturing. It provides the most accurate method to identify and classify objects, making it ideal for quality control.*
CAUTION ALERT	*Avoid using OCR or face detection for defect detection in manufacturing. These features are designed for different use cases, like text extraction and facial identification, not product quality inspection.*

QUESTION 28

Answer - [E] Azure Cognitive Services Vision Service

Option E is the correct choice because Azure Cognitive Services Vision Service offers Optical Character Recognition (OCR) capabilities, allowing for the extraction and translation of text from various document formats while preserving format and layout. Options A, B, C, and D are not specifically designed for maintaining format and layout in document translation.

EXAM FOCUS	*Keep in mind that Azure Cognitive Services Vision preserves document layout and format during OCR and translation tasks, ensuring that the translated output retains the original structure.*
CAUTION ALERT	*Stay cautioned that other Azure services like Translator Text or LUIS are not designed for maintaining the original layout and format in translated documents. OCR from Vision is critical for this task.*

QUESTION 29

Answer - [A] Anonymize customer transaction data before incorporating it into the training dataset

Explanation: A) Anonymizing customer transaction data protects privacy while allowing its use for model training. B) While obtaining consent is important, anonymization provides an additional layer of protection. C) Limiting data scope may hinder model performance and overlook valuable insights. D) Encryption addresses data security but does not guarantee compliance with privacy regulations. E) Excluding transaction data may limit the model's effectiveness and overlook valuable information.

EXAM FOCUS	*You should anonymize customer transaction data before using it in model training to ensure compliance with privacy regulations like GDPR. Anonymization protects sensitive data while allowing effective model training.*

CAUTION ALERT	*Stay clear of using raw customer data without anonymization, as it violates privacy regulations. Encryption protects data security but does not address regulatory compliance requirements like anonymization.*

QUESTION 30

Answer - [A] Insufficient contrast between text and background in the images.

Option A - Insufficient contrast between text and background in the images can lead to inaccuracies in character recognition, as the Azure AI OCR model may struggle to distinguish between text and surrounding elements, especially in low-resolution images. Variability in font types (Option B) may affect recognition accuracy but is less likely to cause systematic inaccuracies. Limited language support (Option C) may impact recognition quality but is not directly related to accuracy issues. An outdated SDK version (Option D) may cause compatibility problems but is not the primary cause of recognition inaccuracies. Lack of integration (Option E) between the app's preprocessing pipeline and Azure AI OCR might affect data flow but is not directly linked to recognition accuracy issues.

EXAM FOCUS	*You need to ensure that images fed into Azure OCR have sufficient contrast between the text and the background. Low-contrast images can cause recognition inaccuracies, especially in low-resolution inputs.*
CAUTION ALERT	*Don't confuse SDK versions or language limitations with accuracy issues related to image quality. Focus on improving the image contrast to help the OCR model better distinguish text from the background.*

QUESTION 31

Answer - [A), B), C), and D)] - Implementing active learning, monitoring model performance, incorporating user feedback, and periodic retraining are essential strategies for continuous model improvement.

E) Incorrect - While transfer learning can be useful, it might not directly address the need for continuous improvement and adaptability to evolving user language patterns.

EXAM FOCUS	*You should implement active learning, monitor performance metrics, and use periodic retraining with updated data to continuously improve your sentiment analysis model's accuracy in production environments. These strategies ensure adaptability to evolving language patterns.*
CAUTION ALERT	*Stay clear of over-relying on transfer learning from unrelated domains. While useful, it may not address the specific need to continually refine a model for real-time data adaptation.*

QUESTION 32

Answer - [A), B), and D)] - Collecting representative training data, implementing fairness-aware algorithms, and employing transfer learning address considerations for handling sentiment variations across different demographic groups and languages.

C) Incorrect - While sensitivity analysis is important for evaluating model performance, it might not directly address the challenge of fine-tuning the model to handle sentiment variations across diverse demographic groups and languages.

EXAM FOCUS	*Always remember to collect diverse training data reflecting user demographics and languages when optimizing for sentiment variations. Implementing fairness-aware algorithms and transfer learning ensures bias mitigation and enhances performance.*
CAUTION ALERT	*Avoid neglecting biases in data. Fairness-aware algorithms should be used to ensure the model performs consistently across different demographic groups and languages.*

QUESTION 33

Answer - [B] Azure Speech Service > Speech API

Option B - Azure Speech Service with the Speech API allows real-time speech-to-text conversion, enabling sentiment analysis of live conversations. Option A is incorrect as Cognitive Search is not suitable for real-time conversation analysis. Option C is incorrect as the Text Analytics API does not directly support live conversation analysis. Option D is incorrect as Computer Vision is focused on image processing, not speech. Option E is incorrect as Content Moderator is not designed for sentiment analysis of live conversations.

EXAM FOCUS	*You should use Azure Speech Service with Speech API for detecting live sentiment in conversations. It converts speech-to-text in real-time, enabling effective sentiment analysis of conversations.*
CAUTION ALERT	*Don't confuse this requirement with Azure Cognitive Search or Text Analytics. They are not designed for real-time conversation analysis, which is critical in this scenario.*

QUESTION 34

Answer - [A), B), and C)] - Best practices for content security and access control include implementing RBAC, encrypting content with Azure Key Vault, and restricting access through Azure Active Directory.

Option A) - Correct: RBAC ensures that only authorized users can moderate content, maintaining security and integrity. Option B) - Correct: Encryption with Azure Key Vault protects content from unauthorized access and data breaches. Option C) - Correct: Restricting access through Azure AD ensures that only authorized users can access the content, enhancing security. Option D) - Incorrect: Sharing content publicly compromises security and violates access control principles. Option E) - Incorrect: Ignoring security measures exposes content to unauthorized access and potential breaches.

EXAM FOCUS	*You need to use role-based access control (RBAC) and Azure Key Vault encryption to protect content in question-answering solutions. These practices ensure that only authorized users can access sensitive data.*
CAUTION ALERT	*Avoid sharing content publicly without authorization controls. Always implement security measures like Azure Active Directory (AD) to prevent unauthorized access.*

QUESTION 35

Answer - [A), B), and D)] - Ensuring high availability and reliability involves deploying content across multiple regions, implementing Azure CDN, and utilizing Azure Traffic Manager for load balancing.

Option A) - Correct: Deploying content across multiple Azure regions enhances redundancy and ensures availability. Option B) - Correct: Azure CDN facilitates global content delivery, enhancing accessibility and reliability. Option C) - Incorrect: Auto-scaling is more relevant for managing resource allocation based on demand but does not directly contribute to high availability. Option D) - Correct: Azure Traffic Manager distributes traffic across regions, improving reliability and reducing latency. Option E) - Incorrect: Optimizing cache settings can enhance performance but does not directly address high availability and reliability concerns.

EXAM FOCUS	*Make sure to deploy content across multiple Azure regions and use Azure CDN for global availability. Using Azure Traffic Manager for load balancing ensures high reliability and minimal downtime.*
CAUTION ALERT	*Stay cautioned against relying solely on auto-scaling for availability. While helpful for resource allocation, it does not guarantee redundancy or failover for content distribution.*

QUESTION 36

Answer - [A, B, C] "mcr.microsoft.com/azure-cognitive-services/speech/recognition"
"--memory 384 --cpus 6"

"--eula accept"

Option A provides the correct URI for the speech recognition model. Option B specifies memory and CPU limits for the container. Option C accepts the end-user license agreement (EULA) during deployment. Options D and E are not relevant for deploying containers.

EXAM FOCUS	*You should include memory and CPU settings along with the correct image repository in your bash deployment statement for speech recognition containers. This ensures optimal resource utilization during deployment.*
CAUTION ALERT	*Avoid forgetting the "--eula accept" parameter, as it is essential for accepting the license agreement when deploying Cognitive Services containers.*

QUESTION 37

Answer - [A, C, E].

A) Using separate models for each language allows better customization and adaptation to language-specific characteristics and nuances. C) Training the model with language-specific tokens helps it learn language-specific patterns and syntax. E) Applying language-specific data augmentation techniques enriches the training data, enhancing the model's ability to generalize across languages. B) Normalizing text input across languages may lead to loss of language-specific features, while limiting the vocabulary size can restrict the model's expressiveness.

EXAM FOCUS	*You need to fine-tune the model with language-specific tokens and apply language-specific data augmentation techniques to support multilingual text generation. This ensures that the model handles different languages effectively.*
CAUTION ALERT	*Stay clear of normalizing text inputs across languages if it leads to the loss of language-specific features. Models should preserve linguistic nuances to maintain performance across different languages.*

QUESTION 38

Answer - [A, B, C].

A) Implementing encryption for data security ensures that sensitive information transmitted and stored by the bot remains protected from unauthorized access. B) Using Azure Key Vault for managing sensitive information enhances security by providing centralized management and secure storage of cryptographic keys. C) Incorporating role-based access control (RBAC) ensures that only authorized individuals can access and modify the bot's data, enhancing compliance with regulations. D) While data anonymization is important for privacy, it may not be sufficient to ensure compliance with regulations alone. E) Conducting regular security audits and vulnerability assessments is essential but may not directly address compliance requirements.

EXAM FOCUS	*You should ensure compliance by using encryption, Azure Key Vault for sensitive information, and RBAC for controlling data access in healthcare applications. These measures help meet data privacy regulations.*
CAUTION ALERT	*Avoid neglecting data anonymization where required for privacy protection. Encryption alone may not be enough to meet privacy laws in certain jurisdictions.*

QUESTION 39

Answer - [A, C] TextAnalyticsClient("<YourSubscriptionKey>", "<YourServiceRegion>")
sentimentResult.Sentiment

Option A initializes the TextAnalyticsClient object with the provided subscription key and service region. Option C retrieves the sentiment result from the sentimentResult object. Options B, D, and E are incorrect or irrelevant for initializing the TextAnalyticsClient or retrieving sentiment.

EXAM FOCUS	*Always remember to use TextAnalyticsClient with the correct subscription key and service region to initialize the client for sentiment analysis in Azure. Retrieve the sentiment score from the result object.*
CAUTION ALERT	*Avoid using incorrect method calls like GetSentiment. The correct method is AnalyzeSentimentAsync for fetching sentiment analysis in Azure AI.*

QUESTION 40

Answer - [D] Azure AI Translator service.

D) Azure AI Translator service provides translation capabilities that can help preprocess customer feedback in multiple languages before sentiment analysis, ensuring accurate detection across language barriers. A) Azure Text Analytics offers sentiment analysis but may not handle multiple languages as effectively as translation services. B) Azure Language Understanding (LUIS) focuses on understanding user intents and entities within a single language and is not specialized for multilingual sentiment analysis. C) Azure Cognitive Search is primarily used for search functionalities and does not provide translation capabilities for multilingual sentiment analysis. E) Azure AI Language Service provides language detection and translation but does not specifically handle sentiment analysis like Azure AI Translator service.

EXAM FOCUS	*You should use Azure AI Translator service to preprocess multilingual customer feedback for sentiment analysis. This ensures the model can accurately detect sentiment across language barriers.*
CAUTION ALERT	*Don't confuse Azure Text Analytics with a translation service. While Text Analytics provides sentiment analysis, it may not handle multilingual preprocessing as efficiently as the Translator service.*

QUESTION 41

Answer - [B] Azure Storage Account.

B) Configuring an Azure Storage Account allows the Cognitive Search service to securely access documents stored in Azure Blob Storage through shared access signatures (SAS) or managed identities, ensuring seamless integration with existing Azure infrastructure. A) Azure Key Vault is used for securely storing keys, secrets, and certificates but is not directly related to accessing Blob Storage. C) Azure Active Directory provides authentication services but may not directly enable access to Blob Storage. D) Azure Virtual Network enables secure communication between Azure resources but is not specifically related to accessing Blob Storage. E) Azure API Management is used for managing APIs and may not directly enable access to Blob Storage.

EXAM FOCUS	*You should always configure Azure Storage Account for Cognitive Search when accessing Blob Storage. Make sure to use Shared Access Signatures (SAS) or Managed Identities to secure access while allowing integration. This ensures security and easy access.*
CAUTION ALERT	*Avoid assuming Azure Active Directory (AAD) alone provides access to Blob Storage. Ensure you configure the Storage Account or you might face issues with service permissions.*

QUESTION 42

Answer - [A] TranslatorTextClient

Option B, ContentModeratorClient, is used for content moderation tasks and is unrelated to language translation with PII preservation. Option C, TextAnalyticsClient, is used for text analytics tasks like sentiment analysis and key phrase extraction, not for language translation. Option D, FormRecognizerClient, is used for extracting information from forms and documents, not for language translation. Option E, LanguageUnderstandingClient, is used for understanding user intents from natural language inputs and does not include translation features. Option A, TranslatorTextClient, is the correct choice as it provides language translation capabilities while ensuring PII preservation.

EXAM FOCUS	*Make sure to choose TranslatorTextClient when preserving Personally Identifiable Information (PII) during language translation. This service can handle text translation while ensuring that PII remains*

CAUTION ALERT	*intact throughout.* *Stay alert not to confuse TextAnalyticsClient with TranslatorTextClient. While Text Analytics can identify key phrases, it does not handle language translation or PII preservation.*

QUESTION 43

Answer - [A] Analyze skill execution logs.

A) Analyzing skill execution logs allows you to identify errors or issues encountered during skill processing, providing insights into potential problems and areas for troubleshooting. B) Increasing the timeout duration may address issues related to skill execution timing out but does not help identify the root cause of errors. C) Checking network connectivity is important but may not directly reveal the cause of skill processing errors. D) Reviewing document format compatibility is essential but may not be the primary cause of skill execution errors. E) Restarting the Azure Cognitive Search service is a drastic measure and is unlikely to resolve specific skill processing errors.

EXAM FOCUS	*You need to analyze skill execution logs thoroughly when debugging custom skill errors in Azure Cognitive Search. These logs provide critical insights into failures and will guide you to the underlying issue.*
CAUTION ALERT	*Don't confuse increasing timeout duration or restarting the service with resolving the root cause. Log analysis is essential to uncover actual skill execution errors, not just timeouts.*

QUESTION 44

Answer - [A] Implement user-specific scoring profiles.

A) Implementing user-specific scoring profiles allows for adjusting search rankings based on user preferences and behavior, enabling personalized search results tailored to individual users. B) While query pipelines can be used for various preprocessing tasks, they do not directly address the requirement for personalized search ranking adjustments. C) Utilizing Azure Machine Learning models for ranking adjustments may be complex and may not provide direct integration with Azure Cognitive Search for personalized ranking. D) Applying custom boosting functions based on user interactions may influence search rankings but may not offer granular control over personalized ranking adjustments. E) Developing custom relevance models for search ranking is a valid approach but may require significant effort and may not provide immediate integration with Azure Cognitive Search.

EXAM FOCUS	*Always remember that user-specific scoring profiles in Azure Cognitive Search are key to personalizing search results. This ensures that user preferences directly influence search rankings, making search more relevant.*
CAUTION ALERT	*Stay clear of assuming query pipelines alone will personalize results. Scoring profiles are essential for adjusting ranking based on user behavior, while pipelines focus on preprocessing queries.*

QUESTION 45

Answer - B) SentimentAnalysisClient.analyzeSentiment()

Option A - TextAnalyticsClient.detectSentiment(): This is a hypothetical method and not part of the Azure Text Analytics SDK.
Option C - TextSentimentClient.analyze(): This is a hypothetical method and not part of the Azure Text Analytics SDK.
Option D - AnalyzeTextClient.detectSentiment(): This is a hypothetical method and not part of the Azure Text Analytics SDK.
Option E - SentimentDetectionClient.analyze(): This is a hypothetical method and not part of the Azure Text Analytics SDK.
Option B is correct because analyzeSentiment() is the method used to determine the sentiment of text in Azure Text

Analytics.

EXAM FOCUS	*You need to use the analyzeSentiment() method in Text Analytics when detecting sentiment. This is the correct method to assess the tone of the text, whether positive, negative, or neutral.*
CAUTION ALERT	*Don't confuse this with methods like detectSentiment() or analyze(), which do not exist in the Azure SDK. Use the precise API method to avoid errors in implementation.*

QUESTION 46

Answer - [C] Understanding pricing models to estimate long-term costs accurately.

A) Understanding pricing models is essential to accurately forecast long-term costs and ensure compliance with budgetary constraints.
B) Opting for a pay-as-you-go model offers flexibility but may not address compliance requirements directly.
C) Selecting the highest pricing tier may lead to unnecessary expenses if the features are not required for the project, and compliance may not be the primary consideration.
D) Utilizing promotional credits may provide initial cost savings but does not ensure compliance with long-term budget requirements.
E) Negotiating custom pricing plans may not always align with compliance regulations and may not be feasible for all projects.

EXAM FOCUS	*You should thoroughly understand pricing models for Azure OpenAI Service to estimate long-term costs and ensure your solution stays within budget and compliance requirements. Look into various pricing tiers before committing.*
CAUTION ALERT	*Stay alert about selecting high-tier pricing unnecessarily. It's important to balance features and cost without opting for higher tiers unless absolutely needed for compliance or functionality.*

QUESTION 47

Answer - [C] Reviewing and refining generated code iteratively based on developer feedback.

C) Iterative review and refinement based on developer feedback ensure that the generated code aligns with quality standards and integrates seamlessly with existing code.
A) Providing comprehensive input prompts enhances code understanding but may not ensure quality or integration.
B) Using pre-trained models without customization may lead to generic code that does not fit specific requirements or integrate well.
D) Ignoring code quality compromises maintainability and may lead to technical debt.
E) Including code generation as a separate phase may disrupt development flow and integration.

EXAM FOCUS	*Make sure to iteratively review and refine generated code when using Azure OpenAI Service for automated code generation. Incorporate developer feedback to maintain code quality and ensure smooth integration with the existing codebase.*
CAUTION ALERT	*Don't ignore generated code quality, even if it appears to meet functional requirements. Unrefined code can introduce security risks or technical debt that may become problematic in the long term.*

QUESTION 48

Answer - D) Statement I, Statement II

Option C - Statement III: This statement is incorrect because Azure AI Language service does not provide support for sentiment analysis.
Option E - Statement II, Statement III: This statement is incorrect because it doesn't include the true statement about

detecting the language used in text (Statement I).
Option A is correct because Azure AI Language service can detect the language used in text, making Statement I true.
Option B is correct because Azure AI Language service can extract key phrases from text, making Statement II true.
Option D is correct as it includes both true statements: Statement I and Statement II.

EXAM FOCUS	*Keep in mind that Azure AI Language Service can detect language and extract key phrases but does not perform sentiment analysis. Use it for tasks like language identification and key phrase extraction in text analytics.*
CAUTION ALERT	*Stay cautioned that sentiment analysis is a feature of Azure Text Analytics, not Azure AI Language Service. Make sure you are using the correct service for the required text processing task.*

QUESTION 49

Answer - [A, D] Implementing role-based access control (RBAC) to restrict access to sensitive fitness data. Hashing user identifiers before storing them in the dataset to anonymize personal information.

A) RBAC restricts access based on roles, ensuring only authorized users can access sensitive fitness data.
D) Hashing user identifiers helps anonymize personal information, enhancing data privacy.
B) Homomorphic encryption is valuable for secure computations but may not directly address dataset usage security.
C) Access log auditing helps identify unauthorized access attempts but may not prevent them proactively.
E) Differential privacy protects individual privacy but may not be directly applicable in this scenario.

EXAM FOCUS	*You need to implement role-based access control (RBAC) and hash user identifiers to maintain privacy when using fitness datasets for generative AI. These measures ensure sensitive data is anonymized and secure.*
CAUTION ALERT	*Don't confuse homomorphic encryption with more direct privacy measures like RBAC or hashing. Homomorphic encryption adds complexity and may not be required for most privacy-preserving scenarios.*

QUESTION 50

Answer - [B] BLEU Score.

A) F1 Score is more commonly used in classification tasks. C) Precision-Recall Curve analysis is mainly used in binary classification tasks. D) Mean Squared Error is typically used for regression problems. E) Semantic Similarity measurement may not be directly applicable for code generation evaluation.

EXAM FOCUS	*Always consider using BLEU Score to evaluate code generation models. This metric evaluates the accuracy of generated code by comparing it to reference code snippets, making it ideal for tasks like code completion.*
CAUTION ALERT	*Avoid relying on metrics like F1 Score or Mean Squared Error for evaluating code generation. These metrics are suited for classification and regression tasks, not for comparing generated and reference code.*

PRACTICE TEST 5 - QUESTIONS ONLY

QUESTION 1

Your organization is developing a question-answering system for a knowledge management platform. The system should be able to understand user queries, retrieve relevant information from a knowledge base, and provide accurate responses. You need to select the Azure AI service that can fulfill the requirements of the question-answering system. Which service should you choose?
Select all answers that apply.

A) Azure Cognitive Services Language Understanding (LUIS)
B) Azure Bot Services
C) Azure Cognitive Services Text Analytics
D) Azure QnA Maker
E) Azure Cognitive Services Personalizer

QUESTION 2

Your organization is implementing a decision support solution for an e-commerce platform to analyze product reviews and provide insights to product managers. The solution needs to extract key phrases, determine sentiment, and identify common customer complaints. Additionally, the solution should integrate seamlessly with existing analytics tools for further analysis.
Which Azure AI service or combination of services should you select to meet these requirements effectively?
Select all answers that apply.

A) Azure AI Text Analytics
B) Azure AI Language Understanding (LUIS)
C) Azure AI Content Moderator
D) Azure AI Form Recognizer
E) Azure AI Cognitive Search

QUESTION 3

In order to integrate Azure AI services into a continuous integration and continuous delivery (CI/CD) pipeline, which Azure CLI command can be used to deploy updates to the service?

```
A) az cognitiveservices account update
B) az cognitiveservices account deploy
C) az cognitiveservices account create
D) az cognitiveservices account import
E) az cognitiveservices account export
```

QUESTION 4

In a scenario where third-party applications need access to Azure AI services on behalf of users, which authentication method provides delegated access with fine-grained permissions?

A) API key
B) OAuth 2.0
C) Azure Active Directory (AAD)
D) Shared access signature (SAS)
E) JSON Web Tokens (JWT)

QUESTION 5

Your organization is planning to deploy a new Azure AI solution for sentiment analysis of social media data to gauge customer opinions about your products and services. As part of the deployment process, you are responsible for creating an Azure AI resource with the necessary services and configurations. The solution should prioritize real-time analysis, accuracy, and compliance with data privacy regulations.

Which steps should you follow to create the Azure AI resource while ensuring real-time analysis, accuracy, and compliance with data privacy regulations?

Select all answers that apply.

A) Choose Azure regions with high-performance computing capabilities to support real-time data processing and analysis.
B) Implement data anonymization techniques to protect user privacy and comply with data protection laws.
C) Enable geo-replication for data redundancy and disaster recovery to ensure data availability and compliance.
D) Configure Azure AI services, such as Azure Text Analytics, for sentiment analysis and accuracy optimization.
E) Establish data retention policies to manage data lifecycle and ensure compliance with privacy regulations.

QUESTION 6

You are deploying an Azure AI solution that incorporates Azure Cognitive Search for indexing and querying data. Your solution needs to ensure secure access to the search service from a virtual machine (VM) in Azure. Which action should you take to achieve this?

A) Create an access policy in Azure Key Vault.
B) Configure a custom role assignment for the VM.
C) Implement an Azure Virtual Network service endpoint.
D) Add a route table to the VM's subnet.
E) Enable Managed Identity for the VM.

QUESTION 7

Your team is tasked with integrating Azure Monitor and Application Insights with Azure AI services for comprehensive monitoring and analysis. Which benefit does this integration provide for managing and securing Azure AI resources?

A) Enabling real-time log analysis
B) Facilitating automated resource provisioning
C) Improving AI model accuracy
D) Reducing latency in data processing
E) Enhancing network security protocols

QUESTION 8

Your organization is implementing Azure AI services for various projects and needs to establish effective cost management practices. Which compliance consideration should influence your decision when implementing cost management practices for Azure AI services?

A) Maximizing resource utilization
B) Minimizing operational overhead
C) Adhering to budget constraints
D) Ignoring cost optimization
E) Focusing solely on performance metrics

QUESTION 9

You are tasked with configuring authentication for an Azure App Services web app named App6. The app needs to authenticate using Microsoft Entra ID with minimal administrative effort and adherence to the principle of least privilege. What action should you take?

A) Generate a client secret and store it securely for App6 authentication.
B) Use Azure Active Directory (Azure AD) authentication and configure App6 to use it.
C) Implement OAuth 2.0 authentication with Azure AD and grant App6 access to Microsoft Entra ID.
D) Enable Managed Service Identity (MSI) for App6 and assign RBAC permissions to Microsoft Entra ID.
E) Configure App6 to use Azure AD single sign-on (SSO).

QUESTION 10

Your organization is concerned about maintaining compliance while implementing text moderation solutions. Which compliance consideration should influence your approach to text moderation implementation?

A) Prioritize text moderation accuracy over regulatory requirements
B) Ensure adherence to industry-specific content standards and regulations
C) Disregard privacy concerns to simplify text moderation processes
D) Overlook compliance considerations for faster deployment
E) Neglect data security standards to reduce operational overhead

QUESTION 11

Your team is tasked with customizing a decision support system for a retail company to optimize inventory management and pricing strategies. What AI modeling approach is most suitable for generating insights and recommendations based on historical sales data and market trends?

A) Implementing supervised learning algorithms for demand forecasting and pricing optimization.
B) Utilizing unsupervised learning techniques for clustering similar products and customer segments.
C) Employing reinforcement learning models for dynamic pricing and inventory replenishment decisions.
D) Integrating deep learning architectures for image-based inventory analysis and shelf optimization.
E) Leveraging natural language processing (NLP) for sentiment analysis of customer reviews and feedback.

QUESTION 12

You are implementing a computer vision solution on Azure AI Vision and need to analyze images for specific features. What steps should you take to achieve this?

A) Select visual features to meet image processing requirements.
B) Extract text from images using Azure AI Vision.
C) Choose between image classification and object detection models.
D) Evaluate custom vision model metrics for performance analysis.
E) Publish a custom vision model for deployment.

QUESTION 13

Your team is responsible for implementing continuous deployment practices for updates to a decision support system (DSS) deployed on Azure. What strategies should you employ to ensure seamless and automated deployment of DSS updates?
Select all answers that apply.

A) Utilize Azure DevOps pipelines to automate build, test, and deployment processes for DSS updates across multiple environments.
B) Implement Azure Functions for serverless deployment and execution of DSS update scripts triggered by code

repository changes.
C) Configure Azure Application Insights to monitor DSS performance and automatically roll back deployments in case of issues.
D) Employ Azure Kubernetes Service (AKS) for containerized deployment of DSS components and rolling updates with minimal downtime.
E) Utilize Azure Blob Storage versioning to maintain a history of DSS artifacts and enable rollback to previous versions if necessary.

QUESTION 14

You are developing an AI solution for a smart city project to analyze traffic camera feeds for congestion detection and traffic management. The solution requires accurate identification of vehicles and traffic flow patterns. Considering the dynamic nature of traffic scenarios, which visual feature detection capability should you prioritize for optimal performance in Azure Computer Vision?
Select all answers that apply.

A) Object tracking
B) Color histogram analysis
C) Motion detection
D) Semantic segmentation
E) Shape analysis

QUESTION 15

During the deployment of an Azure AI decision support solution, you encounter an authentication error when accessing the Azure AI service endpoints. How should you troubleshoot and resolve this issue?

A) Verify that the Azure AI service endpoints are correctly configured and accessible from the deployment environment.
B) Check the authentication credentials used to access the Azure AI service and ensure they are valid and up-to-date.
C) Review the network security group (NSG) rules and firewall settings to allow traffic to and from the Azure AI service endpoints.
D) Upgrade the Azure AI service to a higher tier with enhanced authentication capabilities and stricter security measures.
E) Implement multi-factor authentication (MFA) for accessing the Azure AI service endpoints to enhance security and prevent unauthorized access.

QUESTION 16

You are integrating text extraction capabilities into a workflow automation system. Which compliance consideration should be taken into account to ensure responsible AI principles are followed, particularly regarding the handling of extracted text data?

A) GDPR regulations
B) HIPAA guidelines
C) SOC 2 compliance
D) ISO 27001 certification
E) PCI DSS requirements

QUESTION 17

You are exploring potential applications of image classification models in the healthcare industry. Which application aligns with the use of image classification in healthcare scenarios?

A) Patient scheduling optimization
B) Drug discovery research

C) Tumor detection in medical imaging
D) Clinical trial recruitment
E) Hospital resource allocation

QUESTION 18

You are deploying a computer vision solution using Azure AI Vision, but you encounter an error stating "Invalid image format." What steps should you take to resolve this issue?

A) Validate the image format against the supported formats by Azure AI Vision.
B) Implement image preprocessing techniques to standardize image formats.
C) Check if the Azure AI Vision service has been properly configured with access to image storage.
D) Ensure that the container environment has appropriate permissions to access images.
E) Upgrade the Azure AI Vision service to a higher tier.

QUESTION 19

Your team is tasked with developing a custom computer vision model for detecting anomalies in medical images using Azure AI Vision. During model development, you want to ensure comprehensive monitoring of the model's performance post-deployment to guarantee its effectiveness in clinical settings. Which approach should you adopt to achieve robust performance monitoring and maintenance of the deployed model?

A) Implement Azure Application Insights to track user interactions with the model API, enabling performance analysis and issue detection.
B) Set up Azure Data Factory pipelines to regularly fetch model predictions and compare them against ground truth labels for performance evaluation.
C) Utilize Azure Machine Learning pipelines to automate model retraining based on incoming data and performance metrics, ensuring continuous improvement.
D) Develop custom logging mechanisms within the model code to record inference results and deploy them to Azure Monitor for real-time performance monitoring.
E) Create a manual checklist for clinicians to assess the model's predictions periodically and provide feedback for model refinement and updates.

QUESTION 20

Your team is developing an AI-powered security system for monitoring restricted areas within a facility using video surveillance. The system must detect and track unauthorized personnel entering restricted zones and trigger alerts in real-time. You are responsible for selecting the Azure AI service that enables combining spatial analysis with other video analytics features to enhance security measures effectively. Which Azure AI service should you recommend to meet this requirement and ensure seamless integration with spatial analysis for security monitoring?

A) Azure AI Video Indexer
B) Azure Cognitive Services - Computer Vision
C) Azure Cognitive Services - Video Analyzer
D) Azure AI Vision Spatial Analysis
E) Azure AI Content Moderator

QUESTION 21

You are working on an image processing application using Azure AI Vision. While configuring the service, you encounter an API request with the command: POST https://<resource-name>.cognitiveservices.azure.com/vision/v3.0/analyze. What is the primary purpose of this request?

A) Extracting text from images.
B) Detecting objects and their locations in images.

C) Analyzing facial expressions in images.
D) Generating captions for images.
E) Translating text within images to multiple languages.

QUESTION 22

Your team is developing an enterprise knowledge management system that extracts key information from legal documents for compliance monitoring. The system needs to accurately identify regulatory requirements and obligations mentioned in the documents to ensure adherence to legal standards. Additionally, you need to ensure that the extracted key phrases are securely stored and accessible only to authorized personnel. Which Azure service should you use for extracting key phrases from legal documents and ensuring secure storage, considering compliance and data privacy requirements?

A) Azure Cognitive Search
B) Azure Text Analytics
C) Azure AI Language - Key Phrase Extraction
D) Azure Machine Learning - Natural Language Processing
E) Azure Key Vault

QUESTION 23

Your company is building an AI-driven content moderation system for a global social media platform. The system must classify user-generated content into categories such as positive, negative, or neutral sentiments to ensure a safe online environment. Which approach should you prioritize to achieve accurate sentiment classification?

A) Ensemble learning with multiple sentiment analysis models
B) Rule-based sentiment analysis
C) Pre-trained sentiment analysis models
D) Frequency-based sentiment analysis
E) Lexicon-based sentiment analysis

QUESTION 24

You are experiencing latency issues with the Azure AI Translator service integrated into your application, particularly during peak usage hours. What strategy should you adopt to mitigate latency and ensure consistent service performance?

A) Implementing client-side caching for translated text.
B) Increasing the timeout duration for translation requests.
C) Distributing translation requests across multiple service endpoints.
D) Deploying a load balancer to evenly distribute translation traffic.
E) Optimizing network routing for translation requests.

QUESTION 25

Your team is developing a speech-to-text (STT) solution for a conference transcription service. The service needs to accurately transcribe speakers with various accents and dialects in real-time. Additionally, it should seamlessly handle interruptions and overlapping speech. Which approach would best address these requirements?

A) Implementing speaker diarization to identify and segment speakers.
B) Training separate STT models for each accent and dialect.
C) Leveraging Azure Speech SDK's automatic punctuation feature.
D) Using keyword spotting to detect and handle interruptions.
E) Deploying an ensemble of pre-trained models for diverse speech patterns.

QUESTION 26

Your company is developing a custom speech recognition solution for a mobile application. The solution needs to provide accurate transcription of spoken language while minimizing latency. Which optimization technique should you prioritize to achieve this goal?

A) Implementing a high-complexity neural network architecture for feature extraction.
B) Using a large training dataset to capture diverse speech patterns.
C) Fine-tuning the model parameters based on real-time user feedback.
D) Employing quantization to reduce the model size and inference time.
E) Increasing the number of layers in the neural network to capture more complex patterns.

QUESTION 27

You are developing an application that uses Azure AI Vision for pedestrian detection in surveillance videos. The application should accurately identify and track the movement of pedestrians in real-time. Which Azure AI Vision feature should you utilize to achieve this functionality?

A) Face detection
B) Image Analysis
C) Optical character recognition (OCR)
D) Spatial Analysis
E) Object tracking

QUESTION 28

Your organization is considering automating its document translation workflow and integrating it into existing systems. Which Azure service should you recommend to seamlessly integrate document translation capabilities into other applications and solutions?

A) Azure Cognitive Services Translator Text
B) Azure Cognitive Services Language Understanding (LUIS)
C) Azure Cognitive Services Text Analytics
D) Azure Cognitive Services Speech Service
E) Azure Cognitive Services Vision Service

QUESTION 29

Your team is integrating a custom translation model with Azure AI Translator service to leverage its deployment and scalability features. Which step is essential for seamless integration and interoperability between the custom model and Azure AI Translator service?

A) Convert the custom model into a Docker container for deployment on Azure
B) Ensure compatibility of input and output formats between the custom model and Azure AI Translator service APIs
C) Train the custom model exclusively on Azure AI infrastructure for optimal performance
D) Incorporate Azure AD authentication for secure communication between the custom model and Azure services
E) Implement continuous monitoring and logging to track translation accuracy and performance metrics

QUESTION 30

You are investigating a performance issue with an Azure app that uses Azure AI Translator for real-time language translation. Users report delays in receiving translated text, especially during peak usage hours. What could be a potential cause of this delay?

A) Network latency affecting communication between the app and Azure AI Translator service.
B) Incompatibility between the app's frontend framework and Azure AI Translator SDK.

C) Limited server resources allocated to the Azure AI Translator service.
D) Outdated version of the Azure AI Translator SDK being used in the app.
E) Insufficient permissions granted to the app's Azure resource group.

QUESTION 31

Your team has deployed a language understanding model for a virtual assistant application. You want to leverage analytics to guide enhancements and optimizations for the model's performance. What analytics should you prioritize for this purpose?
Select all answers that apply.

A) User engagement metrics such as session duration and interaction frequency
B) Accuracy and precision of user intents and responses
C) Error rates and confusion patterns in user interactions
D) Distribution of user queries across intents and entities
E) Model training convergence and convergence stability

QUESTION 32

You are tasked with optimizing a language understanding model for a healthcare chatbot application. The model must accurately interpret medical queries and provide relevant responses while ensuring compliance with healthcare regulations. How can you incorporate domain-specific customization into the optimization process to improve the model's performance and adherence to regulatory requirements?
Select all answers that apply.

A) Integrate medical ontologies and terminologies to enhance model understanding of domain-specific concepts
B) Implement anonymization techniques to protect sensitive patient information
C) Apply data masking methods to prevent exposure of confidential data during training
D) Utilize federated learning approaches to train the model on distributed healthcare data sources
E) Conduct regular audits to ensure model compliance with healthcare regulations and guidelines

QUESTION 33

You are developing an Azure app that needs to identify personally identifiable information (PII) in text data and mask it for privacy compliance. Which Azure service and API combination should you use for this purpose?

A) Azure AI Language Service > Text Analytics API
B) Azure Content Moderator > Language API
C) Azure Cognitive Search > Vision API
D) Azure Translator Text > Language API
E) Azure Computer Vision > Vision API

QUESTION 34

How can Azure AI engineers manage content quality and relevance over time effectively in a question answering solution?
Select all answers that apply.

A) Periodically review and update content based on user feedback
B) Utilize Azure AI Content Moderator for automated content analysis
C) Implement machine learning models for content relevance scoring
D) Ignore content updates as long as the solution is functional
E) Rely solely on manual review for content quality control

QUESTION 35

What are essential steps for maintaining knowledge bases in a question answering solution to ensure ongoing effectiveness and relevance?
Select all answers that apply.

A) Regularly update content based on user feedback and insights
B) Perform periodic audits to identify and fill knowledge gaps
C) Implement version control for tracking changes and facilitating rollback
D) Monitor usage patterns and adjust content strategy accordingly
E) Schedule automated backups for data protection and recovery

QUESTION 36

Your organization plans to deploy a custom natural language processing model using Azure containers. Which options should you include in the bash statement to deploy the NLP container successfully?
Select all answers that apply.

```
A) "mcr.microsoft.com/azure-ai/nlp/custommodel"
B) "--memory 512 --cpus 4"
C) "--accept"
D) "--region centralus"
E) "--api-key {API_KEY}"
```

QUESTION 37

You are fine-tuning a language model on Azure for sentiment analysis in customer reviews. During evaluation, you notice that the model performs well on English reviews but struggles with reviews in other languages. What could be a potential solution to improve the model's performance across multiple languages?
Select all answers that apply.

A) Increase the model's training data for other languages
B) Fine-tune the model separately for each language
C) Implement language-specific tokenization techniques
D) Use a language-agnostic pre-trained model
E) Apply transfer learning from English to other languages

QUESTION 38

Your organization is developing a conversational AI solution using Azure Bot Framework for a financial advisory service. To handle complex user interactions effectively, which approach should you prioritize during development?
Select all answers that apply.

A) Implement context switching for seamless topic transitions
B) Utilize adaptive card templates for interactive responses
C) Incorporate natural language generation for dynamic content creation
D) Integrate with Azure Cognitive Services for advanced language understanding
E) Apply hierarchical dialogues for structured conversation flows

QUESTION 39

You are tasked with implementing a speech-to-text functionality in your Azure application. Review the provided code snippet and choose the correct option to complete the code.

```
var recognizer = new SpeechRecognizer(new SpeechConfig("<API_KEY>", "<REGION>"));
```

Which option should you choose for <API_KEY> and <REGION> to successfully initialize the SpeechRecognizer object?

```
A) <API_KEY>: "YourSpeechApiKey"
<REGION>: "eastus"

B) <API_KEY>: "YourSpeechApiKey"
<REGION>: "westus"

C) <API_KEY>: "YourSpeechApiKey"
<REGION>: "centralus"

D) <API_KEY>: "YourSpeechApiKey"
<REGION>: "northcentralus"

E) <API_KEY>: "YourSpeechApiKey"
<REGION>: "southeastasia"
```

QUESTION 40

Your company is developing a sentiment analysis tool that needs to accurately gauge sentiment from customer reviews and social media posts in real-time. Which Azure AI service would you recommend integrating into the tool to achieve real-time sentiment analysis efficiently?

A) Azure Text Analytics
B) Azure Language Understanding (LUIS)
C) Azure Cognitive Search
D) Azure AI Translator service
E) Azure AI Language Service

QUESTION 41

Your team is deploying an Azure Cognitive Search solution to provide search capabilities for a large collection of medical research documents. As part of the deployment process, you need to configure custom skills to extract key information from the documents during indexing. Which Azure Cognitive Search feature should you use to implement custom skills for document processing?

A) Synonyms
B) Tokenization
C) Entity Recognition
D) Skillset
E) Scoring Profile

QUESTION 42

You need to extract structured information from unstructured text inputs, including Personally Identifiable Information (PII). Which Azure AI service should you utilize for this task?

```
A) QnAMakerClient
B) ContentModeratorClient
C) FormRecognizerClient
D) TextAnalyticsClient
E) LanguageUnderstandingClient
```

QUESTION 43

Your team is deploying a custom skill for Azure Cognitive Search to enhance search capabilities for a document management system. The custom skill involves processing documents to extract metadata and improve search relevancy. Which scenario demonstrates how custom skills can enhance search capabilities in Azure Cognitive Search?

A) Extracting key phrases from documents to improve search relevance
B) Converting documents to different formats for better compatibility

C) Identifying duplicate documents within the repository
D) Extracting metadata for administrative purposes
E) Translating documents into multiple languages simultaneously

QUESTION 44

Your organization is developing a recommendation engine for a media streaming platform using Azure Cognitive Search. You need to implement scoring profiles to influence search rankings and enhance content recommendations for users. What should you consider when configuring scoring profiles in Azure Cognitive Search to optimize content recommendations?
Select all answers that apply.

A) Define scoring weights for document attributes
B) Incorporate user feedback signals into scoring profiles
C) Apply temporal decay functions for freshness
D) Implement boosting based on item popularity trends
E) Configure proximity boosting for related content

QUESTION 45

Which method in Azure Text Analytics is used to extract key phrases from text?

```
A) KeyPhraseExtraction()
B) ExtractKeyPhrases()
C) FindKeyPhrases()
D) KeyphraseRecognition()
E) AnalyzeKeyPhrases()
```

QUESTION 46

Your team is deploying an Azure OpenAI model for natural language processing in a healthcare application. Which deployment strategy ensures compliance with regulatory requirements while optimizing performance?

A) Deploying the model as a containerized service using Azure Kubernetes Service (AKS).
B) Utilizing Azure Functions to deploy the model as a serverless function.
C) Implementing the model as an Azure App Service.
D) Integrating the model directly into the application codebase.
E) Using Azure Machine Learning to deploy the model as a web service.

QUESTION 47

As part of a software development project, your team plans to use Azure OpenAI Service to generate code snippets for common programming tasks. What compliance consideration should you prioritize to ensure the generated code adheres to industry standards and legal requirements?

A) Implementing version control to track changes in the generated codebase.
B) Ensuring code snippets are properly licensed for use in the project.
C) Conducting thorough testing to validate the functionality of generated code.
D) Encrypting generated code to protect intellectual property rights.
E) Documenting the code generation process for audit and accountability purposes.

QUESTION 48

Which combination of statements accurately describes features of Azure AI Vision service?

A) Statement I: Azure AI Vision service allows the detection of objects in images.
B) Statement II: Azure AI Vision service supports training custom image classification models.
C) Statement III: Azure AI Vision service provides capabilities for sentiment analysis of images.
D) Statement I, Statement II
E) Statement II, Statement III

QUESTION 49

You are developing a generative AI model to create personalized music playlists based on user preferences. To ensure optimal model performance, what is a best practice for managing and versioning custom music datasets?
Select all answers that apply.

A) Utilizing Azure Data Lake Storage for scalable storage and management of music datasets.
B) Maintaining a changelog to document modifications made to the music dataset over time.
C) Storing metadata separately from audio files to facilitate efficient search and retrieval.
D) Assigning unique identifiers to each music track to track usage and access rights.
E) Implementing Azure Data Factory pipelines to automate data ingestion and preprocessing tasks for music datasets.

QUESTION 50

In a scenario where your organization is continuously collecting new data for a customer sentiment analysis model, which strategy would be most effective for managing model adaptation and preventing model drift over time?

A) Periodic retraining of the model with the new data
B) Implementing a dynamic threshold for model performance
C) Utilizing transfer learning techniques for rapid adaptation
D) Regular monitoring of model performance metrics and triggers for retraining
E) Implementing model versioning and rollback mechanisms

PRACTICE TEST 5 - ANSWERS ONLY

QUESTION 1

Answer - [A, D] Azure Cognitive Services Language Understanding (LUIS), Azure QnA Maker

Option B - Azure Bot Services: Bot Services provides the framework for building chatbots but may not offer specialized capabilities for question-answering systems.
Option C - Azure Cognitive Services Text Analytics: Text Analytics focuses on sentiment analysis and key phrase extraction, which are not directly applicable to retrieving information from a knowledge base.
Option E - Azure Cognitive Services Personalizer: Personalizer is used for personalized content recommendations and does not address the requirements of a question-answering system.
Option A - Azure Cognitive Services Language Understanding (LUIS): LUIS enables the system to understand user intents and extract entities from queries, allowing it to determine the relevant information needed to provide accurate responses.
Option D - Azure QnA Maker: QnA Maker is specifically designed for creating question and answer pairs from a knowledge base, making it an ideal choice for building a question-answering system that retrieves information from structured content.

EXAM FOCUS	*You should use a combination of LUIS and QnA Maker for a question-answering system. LUIS handles understanding intents and entities, while QnA Maker retrieves information from a knowledge base, making them complementary.*
CAUTION ALERT	*Avoid relying on Text Analytics for this use case as it is better suited for sentiment analysis and key phrase extraction, not question-answering.*

QUESTION 2

Answer - [A, E] Azure AI Text Analytics, Azure AI Cognitive Search

Option B - Azure AI Language Understanding (LUIS): Designed for building conversational AI applications, not suited for text analysis.
Option C - Azure AI Content Moderator: Primarily used for content moderation tasks such as detecting offensive content, not suitable for text analysis.
Option D - Azure AI Form Recognizer: Intended for extracting structured data from documents, not suitable for text analysis tasks.

EXAM FOCUS	*Make sure to combine Text Analytics for extracting key phrases and determining sentiment with Cognitive Search for advanced querying and indexing, ensuring seamless integration with analytics tools.*
CAUTION ALERT	*Don't confuse LUIS or Content Moderator for text analysis. These services focus on language understanding and content filtering, respectively, not on extracting and analyzing product reviews.*

QUESTION 3

Answer - A) az cognitiveservices account update

Option B - Incorrect. This command is not used for deploying updates to an existing service but rather for creating new services. Option C - Incorrect. This command is used for creating new cognitive services accounts, not for deploying updates. Option D - Incorrect. This command is used for importing data into a cognitive services account, not for deploying updates. Option E - Incorrect. This command is used for exporting data from a cognitive services account, not for deploying updates.

EXAM	*You should use the command az cognitiveservices account update to deploy updates in a CI/CD pipeline.*

FOCUS	*It ensures your Azure AI service remains updated with new configurations or features.*
CAUTION ALERT	*Stay alert not to use az cognitiveservices account create when updating services. This command is for creating new instances, not for managing updates.*

QUESTION 4

Answer - B) OAuth 2.0

Option A - Incorrect. API keys are typically used for simple authentication scenarios and may not support fine-grained permissions or delegated access. Option C - Incorrect. Azure Active Directory (AAD) provides identity and access management services but may not directly support delegated access in the context of third-party applications. Option D - Incorrect. Shared access signatures are typically used for providing limited access to resources, but they may not support delegated access with fine-grained permissions. Option E - Incorrect. While JSON Web Tokens (JWT) are used for secure transmission of information, they do not inherently provide delegated access with fine-grained permissions.

EXAM FOCUS	*Always remember to use OAuth 2.0 when fine-grained permissions and delegated access are needed for third-party applications. It provides secure and controlled access to resources on behalf of users.*
CAUTION ALERT	*Avoid using API keys or SAS tokens for scenarios requiring delegated access and permission control. They lack the ability to enforce granular permissions.*

QUESTION 5

Answer - [A, B, D, E]

Option A - Choose Azure regions with high-performance computing capabilities to support real-time data processing and analysis: Correct. Selecting regions with high-performance computing capabilities facilitates real-time analysis of social media data.
Option B - Implement data anonymization techniques to protect user privacy and comply with data protection laws: Correct. Data anonymization is essential for safeguarding user privacy and complying with data privacy regulations.
Option C - Enable geo-replication for data redundancy and disaster recovery to ensure data availability and compliance: While important for data availability and disaster recovery, geo-replication may not directly relate to real-time analysis or data privacy compliance.
Option D - Configure Azure AI services, such as Azure Text Analytics, for sentiment analysis and accuracy optimization: Correct. Configuring AI services like Azure Text Analytics ensures accurate sentiment analysis, aligning with solution requirements.
Option E - Establish data retention policies to manage data lifecycle and ensure compliance with privacy regulations: Correct. Data retention policies help manage data lifecycle and ensure compliance with privacy regulations regarding data storage and retention.

EXAM FOCUS	*You need to focus on using high-performance Azure regions, data anonymization, and configuring Text Analytics for accurate sentiment analysis while complying with privacy laws. This ensures real-time, compliant, and secure analysis.*
CAUTION ALERT	*Stay clear of ignoring data retention policies. Failing to configure these can lead to compliance violations, especially under data privacy regulations like GDPR.*

QUESTION 6

Answer - C) Implement an Azure Virtual Network service endpoint.

Option A - Incorrect. Creating an access policy in Azure Key Vault is not relevant for securing access to Azure Cognitive Search from a VM. Option B - Incorrect. Configuring a custom role assignment for the VM may provide access control but does not directly address securing access to Azure Cognitive Search. Option D - Incorrect. Adding a route table to the VM's subnet is not directly related to securing access to Azure Cognitive Search. Option E - Incorrect. Enabling Managed Identity for the VM is not directly related to securing access to Azure Cognitive Search.

EXAM FOCUS	*Make sure to configure an Azure Virtual Network service endpoint for secure access between your VM and Azure Cognitive Search. This enables secure communication without exposing resources to the public internet.*
CAUTION ALERT	*Don't confuse creating access policies in Azure Key Vault with securing access to Cognitive Search. These are different services with different purposes.*

QUESTION 7

Answer - [A] Enabling real-time log analysis.

Enabling real-time log analysis - Integrating Azure Monitor and Application Insights allows for real-time monitoring, analysis, and alerting capabilities, enhancing the management and security of Azure AI resources by providing timely insights into performance and operational status. Options B, C, D, and E may have benefits but are not directly related to the integration of monitoring and analysis tools.

EXAM FOCUS	*You should integrate Azure Monitor and Application Insights to enable real-time log analysis, helping you track the performance and security of AI models and resources in production environments.*
CAUTION ALERT	*Stay alert to the fact that this integration does not directly improve AI model accuracy but rather aids in operational monitoring.*

QUESTION 8

Answer - [C] Adhering to budget constraints.

Adhering to budget constraints - Implementing cost management practices that align with budget constraints ensures efficient allocation of resources and adherence to financial limitations, supporting overall budget compliance and cost control for Azure AI services. Options A, B, D, and E may be relevant but do not specifically address compliance considerations related to budget constraints.

EXAM FOCUS	*You need to prioritize adhering to budget constraints when managing Azure AI services. Implement cost management practices, such as Azure Cost Management, to ensure you stay within your financial limits.*
CAUTION ALERT	*Avoid ignoring cost optimization efforts as operational costs can quickly spiral if not carefully monitored and managed, leading to budget overruns.*

QUESTION 9

Answer - D) Enable Managed Service Identity (MSI) for App6 and assign RBAC permissions to Microsoft Entra ID.

Option A - Incorrect. Storing client secrets may introduce additional security risks and administrative overhead. Option B - Incorrect. While Azure AD authentication is a valid approach, enabling MSI with RBAC permissions directly meets the requirement with minimal administrative overhead. Option C - Incorrect. OAuth 2.0 authentication with Azure AD may not directly support Microsoft Entra ID and may introduce unnecessary complexity. Option E - Incorrect. Azure AD SSO may provide centralized authentication but may not align with the requirement to use Microsoft Entra ID.

EXAM FOCUS	*You should enable Managed Service Identity (MSI) for App6 and assign RBAC permissions to ensure secure access with minimal administrative overhead while adhering to the principle of least privilege.*
CAUTION ALERT	*Don't confuse using Azure AD SSO as a simpler solution. While useful, MSI combined with RBAC provides more secure, fine-grained access control.*

QUESTION 10

Answer - [B] Ensure adherence to industry-specific content standards and regulations.

Ensure adherence to industry-specific content standards and regulations - Compliance with industry-specific content standards and regulations is crucial to avoid legal issues and maintain user trust, unlike options A, C, D, and E, which may lead to regulatory violations or security breaches.

EXAM FOCUS *You should always ensure adherence to industry-specific content standards and regulations when implementing text moderation solutions. Compliance ensures trust, avoids legal risks, and meets regulatory requirements.*

CAUTION ALERT *Avoid overlooking privacy concerns or regulatory compliance for the sake of simplicity or speed, as this can lead to serious legal consequences or breaches of user trust.*

QUESTION 11

Answer - [A] Implementing supervised learning algorithms for demand forecasting and pricing optimization.

Supervised learning algorithms are well-suited for analyzing historical sales data and market trends to generate insights and recommendations for demand forecasting and pricing optimization, aligning with the requirements of the retail industry. Options B, C, D, and E focus on different AI modeling approaches but may not be as directly applicable to inventory management and pricing strategies.

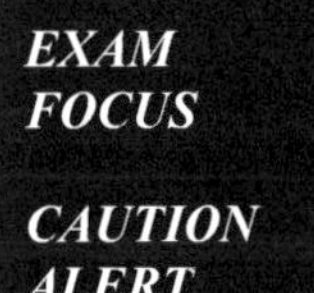

You should choose supervised learning algorithms for demand forecasting and pricing optimization, as they rely on historical data patterns. This approach is most suitable for scenarios requiring predictions based on labeled data.

Avoid using unsupervised or reinforcement learning for this task unless there is insufficient historical data or the business needs dynamic adjustments. Supervised learning is the right fit for structured forecasting.

QUESTION 12

Answer - A) Select visual features to meet image processing requirements.
C) Choose between image classification and object detection models.

Option B - Incorrect. While text extraction is a feature of Azure AI Vision, it may not align with the requirement to analyze images for specific features unrelated to text. Option D - Incorrect. Evaluating custom vision model metrics is important but may not directly relate to the initial steps of analyzing images for specific features. Option E - Incorrect. Publishing a custom vision model is a later step in the process and is not directly related to the initial analysis of images.

Make sure you select the appropriate visual features for your computer vision task. Whether you're analyzing images for object detection or image classification, choosing the right model type ensures accurate results.

Don't confuse text extraction with feature detection. Extracting text is useful for OCR tasks, but for identifying visual features, focus on object detection and classification models.

QUESTION 13

Answer - [A, C, D, E] Options A, C, D, and E are relevant strategies for implementing continuous deployment for DSS updates.

Option A automates build, test, and deployment processes, option C monitors performance and enables automatic rollback, option D facilitates rolling updates with minimal downtime, and option E maintains artifact versions for rollback capability. Option B, Azure Functions, may not be suitable for complex DSS deployments compared to AKS.

EXAM FOCUS	*Always remember to use Azure DevOps pipelines for automating the build, test, and deployment process, and integrate Application Insights for monitoring performance and enabling rollback if needed. This ensures smooth continuous deployment practices.*
CAUTION ALERT	*Stay clear of using Azure Functions for complex DSS deployments. While serverless is useful for lightweight tasks, containerized deployments with AKS are better suited for complex DSS.*

QUESTION 14

Answer - [A, C] Options A and C are crucial for real-time traffic analysis and management in dynamic scenarios. Object tracking (Option A) enables continuous monitoring of vehicles, while motion detection (Option C) detects changes in traffic flow and congestion, essential for timely intervention and management.

Options B, D, and E focus on static features or attributes less critical for dynamic traffic analysis. Color histogram analysis (Option B) and shape analysis (Option E) may provide additional insights but are secondary to tracking and motion detection in dynamic traffic scenarios. Semantic segmentation (Option D) may offer detailed scene understanding but could be computationally intensive for real-time applications.

EXAM FOCUS	*You need to prioritize object tracking and motion detection in traffic management AI solutions. These features provide real-time insights into vehicle movement and traffic flow, which are critical for congestion management.*
CAUTION ALERT	*Don't confuse color histogram analysis or shape analysis with real-time features like object tracking. While useful in static analysis, they don't provide the real-time dynamics needed in traffic flow detection.*

QUESTION 15

Answer - A) Verify that the Azure AI service endpoints are correctly configured and accessible from the deployment environment.
B) Check the authentication credentials used to access the Azure AI service and ensure they are valid and up-to-date.
C) Review the network security group (NSG) rules and firewall settings to allow traffic to and from the Azure AI service endpoints.

Option D - Incorrect. Upgrading the service tier may enhance features but is unlikely to directly resolve authentication errors. Option E - Incorrect. While MFA enhances security, it is not directly related to resolving authentication errors in accessing service endpoints.

EXAM FOCUS	*Keep in mind to validate the configuration of service endpoints, credentials, and NSG rules when encountering authentication errors. Checking these aspects can resolve most connectivity and security-related issues.*
CAUTION ALERT	*Avoid jumping to service tier upgrades before thoroughly troubleshooting the basics like authentication credentials and network configurations.*

QUESTION 16

Answer - [A] GDPR regulations

A) GDPR regulations - Correct. GDPR regulations mandate strict guidelines for the handling of personal data, including text extracted from images. To ensure compliance with responsible AI principles, it is essential to adhere to GDPR requirements regarding data protection, privacy, and consent when processing and storing extracted text data within the workflow automation system.
B) HIPAA guidelines - Incorrect. HIPAA guidelines primarily apply to healthcare data and may not directly relate to the handling of extracted text data in a workflow automation system unless healthcare-related information is involved.
C) SOC 2 compliance - Incorrect. SOC 2 compliance focuses on the security, availability, processing integrity, confidentiality, and privacy of customer data, but it may not specifically address the handling of text extracted from

images.
D) ISO 27001 certification - Incorrect. ISO 27001 certification pertains to information security management systems and may not provide specific guidance on the handling of text extracted from images within a workflow automation system.
E) PCI DSS requirements - Incorrect. PCI DSS requirements are related to payment card data security and may not directly apply to the handling of text extraction data within a workflow automation system unless payment card information is involved.

EXAM FOCUS	*You should always ensure GDPR compliance when handling personal data, especially when it involves text extraction. GDPR ensures that you are handling and processing personal data responsibly.*
CAUTION ALERT	*Stay alert to regulations like HIPAA or PCI DSS—these are only relevant for specific sectors like healthcare or payment data. Focus on GDPR for text data handling.*

QUESTION 17

Answer - [C) Tumor detection in medical imaging]

Image classification in healthcare often involves tasks such as tumor detection in medical imaging, which plays a critical role in diagnosis and treatment planning.
A) Patient scheduling optimization may involve data analysis but not necessarily image classification.
B) Drug discovery research typically involves molecular and chemical analysis rather than image classification.
D) Clinical trial recruitment relies more on patient data analysis than image classification.
E) Hospital resource allocation may involve various factors but not primarily image analysis.

EXAM FOCUS	*Make sure to apply image classification for use cases like tumor detection in medical imaging. It's a widely accepted practice in healthcare for identifying patterns in diagnostic images.*
CAUTION ALERT	*Stay clear of using image classification for tasks like patient scheduling or resource allocation—these tasks involve data analysis, not image-based decision-making.*

QUESTION 18

Answer - [B] Implement image preprocessing techniques to standardize image formats.

Option B - Validating the image format against supported formats (Option A) is important but may not directly resolve the issue if the formats need preprocessing. Checking Azure AI Vision service configuration (Option C) and container environment permissions (Option D) are relevant but might not address the root cause related to image format. Upgrading the Azure AI Vision service (Option E) is not necessary for resolving format issues. Implementing image preprocessing techniques (Option B) to standardize formats ensures compatibility with Azure AI Vision, potentially resolving the error.

EXAM FOCUS	*Always remember to preprocess images and ensure they meet the Azure AI Vision format requirements. Preprocessing images to standardize formats avoids compatibility issues with your AI service.*
CAUTION ALERT	*Avoid assuming that configuration or permission settings alone will resolve image format errors. Standardizing the image formats is the key to solving this issue.*

QUESTION 19

Answer - C) Utilize Azure Machine Learning pipelines to automate model retraining based on incoming data and performance metrics, ensuring continuous improvement.

Option A - Application Insights primarily focuses on application performance monitoring and may not capture detailed model-specific metrics.
Option B - While Data Factory can fetch predictions, it lacks automation for model retraining and continuous improvement.

Option D - Custom logging may provide insights but lacks the automation and scalability of Azure ML pipelines for model maintenance.
Option E - Manual checklists are subjective and may not provide timely feedback or scale well for continuous model monitoring and improvement.

EXAM FOCUS	*Keep in mind that using Azure ML pipelines for retraining and performance monitoring ensures your AI model remains effective over time. It automates the evaluation and retraining process based on live data.*
CAUTION ALERT	*Stay clear of relying solely on manual performance monitoring or static pipelines. For healthcare, automated retraining is critical to adapting to new data patterns.*

QUESTION 20

Answer - C) Azure Cognitive Services - Video Analyzer

Option A - Azure AI Video Indexer focuses more on extracting insights and metadata from videos rather than combining spatial analysis with other video analytics features for security monitoring.
Option B - Azure Cognitive Services - Computer Vision offers image analysis capabilities but may not provide seamless integration with spatial analysis for security monitoring.
Option D - Azure AI Vision Spatial Analysis focuses on spatial analysis but may not offer direct integration with other video analytics features.
Option E - Azure AI Content Moderator is designed for content moderation rather than combining spatial analysis with other video analytics features for security monitoring.

EXAM FOCUS	*You should select Azure Cognitive Services - Video Analyzer for video surveillance that combines spatial analysis with video analytics. This service is designed for security monitoring with real-time insights.*
CAUTION ALERT	*Don't confuse Video Indexer or Computer Vision as comprehensive solutions for spatial analysis. While they excel in specific areas, Video Analyzer provides the real-time tracking and integration needed for security systems.*

QUESTION 21

Answer - [B] Detecting objects and their locations in images.

Option B - This API request is aimed at analyzing images to detect objects within them and determine their locations. It does not involve text extraction (Option A), facial expression analysis (Option C), caption generation (Option D), or text translation (Option E).

EXAM FOCUS	*You should familiarize yourself with the API command structure for Azure AI Vision, as it determines the types of analysis (such as object detection). Knowing these commands will help you configure services effectively.*
CAUTION ALERT	*Stay clear of confusing this API with others like text extraction or facial recognition APIs. Ensure you are targeting the right API for object detection and location analysis.*

QUESTION 22

Answer - C) Azure AI Language - Key Phrase Extraction

Option A - While Azure Cognitive Search can index and search documents, Azure AI Language may provide better accuracy for key phrase extraction in this scenario.
Option B - Azure Text Analytics offers key phrase extraction, but Azure AI Language may provide more customization options and better accuracy.
Option D - Azure Machine Learning requires custom model development, which might not be the most efficient solution for this scenario.

Option E - Azure Key Vault is for securely storing and managing cryptographic keys, secrets, and certificates, not for key phrase extraction and document analysis.

EXAM FOCUS	*Make sure you use Azure AI Language - Key Phrase Extraction for analyzing legal documents, as this service offers specialized accuracy in identifying key phrases that help in compliance monitoring.*
CAUTION ALERT	*Don't confuse Azure Cognitive Search with key phrase extraction. While Cognitive Search is useful for indexing, it may not have the precision needed for compliance monitoring and legal analysis.*

QUESTION 23

Answer - [C] Pre-trained sentiment analysis models.

Pre-trained sentiment analysis models have been trained on diverse datasets and can accurately classify user-generated content into categories such as positive, negative, or neutral sentiments. Ensemble learning may introduce complexity without significant improvement in accuracy. Rule-based, frequency-based, and lexicon-based approaches may not capture nuanced sentiments effectively.

EXAM FOCUS	*You should prioritize using pre-trained sentiment analysis models as they are trained on diverse datasets and perform well out-of-the-box for content moderation tasks like classifying user-generated content.*
CAUTION ALERT	*Avoid using rule-based or frequency-based sentiment analysis for large-scale platforms. These methods may fail to capture the nuances of user sentiments in real-world scenarios.*

QUESTION 24

Answer - [D] Deploying a load balancer to evenly distribute translation traffic.

Option D - Deploying a load balancer to evenly distribute translation traffic among multiple service instances can help mitigate latency by preventing overload on any single endpoint and ensuring consistent service performance during peak usage. Client-side caching (Option A) can reduce repeated requests but does not address latency in service responses. Increasing timeout durations (Option B) may prolong the wait time for users. Distributing requests across multiple endpoints (Option C) requires additional infrastructure setup and may not effectively balance traffic. Optimizing network routing (Option E) can help but is less direct than load balancing for latency mitigation.

EXAM FOCUS	*You need to use a load balancer to manage traffic across multiple instances of the Azure AI Translator service, especially during peak hours. This ensures consistent performance and minimizes latency issues.*
CAUTION ALERT	*Stay alert to network-related issues. Increasing timeout durations or caching may not resolve latency problems caused by overloaded endpoints. Load balancing is the best solution.*

QUESTION 25

Answer - A) Implementing speaker diarization to identify and segment speakers.

Option A - Correct. Implementing speaker diarization helps identify and segment speakers, facilitating accurate transcription in the presence of various accents and dialects.

Option B - Training separate models for each accent and dialect could be resource-intensive and less efficient.

Option C - Automatic punctuation may improve readability but does not specifically address handling interruptions and overlapping speech.

Option D - Keyword spotting is useful for detecting specific phrases but may not address interruptions in real-time transcription.

Option E - While an ensemble of models may improve accuracy, speaker diarization is better suited for identifying and handling various speakers.

EXAM	*Always remember to implement speaker diarization when transcribing conversations with multiple*

FOCUS	*speakers or accents. This technique helps segment and identify speakers, improving transcription accuracy.*
CAUTION ALERT	*Don't confuse automatic punctuation or keyword spotting with handling multiple speakers or overlapping speech. These features are helpful but not central to handling complex speech scenarios.*

QUESTION 26

Answer - [D] Employing quantization to reduce the model size and inference time.

Option D is the most appropriate optimization technique as employing quantization reduces the model size and inference time, leading to decreased latency without sacrificing accuracy significantly. Option A increases complexity but may also increase latency. Option B might improve accuracy but could also increase latency due to longer inference times. Option C addresses fine-tuning but does not directly relate to latency reduction. Option E increases complexity without necessarily addressing latency concerns.

EXAM FOCUS	*You should consider using quantization to optimize your speech recognition model. Reducing model size can lead to lower latency while maintaining transcription accuracy.*
CAUTION ALERT	*Avoid increasing model complexity unnecessarily. Adding more layers or complexity could degrade real-time performance and increase latency, especially in mobile applications.*

QUESTION 27

Answer - [E] Object tracking

Option E - Object tracking allows for the real-time identification and tracking of specific objects, such as pedestrians, within video feeds, making it the most suitable choice for achieving accurate pedestrian detection and movement tracking. Face detection (Option A) focuses on identifying human faces, which is not the primary requirement for this task. Image Analysis (Option B) provides a broad range of image analysis features but does not specifically address object tracking. Optical character recognition (OCR) (Option C) extracts text from images, which is not relevant to pedestrian detection. Spatial Analysis (Option D) analyzes spatial relationships within images but does not track objects over time.

EXAM FOCUS	*Make sure to utilize object tracking in Azure AI Vision for real-time pedestrian detection. This feature is crucial for maintaining continuous tracking of individuals in surveillance video feeds.*
CAUTION ALERT	*Stay clear of using face detection or spatial analysis alone. These may help in certain contexts but do not provide the tracking capabilities needed for pedestrian detection.*

QUESTION 28

Answer - [B] Azure Cognitive Services Language Understanding (LUIS)

Option B is the correct choice because Azure Cognitive Services Language Understanding (LUIS) offers natural language understanding capabilities, enabling seamless integration of document translation capabilities into existing applications and solutions by understanding user intents and entities. Options A, C, D, and E are less suitable for integrating document translation capabilities.

EXAM FOCUS	*You should use Azure Cognitive Services Language Understanding (LUIS) for integrating translation capabilities into a workflow. LUIS allows for seamless integration of document translation while managing user intents and contextual understanding.*
CAUTION ALERT	*Don't confuse other services like Text Analytics or Speech Service as they do not offer the direct integration capabilities for document translation workflows as LUIS does.*

QUESTION 29

Answer - [B] Ensure compatibility of input and output formats between the custom model and Azure AI Translator service APIs

Explanation: B) Compatibility of input and output formats ensures seamless communication between the custom model and Azure AI Translator service, facilitating integration. A) While Docker containers offer deployment flexibility, compatibility with Azure AI Translator service APIs is crucial for integration. C) Training exclusively on Azure AI infrastructure may not directly impact interoperability with Azure services. D) Azure AD authentication enhances security but does not directly address interoperability concerns. E) Continuous monitoring and logging are important but focus on performance rather than integration with Azure AI Translator service.

EXAM FOCUS	*Keep in mind that ensuring input-output format compatibility between your custom model and Azure AI Translator APIs is essential for a seamless integration. Mismatched formats can lead to failures in communication.*
CAUTION ALERT	*Avoid focusing solely on deploying models in Docker containers without considering API compatibility. Even if your model is containerized, it won't work without format alignment with the Translator service.*

QUESTION 30

Answer - [C] Limited server resources allocated to the Azure AI Translator service.

Option C - Limited server resources allocated to the Azure AI Translator service can lead to delays in processing translation requests, especially during peak usage hours when demand exceeds available capacity. Network latency (Option A) might cause delays in communication but is not directly related to service performance. Incompatibility with the frontend framework (Option B) may affect user experience but is not the primary cause of delays in translation. An outdated SDK version (Option D) may lead to compatibility issues but is not the main cause of performance delays. Insufficient permissions (Option E) may result in authentication errors but are unlikely to impact service performance once the requests are received.

EXAM FOCUS	*You need to assess whether server resource allocation for the Azure AI Translator is sufficient during peak usage. If users experience delays, the service may be under-provisioned.*
CAUTION ALERT	*Stay alert to network latency and outdated SDKs, but remember that these factors are less likely to cause the persistent delays experienced during peak times. Resource allocation is key.*

QUESTION 31

Answer - [B), C), and D)] - Prioritizing accuracy and precision of user intents and responses, error rates, confusion patterns, and the distribution of user queries across intents and entities provides insights into areas for model improvement.

A) Incorrect - While user engagement metrics are important, they might not directly inform model enhancements and optimizations.
E) Incorrect - Model training convergence and stability are essential but might not directly guide enhancements for the deployed model's performance.

EXAM FOCUS	*You should track accuracy and precision of user intents as primary indicators for model performance, while also focusing on error patterns to identify areas for improvement. Use query distribution to understand how well the model covers different topics.*
CAUTION ALERT	*Avoid relying solely on user engagement metrics like session duration. While these offer insights into usability, they don't directly correlate with model accuracy or content effectiveness.*

QUESTION 32

Answer - [A), B), and E)] - Integrating medical ontologies, implementing anonymization techniques, and conducting regular audits facilitate domain-specific customization and ensure compliance with healthcare regulations.

D) Incorrect - While federated learning can leverage distributed data sources, it might not directly address the challenge of domain-specific customization and regulatory compliance in healthcare applications.

EXAM FOCUS	*Make sure to integrate medical ontologies to improve the understanding of domain-specific medical queries. Regular compliance audits will ensure adherence to healthcare regulations. Anonymization techniques will protect patient data.*
CAUTION ALERT	*Stay alert when using federated learning. Although useful for distributed data, it may not fully address domain-specific optimization and compliance with healthcare standards.*

QUESTION 33

Answer - [B] Azure Content Moderator > Language API

Option B - Azure Content Moderator provides PII detection and masking functionalities, making it suitable for identifying and masking PII in text data. Option A is incorrect as the Text Analytics API does not include PII detection capabilities. Option C is incorrect as Cognitive Search is not focused on PII detection. Option D is incorrect as Translator Text is for translation, not PII detection. Option E is incorrect as Computer Vision is for image processing, not text analysis.

EXAM FOCUS	*You need to use Azure Content Moderator's Language API for PII detection and masking. This service is designed for privacy compliance, identifying sensitive information in text data and masking it appropriately.*
CAUTION ALERT	*Don't confuse the Text Analytics API with the Content Moderator API. Although Text Analytics offers powerful features, it doesn't focus on PII detection like Content Moderator does.*

QUESTION 34

Answer - [A), B), and C)] - Managing content quality and relevance involves periodically reviewing and updating content, utilizing Azure AI Content Moderator, and implementing machine learning models for relevance scoring.

Option A) - Correct: Periodic review and updates based on user feedback ensure content remains relevant and accurate. Option B) - Correct: Azure AI Content Moderator automates content analysis, enhancing quality control. Option C) - Correct: Machine learning models provide automated scoring for content relevance, improving quality assessment. Option D) - Incorrect: Ignoring content updates may lead to outdated or irrelevant information. Option E) - Incorrect: Manual review alone may not be sufficient for maintaining content quality and relevance.

EXAM FOCUS	*Always remember to review user feedback and periodically update the content in your solution. Automated content analysis tools, like Azure AI Content Moderator, and machine learning models for content relevance scoring will keep the quality high.*
CAUTION ALERT	*Avoid ignoring content updates. Outdated or irrelevant content can reduce the solution's usefulness and lead to poor user experience. Periodic updates are crucial for long-term success.*

QUESTION 35

Answer - [A), B), D), and E)] - Maintaining knowledge bases involves updating content, conducting audits, monitoring usage patterns, and scheduling automated backups.

Option A) - Correct: Regularly updating content based on feedback and insights ensures ongoing relevance and effectiveness. Option B) - Correct: Periodic audits help identify gaps and improve the quality and coverage of the knowledge base. Option C) - Incorrect: While version control is important, it is covered under other options and is not mentioned separately. Option D) - Correct: Monitoring usage patterns allows for adjustments to the content strategy, optimizing user experience. Option E) - Correct: Scheduling automated backups ensures data protection and facilitates recovery in case of data loss or corruption.

EXAM FOCUS	*You should conduct regular audits of your knowledge base to identify gaps and improve content. Monitoring usage patterns will help you adjust your content strategy to better meet user needs. Automated backups ensure data protection.*
CAUTION ALERT	*Stay clear of neglecting knowledge base updates. This can lead to stale or inaccurate information, lowering the effectiveness of your question-answering solution over time.*

QUESTION 36

Answer - [A, B, C] "mcr.microsoft.com/azure-ai/nlp/custommodel"
"--memory 512 --cpus 4"
"--accept"

Option A specifies the correct URI for the NLP custom model container. Option B sets memory and CPU limits. Option C accepts necessary agreements during deployment. Options D and E are not relevant for container deployment.

EXAM FOCUS	*Keep in mind that when deploying NLP models in containers, the correct image URL and resource limits are crucial. Use memory and CPU allocation properly and accept the necessary agreements in your bash deployment command.*
CAUTION ALERT	*Avoid omitting resource allocation settings (memory, CPU) or the --accept flag in your deployment script. Failure to set these could lead to deployment errors or inefficient resource use.*

QUESTION 37

Answer - [B, C, D].

B) Fine-tuning the model separately for each language allows better adaptation to language-specific characteristics and improves performance. C) Implementing language-specific tokenization techniques ensures the model can process different languages effectively. D) Using a language-agnostic pre-trained model can provide a solid foundation for understanding linguistic structures across languages. Increasing the training data for other languages and applying transfer learning from English may help but might not address language-specific nuances adequately.

EXAM FOCUS	*You should consider fine-tuning models separately for each language and use language-specific tokenization techniques. This will ensure your model processes each language effectively. Consider using language-agnostic models for multilingual support.*
CAUTION ALERT	*Stay clear of assuming that increasing data for one language (e.g., English) will generalize well across others. Each language has unique processing requirements that need targeted fine-tuning.*

QUESTION 38

Answer - [A, C, E].

A) Implementing context switching allows the bot to transition seamlessly between different topics within a conversation, enhancing user engagement and satisfaction. C) Incorporating natural language generation enables the bot to dynamically generate content based on user inputs, providing personalized and relevant responses. E) Applying hierarchical dialogues organizes conversation flows into structured layers, allowing for more complex and structured interactions. B) While adaptive card templates offer interactivity, they may not directly address handling complex user interactions. D) Integrating with Azure Cognitive Services enhances language understanding but may not specifically address the complexity of user interactions.

EXAM FOCUS	*Make sure to implement context switching in your bot design. This ensures seamless transitions between topics, which is essential for handling complex user queries. Additionally, hierarchical dialogues allow structured and effective conversation management.*
CAUTION ALERT	*Don't confuse interactive response templates (like adaptive cards) with handling complex interactions. These are useful for UI purposes but don't provide the depth needed for complex, topic-switching conversations.*

QUESTION 39

Answer - [B] <API_KEY>: "YourSpeechApiKey"
<REGION>: "westus"

Option B provides the correct API key and region for Azure Speech service initialization. West US is one of the regions supporting the Speech service. The API key is a placeholder for the actual API key assigned to the Speech service. Options A, C, D, and E either have incorrect region settings or use non-existent regions.

EXAM FOCUS	*You need to ensure your API key and region are correctly configured when using Azure's SpeechRecognizer. This is critical for initializing the service and ensuring your application interacts with the Azure Speech SDK.*
CAUTION ALERT	*Avoid choosing random regions that don't support your service. Each region has specific capabilities, and using the wrong one could result in failed initialization or suboptimal performance.*

QUESTION 40

Answer - [A] Azure Text Analytics.

A) Azure Text Analytics provides sentiment analysis capabilities optimized for real-time processing of customer reviews and social media posts, making it suitable for the requirements of the sentiment analysis tool. B) Azure Language Understanding (LUIS) focuses on understanding user intents and entities within a single language and is not specialized for real-time sentiment analysis. C) Azure Cognitive Search is primarily used for search functionalities and may not provide real-time sentiment analysis capabilities. D) Azure AI Translator service focuses on translation tasks and may not be optimized for real-time sentiment analysis. E) Azure AI Language Service provides language detection and translation but does not specifically handle sentiment analysis like Azure Text Analytics.

EXAM FOCUS	*You should use Azure Text Analytics for real-time sentiment analysis. It's optimized for handling customer reviews and social media posts, making it ideal for applications requiring sentiment detection.*
CAUTION ALERT	*Don't confuse LUIS (Language Understanding) with sentiment analysis. LUIS focuses on understanding user intents, not on determining the emotional tone or sentiment of text data.*

QUESTION 41

Answer - [D] Skillset.

D) Implementing custom skills for document processing is achieved through the use of Skillsets in Azure Cognitive Search, allowing you to define custom logic for extracting key information from documents during indexing. A) Synonyms are used to expand search queries but do not directly relate to document processing. B) Tokenization breaks text into individual tokens but is not specific to custom document processing logic. C) Entity Recognition identifies entities within text but may not cover all aspects of document processing. E) Scoring Profile is used for relevance scoring and does not directly relate to document processing.

EXAM FOCUS	*You should leverage Skillsets in Azure Cognitive Search to define custom skills that process documents during indexing, allowing you to extract key information like metadata or entities. This is crucial for enhancing search relevance.*

CAUTION ALERT	*Stay clear of using features like Synonyms or Tokenization for custom processing. They serve different purposes and won't help in adding processing logic to document indexing.*

QUESTION 42

Answer - [D] TextAnalyticsClient

Option A, QnAMakerClient, is used for building question and answer systems and does not include features for structured information extraction. Option B, ContentModeratorClient, is primarily used for content moderation tasks and may not have specific capabilities for structured information extraction. Option C, FormRecognizerClient, is used for extracting information from forms and documents, not for structured information extraction from unstructured text inputs. Option E, LanguageUnderstandingClient, is used for understanding user intents from natural language inputs and does not include structured information extraction features. Option D, TextAnalyticsClient, is the correct choice as it provides capabilities for extracting structured information, including PII, from unstructured text inputs.

EXAM FOCUS	*Make sure to use TextAnalyticsClient for structured information extraction, including PII. This service provides a robust solution for extracting data from unstructured text inputs, ensuring compliance with privacy standards.*
CAUTION ALERT	*Don't confuse FormRecognizerClient with Text Analytics. Form Recognizer extracts structured data from forms and documents but isn't suitable for general unstructured text analysis.*

QUESTION 43

Answer - [A] Extracting key phrases from documents to improve search relevance.

A) Extracting key phrases from documents enhances search relevance by providing additional context and keywords to improve matching between user queries and document content. B) Converting documents to different formats improves compatibility but may not directly enhance search capabilities. C) Identifying duplicate documents is important for data management but does not directly contribute to search relevancy. D) Extracting metadata for administrative purposes may improve data organization but may not directly enhance search relevancy. E) Translating documents into multiple languages simultaneously expands accessibility but does not directly improve search relevancy.

EXAM FOCUS	*Always remember that extracting key phrases with a custom skill significantly improves search relevance by adding contextual keywords. This is an essential feature in Azure Cognitive Search to enhance document search and retrieval accuracy.*
CAUTION ALERT	*Avoid focusing on administrative tasks like metadata extraction if your primary goal is improving search relevancy. Administrative tasks alone won't enhance the search experience.*

QUESTION 44

Answer - [B, C] Incorporate user feedback signals into scoring profiles.

B) Incorporating user feedback signals into scoring profiles allows for personalized content recommendations based on user interactions, improving the relevance of search results and enhancing the recommendation engine's effectiveness. C) Applying temporal decay functions for freshness ensures that recent content receives higher relevance scores, enhancing content recommendations based on recency. A) While defining scoring weights for document attributes is important, incorporating user feedback signals provides more granular control over personalized content recommendations. D) Implementing boosting based on item popularity trends may enhance general search rankings but does not directly address personalized content recommendations. E) Configuring proximity boosting for related content may improve search relevance but may not provide direct integration with user feedback signals for personalized recommendations.

EXAM FOCUS	*You need to incorporate user feedback and temporal decay functions into scoring profiles to optimize content recommendations. These methods ensure the most relevant and recent content is presented to users.*
CAUTION ALERT	*Don't confuse scoring profiles with popularity trends. While boosting based on item popularity can help, it may not directly relate to user-specific content recommendations.*

QUESTION 45

Answer - B) ExtractKeyPhrases()

Option A - KeyPhraseExtraction(): This is a hypothetical method and not part of the Azure Text Analytics SDK.
Option C - FindKeyPhrases(): This is a hypothetical method and not part of the Azure Text Analytics SDK.
Option D - KeyphraseRecognition(): This is a hypothetical method and not part of the Azure Text Analytics SDK.
Option E - AnalyzeKeyPhrases(): This is a hypothetical method and not part of the Azure Text Analytics SDK.
Option B is correct because ExtractKeyPhrases() is the method used to extract key phrases from text in Azure Text Analytics.

EXAM FOCUS	*Keep in mind that the method for extracting key phrases in Azure Text Analytics is ExtractKeyPhrases(). This method helps analyze documents and extract meaningful concepts to improve search and document understanding.*
CAUTION ALERT	*Stay alert to avoid using incorrect methods like KeyPhraseExtraction() or AnalyzeKeyPhrases() as they are not part of the Azure Text Analytics SDK.*

QUESTION 46

Answer - [A] Deploying the model as a containerized service using Azure Kubernetes Service (AKS).

A) This option offers scalability, isolation, and efficient resource utilization, making it suitable for production environments.
B) While Azure Functions offer serverless deployment, they might not provide the required scalability and isolation for a healthcare application.
C) Azure App Service is primarily for web applications and may not provide the necessary infrastructure for a containerized model.
D) Direct integration into the codebase might lead to maintenance issues and scalability challenges.
E) Azure Machine Learning focuses on ML pipelines rather than direct model deployment for complex AI models.

EXAM FOCUS	*You should prioritize containerized deployment using Azure Kubernetes Service (AKS) for scalable and isolated deployment of AI models in healthcare. This ensures compliance with regulatory requirements while maintaining performance.*
CAUTION ALERT	*Stay cautioned against using Azure Functions or Azure App Service for large-scale healthcare applications. They may not provide the needed infrastructure for complex AI models.*

QUESTION 47

Answer - [B] Ensuring code snippets are properly licensed for use in the project.

B) Ensuring code snippets are properly licensed mitigates legal risks associated with code usage and distribution, ensuring compliance with industry standards and legal requirements.
A) Version control tracks changes but does not address licensing concerns.
C) Testing validates functionality but does not ensure compliance.
D) Encrypting code protects IP but does not address licensing requirements.
E) Documentation aids in transparency but may not directly address licensing compliance.

EXAM FOCUS	*Make sure to check licensing for generated code snippets when using Azure OpenAI Service. This ensures compliance with legal standards and prevents intellectual property issues.*
CAUTION ALERT	*Don't neglect code licensing requirements. Ignoring them can lead to legal complications even if the functionality of the generated code is validated.*

QUESTION 48

Answer - D) Statement I, Statement II

Option C - Statement III: This statement is incorrect because Azure AI Vision service does not provide capabilities for sentiment analysis of images.
Option E - Statement II, Statement III: This statement is incorrect because it doesn't include the true statement about the detection of objects in images (Statement I).
Option A is correct because Azure AI Vision service allows the detection of objects in images, making Statement I true.
Option B is correct because Azure AI Vision service supports training custom image classification models, making Statement II true.
Option D is correct as it includes both true statements: Statement I and Statement II.

EXAM FOCUS	*You should use Azure AI Vision for object detection and custom image classification. These features are essential for processing visual data, but remember it doesn't handle sentiment analysis.*
CAUTION ALERT	*Avoid assuming that Azure AI Vision includes capabilities like sentiment analysis. It's designed for visual tasks, not analyzing emotions or sentiments in images.*

QUESTION 49

Answer - [A, B] Utilizing Azure Data Lake Storage for scalable storage and management of music datasets. Maintaining a changelog to document modifications made to the music dataset over time.

A) Azure Data Lake Storage provides scalable storage and management capabilities suitable for large music datasets.
B) Maintaining a changelog helps track changes and versions in the dataset, aiding reproducibility and accountability.
C) Storing metadata separately can improve search efficiency but may not directly address dataset management and versioning. D) Assigning unique identifiers is valuable but focuses more on access control than dataset versioning.
E) Azure Data Factory is useful for data processing but may not directly address dataset management and versioning.

EXAM FOCUS	*You need to utilize Azure Data Lake Storage for managing and versioning large custom datasets like music collections. Maintaining a detailed changelog will also help track changes in your datasets effectively.*
CAUTION ALERT	*Stay clear of solely relying on metadata storage for managing datasets. While it aids in searchability, it doesn't cover complete dataset versioning and management needs.*

QUESTION 50

Answer - [D] Regular monitoring of model performance metrics and triggers for retraining.

A) Periodic retraining may not be efficient or timely enough to prevent drift. B) A dynamic threshold alone may not address underlying drift issues. C) Transfer learning may not always be applicable or practical for this scenario. E) While versioning and rollback mechanisms are important, they do not directly address drift prevention.

EXAM FOCUS	*Make sure to set up regular performance monitoring and retraining triggers for your sentiment analysis model to prevent drift. This ensures that the model adapts to new data patterns effectively.*
CAUTION ALERT	*Don't rely only on periodic retraining or dynamic thresholds. Without real-time monitoring and retraining triggers, your model may suffer from drift and decrease in performance.*

PRACTICE TEST 6 - QUESTIONS ONLY

QUESTION 1

You are tasked with implementing a natural language processing (NLP) solution for a multinational corporation. The solution needs to analyze customer feedback from various sources, including emails, social media posts, and survey responses. Additionally, the solution should extract key phrases and sentiments accurately to gauge customer satisfaction levels.
Which Azure AI service or combination of services would be most suitable for this scenario?
Select all answers that apply.

A) Azure Cognitive Services Text Analytics
B) Azure Cognitive Services Language Understanding (LUIS)
C) Azure Bot Services
D) Azure AI Translator service
E) Azure Cognitive Services QnA Maker

QUESTION 2

Your company is developing an AI-driven virtual assistant for a global e-commerce platform. The virtual assistant needs to accurately transcribe customer queries in real-time and respond with relevant product information. Additionally, it should support multiple languages to cater to diverse customer bases.
Which Azure AI service or combination of services should you select to meet these requirements effectively?
Select all answers that apply.

A) Azure AI Speech to Text
B) Azure AI Text Analytics
C) Azure AI Translator Text
D) Azure AI Language Understanding (LUIS)
E) Azure AI Text to Speech

QUESTION 3

Which Azure CLI command should be used to create a custom image classification model for Azure AI Vision?

```
A) az cognitiveservices account model create
B) az cognitiveservices account model deploy
C) az cognitiveservices account model train
D) az cognitiveservices account model evaluate
E) az cognitiveservices account model publish
```

QUESTION 4

You are developing an application that utilizes Azure AI services for natural language processing. Which authentication method should you use to ensure secure access to the services and manage user identities?

A) API key
B) Azure Active Directory (AAD)
C) Shared access signature (SAS)
D) Client secret
E) Kerberos

QUESTION 5

In a large-scale enterprise application, you are tasked with deploying an Azure AI service for natural language processing. The architecture demands high availability and scalability. Which criterion is most crucial for determining the default endpoint for the service?

A) Cost-effectiveness
B) Geographical location
C) Traffic distribution
D) Security considerations
E) Latency optimization

QUESTION 6

Your organization is building a language understanding model using Azure AI Language services. You need to ensure that the model can be accessed securely from a web application hosted in Azure App Service. What should you do?

A) Implement Azure Active Directory (AAD) authentication.
B) Enable cross-origin resource sharing (CORS).
C) Use a shared access signature (SAS) token for authentication.
D) Deploy the web application to a virtual machine with a static IP address.
E) Allow anonymous access to the model endpoint.

QUESTION 7

Your team is responsible for monitoring Azure AI resources and ensuring optimal performance for a critical project. Which key performance indicator (KPI) is most relevant for evaluating the performance of Azure AI services?

A) Average CPU utilization
B) Total storage capacity
C) Network bandwidth usage
D) Number of successful API requests
E) Memory usage

QUESTION 8

Your team is tasked with managing account keys for Azure AI services in a large-scale project. Which best practice should you follow to ensure secure key storage and access?

A) Store keys in plaintext files on local servers
B) Share keys openly within the team via email
C) Store keys in Azure Key Vault
D) Embed keys directly in code repositories
E) Write keys on sticky notes and attach them to monitors

QUESTION 9

You are configuring authentication for an Azure App Services web app named App1. The app needs to authenticate using Azure AD while adhering to the principle of least privilege. What is the best course of action?

A) Enable Managed Service Identity (MSI) for App1 and grant RBAC permissions to Azure AD.
B) Implement OAuth 2.0 authentication with Azure AD and grant App1 access to Azure AD.
C) Configure App1 to use Azure AD single sign-on (SSO).
D) Generate a client secret and store it securely for App1 authentication.
E) Enable Azure Active Directory (Azure AD) authentication and configure App1 to use it.

QUESTION 10

You are developing an image-sharing platform that allows users to upload and share photos. To maintain a safe and respectful environment, you need to implement image moderation using Azure Content Moderator. What is a key consideration when implementing image moderation for the platform?

A) Customizing image recognition models to detect specific objects.
B) Integrating with Azure Media Services for real-time content analysis.
C) Setting up workflow automation to handle flagged images efficiently.
D) Ensuring compliance with privacy regulations for user-uploaded images.
E) Using blockchain technology to verify the authenticity of uploaded images.

QUESTION 11

Your team has deployed a decision support system (DSS) for analyzing customer feedback and sentiment to improve product offerings. Which technique should you employ to monitor the performance of the DSS and ensure timely adjustments?

A) Implement Azure Monitor for tracking system health and performance metrics.
B) Utilize Azure Data Factory for orchestrating data pipelines and ETL processes.
C) Configure Azure Logic Apps for workflow automation and integration with external systems.
D) Employ Azure Application Insights for monitoring end-user interactions and application performance.
E) Use Azure DevOps for continuous integration and delivery of AI model updates.

QUESTION 12

You are developing a speech recognition solution using Azure AI Speech. Which actions should you take to implement intent recognition effectively?

A) Train the speech recognition model with a diverse set of utterances representing different intents.
B) Utilize Speech Synthesis Markup Language (SSML) to enhance speech-to-text conversion accuracy.
C) Implement keyword recognition to detect specific phrases within speech input.
D) Configure custom speech solutions to handle complex language patterns and contexts.
E) Fine-tune the model parameters to optimize intent recognition accuracy.

QUESTION 13

You are leading a team of Azure AI engineers tasked with implementing a decision support solution for a large e-commerce platform. The solution aims to enhance customer experience by providing personalized product recommendations based on historical purchase data and user behavior. Which approach should you consider to ensure successful implementation while adhering to best practices?
Select all answers that apply.

A) Utilize Azure AI Metrics Advisor to monitor user engagement metrics and adjust recommendations accordingly.
B) Implement Azure AI Content Moderator to filter out inappropriate product recommendations and maintain brand integrity.
C) Leverage Azure AI Speech service to analyze customer feedback from call center recordings and refine recommendation algorithms.
D) Incorporate Azure AI Translator service to provide multilingual product recommendations for diverse customer segments.
E) Integrate Azure AI Cognitive Search to extract insights from customer reviews and improve recommendation accuracy.

QUESTION 14

You are leading a team tasked with implementing an AI-driven solution for a retail chain to enhance customer experience by enabling smart checkout systems. The solution requires robust object detection capabilities to identify products accurately for automated billing. Which technique should you prioritize to achieve precise object detection in this scenario?

A) YOLO (You Only Look Once)
B) R-CNN (Region-based Convolutional Neural Network)
C) SSD (Single Shot MultiBox Detector)
D) Faster R-CNN
E) Mask R-CNN

QUESTION 15

You are deploying an Azure AI solution using containers. During the deployment process, you encounter an error message indicating "Insufficient memory resources." Which actions should you consider to resolve this issue?

A) Increase the memory allocation for the container.
B) Optimize the Dockerfile to reduce the container image size.
C) Scale up the Azure AI Service plan.
D) Adjust the container runtime settings to optimize memory usage.
E) Upgrade the Azure AI Service resource to a higher tier.

QUESTION 16

You plan to build an app that will use Azure AI Services. You need to identify the methods that can be used to authenticate to Azure AI Services. Which two methods can you use? Each correct answer presents a complete solution.

A) SAML token
B) Subscription key
C) Microsoft Entra ID
D) Kerberos

QUESTION 17

You are tasked with developing a custom object detection model for a retail company to identify specific products on store shelves in real-time. What approach should you take to address the challenges of real-time object detection effectively?
Select all answers that apply.

A) Utilize a lightweight neural network architecture
B) Increase the size of the training dataset
C) Optimize model inference speed using quantization techniques
D) Implement multi-threading for parallel processing
E) Deploy the model on edge devices for on-device inference

QUESTION 18

You are integrating Azure AI Language into your application to analyze text data. You are evaluating an API request using the following command: POST https://<resource-name>.cognitiveservices.azure.com/text/analytics/v3.0/entities/recognition/general. What results can you expect from this request?

A) Sentiment analysis of the text.
B) Extraction of named entities from the text.

C) Translation of the text to a specified language.
D) Identification of key phrases within the text.
E) Conversion of text to speech.

QUESTION 19

Your organization is implementing a video analytics solution to analyze security footage from surveillance cameras placed across different locations. The solution needs to automatically detect and flag suspicious activities such as unauthorized access and intrusions. What Azure AI service should you primarily leverage to achieve this goal while ensuring scalability and real-time processing capabilities?

A) Azure AI Video Indexer
B) Azure AI Vision Spatial Analysis
C) Azure Cognitive Services - Computer Vision
D) Azure Cognitive Services - Video Analyzer
E) Azure Media Services

QUESTION 20

You are tasked with developing an AI-driven traffic management system for a smart city project. The system requires real-time analysis of live video streams from traffic cameras to identify traffic congestion and optimize traffic flow. Which Azure AI service should you recommend to process live video streams efficiently and enable the system to generate real-time alerts for traffic congestion?

A) Azure AI Video Indexer
B) Azure Cognitive Services - Video Analyzer
C) Azure Cognitive Services - Face API
D) Azure AI Vision Spatial Analysis
E) Azure AI Metrics Advisor

QUESTION 21

You are experiencing performance issues with the Azure AI Text Analytics service in your application. Which action should you take to optimize the service?

A) Increase the timeout duration for API requests.
B) Reduce the maximum batch size for processing.
C) Implement caching for frequently accessed data.
D) Upgrade to a higher-tier service plan.
E) Disable diagnostic logging for the service.

QUESTION 22

You are developing an AI solution that requires extracting entities from unstructured text. Which of the following techniques can be used to enhance entity extraction accuracy?

A) Named entity recognition (NER)
B) Entity resolution
C) Custom entity models
D) Rule-based matching
E) Frequency-based extraction

QUESTION 23

You are developing an AI-powered platform for a global e-commerce company. The platform needs to support multiple languages for customer feedback analysis. Which Azure AI service should you recommend to accurately detect the language used in customer reviews, considering the requirement for multilingual support and high accuracy?

A) Azure Text Analytics
B) Azure Translator
C) Azure Language Understanding (LUIS)
D) Azure AI Language
E) Azure Cognitive Search

QUESTION 24

You are developing an application that requires identifying and tagging objects within images. Which Azure AI Vision feature should you utilize for this task?

A) Face detection
B) Optical character recognition (OCR)
C) Object detection
D) Image analysis
E) Spatial analysis

QUESTION 25

You are developing an interactive voice response system that requires dynamic content generation for different user scenarios. Which SSML tag should you use to insert dynamic content into the synthesized speech output?

A) <audio> tag
B) <prosody> tag
C) <say-as> tag
D) <break> tag
E) <sub> tag

QUESTION 26

Your company is developing a virtual assistant for a customer service application. The virtual assistant needs to accurately identify the user's intent to provide relevant assistance. Which Azure AI service is most suitable for implementing intent recognition in this scenario?

A) Azure Cognitive Services Language Understanding (LUIS)
B) Azure Cognitive Services Translator Text
C) Azure Cognitive Services Text Analytics
D) Azure Cognitive Services Speech Service
E) Azure OpenAI Service

QUESTION 27

You are troubleshooting an issue with an Azure app that uses Azure Cognitive Services for language understanding. Users are reporting that the app fails to comprehend complex queries correctly. What could be a potential reason for this issue?

A) Inadequate training data for the language model.
B) Insufficient computational resources allocated to the Azure Cognitive Services instance.
C) Lack of compatibility between the app's frontend framework and Azure Cognitive Services SDK.
D) Outdated version of the Azure Cognitive Services SDK being used.
E) Limited access to external knowledge bases for query enrichment.

QUESTION 28

You are developing a real-time speech translation application for an international conference. The application must synchronize speech input with translated text output seamlessly to ensure effective communication. Which Azure service should you use to achieve this requirement?

A) Azure Speech Translator
B) Azure Speech Studio
C) Azure Translator Text
D) Azure Cognitive Services
E) Azure Language Studio

QUESTION 29

Your team is developing a language understanding model to analyze customer feedback for a retail company. What technique can improve the accuracy of the language model in identifying sentiments expressed in customer reviews?

A) Train the model using only positive sentiments to bias it towards optimistic responses
B) Incorporate sentiment-specific lexicons and dictionaries during model training
C) Ignore sentiment analysis and focus solely on intent recognition
D) Use prebuilt sentiment analysis models without customization
E) Limit the training data to a single genre of customer feedback for simplicity

QUESTION 30

You are tasked with developing an Azure app that leverages Azure AI Speech for real-time transcription of audio streams. The app must support multiple languages and provide accurate transcriptions with minimal latency. Which approach should you take to implement this solution?

A) Utilize Azure AI Speech's real-time transcription API with language auto-detection enabled.
B) Implement a language-specific Azure AI Speech model for each supported language and dynamically switch between models based on detected language.
C) Use Azure AI Translator to translate the audio stream into a single common language before passing it to Azure AI Speech for transcription.
D) Develop a custom language detection module within the app to identify the language of the audio stream and then route it to the corresponding Azure AI Speech model.
E) Implement parallel instances of the Azure AI Speech service, each dedicated to transcribing a specific language, and route audio streams accordingly.

QUESTION 31

You are tasked with deploying a language understanding model for a customer service chatbot application. The model must handle high volumes of user queries while ensuring low latency and high availability. Which best practices should you follow to ensure successful deployment of the language model in this scenario?
Select all answers that apply.

A) Implement auto-scaling to handle fluctuating loads
B) Deploy the model in Azure Kubernetes Service (AKS) for container orchestration
C) Utilize Azure Traffic Manager for load balancing
D) Enable Azure Application Insights for performance monitoring
E) Implement token-based authentication for secure access to the model endpoint

QUESTION 32

You are responsible for managing the language understanding model for a financial institution's chatbot application.

The model plays a crucial role in assisting customers with inquiries regarding their accounts and financial services. What steps should you take to ensure effective backup and recovery of the language model in case of data loss or corruption, while adhering to security and compliance requirements?
Select all answers that apply.

A) Implement regular snapshots of model checkpoints stored in a secure Azure Storage account
B) Utilize version control systems to track changes and revert to previous model versions if necessary
C) Configure automated backups of model configurations and trained data to Azure Blob Storage
D) Implement Azure Key Vault for secure storage of encryption keys used to protect model data
E) Maintain offline backups of model weights and parameters on encrypted storage devices

QUESTION 33

Your team is developing an Azure app that requires real-time translation of text from one language to another. Which Azure service and API combination should you use to accomplish this task?

A) Azure AI Language Service > Text Analytics API
B) Azure Translator Text > Language API
C) Azure Computer Vision > Vision API
D) Azure Content Moderator > Language API
E) Azure QnA Maker > Decision API

QUESTION 34

What techniques are essential for effective knowledge base training in a question answering solution?
Select all answers that apply.

A) Utilize diverse datasets for comprehensive coverage
B) Implement active learning for iterative improvement
C) Incorporate user feedback to refine knowledge base
D) Apply reinforcement learning for dynamic adaptation
E) Ignore training data and rely solely on prebuilt models

QUESTION 35

In designing multi-turn conversation flows for a question answering solution, what techniques can Azure AI engineers employ to maintain context over multiple interactions effectively?
Select all answers that apply.

A) Utilize session management to track user context
B) Implement stateful conversation handling
C) Store conversation history in a persistent data store
D) Apply reinforcement learning for dynamic conversation paths
E) Implement context switches based on user prompts

QUESTION 36

You are tasked with deploying a custom natural language understanding (NLU) model in an Azure container environment. Which options should you select to complete the provided bash statement?
Select all answers that apply.

```
A) "mcr.microsoft.com/azure-cognitive-services/language/nlu"
 B) "--memory 256 --cpus 4"
 C) "--accept"
```

```
D) "--region eastus"
E) "--api-key {API_KEY}"
```

QUESTION 37

Your organization is deploying a custom natural language processing (NLP) model on Azure to analyze customer feedback for sentiment analysis. Which steps should be included in the deployment process to ensure security and scalability?
Select all answers that apply.

A) Implement role-based access control (RBAC)
B) Configure auto-scaling based on workload
C) Encrypt data at rest and in transit
D) Monitor model performance using Azure Monitor
E) Optimize resource utilization using serverless architecture

QUESTION 38

Your company is developing a voice assistant solution for a smart home IoT platform using Azure Cognitive Services. As part of the design process, you need to ensure effective management of user context to personalize interactions. What approach should you prioritize to achieve this?
Select all answers that apply.

A) Implement session persistence for maintaining user state
B) Utilize Azure Bot Framework for multi-channel integration
C) Integrate Azure Active Directory for user authentication
D) Employ natural language understanding for context extraction
E) Implement role-based access control (RBAC) for user permissions

QUESTION 39

You need to integrate Azure Text Analytics into your application for sentiment analysis. Choose the appropriate class to represent the Text Analytics client in the provided code snippet.

```
var textAnalyticsClient = new TextAnalyticsClient(new
TextAnalyticsApiKeyCredential("<API_KEY>"), new TextAnalyticsClientOptions { Endpoint =
"<ENDPOINT>" });
```

```
A) TextAnalyticsApiKeyCredential
B) TextAnalyticsClientOptions
C) TextAnalyticsClient
D) TextAnalyticsClientCredential
E) TextAnalyticsApiKeyCredentialOptions
```

QUESTION 40

Your team is developing a natural language processing (NLP) application that aims to analyze customer feedback to improve product offerings. Ethical considerations are paramount in ensuring the fairness and transparency of the analysis. Which Azure AI service should you integrate into the application to address bias and ensure fairness in the language models?

A) Azure Text Analytics
B) Azure Language Understanding (LUIS)
C) Azure AI Translator service
D) Azure Cognitive Services
E) Azure Machine Learning

QUESTION 41

Your organization is planning to implement Azure Cognitive Search to enable efficient search capabilities for a diverse range of documents, including PDFs, Word documents, and CSV files. As the Azure AI engineer responsible for creating data sources, you need to select the appropriate data source types to ensure seamless ingestion of these documents into the search index. Which data source types should you choose?
Select all answers that apply.

A) Azure Blob Storage
B) Azure SQL Database
C) Azure Cosmos DB
D) Azure Data Lake Storage
E) Azure Table Storage

QUESTION 42

You are developing an application that utilizes Azure Cognitive Services to analyze text for sentiment analysis. Which code snippet should you use to call the sentiment analysis API?

A) Azure.AI.TextAnalytics.SentimentAnalysisClient
B) Microsoft.Azure.CognitiveServices.Language.TextAnalytics.Sentiment
C) Azure.AI.TextAnalytics.TextAnalyticsClient
D) Microsoft.Azure.CognitiveServices.Language.TextAnalytics.TextAnalyticsAPI
E) Microsoft.Azure.CognitiveServices.Language.TextAnalytics.TextAnalyticsClient

QUESTION 43

Your organization is implementing Azure Cognitive Search to index a large volume of documents from various sources. As part of the deployment, you need to configure indexers to automate data ingestion and enrichment processes. Which approach should you take to ensure efficient data ingestion and enrichment in Azure Cognitive Search?

A) Schedule indexers to run at fixed intervals
B) Use Azure Logic Apps to trigger indexer execution
C) Manually trigger indexers after data updates
D) Configure webhooks to notify indexers of data changes
E) Implement Azure Functions to monitor and trigger indexers

QUESTION 44

You are tasked with implementing an Azure Cognitive Search solution for a large e-commerce platform. The platform requires advanced search capabilities, including faceted search and personalized search results for users. As part of the implementation, you need to configure Knowledge Store projections to optimize data retrieval and analysis. Which approach should you take to configure Knowledge Store projections effectively?

A) Configure Knowledge Store projections to include only raw data
B) Design projections to store enriched data in file format
C) Implement projections for object storage with minimal metadata
D) Store projected data in a relational table format
E) Include both raw and enriched data in Knowledge Store projections

QUESTION 45

In Azure Speech service, which method should you use to convert text to speech with the ability to control pronunciation, intonation, and timing?

```
A) TextToSpeechService.convertText()
B) Speak()
C) Synthesize()
D) SSML()
E) GenerateSpeech()
```

QUESTION 46

While deploying an Azure OpenAI model, you need to ensure seamless integration with your existing Azure infrastructure. Which deployment approach would best facilitate this integration, considering the existing infrastructure is primarily based on Azure Virtual Machines (VMs)?

A) Deploying the model as a Docker container on Azure Container Instances (ACI).
B) Implementing the model as an Azure Function.
C) Deploying the model as an Azure Cognitive Service.
D) Integrating the model into an Azure Virtual Network (VNet).
E) Using Azure DevOps to manage the deployment pipeline.

QUESTION 47

Your team is integrating code generation capabilities into a collaborative coding platform using Azure OpenAI Service. Which approach should you prioritize to customize the code generation process for different programming languages and optimize developer productivity?

A) Providing language-specific templates for common coding tasks.
B) Requiring developers to manually specify programming languages for code generation.
C) Limiting code generation to a single programming language for consistency.
D) Implementing automatic language detection for seamless code generation.
E) Using a third-party library for language translation of generated code.

QUESTION 48

When working with Azure AI Language service for language understanding models, which combination of statements is true?

A) Statement I: Language understanding models support intent recognition.
B) Statement II: Language understanding models support text-to-speech conversion.
C) Statement III: Language understanding models support language translation.
D) Statement I, Statement II
E) Statement I, Statement III

QUESTION 49

In a project aiming to generate personalized short stories using generative AI, you are evaluating the impact of different narrative datasets on story quality. What is a recommended approach to measure the effectiveness of custom data in enhancing generative outcomes?
Select all answers that apply.

A) Assessing the length of generated stories to determine the dataset's impact on story duration.
B) Analyzing the sentiment of reader feedback on stories generated from different datasets.
C) Implementing cluster analysis to identify patterns and variations in story themes across datasets.

D) Conducting comparative analysis of story coherence and plot development using different datasets.
E) Monitoring computational resource usage during model training with each dataset.

QUESTION 50

Your team is tasked with fine-tuning an Azure OpenAI model to generate custom images based on textual descriptions. During the process, you encounter challenges with maintaining diversity and quality in the generated images. Which approach would best address these challenges?

A) Adjusting model hyperparameters to balance diversity and quality
B) Implementing additional constraints during training to enforce diversity
C) Incorporating a feedback loop mechanism for continuous improvement
D) Augmenting the training dataset with diverse image samples
E) Fine-tuning separate models for different image categories

PRACTICE TEST 6 - ANSWERS ONLY

QUESTION 1

Answer - [A, B] Azure Cognitive Services Text Analytics, Azure Cognitive Services Language Understanding (LUIS)

Option C - Azure Bot Services: While capable of processing natural language, it's more focused on building conversational AI and not ideal for sentiment analysis or key phrase extraction.
Option D - Azure AI Translator service: Primarily used for language translation and not designed for sentiment analysis or key phrase extraction.
Option E - Azure Cognitive Services QnA Maker: Designed for creating question-and-answer bots, not sentiment analysis or key phrase extraction.
Option A - Azure Cognitive Services Text Analytics: Provides sentiment analysis and key phrase extraction functionalities, suitable for analyzing customer feedback.
Option B - Azure Cognitive Services Language Understanding (LUIS): Allows for building custom language understanding models, ideal for extracting intents and entities from customer feedback.

EXAM FOCUS	*You should utilize Azure Cognitive Services Text Analytics for sentiment analysis and key phrase extraction. Pair it with LUIS for extracting intents and entities from diverse customer feedback. These services complement each other for NLP solutions across multiple input sources.*
CAUTION ALERT	*Stay clear of choosing services like Azure Bot Services or QnA Maker if your focus is on analyzing customer feedback rather than building conversational bots.*

QUESTION 2

Answer - [A, C] Azure AI Speech to Text, Azure AI Translator Text

Option B - Azure AI Text Analytics: Primarily for text analysis tasks such as sentiment analysis, not suitable for real-time transcription.
Option D - Azure AI Language Understanding (LUIS): Designed for intent recognition in conversational AI, not suited for real-time transcription.
Option E - Azure AI Text to Speech: Converts text to spoken audio, not suitable for transcribing customer queries.

EXAM FOCUS	*Make sure to combine Azure AI Speech to Text for real-time transcription and Azure Translator Text for multilingual support. These are essential for global applications that need to cater to diverse customer bases.*
CAUTION ALERT	*Avoid relying solely on LUIS or Text Analytics for transcription or multilingual support, as they are more suited for text analysis and intent extraction rather than real-time transcription.*

QUESTION 3

Answer - C) az cognitiveservices account model train

Option A - Incorrect. This command is not used for creating custom models but rather for managing the account itself. Option B - Incorrect. This command is used for deploying models, not for creating them. Option D - Incorrect. This command is used for evaluating models, not for creating them. Option E - Incorrect. This command is used for publishing models, not for creating them.

EXAM FOCUS	*You need to use the command az cognitiveservices account model train for creating custom image classification models in Azure AI Vision. Training is a crucial step in building a performant model.*
CAUTION ALERT	*Don't confuse this with commands like model deploy or model evaluate, which are for deploying and evaluating models, not training them.*

QUESTION 4

Answer - B) Azure Active Directory (AAD)

Option A - Incorrect. API keys are typically used for simple authentication scenarios but may not provide comprehensive user identity management. Option C - Incorrect. Shared access signatures are more suitable for granting limited access to resources rather than managing user identities. Option D - Incorrect. Client secrets are used in OAuth 2.0 flow but may not provide comprehensive user identity management. Option E - Incorrect. Kerberos is not typically used for authentication to Azure AI services and does not integrate well with Azure Active Directory.

EXAM FOCUS	*Always remember that Azure Active Directory (AAD) provides the most secure and scalable way to manage user identities and authenticate access to Azure AI services. It integrates well with Azure's identity management infrastructure.*
CAUTION ALERT	*Stay cautioned against using API keys or SAS tokens for complex authentication needs. These options may not offer the comprehensive security and user management that AAD provides.*

QUESTION 5

Answer - [E] Latency optimization.

Latency optimization - In a large-scale enterprise application, especially one requiring high availability and scalability, minimizing latency is crucial for ensuring smooth user experience. Default endpoints should be chosen based on geographical proximity to users, network latency considerations, and efficient traffic distribution to minimize latency. Options A, B, C, and D might influence certain aspects of endpoint selection but are not as critical as ensuring low latency.

EXAM FOCUS	*Keep in mind that latency optimization should be your top priority when choosing an endpoint for AI services in large-scale applications. Proximity to users can make a significant difference in user experience.*
CAUTION ALERT	*Avoid prioritizing cost over latency when deploying enterprise-scale applications. High latency can lead to poor performance and user dissatisfaction.*

QUESTION 6

Answer - A) Implement Azure Active Directory (AAD) authentication.

Option B - Incorrect. Enabling cross-origin resource sharing (CORS) does not provide user authentication for accessing the language understanding model. Option C - Incorrect. Using a shared access signature (SAS) token may not provide comprehensive user authentication for accessing the model from a web application. Option D - Incorrect. Deploying the web application to a virtual machine with a static IP address does not address user authentication requirements. Option E - Incorrect. Allowing anonymous access may compromise security and does not provide user authentication.

EXAM FOCUS	*You should implement Azure Active Directory (AAD) authentication for securely accessing AI models from Azure App Service. It ensures comprehensive access control and identity management.*
CAUTION ALERT	*Don't rely on CORS or SAS tokens for secure access to AI models. They don't provide the level of security and user identity management required for enterprise applications.*

QUESTION 7

Answer - [D] Number of successful API requests.

Number of successful API requests - Evaluating the number of successful API requests provides insights into the usage and performance of Azure AI services, indicating their effectiveness in processing requests and delivering results. Options A, B, C, and E may be relevant but do not directly measure the performance of AI services in handling requests.

EXAM FOCUS	*You need to monitor the number of successful API requests as a key performance indicator for evaluating the reliability and performance of Azure AI services. This helps you track service usage and efficiency.*
CAUTION ALERT	*Avoid focusing on metrics like CPU utilization or storage capacity for performance evaluation. These may not provide direct insights into the effectiveness of your AI services.*

QUESTION 8

Answer - [C] Store keys in Azure Key Vault.

Store keys in Azure Key Vault - Azure Key Vault provides a secure and centralized solution for storing and managing keys, certificates, and secrets, ensuring encryption, access control, and auditability, thereby mitigating the risks associated with storing keys in plaintext files, sharing them openly, embedding them in code repositories, or writing them on sticky notes.

EXAM FOCUS	*Make sure to store your keys securely in Azure Key Vault. It offers encryption, access control, and audit capabilities, which are critical for secure key management in large-scale projects.*
CAUTION ALERT	*Stay clear of storing keys in plaintext files, code repositories, or sharing them via email. This can lead to severe security breaches and compromise your Azure AI services.*

QUESTION 9

Answer - A) Enable Managed Service Identity (MSI) for App1 and grant RBAC permissions to Azure AD.

Option B - Incorrect. While OAuth 2.0 authentication with Azure AD is a valid approach, enabling MSI with RBAC permissions directly meets the requirement with minimal administrative overhead. Option C - Incorrect. Azure AD SSO may provide centralized authentication but may not align with the requirement to use Azure AD directly. Option D - Incorrect. Storing client secrets may introduce additional security risks and administrative overhead. Option E - Incorrect. While Azure AD authentication is a valid approach, enabling MSI with RBAC permissions directly meets the requirement with minimal administrative overhead.

EXAM FOCUS	*Always consider enabling Managed Service Identity (MSI) and granting Role-Based Access Control (RBAC) permissions for Azure AD authentication in your apps. This simplifies authentication while maintaining security.*
CAUTION ALERT	*Don't confuse MSI with other options like OAuth 2.0 or client secrets, which may require more manual management and overhead compared to MSI's built-in identity management.*

QUESTION 10

Answer - [C] Setting up workflow automation to handle flagged images efficiently.

Setting up workflow automation ensures that flagged images are addressed promptly and efficiently, enhancing the moderation process. Options A, B, D, and E address different aspects but may not directly contribute to improving the efficiency of handling flagged images.

EXAM FOCUS	*You should set up workflow automation with Azure Content Moderator to handle flagged images efficiently. This ensures prompt moderation and keeps the platform safe and compliant.*
CAUTION ALERT	*Stay alert to privacy regulations while using AI for image moderation. Ensure that user-uploaded images are handled according to data privacy laws like GDPR or CCPA.*

QUESTION 11

Answer - [A] Implement Azure Monitor for tracking system health and performance metrics.

Azure Monitor provides comprehensive monitoring capabilities for tracking system health, performance metrics, and resource utilization, making it ideal for monitoring the performance of a decision support system and facilitating timely adjustments. Options B, C, D, and E focus on different Azure services but may not provide the same level of monitoring functionality required for a DSS.

EXAM FOCUS	*You should implement Azure Monitor for comprehensive tracking of system health and performance metrics in your decision support system (DSS). It allows you to set up alerts and track resource utilization in real time, ensuring smooth system performance.*
CAUTION ALERT	*Avoid relying solely on basic service logs or manual checks. Azure Monitor provides a centralized, automated way to monitor all critical aspects of your DSS.*

QUESTION 12

Answer - A) Train the speech recognition model with a diverse set of utterances representing different intents.
D) Configure custom speech solutions to handle complex language patterns and contexts.

Option B - Incorrect. SSML primarily focuses on text-to-speech conversion and may not directly impact intent recognition accuracy. Option C - Incorrect. Keyword recognition is useful for detecting specific phrases but may not be sufficient for identifying various intents within speech input. Option E - Incorrect. While fine-tuning model parameters is important, it may not be categorized as necessary for implementing intent recognition effectively.

EXAM FOCUS	*Make sure to train the speech recognition model with a diverse set of utterances to cover all potential intents. Custom Speech can help you handle complex language patterns, enhancing recognition accuracy.*
CAUTION ALERT	*Don't confuse using Speech Synthesis Markup Language (SSML) with improving recognition accuracy—it is primarily for enhancing text-to-speech output, not speech-to-text conversion.*

QUESTION 13

Answer - [B, E] Options B (Azure AI Content Moderator) and E (Azure AI Cognitive Search) align with the scenario of enhancing customer experience through personalized product recommendations while ensuring brand integrity and improving recommendation accuracy based on customer feedback and reviews.

Options A, C, and D are not directly related to the specific requirements of implementing a decision support solution for personalized product recommendations in an e-commerce platform. Option A focuses on user engagement monitoring but doesn't address content moderation or recommendation accuracy. Option C deals with analyzing customer feedback but doesn't directly contribute to personalized recommendations. Option D addresses multilingual support but doesn't directly improve recommendation accuracy or content moderation.

EXAM FOCUS	*Keep in mind that Azure AI Content Moderator helps filter inappropriate content, maintaining brand integrity, while Azure Cognitive Search enhances recommendation algorithms by extracting valuable insights from customer reviews.*
CAUTION ALERT	*Stay alert to not overuse tools like Azure Metrics Advisor for recommendation accuracy. Metrics are useful for engagement monitoring, but Cognitive Search directly impacts recommendation relevance.*

QUESTION 14

Answer - [B] Option B (R-CNN) should be prioritized for precise object detection in the context of smart checkout systems. R-CNN performs region-based analysis, identifying objects within specific regions of an image, making it suitable for accurately detecting products for automated billing.

Options A, C, D, and E represent alternative object detection techniques, but R-CNN (Option B) is preferred for its effectiveness in identifying object regions, which aligns with the requirements of the smart checkout system scenario.

EXAM FOCUS	*You need to prioritize R-CNN (Region-based Convolutional Neural Network) for precise object detection in smart checkout systems. It excels in identifying object regions, making it ideal for retail scenarios.*
CAUTION ALERT	*Stay clear of relying on models like YOLO in scenarios where precision outweighs speed. YOLO might process faster but may not offer the same accuracy as R-CNN for complex retail environments.*

QUESTION 15

Answer - [D] Adjust the container runtime settings to optimize memory usage.

Option D - Increasing the memory allocation for the container (Option A) might not resolve the issue efficiently as it could still lead to memory contention. Optimizing the Dockerfile (Option B) can improve performance but might not directly address memory constraints. Scaling up the Azure AI Service plan (Option C) may not be necessary and could result in increased costs. Upgrading the Azure AI Service resource to a higher tier (Option E) is not the most efficient solution initially. Adjusting the container runtime settings (Option D) to optimize memory usage is the most appropriate action as it directly addresses the memory resource issue.

EXAM FOCUS	*Always consider adjusting container runtime settings to optimize memory usage first. This often resolves resource issues efficiently without additional cost.*
CAUTION ALERT	*Avoid scaling up the service plan or increasing memory allocation unnecessarily. These are costly solutions that might not address the root of the issue, which could be poor memory management in the runtime settings.*

QUESTION 16

Answer - [B) Subscription key, C) Microsoft Entra ID]

Azure AI Services can be authenticated using a subscription key or Microsoft Entra ID.
A) SAML token - While SAML tokens are used for authentication, they are not specific to Azure AI Services.
D) Kerberos - Kerberos is a network authentication protocol, but it's not typically used for authenticating to Azure AI Services.

EXAM FOCUS	*You should use Subscription Keys and Microsoft Entra ID for secure and flexible authentication when accessing Azure AI Services. These methods integrate well with Azure's identity management and access control features.*
CAUTION ALERT	*Don't confuse this with using SAML tokens or Kerberos—while useful for other types of authentication, they are not typically employed for Azure AI Services.*

QUESTION 17

Answer - [A) Utilize a lightweight neural network architecture, C) Optimize model inference speed using quantization techniques, D) Implement multi-threading for parallel processing]

A lightweight neural network architecture helps in reducing inference time without compromising performance, making it suitable for real-time object detection. Quantization techniques further optimize model inference speed, and multi-threading enables parallel processing to enhance real-time performance.
B) Increasing the size of the training dataset may improve model accuracy but does not directly address real-time challenges.
E) While deploying the model on edge devices may enhance inference speed, it might not be sufficient to achieve real-time performance without addressing other optimization techniques.

EXAM FOCUS	*You need to use a lightweight neural network architecture and apply quantization techniques to optimize model inference speed. This reduces the model's size without sacrificing accuracy, crucial for real-time object detection.*

CAUTION ALERT	*Stay clear of focusing only on increasing training dataset size. While more data can improve accuracy, real-time detection requires more focus on model efficiency and performance optimization.*

QUESTION 18

Answer - [B] Extraction of named entities from the text.

Option B - This API request specifically targets the recognition of named entities within the text, providing information about entities such as people, organizations, locations, etc. Sentiment analysis (Option A) and translation (Option C) are not the intended outcomes of this request. Key phrase extraction (Option D) and text-to-speech conversion (Option E) are unrelated to entity recognition and are not part of this API endpoint's functionality.

EXAM FOCUS	*Keep in mind that the API request targets named entity recognition, extracting entities such as people, organizations, and locations. This is crucial for applications that need to understand structured data from text.*
CAUTION ALERT	*Avoid assuming this request handles sentiment analysis or key phrase extraction. While related, they require different endpoints or services within Azure AI.*

QUESTION 19

Answer - D) Azure Cognitive Services - Video Analyzer

Option A - Azure AI Video Indexer is more focused on extracting insights and metadata from videos but may not offer real-time detection capabilities.
Option B - Azure AI Vision Spatial Analysis is suitable for analyzing static images rather than real-time video streams.
Option C - Azure Cognitive Services - Computer Vision is designed for image analysis and lacks comprehensive video processing features.
Option E - Azure Media Services provides video streaming and encoding capabilities but does not offer built-in video analytics for real-time activity detection.

EXAM FOCUS	*You should leverage Azure Cognitive Services - Video Analyzer for real-time video analytics. It's designed to handle the demands of processing live video streams and generating actionable insights such as detecting suspicious activities.*
CAUTION ALERT	*Don't confuse this with Azure AI Video Indexer, which focuses more on metadata extraction rather than real-time analysis. The correct tool for real-time detection and alerts is Video Analyzer.*

QUESTION 20

Answer - B) Azure Cognitive Services - Video Analyzer

Option A - Azure AI Video Indexer focuses more on extracting insights and metadata from videos rather than real-time analysis for traffic congestion.
Option C - Azure Cognitive Services - Face API is tailored for facial recognition and detection, not traffic congestion analysis.
Option D - Azure AI Vision Spatial Analysis is more suitable for detecting spatial patterns and movements in videos rather than traffic congestion analysis.
Option E - Azure AI Metrics Advisor is designed for monitoring and analyzing metrics data, not real-time traffic analysis.

EXAM FOCUS	*Make sure to use Azure Cognitive Services - Video Analyzer for efficient processing of live traffic feeds. It allows for real-time detection and alerting, essential for smart city traffic management systems.*
CAUTION ALERT	*Stay clear of using Azure AI Video Indexer or Face API—while useful in other contexts, they lack the real-time video analytics needed for traffic congestion detection and optimization.*

QUESTION 21

Answer - [C] Implement caching for frequently accessed data.

Option C - Implementing caching for frequently accessed data can significantly improve performance by reducing the need for repeated processing or requests to the AI service. Increasing timeout duration (Option A) or reducing batch size (Option B) may not directly address the root cause of performance issues. Upgrading service plans (Option D) might provide additional resources but does not necessarily optimize performance. Disabling diagnostic logging (Option E) can hinder troubleshooting efforts without addressing performance directly.

EXAM FOCUS	*You should implement caching for frequently accessed data to improve performance. Caching reduces redundant processing, especially when dealing with repetitive requests or commonly requested data.*
CAUTION ALERT	*Avoid assuming that increasing timeout duration or reducing batch sizes will directly resolve performance issues. These tactics may not address the root cause of inefficiencies.*

QUESTION 22

Answer - [C] Custom entity models.

Custom entity models can be tailored to specific domains or contexts, improving accuracy by focusing on relevant entities. Named entity recognition (NER) is a more general approach and may not capture domain-specific entities effectively. Entity resolution is about disambiguating references to entities and is not directly related to extraction. Rule-based matching and frequency-based extraction are limited in flexibility compared to custom models.

EXAM FOCUS	*Make sure to use custom entity models when working with domain-specific text. This approach improves accuracy by focusing on relevant entities that generic models might overlook.*
CAUTION ALERT	*Stay alert when relying solely on named entity recognition (NER). While effective for general use, it may not handle specialized terminology in niche fields like legal or medical texts.*

QUESTION 23

Answer - [B] Azure Translator.

While Azure Text Analytics provides language detection capabilities, Azure Translator is specifically designed for multilingual support and high accuracy in translation tasks. Azure Language Understanding (LUIS) focuses on intent classification and entity recognition, not language detection. Azure AI Language is a broad category covering various natural language processing services but does not specialize in language detection. Azure Cognitive Search is designed for indexing and searching text data, not language detection.

EXAM FOCUS	*You need to use Azure Translator for multilingual customer feedback analysis. It's optimized for detecting and translating multiple languages, providing higher accuracy in a global context.*
CAUTION ALERT	*Don't confuse language detection with other services like LUIS, which focuses on intent recognition, or Text Analytics, which handles broader text processing but not translation.*

QUESTION 24

Answer - [C] Object detection

Option C - Object detection is specifically designed to identify and tag objects within images, making it the most suitable choice for this task. Face detection (Option A) focuses on detecting human faces, while OCR (Option B) extracts text from images. Image analysis (Option D) and spatial analysis (Option E) have broader applications and are not specialized for object detection.

EXAM	*Always remember to use Object detection in Azure AI Vision for identifying and tagging objects in*

FOCUS	*images. It is specifically designed for such tasks, making it the best choice for this scenario.*
CAUTION ALERT	*Stay clear of using broader image analysis features if you are looking for specific object identification. Tools like OCR or Face detection won't meet your object detection requirements.*

QUESTION 25

Answer - C) <say-as> tag

Option A - The <audio> tag is used to include pre-recorded audio files in the speech output, not for dynamically generated content.
Option B - The <prosody> tag is used to modify the pitch, rate, and volume of the speech, but it does not insert dynamic content.
Option C - Correct. The <say-as> tag is used to insert dynamic content such as numbers, dates, or other structured information into the synthesized speech output.
Option D - The <break> tag is used to insert pauses in the speech output and is not meant for dynamic content insertion.
Option E - The <sub> tag is used for substituting one word or phrase with another, which is not relevant for dynamic content generation.

EXAM FOCUS	*Keep in mind that the <say-as> tag in SSML is used for inserting dynamic content, such as numbers, dates, and structured data, ensuring your interactive voice response system remains dynamic and user-friendly.*
CAUTION ALERT	*Stay alert not to confuse the <prosody> or <audio> tags with dynamic content generation. These tags modify tone and play pre-recorded audio, which are different from dynamic content insertion.*

QUESTION 26

Answer - [A] Azure Cognitive Services Language Understanding (LUIS)

Option A is correct as Azure Cognitive Services Language Understanding (LUIS) provides natural language understanding to build conversational AI applications, including intent recognition. Options B, C, and D are unrelated to intent recognition and focus on translation, text analytics, and speech processing, respectively. Option E refers to Azure OpenAI Service, which is not specifically designed for intent recognition but for generating content.

EXAM FOCUS	*You need to use Azure Cognitive Services LUIS for intent recognition in customer service virtual assistants. It provides robust language understanding to interpret user queries accurately.*
CAUTION ALERT	*Avoid using services like Text Analytics or Speech Service for intent recognition, as these are more suited for text analytics and speech processing rather than understanding user intents.*

QUESTION 27

Answer - [A] Inadequate training data for the language model.

Option A - Inadequate training data for the language model can lead to poor comprehension of complex queries as the model may not have learned the necessary patterns and nuances. Insufficient computational resources (Option B) might cause performance issues but are less likely to impact comprehension directly. Compatibility issues (Option C) between frontend frameworks and SDKs may cause integration problems but not necessarily affect language understanding. Similarly, an outdated SDK version (Option D) may cause compatibility issues but should not directly impact comprehension. Limited access to external knowledge bases (Option E) may affect query enrichment but is not the primary cause of comprehension issues.

EXAM	*Make sure to provide adequate and diverse training data for your language model. Inadequate data is one*

FOCUS	*of the most common reasons for poor comprehension of complex queries.*
CAUTION ALERT	*Stay clear of assuming that upgrading the service tier or SDK version will solve comprehension problems. These issues are typically linked to insufficient training data or poorly designed models.*

QUESTION 28

Answer - [A] Azure Speech Translator

Explanation: This service provides real-time translation of speech input into multiple languages with synchronization between speech and translated text. Azure Speech Studio, Azure Translator Text, Azure Cognitive Services, and Azure Language Studio do not offer the specific capabilities required for real-time speech translation with synchronization.

EXAM FOCUS	*Always consider using Azure Speech Translator for real-time, synchronized speech translation in multilingual environments. It provides the necessary tools for translating speech in real time, ensuring seamless communication.*
CAUTION ALERT	*Don't confuse this service with Azure Translator Text, which focuses on written text translation. You need Speech Translator for audio translation.*

QUESTION 29

Answer - [B] Incorporate sentiment-specific lexicons and dictionaries during model training

Explanation: B) Incorporating sentiment-specific lexicons and dictionaries during training enhances the model's ability to recognize and classify sentiments accurately. A) Training with only positive sentiments introduces bias and may lead to inaccurate sentiment analysis. C) Ignoring sentiment analysis overlooks valuable insights from customer feedback, reducing the model's effectiveness. D) Prebuilt models may not capture the nuances of sentiment specific to the retail industry. E) Limiting training data to a single genre may result in a lack of diversity and may not adequately represent the range of sentiments expressed in customer feedback.

EXAM FOCUS	*You should incorporate sentiment-specific lexicons and dictionaries during training to improve the accuracy of sentiment analysis models. Tailored sentiment analysis is key to extracting meaningful insights from customer feedback.*
CAUTION ALERT	*Avoid training the model with only positive sentiments. This introduces bias, and the model will struggle with negative or neutral sentiment classification, reducing its reliability.*

QUESTION 30

Answer - [A] Utilize Azure AI Speech's real-time transcription API with language auto-detection enabled.

Option A - Utilizing Azure AI Speech's real-time transcription API with language auto-detection enabled ensures that the app can transcribe audio streams in multiple languages without the need for language-specific configuration, minimizing latency and complexity. Option B requires maintaining multiple language-specific models, increasing development overhead and latency. Option C introduces additional translation overhead and may impact transcription accuracy. Option D adds complexity and latency due to language detection logic. Option E involves unnecessary duplication of resources and complexity in managing parallel services.

EXAM FOCUS	*You need to leverage Azure AI Speech's real-time transcription API with language auto-detection to support multiple languages efficiently. This approach minimizes latency while offering multilingual support without manual intervention.*
CAUTION ALERT	*Don't confuse real-time transcription with translation tasks. Translating audio before transcription (as in Option C) adds unnecessary overhead and reduces accuracy.*

QUESTION 31

Answer - [A), B), C), and D)] - Implementing auto-scaling, deploying in AKS, utilizing Azure Traffic Manager, and enabling Azure Application Insights align with best practices for ensuring low latency, high availability, load balancing, and performance monitoring in deployment.

E) Incorrect - While token-based authentication is important for security, it might not directly address deployment considerations such as scalability and performance.

EXAM FOCUS	*You should implement auto-scaling, deploy using AKS, and use Azure Traffic Manager to ensure low latency and high availability. Azure Application Insights will help you track performance and identify bottlenecks.*
CAUTION ALERT	*Stay cautioned that using only token-based authentication addresses security, but not scalability or performance. Focus on the architecture's ability to handle high traffic.*

QUESTION 32

Answer - [A), C), and D)] - Implementing regular snapshots, automated backups, and secure storage with Azure Key Vault ensures effective backup and recovery of the language model while addressing security and compliance requirements.

B) Incorrect - While version control systems are useful for tracking changes, they might not provide efficient backup and recovery mechanisms specifically tailored for language model data and configurations.

EXAM FOCUS	*Make sure to implement regular snapshots and automated backups to Azure Blob Storage for secure and effective recovery. Use Azure Key Vault for secure encryption key storage.*
CAUTION ALERT	*Stay alert to not rely solely on version control systems for backups. These systems track changes but may not handle full backup and recovery needs efficiently.*

QUESTION 33

Answer - [B] Azure Translator Text > Language API

Option B - Azure Translator Text service provides real-time translation capabilities, making it the best choice for translating text from one language to another. Option A is incorrect as the Text Analytics API is not designed for translation tasks. Option C is incorrect as Computer Vision is for image processing. Option D is incorrect as Content Moderator is more focused on content moderation. Option E is incorrect as QnA Maker is for question and answer functionality.

EXAM FOCUS	*You need to use Azure Translator Text and Language API for real-time translation of text. It's optimized for high accuracy and multilingual support.*
CAUTION ALERT	*Avoid choosing APIs like Text Analytics or QnA Maker that focus on other tasks like text analysis and question-answering, not translation.*

QUESTION 34

Answer - [A), B), and C)] - Effective knowledge base training involves utilizing diverse datasets, implementing active learning, and incorporating user feedback for refinement.

Option A) - Correct: Utilizing diverse datasets ensures comprehensive coverage and minimizes bias. Option B) - Correct: Active learning facilitates iterative improvement by focusing on informative data points. Option C) - Correct: Incorporating user feedback enables continuous refinement based on real-world interactions. Option D) - Incorrect: Reinforcement learning may not be suitable for knowledge base training in this context. Option E) - Incorrect: Ignoring training data limits the adaptability and relevance of the knowledge base.

EXAM FOCUS	*Always remember to use a diverse dataset and implement active learning. User feedback is crucial to refine your knowledge base continuously, improving real-world application.*
CAUTION ALERT	*Don't confuse prebuilt models with training data. Ignoring real-world data will make your model less adaptive to specific queries and less effective in live scenarios.*

QUESTION 35

Answer - [A), B), and C)] - Maintaining context over multiple interactions involves utilizing session management, stateful conversation handling, and storing conversation history.

Option A) - Correct: Utilizing session management helps track user context across multiple interactions. Option B) - Correct: Implementing stateful conversation handling allows for retaining context throughout the conversation. Option C) - Correct: Storing conversation history in a persistent data store enables referencing past interactions to maintain context. Option D) - Incorrect: While reinforcement learning can optimize conversation paths, it may not directly address maintaining context over multiple interactions. Option E) - Incorrect: Context switches based on user prompts may disrupt continuity and are not necessarily conducive to maintaining context.

EXAM FOCUS	*Keep in mind that session management and stateful handling are critical for maintaining context in multi-turn conversations. Store conversation history to enable smooth transitions and maintain relevance.*
CAUTION ALERT	*Stay clear of over-reliance on context switches based on user prompts, as this can disrupt the natural flow of the conversation and lose continuity.*

QUESTION 36

Answer - [A, B, E] "mcr.microsoft.com/azure-cognitive-services/language/nlu"
"--memory 256 --cpus 4"
"--api-key {API_KEY}"

Option A provides the correct URI for the NLU model container. Option B sets memory and CPU limits. Option E specifies the API key required for authentication. Options C and D are irrelevant for container deployment.

EXAM FOCUS	*You need to correctly configure your container using the appropriate memory, CPU, API key, and the correct container image for the model. This ensures a smooth deployment process.*
CAUTION ALERT	*Avoid overlooking the configuration parameters like memory allocation or API keys, as incorrect setup can cause deployment failures or resource shortages.*

QUESTION 37

Answer - [A, B, C].

A) Implementing role-based access control (RBAC) ensures that only authorized personnel can access and modify the deployed model, enhancing security. B) Configuring auto-scaling ensures that the deployed model can handle fluctuations in workload efficiently, enhancing scalability. C) Encrypting data at rest and in transit protects sensitive information from unauthorized access or interception, contributing to security. D) Monitoring model performance using Azure Monitor is crucial for maintaining optimal performance but is not directly related to security and scalability. E) Optimizing resource utilization using serverless architecture is beneficial for cost efficiency but does not directly address security and scalability concerns.

EXAM FOCUS	*Make sure to implement RBAC, configure auto-scaling, and encrypt data for security and scalability. Monitoring performance helps ensure the deployed model maintains optimal results.*
CAUTION ALERT	*Stay alert not to neglect security best practices like encryption. Focusing only on scalability without addressing security could expose sensitive data.*

QUESTION 38

Answer - [A, D].

A) Implementing session persistence ensures that user context and preferences are retained across interactions, enabling personalized responses and experiences. D) Employing natural language understanding enables the voice assistant to extract relevant context from user inputs, facilitating more accurate and context-aware interactions. B) While Azure Bot Framework supports multi-channel integration, it may not directly address user context management for personalization. C) Integrating Azure Active Directory focuses on user authentication and access control, but it may not directly relate to context management. E) Role-based access control (RBAC) is important for security but may not be directly related to managing user context for personalization.

EXAM FOCUS	*You should prioritize session persistence and NLU to maintain and utilize user context effectively for personalizing voice assistant interactions. This enhances user experience across multiple sessions.*
CAUTION ALERT	*Don't confuse session persistence with RBAC or multi-channel integration. While these are important, they don't directly contribute to maintaining personalized context.*

QUESTION 39

Answer - [C] TextAnalyticsClient

Choice A - TextAnalyticsApiKeyCredential: Incorrect. This choice represents the credential class for the Text Analytics service, not the client itself.
Choice B - TextAnalyticsClientOptions: Incorrect. This choice represents options for configuring the Text Analytics client, not the client itself.
Choice C - TextAnalyticsClient: Correct. This choice represents the client class for interacting with Azure Text Analytics service.
Choice D - TextAnalyticsClientCredential: Incorrect. This choice is not a valid class related to the Text Analytics client.
Choice E - TextAnalyticsApiKeyCredentialOptions: Incorrect. This choice is related to options for configuring API key credentials, not the client itself.

EXAM FOCUS	*Always remember that TextAnalyticsClient is the correct class for interacting with the Text Analytics service. Ensure that your API keys and options are correctly configured for seamless integration.*
CAUTION ALERT	*Stay clear of using the wrong credential classes like TextAnalyticsApiKeyCredential as they don't represent the actual client class, leading to connection issues.*

QUESTION 40

Answer - [D] Azure Cognitive Services.

D) Azure Cognitive Services provides capabilities for detecting and mitigating bias in language models, ensuring fairness and transparency in NLP applications. A) Azure Text Analytics offers basic sentiment analysis but does not specialize in bias detection. B) Azure Language Understanding (LUIS) focuses on understanding user intents and entities and does not specifically address bias in language models. C) Azure AI Translator service is used for translation tasks and does not provide bias detection features. E) Azure Machine Learning can be used for training and deploying models but may require additional customization for bias detection.

EXAM FOCUS	*You should integrate Azure Cognitive Services to detect and mitigate bias in your NLP models. Ensuring fairness in your application will help gain user trust and meet ethical standards.*
CAUTION ALERT	*Don't confuse this with services like LUIS or Text Analytics, which focus on language understanding and sentiment analysis without addressing bias detection specifically.*

QUESTION 41

Answer - [A, D] Azure Blob Storage, Azure Data Lake Storage.

A) Azure Blob Storage is suitable for storing various file types, including PDFs, Word documents, and CSV files, making it an ideal choice for ingesting diverse document formats into Azure Cognitive Search. D) Azure Data Lake Storage is also capable of storing a wide range of file formats and is suitable for large-scale data ingestion, complementing Azure Blob Storage for handling diverse document types. B) Azure SQL Database is primarily for structured data and may not handle unstructured document formats efficiently. C) Azure Cosmos DB is designed for NoSQL databases and may not be suitable for document storage and indexing. E) Azure Table Storage is suitable for structured data but may not efficiently handle diverse document formats like PDFs and Word documents.

EXAM FOCUS	*You should select Azure Blob Storage and Azure Data Lake Storage to efficiently handle diverse document formats like PDFs, Word documents, and CSV files for Cognitive Search ingestion. These are optimal for unstructured data.*
CAUTION ALERT	*Stay clear of using data sources like Azure SQL Database or Azure Table Storage, as they are designed for structured data and may not handle unstructured document formats effectively.*

QUESTION 42

Answer - [C] Azure.AI.TextAnalytics.TextAnalyticsClient

Option A is incorrect because SentimentAnalysisClient is not a valid class in the Azure.AI.TextAnalytics namespace. Option B is incorrect because Microsoft.Azure.CognitiveServices.Language.TextAnalytics.Sentiment is not a valid class for calling the sentiment analysis API in Azure Cognitive Services. Option D is incorrect because TextAnalyticsAPI is not a valid class in the Microsoft.Azure.CognitiveServices.Language.TextAnalytics namespace. Option E is incorrect because TextAnalyticsClient is the correct class for calling the sentiment analysis API in Azure Cognitive Services.

EXAM FOCUS	*Keep in mind that Azure.AI.TextAnalytics.TextAnalyticsClient is the correct class for calling the sentiment analysis API. Ensure your API calls are optimized for the best performance in sentiment analysis tasks.*
CAUTION ALERT	*Stay cautioned against using incorrect classes like SentimentAnalysisClient or TextAnalyticsAPI, as these are not valid for interacting with Azure's Text Analytics API and will result in errors.*

QUESTION 43

Answer - [D] Configure webhooks to notify indexers of data changes.

D) Configuring webhooks to notify indexers of data changes ensures timely and efficient data ingestion and enrichment by automatically triggering indexer execution upon data updates, eliminating the need for manual intervention. A) Scheduling indexers at fixed intervals may lead to delays in processing updated data and may not align with real-time requirements. B) Using Azure Logic Apps to trigger indexer execution adds unnecessary complexity and may not provide direct integration with data sources. C) Manually triggering indexers after data updates is not scalable and may introduce delays in indexing processes. E) While Azure Functions can be used to monitor and trigger indexers, configuring webhooks provides a more direct and streamlined approach to handle data changes.

EXAM FOCUS	*You should configure webhooks to notify indexers of data changes for real-time and efficient data ingestion in Azure Cognitive Search. This automation ensures timely updates without manual intervention.*
CAUTION ALERT	*Avoid relying solely on scheduled or manual indexer triggers, as they may introduce delays in data ingestion and lead to outdated search results. Webhooks offer a more dynamic solution.*

QUESTION 44

Answer - [E] Include both raw and enriched data in Knowledge Store projections.

E) Including both raw and enriched data in Knowledge Store projections allows for comprehensive data analysis and retrieval, providing the necessary flexibility for implementing advanced search capabilities such as faceted search and personalized results. A) Configuring Knowledge Store projections to include only raw data may limit the ability to perform advanced analytics and search functionalities that require enriched data. B) Designing projections to store enriched data in file format may not be optimal for efficient data retrieval and analysis compared to storing in a structured format like tables. C) Implementing projections for object storage with minimal metadata may not provide sufficient context for effective search and analysis. D) Storing projected data in a relational table format can be suitable for certain scenarios but may not fully leverage the capabilities of Knowledge Store for optimizing search and analysis in this context.

EXAM FOCUS	*Always remember to include both raw and enriched data in Knowledge Store projections for comprehensive data analysis. This provides flexibility for advanced search capabilities such as faceted and personalized search results.*
CAUTION ALERT	*Don't confuse storing data in file format or object storage with metadata as a suitable option for advanced search; this approach can limit the analytical capabilities of your Cognitive Search solution.*

QUESTION 45

Answer - D) SSML()

Option A - TextToSpeechService.convertText(): This is a hypothetical method and not part of the Azure Speech service SDK.
Option B - Speak(): This is a hypothetical method and not part of the Azure Speech service SDK.
Option C - Synthesize(): This is a hypothetical method and not part of the Azure Speech service SDK.
Option E - GenerateSpeech(): This is a hypothetical method and not part of the Azure Speech service SDK.
Option D is correct because SSML (Speech Synthesis Markup Language) is used in Azure Speech service to control pronunciation, intonation, and timing during text-to-speech conversion.

EXAM FOCUS	*Make sure to use SSML (Speech Synthesis Markup Language) when controlling pronunciation, intonation, and timing in Azure Speech service. This provides the flexibility needed for generating more natural and customized speech output.*
CAUTION ALERT	*Stay alert not to rely on hypothetical methods like convertText() or Synthesize() as they do not exist in the SDK. Focus on using valid SSML features for text-to-speech conversion.*

QUESTION 46

Answer - [D] Integrating the model into an Azure Virtual Network (VNet).

D) This option allows for secure communication and integration with existing Azure VMs within a controlled network environment.
A) ACI deployment might not offer the necessary network integration required by existing VMs.
B) Azure Functions are suitable for serverless applications but may not integrate seamlessly with existing VM-based infrastructure.
C) Azure Cognitive Services are managed services and may not align with existing VM-based deployments.
E) Azure DevOps is a CI/CD tool and does not directly address integration with existing VM infrastructure.

EXAM FOCUS	*You should integrate your Azure OpenAI model into an Azure Virtual Network (VNet) to ensure secure communication and seamless integration with existing infrastructure based on Azure VMs. This enhances security and performance.*
CAUTION ALERT	*Avoid deploying on Azure Functions or ACI if you need tight network integration with existing VMs. These approaches may not provide the necessary flexibility and network control.*

QUESTION 47

Answer - [A] Providing language-specific templates for common coding tasks.

A) Providing language-specific templates ensures customization and optimization of the code generation process for different programming languages, enhancing developer productivity.
B) Manual language specification may lead to errors and inefficiencies.
C) Limiting to a single language restricts flexibility and may not meet diverse requirements.
D) Automatic language detection introduces complexity and may not accurately identify the intended language.
E) Third-party libraries for translation may introduce dependencies and compatibility issues.

EXAM FOCUS	*You need to prioritize providing language-specific templates for common coding tasks when integrating Azure OpenAI Service into your coding platform. This improves customization and developer productivity across multiple programming languages.*
CAUTION ALERT	*Stay clear of using a one-size-fits-all approach like limiting to a single programming language, as this restricts flexibility and fails to meet the needs of diverse users.*

QUESTION 48

Answer - D) Statement I, Statement II

Option A - Statement I: Language understanding models indeed support intent recognition, making Statement I true.
Option B - Statement II: Language understanding models do not directly support text-to-speech conversion, making Statement II false.
Option C - Statement III: Language understanding models do not directly support language translation, making Statement III false.
Option D is correct because Statement I is true and Statement II is false.
Option E - Statement III: Language understanding models do not directly support language translation, making Statement III false.

EXAM FOCUS	*Make sure you understand that language understanding models support intent recognition but do not provide text-to-speech or translation functionalities. Focus on their primary role in identifying user intents and entities.*
CAUTION ALERT	*Avoid confusing language understanding models with other services like Azure Speech or Translator. These models are designed for natural language understanding, not for speech synthesis or translation.*

QUESTION 49

Answer - [B, D] Analyzing the sentiment of reader feedback on stories generated from different datasets. Conducting comparative analysis of story coherence and plot development using different datasets.

B) Analyzing reader sentiment provides insight into the emotional response evoked by stories from different datasets, indicating their effectiveness.
D) Comparative analysis of story coherence and plot development directly assesses the quality of narratives generated from different datasets.
A) Assessing story length may not capture the qualitative aspects of story improvement.
C) Cluster analysis focuses on thematic variations but may not directly measure narrative quality.
E) Monitoring computational resources usage does not directly assess the impact of datasets on generative outcomes.

EXAM FOCUS	*You should use sentiment analysis of reader feedback and comparative analysis of story coherence to assess the effectiveness of datasets used for generating personalized stories. This provides valuable insights into narrative quality.*
CAUTION ALERT	*Don't confuse story length with narrative quality; it's important to focus on the depth and structure of the story rather than just its duration when evaluating generative AI outputs.*

QUESTION 50

Answer - [B] Implementing additional constraints during training to enforce diversity.

A) Adjusting hyperparameters alone may not effectively balance diversity and quality. C) While a feedback loop is valuable, it may not directly address diversity and quality issues. D) Augmenting the dataset helps, but enforcing diversity during training can be more effective. E) Fine-tuning separate models might be impractical and may not guarantee diversity across all categories.

EXAM FOCUS	*Always remember to implement additional constraints during training to enforce diversity when fine-tuning a generative AI model for image generation. This helps maintain both diversity and quality in the outputs.*
CAUTION ALERT	*Stay alert that merely adjusting hyperparameters or fine-tuning separate models may not effectively solve diversity and quality issues in generated images. Focus on training constraints for better results.*

PRACTICE TEST 7 - QUESTIONS ONLY

QUESTION 1

Your company is developing a chatbot to provide customer support for an e-commerce platform. The chatbot needs to understand user queries, provide relevant responses, and escalate complex issues to human agents when necessary. Additionally, the chatbot should continuously learn from user interactions to improve its performance over time.
Which Azure AI service or combination of services would be most appropriate for this chatbot scenario?
Select all answers that apply.

A) Azure Cognitive Services Text Analytics
B) Azure Cognitive Services Language Understanding (LUIS)
C) Azure Bot Services
D) Azure AI Translator service
E) Azure Cognitive Services QnA Maker

QUESTION 2

Your organization is building a mobile application that assists users with navigation in urban areas. The application needs to provide spoken directions to users based on their current location and destination, supporting natural language inputs for navigation commands.
Which Azure AI service should you choose to fulfill these requirements effectively?

A) Azure AI Speech to Text
B) Azure AI Text Analytics
C) Azure AI Language Understanding (LUIS)
D) Azure AI Text to Speech
E) Azure AI Translator Text

QUESTION 3

When configuring diagnostic logging for an Azure AI service, which Azure CLI command should be used to enable logging for a specific category?

```
A) az monitor diagnostic-settings create
B) az monitor diagnostic-settings update
C) az monitor diagnostic-settings add
D) az monitor diagnostic-settings set
E) az monitor diagnostic-settings enable
```

QUESTION 4

In a scenario where a mobile application needs to authenticate users and access Azure AI services securely, which authentication method provides the necessary flexibility and security?

A) Basic authentication
B) OAuth 2.0
C) Azure Key Vault
D) Shared access signature (SAS)
E) SAML token

QUESTION 5

Your team is deploying a decision support solution using Azure AI services. The solution requires continuous integration and continuous delivery (CI/CD) pipeline integration. Which factor is paramount while integrating Azure AI services into the CI/CD pipeline?

A) Service authentication
B) Dependency management
C) Service versioning
D) Containerization
E) Automated testing

QUESTION 6

You are developing a computer vision solution using Azure AI services and deploying it to an Azure Kubernetes Service (AKS) cluster. You want to ensure that only authorized AKS nodes can access the AI services securely. What should you do?

A) Configure network security groups (NSGs) for the AKS cluster nodes.
B) Use Azure Active Directory (AAD) integration for the AKS cluster.
C) Implement service principal authentication for the AKS cluster.
D) Set up a custom role assignment for the AKS cluster.
E) Enable private endpoints for the AI services.

QUESTION 7

As part of your Azure AI resource monitoring strategy, you need to configure alerts and notifications to ensure timely response to performance issues. What is a best practice for setting up alerts and notifications for Azure AI services?

A) Configuring alerts based on static thresholds
B) Defining alerts for all resource metrics
C) Establishing alerts with long delay times
D) Sending notifications only during business hours
E) Setting up alerts for both performance and availability metrics

QUESTION 8

During the deployment of an Azure AI service, you need to implement authentication mechanisms to ensure secure access to resources. Which approach should you adopt to achieve this goal effectively?

A) Use unsecured HTTP connections for communication
B) Implement basic authentication with hardcoded credentials
C) Utilize Azure Active Directory (Azure AD) for authentication
D) Share authentication tokens publicly
E) Implement no authentication mechanism

QUESTION 9

You need to configure authentication for an Azure App Services web app named App2. The app must authenticate using Azure AD while minimizing administrative effort and adhering to the principle of least privilege. What should you do?

A) Enable Managed Service Identity (MSI) for App2 and assign RBAC permissions to Azure AD.
B) Implement OAuth 2.0 authentication with Azure AD and grant App2 access to Azure AD.
C) Configure App2 to use Azure AD single sign-on (SSO).
D) Enable Azure Active Directory (Azure AD) authentication and configure App2 to use it.
E) Generate a client secret and store it securely for App2 authentication.

QUESTION 10

Your team is building an e-commerce platform that allows users to upload product images for listing. To ensure compliance with platform policies and regulatory standards, you need to implement image moderation using Azure Content Moderator. What is a critical aspect to consider when designing the image moderation process?

A) Integrating with Azure Active Directory for user authentication and authorization.
B) Implementing role-based access control (RBAC) to manage moderation permissions.
C) Defining clear guidelines and criteria for acceptable product images.
D) Encrypting image data at rest and in transit to protect user privacy.
E) Leveraging Azure Functions for serverless image processing and moderation.

QUESTION 11

Your organization is utilizing Azure AI services for a decision support system (DSS) that analyzes financial market data and provides investment recommendations. What approach should you take to optimize the scalability and cost management of the DSS?

A) Implement Azure Data Lake Storage for cost-effective storage of large volumes of financial data.
B) Utilize Azure Functions for serverless event-driven compute and cost optimization.
C) Configure Azure Kubernetes Service (AKS) for containerized deployment and resource scalability.
D) Employ Azure Synapse Analytics for scalable data warehousing and analytics.
E) Use Azure Cosmos DB for globally distributed, highly scalable NoSQL databases.

QUESTION 12

You are deploying a custom computer vision model on Azure AI Vision for image classification tasks. What steps should you take to ensure the model's performance and accuracy?

A) Label images accurately to provide clear training data for the classification model.
B) Evaluate custom vision model metrics to assess its performance on validation datasets.
C) Publish the custom vision model and integrate it into client applications for real-time classification.
D) Use Azure AI Video Indexer to extract insights from videos and enhance the classification model.
E) Choose visual features that align with the specific classification requirements and objectives.

QUESTION 13

Your team is tasked with deploying a decision support solution for a healthcare provider to optimize patient scheduling and resource allocation. The solution should incorporate real-time data analytics and predictive modeling to anticipate patient demand and allocate resources efficiently. Which Azure AI service should you select to meet the requirements of this scenario?

A) Azure AI Metrics Advisor
B) Azure AI Video Indexer
C) Azure Cognitive Search
D) Azure Machine Learning
E) Azure AI Document Intelligence

QUESTION 14

Your team is developing an AI solution for a logistics company to optimize warehouse operations by automating inventory management through object detection in real-time. The solution must handle a diverse range of objects, including packages of various sizes and shapes. Considering the dynamic warehouse environment, which aspect of object detection should you focus on to ensure adaptability and accuracy?
Select all answers that apply.

A) Multi-scale feature extraction
B) Non-maximum suppression
C) Data augmentation techniques
D) Transfer learning
E) Adaptive thresholding

QUESTION 15

While developing a language understanding model with Azure AI Language, you encounter a performance issue where the responses from the model are delayed significantly. What actions could help mitigate this problem?

A) Increase the size of the Azure AI Language resource.
B) Optimize the training data for the language understanding model.
C) Implement caching mechanisms to store frequently requested responses.
D) Scale out the deployment of the language understanding model.
E) Upgrade the Azure AI Language resource to a higher tier.

QUESTION 16

You have an Azure App Services web app named App1. You need to configure App1 to use Azure AI Services to authenticate by using Microsoft Entra ID. The solution must meet the following requirements: Minimize administrative effort. Use the principle of least privilege. What should you do?

A) Create a secret and store the secret in an Azure key vault. Assign App1 role-based access control (RBAC) permissions to the secret.
B) Create a Microsoft Entra app registration and enable certificate-based authentication.
C) From App1, enable a managed identity and assign role-based access control (RBAC) permissions to Azure AI Services.
D) From PowerShell, create a secret that never expires.

QUESTION 17

Your team is preparing a dataset for training a custom object detection model to detect defects in manufacturing processes. Which technique should you employ to augment the dataset effectively?
Select all answers that apply.

A) Random rotation of images
B) Adding Gaussian noise to images
C) Applying random brightness adjustments
D) Flipping images horizontally
E) Cropping random regions from images

QUESTION 18

You are utilizing Azure AI Speech service to process audio data in your application. While configuring the service, you come across an API request using the command: GET https://<resource-name>.cognitiveservices.azure.com/stt/v1.0/diagnostics/speechRecognition. What will be the outcome of this request?

A) Retrieval of speech recognition results.
B) Analysis of speech quality metrics.
C) Generation of synthesized speech from text.
D) Detection of audio sentiment.
E) Translation of speech to text.

QUESTION 19

Your company is exploring the use of video analytics to enhance customer experience in retail stores by analyzing customer behavior and preferences. You need to select a solution that can extract insights from videos to identify popular product areas, customer traffic patterns, and demographics. Which Azure AI service would be most appropriate for this scenario, considering its ability to analyze large volumes of video data and provide actionable insights for business decision-making?

A) Azure AI Video Indexer
B) Azure Cognitive Services - Video Analyzer
C) Azure Cognitive Services - Computer Vision
D) Azure AI Vision Spatial Analysis
E) Azure Media Services

QUESTION 20

Your organization is developing an AI-based security system for monitoring factory operations in real-time. The system requires analyzing live video feeds from security cameras to detect unauthorized access to restricted areas and trigger alerts immediately. Which Azure AI service should you recommend to implement real-time alerting based on the analysis of live video streams for unauthorized access detection?

A) Azure Cognitive Services - Face API
B) Azure Cognitive Services - Video Analyzer
C) Azure AI Vision Spatial Analysis
D) Azure AI Video Indexer
E) Azure AI Metrics Advisor

QUESTION 21

You are encountering interaction issues with the Azure AI Translator service integrated into your application. Which approach should you consider to resolve these issues?

A) Adjusting API request headers for compatibility.
B) Increasing the retry count for failed requests.
C) Reviewing and updating client application dependencies.
D) Optimizing network bandwidth allocation.
E) Modifying service endpoint configurations.

QUESTION 22

Your AI solution involves extracting entities from multilingual documents. Which approach is suitable for handling entity extraction in different languages and dialects effectively?

A) Named entity recognition (NER)
B) Language detection
C) Custom entity models
D) Rule-based matching
E) Entity linking

QUESTION 23

Your organization is implementing a chatbot solution for customer support across multiple regions. The chatbot needs to automatically switch between languages based on user input to provide seamless multilingual support. Which Azure AI service should you use to detect the language of incoming messages and enable the chatbot to respond appropriately in the detected language?

A) Azure Translator
B) Azure Text Analytics
C) Azure AI Language
D) Azure Language Understanding (LUIS)
E) Azure Cognitive Search

QUESTION 24

You are building an application that requires extracting text from images to analyze and process textual content. Which Azure AI Vision feature should you utilize to achieve this functionality?

A) Face detection
B) Object detection
C) Image analysis
D) Optical character recognition (OCR)
E) Spatial analysis

QUESTION 25

You are designing a speech-enabled application that requires precise control over the pronunciation and emphasis of certain words in the synthesized speech output. Which SSML tag should you use for this purpose?

```
A) <phoneme> tag
B) <emphasis> tag
C) <prosody> tag
D) <say-as> tag
E) <break> tag
```

QUESTION 26

Your team is developing a chatbot for a retail website to assist customers with product inquiries. The chatbot must accurately interpret user queries and direct them to relevant product information. Which Azure AI service is best suited for implementing intent recognition in this scenario?

A) Azure Cognitive Services Form Recognizer
B) Azure Cognitive Services QnA Maker
C) Azure Cognitive Services Text Analytics
D) Azure Cognitive Services Language Understanding (LUIS)
E) Azure Cognitive Services Translator Text

QUESTION 27

You are diagnosing an issue with an Azure app that leverages Azure AI Video Indexer to extract insights from a large volume of video content. Users complain about delays in processing videos, impacting the real-time nature of the application. What could be a potential cause of this delay?

A) Network latency affecting communication with the Azure AI Video Indexer service.
B) Lack of integration between the Azure app and the CDN used for video content delivery.
C) Insufficient concurrency settings in the Azure AI Video Indexer configuration.
D) Excessive computational complexity of the video content.
E) Limited bandwidth allocated to the Azure AI Video Indexer service.

QUESTION 28

Your team is developing a speech translation solution for a multinational corporation. They aim to deploy the solution across various devices and platforms to facilitate international communication. Which of the following considerations should they focus on to enhance the user experience?
Select all answers that apply.

A) Latency reduction in translation
B) Optimizing speech recognition accuracy
C) Implementing speech synthesis markup language (SSML)
D) Ensuring compliance with GDPR regulations
E) Integration with Azure Key Vault for secure communication

QUESTION 29

Your organization is integrating a language understanding model with a chatbot to automate customer service inquiries. What is a recommended best practice for managing version control and updates in the language model to ensure smooth integration with the chatbot?

A) Deploy updates to the language model without testing in a production environment
B) Maintain multiple versions of the language model concurrently to avoid compatibility issues
C) Use a version control system to track changes and rollback updates if necessary
D) Implement updates to the language model without considering potential impact on the chatbot
E) Allow developers to make ad-hoc changes to the language model without documentation

QUESTION 30

You are designing an Azure app that will utilize Azure AI Translator for translating text between multiple languages. The app must ensure accurate translations while minimizing costs. How should you implement the translation functionality to meet these requirements?

A) Utilize Azure AI Translator's containerized deployment option with custom translation models for each language pair.
B) Implement direct API calls to Azure AI Translator for each translation request, dynamically selecting the target language based on user input.
C) Pre-translate commonly used phrases and sentences offline and store them in a local database for quick retrieval during runtime.
D) Leverage Azure AI Translator's neural machine translation (NMT) models with automatic language detection enabled for on-the-fly translation.
E) Develop custom translation models using Azure AI Language that are specifically optimized for the app's supported languages.

QUESTION 31

Your team is developing a language understanding model for a healthcare application. The model will be consumed by multiple frontend applications for patient interactions. What strategies should you employ for effective model consumption and integration in this scenario to ensure HIPAA compliance and data privacy?
Select all answers that apply.

A) Implement role-based access control (RBAC) for restricting access to sensitive data
B) Encrypt communication between frontend applications and the model using Transport Layer Security (TLS)
C) Use Azure Key Vault to securely store and manage sensitive information
D) Deploy the model in an isolated Virtual Network (VNet)
E) Regularly audit access logs and monitor data usage patterns

QUESTION 32

Your team is developing a language understanding model for a healthcare provider's virtual assistant application. The model is critical for accurately interpreting patient inquiries and providing relevant medical information. What best practices should you follow to ensure efficient versioning and rollback capabilities for the language model, considering the importance of maintaining data integrity and regulatory compliance in the healthcare domain?
Select all answers that apply.

A) Implement a robust change management process with documented approval workflows for model updates
B) Utilize Azure DevOps pipelines to automate versioning and rollback processes for model deployments
C) Establish a testing environment to validate model changes before promoting them to production
D) Integrate continuous monitoring mechanisms to detect deviations in model performance or compliance violations
E) Apply differential backups to track changes in model configurations and data between versions

QUESTION 33

You are building an Azure app that requires detecting and identifying faces in images uploaded by users. Which Azure service and API combination should you use to achieve this functionality?

A) Azure Cognitive Search > Vision API
B) Azure Content Moderator > Decision API
C) Azure AI Language Service > Text Analytics API
D) Azure Computer Vision > Vision API
E) Azure QnA Maker > Language API

QUESTION 34

What tools and metrics can Azure AI engineers use to evaluate knowledge base performance in a question answering solution?
Select all answers that apply.

A) Implement Azure Metrics Advisor for performance monitoring
B) Utilize Azure AI Content Moderator for quality assessment
C) Measure accuracy, recall, and precision metrics
D) Apply Azure Machine Learning for predictive analytics
E) Rely on subjective user feedback for evaluation

QUESTION 35

What challenges do Azure AI engineers face when implementing multi-turn logic in a question answering solution, and how can they address these challenges effectively?
Select all answers that apply.

A) Handling complex user queries with varying context
B) Managing state transitions between conversational turns
C) Ensuring timely responses without sacrificing accuracy
D) Balancing between personalization and privacy concerns
E) Integrating third-party APIs for additional functionalities

QUESTION 36

Your organization is deploying a custom generative AI model in an Azure container. Which options should you include in the provided bash statement to accomplish this task?
Select all answers that apply.

```
A) "mcr.microsoft.com/azure-ai/generative/model"
 B) "--memory 512 --cpus 8"
 C) "--accept"
 D) "--region westus"
 E) "--api-key {API_KEY}"
```

QUESTION 37

In your AI project, you are integrating a custom NLP model with Azure services for text analysis. Which integration approach ensures seamless interaction between the custom model and Azure services?
Select all answers that apply.

A) Expose the model as a RESTful API using Azure Functions
B) Deploy the model as a Docker container on Azure Kubernetes Service (AKS)
C) Utilize Azure Logic Apps for event-driven model execution
D) Embed the model within an Azure Virtual Machine (VM)
E) Incorporate the model into an Azure Databricks notebook

QUESTION 38

Your team is designing a voice user interface (UI) for a banking mobile application, leveraging Azure Cognitive Services for voice recognition and processing. To ensure seamless interaction across multiple channels, what strategy should you adopt?
Select all answers that apply.

A) Implement channel-specific voice models for optimized performance
B) Utilize Azure Functions for serverless voice processing capabilities
C) Employ Azure Logic Apps for orchestrating voice interactions across channels
D) Implement responsive design principles for cross-device compatibility
E) Utilize Azure Speech SDK for consistent voice recognition across platforms

QUESTION 39

You are developing an Azure application that needs to authenticate users using Azure Active Directory (AAD). Which class should you use to authenticate the user in the provided code snippet?

```
 var credential = new ClientSecretCredential("<TENANT_ID>", "<CLIENT_ID>",
"<CLIENT_SECRET>");
```

```
 A) ClientCredential
 B) ClientAssertionCredential
 C) UsernamePasswordCredential
 D) DeviceCodeCredential
 E) ClientSecretCredential
```

QUESTION 40

Your company is developing a speech-to-text application that transcribes audio recordings of customer service calls for analysis. Data privacy and user consent are critical considerations in processing sensitive speech data. Which Azure AI service should you use to ensure compliance with data privacy regulations and obtain user consent for speech processing?

A) Azure Text Analytics
B) Azure Language Understanding (LUIS)
C) Azure AI Translator service
D) Azure Cognitive Services
E) Azure Key Vault

QUESTION 41

Your team is tasked with automating the ingestion of data from an on-premises SQL Server database into Azure Cognitive Search. As the Azure AI engineer responsible for data ingestion, you need to implement a solution that ensures timely updates and refreshes of the search index to reflect changes in the source database. Which approach should you adopt to handle data source updates and refreshes efficiently?

A) Implement a scheduled Azure Function to trigger data refreshes
B) Utilize Azure Data Factory to orchestrate data pipeline for incremental updates
C) Configure Change Tracking feature in SQL Server and Azure Cognitive Search
D) Use Azure Logic Apps to monitor database changes and trigger index updates
E) Set up a custom webhook to notify Azure Cognitive Search of database changes

QUESTION 42

Your application needs to translate text from English to French using Azure Cognitive Services Translator. Which code snippet should you use to call the translation API?

```
A) Microsoft.Azure.CognitiveServices.Translator.Text.TranslatorClient
B) Azure.AI.Translation.TranslationClient
C) Microsoft.Azure.CognitiveServices.Translator.TranslationAPI
D) Azure.AI.Translation.TranslationAPI
E) Azure.CognitiveServices.Translator.TranslatorClient
```

QUESTION 43

Your team is tasked with implementing Azure Cognitive Search to index a diverse range of documents, including text files, PDFs, and images. To ensure continuous updates to the search index, you need to schedule and run indexers efficiently. Which strategy should you employ to schedule and run indexers for continuous updates in Azure Cognitive Search?

A) Utilize Azure Logic Apps to schedule indexer execution
B) Trigger indexers based on predefined time intervals
C) Configure indexers to run on-demand
D) Implement Azure Data Factory pipelines to orchestrate indexer execution
E) Schedule indexers based on data change notifications

QUESTION 44

Your organization is deploying an Azure Cognitive Search solution to index a large volume of documents for a legal research platform. As part of the implementation, you need to ensure secure access control for projected data stored in Knowledge Store. What is the recommended approach for implementing security and access control for projected data in Knowledge Store?

A) Grant public read access to all projected data
B) Implement role-based access control (RBAC) for fine-grained access management
C) Store all projected data in an open-access repository
D) Encrypt projected data using a symmetric encryption algorithm
E) Share access keys with external collaborators for data retrieval

QUESTION 45

When using Azure Translator service to translate text between languages, which method should you use to detect the language of the input text?

```
A) Translate()
```

```
B) DetectLanguage()
C) IdentifyLanguage()
D) LanguageDetection()
E) GetLanguage()
```

QUESTION 46

You are tasked with customizing an Azure OpenAI language model to better suit the needs of your organization. Which approach ensures efficient customization while maintaining compatibility with future model updates?
Select all answers that apply.

A) Modifying the model architecture to suit specific requirements.
B) Training the model on a representative dataset using Azure Machine Learning.
C) Adding custom prompts to guide model responses.
D) Implementing post-processing techniques to refine model outputs.
E) Rewriting the model's core algorithms to meet unique specifications.

QUESTION 47

Your team is evaluating the usability of code generated by Azure OpenAI Service for a software development project. What key factor should you consider to assess the quality and effectiveness of the generated code in meeting project requirements?

A) The length of the generated code snippets.
B) The readability and maintainability of the generated code.
C) The execution speed of code generated by Azure OpenAI Service.
D) The number of programming languages supported by the code generation models.
E) The availability of technical support for addressing code generation issues.

QUESTION 48

When utilizing Azure AI Speech service for speech processing, which combination of statements is accurate?

A) Statement I: Azure AI Speech service supports speech-to-text conversion.
B) Statement II: Azure AI Speech service provides image recognition capabilities.
C) Statement III: Azure AI Speech service offers text moderation functionalities.
D) Statement II, Statement III
E) Statement I, Statement III

QUESTION 49

You are tasked with fine-tuning an Azure OpenAI model to generate product descriptions for an e-commerce platform. Which process is recommended for tracking and evaluating the model's performance post-fine-tuning to ensure its effectiveness in enhancing product descriptions?
Select all answers that apply.

A) Conducting A/B testing with a subset of product listings to compare the original and fine-tuned model outputs.
B) Implementing periodic retraining of the model with updated product data to maintain relevancy.
C) Monitoring customer engagement metrics, such as click-through rates, on pages featuring descriptions generated by the fine-tuned model.
D) Analyzing the model's loss function during training to assess convergence and stability post-fine-tuning.
E) Establishing a feedback loop with domain experts to gather qualitative feedback on the quality and relevance of generated descriptions.

QUESTION 50

In a scenario where your team is fine-tuning an Azure OpenAI language model to generate personalized product recommendations for an e-commerce platform, what compliance consideration should you prioritize during the fine-tuning process?

A) Ensuring GDPR compliance for user data privacy
B) Implementing explainability mechanisms for transparency
C) Adhering to industry-specific regulations for recommendation systems
D) Securing model checkpoints and training data
E) Managing bias and fairness in recommendation outcomes

PRACTICE TEST 7 - ANSWERS ONLY

QUESTION 1

Answer - [B, C, E] Azure Cognitive Services Language Understanding (LUIS), Azure Bot Services, Azure Cognitive Services QnA Maker

Option A - Azure Cognitive Services Text Analytics: Primarily used for sentiment analysis and key phrase extraction, not for understanding user queries in a chatbot scenario.
Option D - Azure AI Translator service: Designed for language translation and not for understanding user intents or building chatbots.
Option B - Azure Cognitive Services Language Understanding (LUIS): Ideal for understanding user intents and entities, essential for developing conversational chatbots.
Option C - Azure Bot Services: Specifically designed for building and deploying chatbots, integrating with LUIS for natural language understanding.
Option E - Azure Cognitive Services QnA Maker: Useful for creating question-and-answer bots, allowing the chatbot to respond to frequently asked questions.

You should use Azure Cognitive Services LUIS, Azure Bot Services, and Azure Cognitive Services QnA Maker together to build a chatbot that understands user queries, responds appropriately, and can escalate complex issues to human agents.

Stay cautioned that Azure Text Analytics and Azure Translator service are not designed for full conversational capabilities in chatbots. They handle specific tasks but not conversational flow or intent recognition.

QUESTION 2

Answer - [D] Azure AI Text to Speech

Option A - Azure AI Speech to Text: Converts speech to text, not suitable for providing spoken directions.
Option B - Azure AI Text Analytics: Used for text analysis tasks like sentiment analysis, not suitable for spoken directions.
Option C - Azure AI Language Understanding (LUIS): Designed for intent recognition in conversational AI applications, not suited for providing spoken directions.
Option E - Azure AI Translator Text: Translates text between languages, not suitable for providing spoken directions.

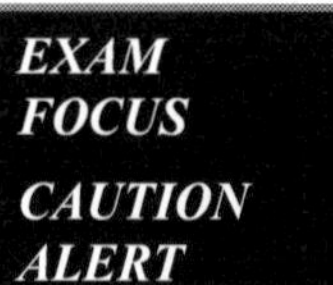

You need to choose Azure AI Text to Speech for spoken directions in a navigation app, as it provides natural-sounding voice output for location-based instructions.

Stay clear of options like Azure AI Speech to Text or Azure AI Text Analytics for this use case, as they handle different tasks such as transcription and text analysis, not speech output.

QUESTION 3

Answer - B) az monitor diagnostic-settings update

Option A - Incorrect. This command is used for creating new diagnostic settings, not for updating existing ones. Option C - Incorrect. This command is not a valid option for modifying diagnostic settings. Option D - Incorrect. This command is used for setting properties of diagnostic settings, not for enabling logging for specific categories. Option E - Incorrect. This command does not exist in the Azure CLI for managing diagnostic settings.

Make sure to use az monitor diagnostic-settings update to modify and enable logging for specific diagnostic categories when configuring Azure AI service monitoring. This ensures proper tracking of diagnostic data.

CAUTION ALERT	*Don't confuse this with az monitor diagnostic-settings create, which is used for creating new diagnostic settings, not updating them.*

QUESTION 4

Answer - B) OAuth 2.0

Option A - Incorrect. Basic authentication may not be suitable for mobile applications due to security concerns and lack of flexibility. Option C - Incorrect. Azure Key Vault is used for storing secrets securely but is not an authentication method. Option D - Incorrect. Shared access signatures are typically used for granting limited access to resources and may not provide user authentication for mobile applications. Option E - Incorrect. SAML tokens are not commonly used for mobile application authentication and may not provide the necessary flexibility.

EXAM FOCUS	*You should implement OAuth 2.0 for secure, flexible user authentication in mobile apps accessing Azure AI services. OAuth 2.0 is widely used for secure API authentication across platforms.*
CAUTION ALERT	*Stay alert that basic authentication is insecure for mobile applications, and SAML tokens may not offer the flexibility needed for mobile environments.*

QUESTION 5

Answer - [C] Service versioning.

Service versioning - In a CI/CD pipeline, maintaining service versions ensures consistency and reliability in deployments. It allows for easier rollback and facilitates testing of specific service versions. Options A, B, D, and E are important aspects but not as crucial as ensuring proper versioning for seamless integration.

EXAM FOCUS	*Always remember that service versioning is critical for integrating Azure AI services into a CI/CD pipeline. It ensures consistency, allows rollback, and supports reliable testing across environments.*
CAUTION ALERT	*Avoid overlooking service versioning, as this could lead to inconsistencies and errors during the CI/CD process, especially when rolling out updates.*

QUESTION 6

Answer - E) Enable private endpoints for the AI services.

Option A - Incorrect. Configuring network security groups (NSGs) may provide network-level security but does not directly address securing access to AI services for AKS nodes. Option B - Incorrect. Azure Active Directory (AAD) integration is more relevant for user authentication than securing access for AKS nodes. Option C - Incorrect. Service principal authentication is more relevant for authenticating applications than securing access for AKS nodes. Option D - Incorrect. Setting up a custom role assignment may provide access control but does not directly address securing access to AI services for AKS nodes.

EXAM FOCUS	*Make sure to enable private endpoints for securing access between your Azure Kubernetes Service (AKS) nodes and Azure AI services, ensuring that traffic stays within your private network.*
CAUTION ALERT	*Don't confuse this with using network security groups (NSGs), which provide network security but don't specifically protect Azure AI services or enforce secure access for AKS nodes.*

QUESTION 7

Answer - [E] Setting up alerts for both performance and availability metrics.

Setting up alerts for both performance and availability metrics - Configuring alerts for performance and availability metrics allows for comprehensive monitoring and timely response to issues affecting Azure AI services, ensuring proactive incident management and service reliability. Options A, B, C, and D may lead to inadequate or delayed alerting, impacting the ability to address performance issues promptly.

EXAM FOCUS	*You need to configure alerts for both performance and availability metrics when monitoring Azure AI services. This approach ensures comprehensive coverage and timely notifications of any potential issues.*
CAUTION ALERT	*Avoid configuring alerts based only on static thresholds or sending notifications only during business hours, as this might lead to delayed responses to critical issues.*

QUESTION 8

Answer - [C] Utilize Azure Active Directory (Azure AD) for authentication.

Utilize Azure Active Directory (Azure AD) for authentication - Integrating Azure AD enables centralized authentication and access control for Azure AI services, leveraging features such as multi-factor authentication (MFA), conditional access, and role-based access control (RBAC) to enhance security posture, unlike options A, B, D, and E, which may compromise security.

EXAM FOCUS	*Make sure to utilize Azure Active Directory (Azure AD) for authentication when securing access to Azure AI services. It offers robust access control and multi-factor authentication.*
CAUTION ALERT	*Stay clear of using unsecured methods like HTTP connections or hardcoded credentials, as they severely compromise security.*

QUESTION 9

Answer - A) Enable Managed Service Identity (MSI) for App2 and assign RBAC permissions to Azure AD.

Option B - Incorrect. While OAuth 2.0 authentication with Azure AD is a valid approach, enabling MSI with RBAC permissions directly meets the requirement with minimal administrative overhead. Option C - Incorrect. Azure AD SSO may provide centralized authentication but may not align with the requirement to use Azure AD directly. Option D - Incorrect. While Azure AD authentication is a valid approach, enabling MSI with RBAC permissions directly meets the requirement with minimal administrative overhead. Option E - Incorrect. Storing client secrets may introduce additional security risks and administrative overhead.

EXAM FOCUS	*You should enable Managed Service Identity (MSI) and assign RBAC permissions to minimize administrative effort and secure your app's access to Azure AD. This approach aligns with the principle of least privilege.*
CAUTION ALERT	*Avoid using client secrets for app authentication, as they can increase security risks and administrative overhead when compared to MSI and RBAC.*

QUESTION 10

Answer - [C] Defining clear guidelines and criteria for acceptable product images.

Clear guidelines and criteria for acceptable product images are crucial for ensuring consistent and effective moderation, aligning with platform policies and regulatory standards. Options A, B, D, and E focus on security, authentication, and infrastructure but may not directly address the moderation process itself.

EXAM FOCUS	*You should clearly define guidelines and criteria for acceptable product images when using Azure Content Moderator for image moderation, ensuring compliance with platform policies.*
CAUTION ALERT	*Stay alert that focusing solely on security aspects like encryption or authentication does not address the core requirement of defining clear moderation standards.*

QUESTION 11

Answer - [B] Utilize Azure Functions for serverless event-driven compute and cost optimization.

Azure Functions offer serverless compute capabilities, enabling cost optimization by automatically scaling resources based on demand and minimizing idle compute time, which is crucial for optimizing the scalability and cost management of a decision support system. Options A, C, D, and E focus on different Azure services but may not provide the same level of cost efficiency and scalability as Azure Functions for this scenario.

EXAM FOCUS	*You should consider using Azure Functions for serverless event-driven compute when optimizing cost and scalability in decision support systems, as it allows for auto-scaling and reduces idle resource costs.*
CAUTION ALERT	*Stay clear of assuming that other services like Azure Cosmos DB or Azure Synapse Analytics will optimize both cost and scalability as efficiently as Azure Functions for serverless workflows.*

QUESTION 12

Answer - A) Label images accurately to provide clear training data for the classification model.
B) Evaluate custom vision model metrics to assess its performance on validation datasets.

Option C - Incorrect. While integrating the model into client applications is important, it may not directly impact the performance and accuracy of the model during training and evaluation. Option D - Incorrect. Azure AI Video Indexer is primarily used for video analysis and may not directly contribute to improving image classification models. Option E - Incorrect. Choosing visual features is essential but is typically done during model configuration and may not directly relate to ensuring model performance and accuracy.

EXAM FOCUS	*Make sure to label images accurately for training a custom computer vision model. Proper labeling is critical for high-performance and accurate classification, and this step ensures the model learns correctly.*
CAUTION ALERT	*Avoid skipping proper validation metrics after training. While publishing the model is important, evaluating performance through validation datasets is crucial before deployment.*

QUESTION 13

Answer - [D] Option D (Azure Machine Learning) is the most suitable choice for deploying a decision support solution that requires real-time data analytics, predictive modeling, and resource allocation optimization in a healthcare setting.

Options A, B, C, and E are not specifically designed for the requirements mentioned in the scenario. Option A focuses on metrics monitoring, Option B deals with video analytics, Option C is for text search and analytics, and Option E is for document processing and insights extraction.

EXAM FOCUS	*You should utilize Azure Machine Learning to incorporate real-time analytics and predictive modeling for healthcare applications. It offers capabilities like training and deploying models for resource optimization.*
CAUTION ALERT	*Don't confuse services like Azure Cognitive Search or Metrics Advisor for real-time predictive modeling; they serve different purposes, such as search and metric monitoring, respectively.*

QUESTION 14

Answer - [A, D] Options A and D are critical for ensuring adaptability and accuracy in object detection for diverse objects and dynamic environments. Multi-scale feature extraction (Option A) allows the model to detect objects of different sizes effectively, while transfer learning (Option D) enables the model to leverage pre-trained knowledge for improved performance in new environments.

Options B, C, and E are less relevant for the scenario described. Non-maximum suppression (Option B) helps reduce duplicate detections, data augmentation techniques (Option C) enhance model robustness but may not directly address adaptability to diverse objects, and adaptive thresholding (Option E) is primarily used for binarization and may not suit the complexity of object detection in a dynamic warehouse environment.

EXAM FOCUS	*Keep in mind that using multi-scale feature extraction and transfer learning ensures adaptability in object detection across diverse environments. These techniques allow the model to perform well across various object sizes and conditions.*
CAUTION ALERT	*Avoid relying solely on techniques like data augmentation or adaptive thresholding for a dynamic environment, as these may not address the core challenge of diverse object detection.*

QUESTION 15

Answer - [D] Scale out the deployment of the language understanding model.

Option D - Increasing the size of the Azure AI Language resource (Option A) may not directly address the delay in responses and could incur additional costs. While optimizing the training data (Option B) can improve model accuracy, it might not necessarily reduce response delays. Implementing caching mechanisms (Option C) can help with frequently requested responses but may not resolve the underlying performance issue. Upgrading the Azure AI Language resource (Option E) is not the most efficient solution initially. Scaling out the deployment of the language understanding model (Option D) is the most suitable action as it can distribute the workload and improve response times.

EXAM FOCUS	*Always remember that scaling out deployment is often a better approach to handle response delays in language understanding models, as it distributes the load across multiple instances and reduces latency.*
CAUTION ALERT	*Stay cautioned that simply increasing resource size or upgrading tiers may increase costs without solving the underlying issue of delayed responses. Focus on scaling out for efficiency.*

QUESTION 16

Answer - [C) From App1, enable a managed identity and assign role-based access control (RBAC) permissions to Azure AI Services.]

Enabling a managed identity in App1 and assigning role-based access control (RBAC) permissions to Azure AI Services meets the requirements of minimizing administrative effort and following the principle of least privilege.
A) Creating a secret in Azure Key Vault introduces additional administrative overhead.
B) Certificate-based authentication may not align with the requirement of minimizing administrative effort.
D) Creating a secret from PowerShell does not leverage Azure AD authentication and managed identities.

EXAM FOCUS	*You should enable Managed Identity for App1 and assign RBAC permissions. This minimizes administrative effort and adheres to the principle of least privilege, ensuring secure and efficient authentication to Azure AI services.*
CAUTION ALERT	*Don't confuse the use of managed identities with creating secrets or certificates, as the latter can introduce unnecessary complexity and increase the risk of security issues.*

QUESTION 17

Answer - [A) Random rotation of images, C) Applying random brightness adjustments, D) Flipping images horizontally, E) Cropping random regions from images]

Augmenting the dataset with various transformations like random rotation, brightness adjustments, horizontal flipping, and cropping random regions helps improve model generalization and robustness.
B) Adding Gaussian noise may not be as relevant for object detection tasks compared to other augmentation techniques.

EXAM	*You need to use diverse augmentation techniques such as rotation, brightness adjustment, cropping, and*

FOCUS	*flipping to improve object detection accuracy and model generalization, particularly for detecting defects in manufacturing processes.*
CAUTION ALERT	*Stay clear of using noise-based augmentations like Gaussian noise, as they might not improve the model's ability to detect object defects effectively.*

QUESTION 18

Answer - [B] Analysis of speech quality metrics.

Option B - This API request is designed to provide diagnostic information regarding the quality of speech recognition, such as metrics related to accuracy, clarity, and other performance indicators. Retrieval of speech recognition results (Option A), synthesis of speech from text (Option C), detection of audio sentiment (Option D), and translation of speech to text (Option E) are not the objectives of this specific endpoint.

EXAM FOCUS	*Always remember that diagnostics API requests, such as speech recognition diagnostics, provide key metrics for assessing the quality of speech recognition systems, helping you fine-tune system performance.*
CAUTION ALERT	*Stay alert not to confuse diagnostic APIs with those used for speech-to-text translation or sentiment detection, as their purposes differ significantly.*

QUESTION 19

Answer - A) Azure AI Video Indexer

Option B - Azure Cognitive Services - Video Analyzer focuses more on real-time video processing and activity detection rather than detailed behavioral analysis.
Option C - Azure Cognitive Services - Computer Vision is more suited for image analysis and lacks the comprehensive video analytics capabilities required for this scenario.
Option D - Azure AI Vision Spatial Analysis is designed for static image analysis rather than in-depth video behavior insights.
Option E - Azure Media Services primarily deals with video streaming and encoding rather than video analytics and insights extraction.

EXAM FOCUS	*You should choose Azure AI Video Indexer to analyze video data for insights like customer behavior, traffic patterns, and demographics in retail. It specializes in extracting insights from large volumes of video data.*
CAUTION ALERT	*Don't confuse Video Indexer with Computer Vision or Video Analyzer, as the latter services focus on image analysis and real-time processing, not business insights from customer behavior.*

QUESTION 20

Answer - B) Azure Cognitive Services - Video Analyzer

Option A - Azure Cognitive Services - Face API is designed for facial recognition and detection, not real-time video analysis for unauthorized access detection.
Option C - Azure AI Vision Spatial Analysis focuses on detecting spatial patterns and movements in videos but may not offer specific features for unauthorized access detection in real-time.
Option D - Azure AI Video Indexer is more suited for extracting insights and metadata from videos rather than real-time alerting for security purposes.
Option E - Azure AI Metrics Advisor is designed for monitoring and analyzing metrics data, not real-time video analysis for security monitoring.

EXAM FOCUS	*Make sure to use Azure Cognitive Services - Video Analyzer for real-time security monitoring in factory environments. It processes live video feeds and can detect unauthorized access or suspicious activity.*

CAUTION ALERT	*Avoid using Face API or AI Vision Spatial Analysis for this use case, as they focus on specific tasks like facial recognition or static spatial analysis, not real-time alerting based on video feeds.*

QUESTION 21

Answer - [C] Reviewing and updating client application dependencies.

Option C - Reviewing and updating client application dependencies can address compatibility issues or conflicts that may cause interaction issues with the AI service. Adjusting API request headers (Option A) might be necessary in some cases but typically addresses specific requirements rather than interaction issues. Increasing retry count (Option B) may not resolve underlying compatibility or dependency issues. Optimizing network bandwidth (Option D) and modifying service endpoints (Option E) are less likely to resolve interaction issues related to client application dependencies.

EXAM FOCUS	*You should review and update client application dependencies when encountering interaction issues with Azure services. This ensures compatibility and reduces potential conflicts that may affect service performance.*
CAUTION ALERT	*Stay alert and avoid increasing retry counts without addressing the root cause. Retry logic helps with transient failures but won't fix dependency or compatibility issues.*

QUESTION 22

Answer - [C] Custom entity models.

Custom entity models can be trained and fine-tuned for specific languages and dialects, providing better accuracy compared to general-purpose techniques like NER or rule-based matching. Language detection is helpful in identifying the language used but does not directly aid in entity extraction. Entity linking associates entities with knowledge bases but does not directly address the language variability. Rule-based matching may not handle language nuances well.

EXAM FOCUS	*Make sure to use custom entity models when handling entity extraction across different languages and dialects. This allows for more accurate extractions, especially when general models are insufficient for specific language nuances.*
CAUTION ALERT	*Stay clear of over-reliance on rule-based matching for entity extraction in multilingual contexts, as it might not capture the intricacies of different languages effectively.*

QUESTION 23

Answer - [D] Azure Language Understanding (LUIS).

Azure Language Understanding (LUIS) is designed to understand and interpret user intents and entities in natural language input, making it suitable for detecting the language of incoming messages for multilingual chatbot support. Azure Translator focuses on translation tasks, not language detection. Azure Text Analytics provides language detection capabilities but is not tailored for chatbot integration. Azure AI Language is a broad category covering various natural language processing services but does not specialize in language detection. Azure Cognitive Search is designed for indexing and searching text data, not language detection.

EXAM FOCUS	*You need to use Azure Language Understanding (LUIS) for detecting language and intent in chatbot applications. It's optimized for natural language understanding and can detect user language and intent in real time.*
CAUTION ALERT	*Don't confuse Azure Translator or Text Analytics with LUIS. While they provide translation and language detection, they are not designed for intent recognition in conversational AI systems.*

QUESTION 24

Answer - [D] Optical character recognition (OCR)

Option D - Optical character recognition (OCR) is specifically designed to extract text from images, making it the most suitable choice for analyzing and processing textual content within images. Face detection (Option A) and object detection (Option B) focus on identifying faces and objects, respectively. Image analysis (Option C) and spatial analysis (Option E) have broader applications and do not specialize in text extraction.

EXAM FOCUS	*Always remember that Optical Character Recognition (OCR) in Azure AI Vision is the key feature for extracting text from images. It's specifically designed for this purpose and works across a variety of image types.*
CAUTION ALERT	*Avoid using other vision features like face detection or image analysis for text extraction, as they are not optimized for textual content within images.*

QUESTION 25

Answer - B) <emphasis> tag

Option A - The <phoneme> tag is used to specify the phonetic pronunciation of a word, which is not related to emphasis in speech output.

Option B - Correct. The <emphasis> tag is used to indicate emphasis or stress on specific words or phrases in the synthesized speech output.

Option C - The <prosody> tag is used to modify the pitch, rate, and volume of speech but does not emphasize specific words.

Option D - The <say-as> tag is used to insert dynamic content, such as numbers or dates, into the speech output.

Option E - The <break> tag is used to insert pauses in the speech output and is not related to emphasis.

EXAM FOCUS	*Keep in mind that the <emphasis> tag in SSML is designed to control pronunciation emphasis in speech synthesis. Use this to highlight words or phrases for clear communication in speech-enabled applications.*
CAUTION ALERT	*Don't confuse this with the <phoneme> tag, which handles pronunciation via phonetic spelling but doesn't control emphasis or stress in synthesized speech.*

QUESTION 26

Answer - [D] Azure Cognitive Services Language Understanding (LUIS)

Option D is the correct choice as Azure Cognitive Services Language Understanding (LUIS) is designed for natural language understanding and intent recognition, making it ideal for interpreting user queries in a chatbot application. Options A, B, C, and E are unrelated to intent recognition and focus on other aspects of AI processing.

EXAM FOCUS	*Make sure to use Azure Cognitive Services Language Understanding (LUIS) for intent recognition. It's purpose-built for identifying and handling user intents in natural language, especially in chatbot scenarios.*
CAUTION ALERT	*Stay cautioned that using QnA Maker or Text Analytics won't provide accurate intent recognition. They are meant for specific use cases like question-answering and text analysis, not understanding intent.*

QUESTION 27

Answer - [C] Insufficient concurrency settings in the Azure AI Video Indexer configuration.

Option C - Insufficient concurrency settings in the Azure AI Video Indexer configuration can lead to delays in processing video content, especially when dealing with a large volume of videos simultaneously. Network latency (Option A) might affect communication but is less likely to cause significant delays. Lack of integration with the CDN (Option B) may impact content delivery but not necessarily processing delays. The computational complexity of the content (Option D) can affect processing time but is not related to Azure AI Video Indexer configuration. Limited bandwidth (Option E) may affect data transfer speeds but should not cause delays in processing.

EXAM FOCUS	*You should check and optimize the concurrency settings in Azure AI Video Indexer to improve processing speed. Proper configuration allows the system to handle large volumes of video data more efficiently.*
CAUTION ALERT	*Avoid assuming that network latency or computational complexity alone are the causes of video processing delays. Often, it's the configuration within the AI service itself that needs adjustment.*

QUESTION 28

Answer - [A, C] Latency reduction in translation, C) Implementing speech synthesis markup language (SSML)

Explanation: A) Reduced latency ensures smooth and responsive communication, enhancing the user experience. C) SSML allows fine-tuning of speech output, improving the naturalness of translated speech and enhancing user experience. Options B, D, and E are not directly related to enhancing user experience in speech translation.

EXAM FOCUS	*You need to focus on latency reduction and implementing SSML to enhance user experience in multilingual speech translation solutions. Reducing delays ensures smoother communication, while SSML adds naturalness to speech.*
CAUTION ALERT	*Stay clear of underestimating the impact of latency in real-time translation applications. It can disrupt user experience and reduce the effectiveness of the solution.*

QUESTION 29

Answer - [C] Use a version control system to track changes and rollback updates if necessary

Explanation: C) Using a version control system enables tracking of changes, facilitates collaboration, and allows for rollback of updates if issues arise during integration with the chatbot. A) Deploying updates without testing may introduce errors and disrupt chatbot functionality. B) Maintaining multiple versions concurrently increases complexity and may lead to compatibility issues. D) Implementing updates without considering impact risks compatibility issues and functional errors. E) Ad-hoc changes without documentation compromise transparency and reproducibility, hindering troubleshooting efforts.

EXAM FOCUS	*Always use a version control system to manage updates and changes to your language models. This ensures smooth integration and rollback capabilities if issues arise after updates.*
CAUTION ALERT	*Avoid making ad-hoc changes or deploying updates without proper testing and version control, as this can introduce bugs and negatively impact the chatbot's functionality.*

QUESTION 30

Answer - [D] Leverage Azure AI Translator's neural machine translation (NMT) models with automatic language detection enabled for on-the-fly translation.

Option D - Leveraging Azure AI Translator's neural machine translation (NMT) models with automatic language detection enabled ensures accurate translations with minimal latency and cost overhead, as the service dynamically adapts to the source language and context. Option A introduces complexity and maintenance overhead with containerized deployment and custom models. Option B requires handling language selection logic and individual API calls for each translation, potentially increasing latency and costs. Option C may not cover all possible translations and could lead to inaccuracies for less common phrases. Option E involves unnecessary custom model development and maintenance for translation tasks already supported by Azure AI Translator.

EXAM	*Keep in mind that leveraging Azure AI Translator's NMT models with automatic language detection is the*

FOCUS	*most efficient way to handle multiple languages while minimizing costs and ensuring accuracy.*
CAUTION ALERT	*Don't confuse using custom translation models or pre-translation approaches with Azure AI Translator's built-in models, as they introduce unnecessary complexity and higher costs.*

QUESTION 31

Answer - [A), B), and D)] - Implementing RBAC, encrypting communication, and deploying in an isolated VNet are essential strategies for ensuring HIPAA compliance and data privacy in model consumption.

C) Incorrect - While Azure Key Vault is important for securely managing sensitive information, it might not directly address compliance and privacy considerations related to model consumption and integration.

EXAM FOCUS	*You should implement RBAC and deploy the model in a Virtual Network (VNet) to ensure restricted access and privacy for healthcare applications. Encryption of data (TLS) is critical to maintaining HIPAA compliance.*
CAUTION ALERT	*Stay clear of assuming Azure Key Vault alone can ensure compliance. While important for key management, VNet isolation and encryption provide additional necessary privacy safeguards.*

QUESTION 32

Answer - [A), C), and D)] - Implementing a change management process, establishing a testing environment, and integrating continuous monitoring ensure efficient versioning and rollback capabilities while addressing data integrity and compliance considerations in the healthcare domain.

B) Incorrect - While Azure DevOps pipelines can facilitate automation, they might not directly address the importance of maintaining data integrity and regulatory compliance specific to the healthcare domain.

EXAM FOCUS	*You need to establish a change management process and set up a testing environment to validate model updates before production. Continuous monitoring for performance deviations ensures no compliance violations occur.*
CAUTION ALERT	*Avoid deploying model updates without a robust testing environment, as this can introduce errors or violations in a healthcare setting, where data integrity is crucial.*

QUESTION 33

Answer - [D] Azure Computer Vision > Vision API

Option D - Azure Computer Vision service with the Vision API enables face detection and identification, making it the most suitable choice for this task. Option A is incorrect as Cognitive Search is not designed for image processing tasks. Option B is incorrect as Content Moderator is focused on content moderation. Option C is incorrect as the Text Analytics API does not include image processing features. Option E is incorrect as QnA Maker is for question and answer functionality, not image processing.

EXAM FOCUS	*Make sure to use Azure Computer Vision > Vision API for face detection and identification. This is optimized for image-based tasks like face recognition in applications requiring visual processing.*
CAUTION ALERT	*Stay cautioned against using services like Cognitive Search or QnA Maker, which are not intended for image processing tasks. Always choose the API that aligns with the task requirements.*

QUESTION 34

Answer - [A), B), and C)] - Tools and metrics for evaluating knowledge base performance include Azure Metrics Advisor, Azure AI Content Moderator, and accuracy, recall, and precision metrics.

Option A) - Correct: Azure Metrics Advisor provides performance monitoring capabilities, facilitating continuous improvement. Option B) - Correct: Azure AI Content Moderator assists in quality assessment, ensuring compliance with content standards. Option C) - Correct: Accuracy, recall, and precision metrics offer quantitative insights into the effectiveness of the knowledge base. Option D) - Incorrect: Azure Machine Learning focuses on predictive analytics and may not be directly applicable for evaluating knowledge base performance. Option E) - Incorrect: Relying solely on subjective user feedback may introduce bias and overlook objective performance metrics.

EXAM FOCUS	*Always remember that accuracy, recall, and precision are critical metrics for evaluating the performance of question-answering solutions. Azure Metrics Advisor can provide insights into these metrics for continuous monitoring.*
CAUTION ALERT	*Avoid relying solely on subjective feedback or predictive analytics from Azure Machine Learning, as these may not provide comprehensive performance insights for knowledge base solutions.*

QUESTION 35

Answer - [A), B), and C)] - Implementing multi-turn logic involves addressing challenges related to handling complex queries, managing state transitions, and ensuring timely responses.

Option A) - Correct: Handling complex user queries with varying context poses a challenge in maintaining conversation flow and relevance. Option B) - Correct: Managing state transitions is crucial for retaining context and guiding the conversation effectively. Option C) - Correct: Ensuring timely responses while maintaining accuracy is essential for a seamless user experience. Option D) - Incorrect: Balancing personalization and privacy concerns is important but may not directly relate to implementing multi-turn logic. Option E) - Incorrect: Integrating third-party APIs can enhance functionality but does not directly address challenges specific to multi-turn logic implementation.

EXAM FOCUS	*You should focus on managing state transitions and handling complex user queries to implement effective multi-turn conversation logic. Proper state management ensures accurate and timely responses across multiple turns.*
CAUTION ALERT	*Stay alert to the challenges of maintaining context in multi-turn conversations. Failing to handle state transitions can disrupt the flow and result in irrelevant responses to user queries.*

QUESTION 36

Answer - [A, B, C] "mcr.microsoft.com/azure-ai/generative/model"
"--memory 512 --cpus 8"
"--accept"

Option A specifies the correct URI for the generative AI model container. Option B sets memory and CPU limits. Option C accepts necessary agreements during deployment. Options D and E are not relevant for container deployment.

EXAM FOCUS	*You need to use the correct container image for deploying generative AI models in Azure. Set appropriate CPU and memory limits for efficient container execution, and always include the --accept option during deployment to streamline the process.*
CAUTION ALERT	*Stay clear of deploying without memory and CPU configurations, as improper resource allocation can lead to performance bottlenecks during container execution.*

QUESTION 37

Answer - [A, C].

A) Exposing the model as a RESTful API using Azure Functions enables seamless interaction with other Azure services through HTTP endpoints. C) Utilizing Azure Logic Apps allows for event-driven execution of the model based on triggers from various Azure services, facilitating integration. B) Deploying the model as a Docker container on AKS and embedding it within a VM or Databricks notebook may require additional configuration for integration.

EXAM FOCUS	*Make sure to expose your custom NLP model as a REST API using Azure Functions and integrate with Azure Logic Apps for event-driven execution. This ensures seamless interaction with Azure services.*
CAUTION ALERT	*Avoid embedding the model in VMs or Databricks notebooks unless necessary, as this increases the complexity of the integration and limits scalability compared to serverless approaches like Azure Functions.*

QUESTION 38

Answer - [C, D, E].

C) Employing Azure Logic Apps allows for orchestrating voice interactions across different channels seamlessly, ensuring consistent user experiences across devices and platforms. D) Implementing responsive design principles ensures that the voice UI adapts to various screen sizes and devices, enhancing usability and accessibility. E) Utilizing Azure Speech SDK provides consistent voice recognition capabilities across different platforms, maintaining a unified user experience. A) Implementing channel-specific voice models may lead to inconsistency and complexity across channels, impacting user experience negatively. B) While Azure Functions offer serverless capabilities, they may not directly address the need for cross-channel interaction management.

EXAM FOCUS	*Keep in mind that Azure Logic Apps help orchestrate voice interactions across channels for consistent multi-platform user experiences. Ensure your app implements responsive design principles and uses Azure Speech SDK for cross-platform consistency.*
CAUTION ALERT	*Stay cautioned against using channel-specific voice models. This could introduce unnecessary complexity and inconsistencies across different devices or platforms, harming the user experience.*

QUESTION 39

Answer - [E] ClientSecretCredential

Choice A - ClientCredential: Incorrect. This choice is not suitable for authenticating with Azure Active Directory using a client secret.
Choice B - ClientAssertionCredential: Incorrect. This choice is used for client assertion authentication, not for client secret authentication.
Choice C - UsernamePasswordCredential: Incorrect. This choice is used for username-password authentication, not for client secret authentication.
Choice D - DeviceCodeCredential: Incorrect. This choice is used for device code authentication, not for client secret authentication.
Choice E - ClientSecretCredential: Correct. This choice is specifically designed for authenticating with Azure Active Directory using a client secret.

EXAM FOCUS	*You should use ClientSecretCredential for authenticating applications with Azure AD. This ensures secure access to Azure services and facilitates proper authentication workflows in your Azure app.*
CAUTION ALERT	*Avoid confusing other credential types like ClientAssertionCredential or UsernamePasswordCredential, which are not suitable for client secret-based authentication scenarios.*

QUESTION 40

Answer - [D] Azure Cognitive Services.

D) Azure Cognitive Services offers capabilities for speech-to-text processing while ensuring compliance with data privacy regulations and obtaining user consent for speech processing. A) Azure Text Analytics focuses on text analysis and does not provide speech processing capabilities. B) Azure Language Understanding (LUIS) is used for understanding user intents and entities in text and does not handle speech data privacy. C) Azure AI Translator service is focused on translation tasks and does not address speech data privacy concerns. E) Azure Key Vault is used for securely storing and managing keys, secrets, and certificates but does not handle speech data privacy or user consent.

EXAM FOCUS	*Always remember that Azure Cognitive Services provides the necessary compliance for speech-to-text solutions, ensuring adherence to data privacy regulations and enabling user consent. This is crucial in handling sensitive customer data.*
CAUTION ALERT	*Stay clear of overlooking data privacy regulations when processing speech data. Azure Key Vault helps manage keys, but you need to ensure that speech processing itself is compliant with privacy laws like GDPR.*

QUESTION 41

Answer - [B] Utilize Azure Data Factory to orchestrate data pipeline for incremental updates.

B) Azure Data Factory provides robust capabilities for orchestrating data pipelines and supports incremental updates, making it suitable for automating the ingestion of data from an on-premises SQL Server database into Azure Cognitive Search while ensuring timely updates and refreshes of the search index. A) Implementing a scheduled Azure Function may lack the built-in capabilities for incremental updates and may require additional development effort. C) Change Tracking feature in SQL Server and Azure Cognitive Search may not provide seamless integration for data ingestion automation. D) Azure Logic Apps offer workflow automation but may not provide native support for incremental updates and data pipeline orchestration. E) Custom webhooks require additional configuration and may not offer the comprehensive capabilities of Azure Data Factory for handling data source updates efficiently.

EXAM FOCUS	*You should utilize Azure Data Factory to handle data pipelines efficiently for incremental updates and ensure timely index refreshes. Data Factory provides the automation and orchestration you need for large-scale data ingestion.*
CAUTION ALERT	*Stay clear of using custom webhooks or Azure Functions unless you need manual handling. Data Factory's built-in orchestration is more scalable for incremental updates.*

QUESTION 42

Answer - [B] Azure.AI.Translation.TranslationClient

Option A is incorrect because Microsoft.Azure.CognitiveServices.Translator.Text.TranslatorClient is not the correct class for calling the translation API. Option C is incorrect because Microsoft.Azure.CognitiveServices.Translator.TranslationAPI is not the correct class for calling the translation API. Option D is incorrect because Azure.AI.Translation.TranslationAPI is not the correct class for calling the translation API. Option E is incorrect because Azure.CognitiveServices.Translator.TranslatorClient is not the correct class for calling the translation API. Option B is the correct choice as TranslationClient is the class for calling the translation API in the Azure.AI.Translation namespace.

EXAM FOCUS	*Make sure to use the correct class and API namespace when working with Azure AI Translation services. The correct class is Azure.AI.Translation.TranslationClient, which allows seamless API communication.*
CAUTION ALERT	*Don't confuse the class names with similar-sounding ones. Using incorrect namespaces or classes, such as Microsoft.Azure.CognitiveServices, will lead to code errors.*

QUESTION 43

Answer - [E] Schedule indexers based on data change notifications.

E) Scheduling indexers based on data change notifications ensures that indexers are triggered automatically whenever there are updates to the source data, enabling continuous updates to the search index without manual intervention. A) Utilizing Azure Logic Apps may introduce unnecessary complexity and may not provide direct integration with data change events. B) Triggering indexers based on predefined time intervals may lead to unnecessary indexing operations when data remains unchanged. C) Configuring indexers to run on-demand may not align with the requirement for continuous updates and may result in delays in indexing. D) Azure Data Factory is primarily used for data integration and orchestration but may not provide native support for scheduling indexer execution based on data change notifications.

EXAM FOCUS	*Always remember to schedule indexers in Azure Cognitive Search based on data change notifications. This ensures that indexing occurs only when there are actual updates, saving resources and improving efficiency.*
CAUTION ALERT	*Avoid scheduling indexers on time intervals alone. This could lead to unnecessary index refreshes, even when there are no data changes, wasting computational resources.*

QUESTION 44

Answer - [B] Implement role-based access control (RBAC) for fine-grained access management.

B) Implementing role-based access control (RBAC) allows for fine-grained access management, ensuring that only authorized users or roles have access to specific projected data based on their permissions. A) Granting public read access to all projected data poses significant security risks and may lead to unauthorized access or data breaches. C) Storing all projected data in an open-access repository disregards security concerns and may expose sensitive information to unauthorized users. D) Encrypting projected data using a symmetric encryption algorithm provides data confidentiality but may not address access control requirements for specific users or roles. E) Sharing access keys with external collaborators may lead to unauthorized access and compromise data security if not managed properly, making it a less secure option for access control.

EXAM FOCUS	*You need to implement role-based access control (RBAC) for fine-grained security management in Azure Cognitive Search Knowledge Store. This ensures secure, authorized access to critical documents.*
CAUTION ALERT	*Stay alert to the risks of granting public read access or sharing access keys. These can lead to data exposure and serious security vulnerabilities.*

QUESTION 45

Answer - B) DetectLanguage()

Option A - Translate(): This is a hypothetical method and not part of the Azure Translator service SDK.
Option C - IdentifyLanguage(): This is a hypothetical method and not part of the Azure Translator service SDK.
Option D - LanguageDetection(): This is a hypothetical method and not part of the Azure Translator service SDK.
Option E - GetLanguage(): This is a hypothetical method and not part of the Azure Translator service SDK.
Option B is correct because DetectLanguage() is used to detect the language of the input text in Azure Translator service.

EXAM FOCUS	*Keep in mind that the DetectLanguage() method is your go-to for identifying the language of input text when using the Azure Translator service. It's designed for quick and accurate language detection.*
CAUTION ALERT	*Stay cautioned against relying on fictional methods like IdentifyLanguage() or LanguageDetection()—these don't exist in Azure's Translator SDK.*

QUESTION 46

Answer - [B, C] Training the model on a representative dataset using Azure Machine Learning. Adding custom prompts to guide model responses.

B) Training on a representative dataset allows the model to learn from specific organizational data while maintaining

compatibility with future updates.
C) Adding custom prompts guides the model to produce responses aligned with organizational requirements.
A) Modifying the model architecture could lead to compatibility issues with future updates.
D) Post-processing techniques are applied after model inference and do not directly influence model customization.
E) Rewriting core algorithms introduces complexity and may not align with future updates or model improvements.

EXAM FOCUS	*You should train your Azure OpenAI model on a representative dataset and use custom prompts to guide its behavior while ensuring compatibility with future updates. This keeps the customization flexible and manageable.*
CAUTION ALERT	*Avoid modifying the model architecture or core algorithms, as this can cause compatibility issues with future updates and increase the complexity of maintenance.*

QUESTION 47

Answer - [B] The readability and maintainability of the generated code.

B) Readability and maintainability are critical factors in assessing the quality and effectiveness of generated code, ensuring ease of understanding and future modifications.
A) Code length may not correlate with quality and may vary based on task complexity.
C) Execution speed is important but does not directly reflect code quality.
D) Language support is relevant but does not assess code quality.
E) Technical support is valuable but does not directly influence code quality assessment.

EXAM FOCUS	*Make sure to prioritize readability and maintainability when evaluating generated code from Azure OpenAI Service. Clean and maintainable code ensures long-term efficiency and ease of updates.*
CAUTION ALERT	*Avoid focusing solely on code length or execution speed—these factors don't necessarily correlate with quality or project alignment.*

QUESTION 48

Answer - E) Statement I, Statement III

Option A - Statement I: Azure AI Speech service indeed supports speech-to-text conversion, making Statement I true.
Option B - Statement II: Azure AI Speech service does not provide image recognition capabilities, making Statement II false.
Option C - Statement III: Azure AI Speech service does not offer text moderation functionalities, making Statement III false.
Option D - Statement II: Azure AI Speech service does not provide image recognition capabilities, making Statement II false.
Option E is correct because Statement I is true and Statement III is false.

EXAM FOCUS	*Always remember that the Azure AI Speech service supports speech-to-text conversion. This core feature is critical in many speech-based applications.*
CAUTION ALERT	*Stay clear of thinking that speech services include image recognition or text moderation; they are distinct and unrelated services.*

QUESTION 49

Answer - [A, C] Conducting A/B testing with a subset of product listings to compare the original and fine-tuned model outputs. Monitoring customer engagement metrics, such as click-through rates, on pages featuring descriptions generated by the fine-tuned model.

A) A/B testing allows direct comparison between the original and fine-tuned model outputs, providing quantitative insights into performance improvement.

C) Monitoring customer engagement metrics offers real-world feedback on the effectiveness of the fine-tuned model in driving user interaction.

B) Periodic retraining is important but focuses on model maintenance rather than post-fine-tuning evaluation.

D) Analyzing loss function convergence is relevant during training but may not fully capture performance post-fine-tuning.

E) Establishing a feedback loop is valuable but may not provide immediate performance evaluation metrics.

EXAM FOCUS	*You should conduct A/B testing and monitor engagement metrics (like click-through rates) to assess the performance of fine-tuned models for generating product descriptions. This provides real-world insights into effectiveness.*
CAUTION ALERT	*Avoid relying solely on loss function analysis during training; while useful, it doesn't capture post-deployment performance or user engagement metrics.*

QUESTION 50

Answer - [E] Managing bias and fairness in recommendation outcomes.

A) While GDPR compliance is important, it may not directly relate to model fine-tuning. B) Explainability is crucial but may not be the top priority during fine-tuning. C) Industry regulations are important but may not specifically address model fine-tuning concerns. D) Securing checkpoints and data is essential but not directly related to bias and fairness in recommendations.

EXAM FOCUS	*Make sure to manage bias and fairness in your fine-tuned Azure OpenAI models, especially when creating personalized recommendations. This ensures ethical AI practices and a positive user experience.*
CAUTION ALERT	*Don't confuse compliance with GDPR and other data regulations as the only priority—bias management and fairness are equally critical during model fine-tuning.*

PRACTICE TEST 8 - QUESTIONS ONLY

QUESTION 1

Your team is working on a project that involves analyzing large volumes of text data to identify trends and patterns in customer feedback. The project requires extracting key phrases, determining sentiment, and categorizing feedback into predefined topics. Furthermore, the solution should be scalable and support multiple languages.
Which Azure AI service or combination of services would best meet these requirements? Select all answers that apply.

A) Azure Cognitive Services Text Analytics
B) Azure Cognitive Services Language Understanding (LUIS)
C) Azure Bot Services
D) Azure AI Translator service
E) Azure Cognitive Services QnA Maker

QUESTION 2

Your team is developing a call center solution for a telecommunications company. The solution needs to transcribe customer calls in real-time, identify customer sentiment, and escalate calls based on predefined criteria. Additionally, it should support integration with existing CRM systems for call routing.
Which Azure AI service or combination of services should you select to meet these requirements effectively?
Select all answers that apply.

A) Azure AI Speech to Text
B) Azure AI Text Analytics
C) Azure AI Language Understanding (LUIS)
D) Azure AI Text to Speech
E) Azure AI Translator Text

QUESTION 3

To view the details of a custom translation model deployed on Azure AI Translator service, which Azure CLI command should be used?

A) az translator model show
B) az translator model list
C) az translator model get
D) az translator model view
E) az translator model info

QUESTION 4

You are implementing a chatbot solution that integrates Azure AI Language services. Which authentication method should you use to ensure that the chatbot can securely access the language processing capabilities without exposing sensitive information?

A) Azure Active Directory (AAD)
B) API key
C) OAuth 2.0
D) Shared access signature (SAS)
E) Certificate authentication

QUESTION 5

You are designing a container deployment strategy for an Azure AI service that requires frequent updates and scalability. Which aspect should be prioritized to optimize container deployment for this scenario?

A) Container orchestration
B) Image size optimization
C) Resource utilization monitoring
D) Network security
E) Service discovery

QUESTION 6

You are designing an Azure AI solution that incorporates Azure Cognitive Services for language processing. The solution requires access from on-premises servers to the cognitive services securely. What should you do?

A) Configure ExpressRoute for private network connectivity.
B) Use a shared access signature (SAS) token for authentication.
C) Set up a VPN gateway for secure tunneling.
D) Implement Azure Key Vault for storing authentication credentials.
E) Expose the cognitive services endpoints to the public internet.

QUESTION 7

Your organization needs to analyze usage patterns of Azure AI resources to optimize resource allocation and cost efficiency. Which tool should you utilize for real-time monitoring and analysis of Azure AI service usage?

A) Azure Monitor Logs
B) Azure Data Factory
C) Azure Resource Graph
D) Azure Cost Management
E) Azure Application Insights

QUESTION 8

Your team is developing an Azure AI solution that requires secure communication between various components. Which strategy should you employ to ensure secure communication between Azure AI services?

A) Use plaintext communication for simplicity
B) Implement Transport Layer Security (TLS) encryption
C) Share sensitive data openly over the network
D) Disable encryption to improve performance
E) Rely on third-party encryption tools

QUESTION 9

You are tasked with configuring authentication for an Azure App Services web app named App3. The app needs to authenticate using Azure AD with minimal administrative effort and adherence to the principle of least privilege. What action should you take?

A) Generate a client secret and store it securely for App3 authentication.
B) Use Azure Active Directory (Azure AD) authentication and configure App3 to use it.
C) Implement OAuth 2.0 authentication with Azure AD and grant App3 access to Azure AD.
D) Enable Managed Service Identity (MSI) for App3 and assign RBAC permissions to Azure AD.
E) Configure App3 to use Azure AD single sign-on (SSO).

QUESTION 10

You are tasked with implementing image moderation for a social media platform that experiences a high volume of image uploads daily. Which approach can help efficiently process and moderate large volumes of images while maintaining low latency?

A) Utilizing Azure Kubernetes Service (AKS) for containerized image moderation.
B) Implementing Azure Functions with Azure Queue Storage for asynchronous image processing.
C) Deploying Azure Virtual Machines with GPU acceleration for parallel image analysis.
D) Leveraging Azure CDN for caching and delivering moderated images globally.
E) Integrating Azure Logic Apps for orchestrating image moderation workflows.

QUESTION 11

Your team is responsible for maintaining a decision support system (DSS) that analyzes healthcare data to optimize patient care. What is a key consideration when adjusting AI models based on performance feedback to ensure regulatory compliance and patient privacy?

A) Incorporating federated learning techniques to train AI models on decentralized healthcare data sources.
B) Ensuring compliance with HIPAA regulations for handling sensitive patient information and data privacy.
C) Implementing differential privacy mechanisms to protect individual patient data and maintain anonymity.
D) Utilizing homomorphic encryption for secure computation on encrypted healthcare data.
E) Employing blockchain technology for maintaining an immutable audit trail of AI model updates and data access.

QUESTION 12

You are responsible for implementing a decision support solution on Azure AI Metrics Advisor for data monitoring. Which actions should you take to effectively configure and manage the solution?

A) Provision a Metrics Advisor resource and define data sources for monitoring.
B) Implement custom moderation policies to filter out irrelevant data from the monitoring process.
C) Define key metrics and anomaly detection thresholds to trigger alerts for potential issues.
D) Utilize Azure Cognitive Search to index and search through historical monitoring data for analysis.
E) Configure automated actions to respond to detected anomalies and optimize system performance.

QUESTION 13

As a senior Azure AI engineer, you are reviewing the architecture of a decision support solution developed by your team. The solution integrates multiple Azure AI services to analyze customer feedback and sentiment from social media channels to drive marketing strategies. During the review, you notice that the solution lacks proper encryption of sensitive data transmitted between services. Which action should you recommend to address this security concern?

A) Implement Azure Key Vault to store and manage encryption keys used by Azure AI services.
B) Enable Azure Active Directory (Azure AD) authentication for all Azure AI services involved in data transmission.
C) Configure Azure Private Link to establish private communication channels between Azure AI services.
D) Apply Azure Role-Based Access Control (RBAC) to restrict access to sensitive data within Azure AI services.
E) Deploy Azure Virtual Network Service Endpoints to isolate Azure AI services from public internet access.

QUESTION 14

You are architecting an AI solution for a smart city project aimed at enhancing public safety through real-time surveillance and threat detection. The solution requires object detection capabilities to identify potential security threats, such as abandoned objects or suspicious behavior. Which factor should you consider to optimize object detection performance for this scenario?
Select all answers that apply.

A) Minimizing false positives
B) Maximizing recall rate
C) Reducing model complexity
D) Enhancing object localization accuracy
E) Increasing inference speed

QUESTION 15

During the deployment of a custom computer vision model using Azure AI Vision, you encounter an error stating "Model not found." Which actions should you take to troubleshoot and resolve this issue?

A) Verify the permissions of the Azure AI Vision resource.
B) Check if the custom vision model has been properly trained and published.
C) Review the configuration settings of the Azure AI Vision resource.
D) Ensure that the container environment has access to the Azure AI Vision API endpoint.
E) Upgrade the Azure AI Vision resource to a higher tier.

QUESTION 16

You have an Azure AI Services resource. You need to enable diagnostic logging. What are two prerequisites for diagnostic logging? Each correct answer presents a complete solution.
Select all answers that apply.

A) Log Analytics workspace
B) An Azure Cosmos DB for NoSQL account
C) An Azure Key Vault
D) An Azure SQL database
E) An Azure Storage account

QUESTION 17

You are evaluating the performance of a custom object detection model trained on Azure AI Vision for detecting vehicles in surveillance footage. Which cross-validation technique should you employ to ensure reliable model evaluation?

A) Holdout validation
B) K-fold cross-validation
C) Leave-one-out cross-validation
D) Stratified cross-validation
E) Time series cross-validation

QUESTION 18

In your application, you are utilizing Azure Cognitive Search for implementing search functionality. While configuring the service, you encounter an API request using the command: POST https://<resource-name>.search.windows.net/indexes/<index-name>/docs/search. What outcome can you expect from this request?

A) Indexing of documents in the search service.
B) Retrieval of search results based on specified criteria.
C) Analysis of search performance metrics.
D) Translation of search queries to multiple languages.
E) Synthesis of search results into a structured format.

QUESTION 19

Your team is tasked with implementing a solution to analyze video recordings of manufacturing processes to identify defects and optimize production efficiency. The solution requires the ability to track specific objects and detect irregularities in assembly lines. Considering the need for precision and accuracy, which Azure AI service should you choose to perform object tracking and anomaly detection effectively?

A) Azure AI Video Indexer
B) Azure Cognitive Services - Computer Vision
C) Azure Cognitive Services - Video Analyzer
D) Azure AI Vision Spatial Analysis
E) Azure Media Services

QUESTION 20

Your team is working on a project to develop an AI-powered wildlife monitoring system for a national park. The system requires analyzing live video streams from remote cameras to detect and track animal movements and behavior patterns. To ensure scalability and efficient processing of live video feeds, which Azure AI service should you recommend that supports the incorporation of custom AI models for wildlife analysis in real-time?

A) Azure Cognitive Services - Video Analyzer
B) Azure AI Vision Spatial Analysis
C) Azure AI Video Indexer
D) Azure Cognitive Services - Custom Vision
E) Azure Machine Learning service

QUESTION 21

You are encountering errors related to authentication when accessing the Azure AI Speech service in your application. Which action should you take to resolve this issue?

A) Refreshing the authentication token at regular intervals.
B) Reviewing and updating API request parameters.
C) Renewing the service account credentials.
D) Implementing multi-factor authentication for service access.
E) Adding IP restrictions to the service configuration.

QUESTION 22

You are designing an AI solution to extract entities from noisy and inconsistent text data. Which technique can help mitigate challenges in entity extraction from such unstructured text?

A) Named entity recognition (NER)
B) Custom entity models
C) Sentiment analysis
D) Machine learning
E) Rule-based matching

QUESTION 23

Your team is building an AI-driven content moderation system for a social media platform. The system needs to accurately identify and filter out inappropriate content across multiple languages. Which approach should you prioritize to ensure effective language detection and content moderation in a multilingual environment?

A) Rule-based language detection
B) Pre-trained language detection models

C) Custom language detection models
D) Frequency-based language detection
E) Lexicon-based language detection

QUESTION 24

You are tasked with developing an application that needs to detect the presence of people in images. Which Azure AI Vision feature should you leverage for this requirement?

A) Face detection
B) Image analysis
C) Optical character recognition (OCR)
D) Object detection
E) Spatial analysis

QUESTION 25

You are developing a speech synthesis application that requires inserting pauses of varying lengths between words in the synthesized speech output. Which SSML tag should you use to achieve this?

A) <audio> tag
B) <break> tag
C) <prosody> tag
D) <sub> tag
E) <emphasis> tag

QUESTION 26

Your organization is developing a voice-controlled smart home system. The system needs to understand spoken commands to control various IoT devices in the home. Which Azure AI service should you use to implement intent recognition for processing voice commands?

A) Azure Cognitive Services Translator Text
B) Azure Cognitive Services Text Analytics
C) Azure Cognitive Services Language Understanding (LUIS)
D) Azure Cognitive Services Speech Service
E) Azure OpenAI Service

QUESTION 27

You are investigating a performance issue with an Azure app that utilizes Azure AI Translator for real-time language translation. Users notice a delay in translation responses, affecting the app's responsiveness. What could be a possible reason for this delay?

A) Insufficient permissions assigned to the Azure AI Translator service.
B) Incompatibility between the app's frontend technology and the Azure AI Translator SDK.
C) Network congestion impacting data transmission to and from the Azure AI Translator service.
D) Insufficient memory allocated to the Azure AI Translator service instance.
E) Outdated version of the Azure AI Translator SDK being used in the app.

QUESTION 28

Your company is exploring the integration of speech translation capabilities into its customer service chatbot to cater to a global customer base. Which challenge should your team consider while achieving high-quality speech translation in this scenario?

A) Scalability of the translation service
B) Availability of language models
C) Accuracy of sentiment analysis
D) Compatibility with legacy systems
E) Integration with social media platforms

QUESTION 29

Your team is tasked with creating a language understanding model in Azure to enhance customer support interactions for a multinational e-commerce platform. Which step is essential during the creation of the language understanding model to ensure accurate intent recognition and entity extraction?

A) Include a diverse set of training phrases for each intent
B) Define intents based solely on customer feedback
C) Limit the number of entities to improve model efficiency
D) Use prebuilt language models without customization
E) Ignore entity extraction and focus solely on intent recognition

QUESTION 30

You are developing an Azure app that will use Azure AI Computer Vision for image analysis. The app must be capable of detecting and extracting text from images captured by users' devices. What would be the most suitable approach to implement this functionality?

A) Utilize Azure AI Computer Vision's OCR API to extract text directly from uploaded images.
B) Implement an image preprocessing pipeline in the app to enhance text visibility and then use Azure AI Computer Vision's OCR API for text extraction.
C) Leverage Azure AI Translator to translate the captured text into a standardized format before passing it to Azure AI Computer Vision for analysis.
D) Develop a custom deep learning model using Azure AI Vision to specifically target text extraction from images.
E) Utilize Azure AI Language to perform optical character recognition (OCR) on the images and extract text directly within the app.

QUESTION 31

Your team has deployed a language understanding model for a finance application, and you need to ensure continuous monitoring and management of its performance in production. Which practices should you implement to achieve this goal effectively while minimizing service disruptions?
Select all answers that apply.

A) Implement automated anomaly detection for identifying performance deviations
B) Set up alerts for threshold breaches in model response times
C) Utilize Azure DevOps for version control and rollback capabilities
D) Schedule regular performance testing and optimization cycles
E) Implement canary deployments for gradual rollout of model updates

QUESTION 32

As part of a language understanding model deployment for an e-commerce chatbot, you need to ensure effective backup and recovery strategies to mitigate the risk of data loss or corruption. Additionally, compliance with data protection regulations is paramount. What steps should you take to address these requirements and ensure seamless restoration of the language model in case of unexpected incidents or failures?
Select all answers that apply.

A) Configure regular backups of model checkpoints and training data to Azure Blob Storage with encryption enabled

B) Implement versioning of model configurations and maintain a rollback mechanism for reverting to previous states
C) Utilize Azure Key Vault for secure storage of authentication credentials and encryption keys used to access model data
D) Integrate automated testing routines to verify the integrity and functionality of backup data and recovery processes
E) Establish access controls and audit trails to monitor changes to model configurations and backups

QUESTION 33

Your organization is developing an Azure app that needs to transcribe audio files into text format. Which Azure service and API combination should you implement to achieve this requirement?

A) Azure Cognitive Search > Language API
B) Azure Speech Service > Speech API
C) Azure AI Language Service > Text Analytics API
D) Azure Computer Vision > Vision API
E) Azure Content Moderator > Language API

QUESTION 34

How can Azure AI engineers address gaps in knowledge coverage effectively in a question answering solution?
Select all answers that apply.

A) Conduct regular audits to identify and fill knowledge gaps
B) Implement user profiling for personalized recommendations
C) Ignore minor gaps to focus on broader content areas
D) Utilize machine learning to predict potential knowledge gaps
E) Integrate third-party knowledge bases for comprehensive coverage

QUESTION 35

How can Azure AI engineers enhance user experience through multi-turn capability in a question answering solution, considering technical aspects and usability principles?
Select all answers that apply.

A) Implement context-aware response generation
B) Utilize sentiment analysis for adaptive interaction
C) Offer personalized recommendations based on user history
D) Enable seamless handoff to human agents when needed
E) Ensure compatibility with various communication channels

QUESTION 36

You are deploying a custom image classification model in an Azure container environment. Which options should you select to complete the provided bash statement?
Select all answers that apply.

```
A) "mcr.microsoft.com/azure-cognitive-services/vision/classification"
B) "--memory 384 --cpus 6"
C) "--accept"
D) "--region centralus"
E) "--api-key {API_KEY}"
```

QUESTION 37

Your team is tasked with monitoring and managing a custom NLP model deployed on Azure for sentiment analysis.

Which actions should be prioritized to ensure the model's effectiveness and reliability in production?
Select all answers that apply.

A) Set up alerts for abnormal model behavior
B) Perform regular performance optimization
C) Implement version control for model updates
D) Conduct periodic retraining with new data
E) Establish failover mechanisms for model availability

QUESTION 38

Your organization is developing a voice assistant for a retail e-commerce website, aiming to provide personalized recommendations and support for users. What challenge in voice interaction design should you prioritize addressing to enhance user engagement and satisfaction?
Select all answers that apply.

A) Handling noisy environments for accurate voice recognition
B) Providing real-time feedback during voice interactions
C) Integrating natural language understanding for context-aware responses
D) Managing latency for responsive voice assistant performance
E) Implementing multimodal interaction for enhanced user experiences

QUESTION 39

You are working on a project that involves training and deploying custom machine learning models using Azure Machine Learning service. In the provided code snippet, which class should you use to interact with Azure Machine Learning service?

```
var mlClient = new MachineLearningManagementClient(new TokenCredentials("<TOKEN>"), new Uri("<ML_ENDPOINT>"));
```

```
A) TokenCredentials
B) MachineLearningManagementClient
C) MachineLearningClient
D) AzureMachineLearningCredential
E) AzureMachineLearningClient
```

QUESTION 40

Your team is developing a language understanding model for a chatbot that interacts with customers to provide support. Transparency and explainability of the model's decisions are crucial for building trust with users. Which Azure AI service should you use to ensure transparency and explainability in the language understanding model?

A) Azure Text Analytics
B) Azure Language Understanding (LUIS)
C) Azure AI Translator service
D) Azure Cognitive Services
E) Azure Machine Learning

QUESTION 41

Your organization is deploying an Azure Cognitive Search solution to index and search a large volume of documents stored in Azure Blob Storage. As the Azure AI engineer responsible for optimizing data ingestion performance, you need to implement strategies that ensure efficient ingestion of documents into the search index. Which strategy should you prioritize to optimize data ingestion performance for Azure Cognitive Search?

A) Parallelize document ingestion using Azure Data Factory

B) Optimize document metadata for efficient indexing
C) Configure indexers with appropriate batch sizes and concurrency settings
D) Utilize Azure Queue Storage for asynchronous document processing
E) Implement caching mechanisms to reduce latency during document retrieval

QUESTION 42

You are implementing a feature in your application that utilizes Azure Speech service for text-to-speech conversion. Which code snippet should you use to create a SpeechSynthesizer object?

A) Microsoft.CognitiveServices.Speech.SpeechSynthesis.SpeechSynthesizer.CreateSpeechSynthesizer()
B) Microsoft.Azure.CognitiveServices.Speech.SpeechSynthesizer.CreateSynthesizer()
C) Azure.AI.Speech.SpeechSynthesizer.CreateSpeechSynthesizer()
D) Azure.CognitiveServices.Speech.SpeechSynthesis.SpeechSynthesizer.CreateSynthesizer()
E) Microsoft.Azure.CognitiveServices.Speech.SpeechSynthesis.SpeechSynthesizer.CreateSpeechSynthesizer()

QUESTION 43

Your organization is deploying Azure Cognitive Search to index a large volume of structured and unstructured data from various sources. During indexer execution, you encounter errors and exceptions that impact the indexing process. What should you do to handle errors and exceptions effectively during indexer execution in Azure Cognitive Search?

A) Implement retry logic within indexers
B) Manually re-run indexers after resolving errors
C) Increase the indexer timeout duration
D) Configure alerting for indexer failures
E) Optimize data source connections for reliability

QUESTION 44

You are designing an Azure Cognitive Search solution for a healthcare organization to index patient records and medical documents. The organization requires efficient retrieval of structured data stored in Knowledge Store for analytics and reporting purposes. What is the recommended storage format for projecting structured data in Knowledge Store to meet the organization's requirements?

A) Store structured data as plain text files
B) Utilize object storage for structured data projection
C) Opt for JSON format to store structured data
D) Store structured data in relational tables
E) Use XML format for structured data storage

QUESTION 45

In Azure AI Language service, which method should you use to analyze text and extract key phrases?

```
A) Extract()
B) AnalyzeText()
C) ExtractKeyPhrases()
D) IdentifyPhrases()
E) KeyPhraseExtraction()
```

QUESTION 46

When monitoring and maintaining the performance of an Azure OpenAI model, which key metric should you prioritize to ensure the model continues to meet business requirements?

A) Latency: The time taken for the model to process a single inference request.
B) Throughput: The number of inference requests the model can handle per unit of time.
C) Accuracy: The percentage of correct predictions made by the model on unseen data.
D) Memory usage: The amount of memory consumed by the model during inference.
E) Cost: The total expenses incurred for deploying and running the model in production.

QUESTION 47

Your team is incorporating code generation into the continuous integration and continuous deployment (CI/CD) pipeline using Azure OpenAI Service. What strategy should you prioritize to ensure seamless integration of generated code with automated testing and deployment processes?

A) Generating code only after manual approval to minimize deployment risks.
B) Integrating code generation as a standalone step in the CI/CD pipeline.
C) Implementing version control for tracking changes in the generated codebase.
D) Automating code generation triggered by specific events in the development workflow.
E) Conducting code reviews for every generated code snippet before deployment.

QUESTION 48

In Azure AI Translator service for language translation, which combination of statements holds true?

A) Statement I: Azure AI Translator service supports translation between spoken languages.
B) Statement II: Azure AI Translator service allows translation of text and documents.
C) Statement III: Azure AI Translator service provides sentiment analysis.
D) Statement I, Statement III
E) Statement II, Statement III

QUESTION 49

Your team is fine-tuning an Azure OpenAI model to generate personalized email responses based on customer inquiries. What is a recommended strategy for managing model drift and ensuring the continued relevance of generated responses over time?
Select all answers that apply.

A) Implementing an automated monitoring system to track model performance metrics and trigger retraining when performance degrades.
B) Regularly updating the model with new customer inquiry data to capture evolving language patterns and trends.
C) Conducting periodic audits of generated responses to identify discrepancies or outdated information.
D) Employing an ensemble learning approach to combine predictions from multiple versions of the model.
E) Utilizing reinforcement learning techniques to adapt the model's behavior based on user feedback.

QUESTION 50

Your team is tasked with fine-tuning an Azure OpenAI model to generate personalized responses for a virtual assistant application. During the fine-tuning process, you encounter challenges with maintaining coherence and relevance in the generated responses. Which approach would best address these challenges?

A) Implementing a reward mechanism to encourage coherent responses
B) Incorporating a context-awareness module to enhance relevance
C) Adjusting the temperature parameter to control response variability
D) Fine-tuning with transfer learning on a domain-specific corpus
E) Using pre-trained language models for generating responses

PRACTICE TEST 8 - ANSWERS ONLY

QUESTION 1

Answer - [A, B, D] Azure Cognitive Services Text Analytics, Azure Cognitive Services Language Understanding (LUIS), Azure AI Translator service

Option C - Azure Bot Services: Primarily focused on building conversational chatbots, not suitable for large-scale text analysis.
Option E - Azure Cognitive Services QnA Maker: Designed for creating question-and-answer bots, not ideal for text analytics or sentiment analysis.
Option A - Azure Cognitive Services Text Analytics: Provides sentiment analysis, key phrase extraction, and topic detection capabilities, suitable for analyzing customer feedback.
Option B - Azure Cognitive Services Language Understanding (LUIS): Useful for building custom language understanding models to categorize feedback into predefined topics.
Option D - Azure AI Translator service: Allows for translating text into multiple languages, supporting the project's requirement for analyzing feedback in various languages.

EXAM FOCUS	*You should use Azure Cognitive Services Text Analytics for sentiment analysis and key phrase extraction and combine it with LUIS to categorize feedback into topics, while Azure Translator supports multiple languages. This combination is scalable and covers all aspects.*
CAUTION ALERT	*Stay clear of using Azure Bot Services or QnA Maker for large-scale text analysis. These are built for conversational interfaces, not for comprehensive sentiment or language analysis.*

QUESTION 2

Answer - [A, B, C] Azure AI Speech to Text, Azure AI Text Analytics, Azure AI Language Understanding (LUIS)

Option D - Azure AI Text to Speech: Converts text to spoken audio, not suitable for transcribing customer calls.
Option E - Azure AI Translator Text: Translates text between languages, not suitable for real-time transcription.

EXAM FOCUS	*Always remember to integrate Azure AI Speech to Text for real-time transcription, Text Analytics for sentiment analysis, and LUIS for intent detection. These services work together to analyze and route customer calls efficiently.*
CAUTION ALERT	*Don't confuse Text to Speech with Speech to Text—the former is for converting text to speech, not for transcribing calls.*

QUESTION 3

Answer - A) az translator model show

Option B - Incorrect. This command lists all available translation models, not specific details of a deployed model. Option C - Incorrect. This command is not a valid option for viewing details of a deployed model. Option D - Incorrect. This command does not exist in the Azure CLI for viewing model details. Option E - Incorrect. This command is not a valid option for viewing details of a deployed model.

EXAM FOCUS	*You need to use az translator model show to view specific details of custom translation models deployed on Azure AI Translator. This command provides necessary insights for monitoring and management.*
CAUTION ALERT	*Avoid using incorrect CLI commands such as az translator model list or az translator model view, as they won't show detailed model information.*

QUESTION 4

Answer - A) Azure Active Directory (AAD)

Option B - Incorrect. API keys may not provide the necessary security measures for accessing sensitive language processing capabilities. Option C - Incorrect. OAuth 2.0 is typically used for user authentication and authorization, which may not be suitable for service-to-service communication in a chatbot scenario. Option D - Incorrect. Shared access signatures are typically used for granting limited access to resources and may not provide the necessary user authentication for a chatbot solution. Option E - Incorrect. Certificate authentication may be overly complex and not well-suited for service-to-service communication in a chatbot scenario.

EXAM FOCUS	*You should implement Azure Active Directory (AAD) for authentication in a chatbot solution. This method ensures secure service-to-service communication without exposing sensitive information, supporting enterprise-level security.*
CAUTION ALERT	*Stay alert—using API keys or shared access signatures can expose sensitive data, and they don't provide the same level of security as AAD for access to Azure AI services.*

QUESTION 5

Answer - [A] Container orchestration.

Container orchestration - In scenarios requiring frequent updates and scalability, container orchestration tools like Kubernetes provide automated management, scaling, and deployment of containerized applications, ensuring high availability and efficiency. Options B, C, D, and E are relevant but not as critical for optimizing container deployment in this context.

EXAM FOCUS	*Make sure to prioritize container orchestration when deploying Azure AI services that require frequent updates and scalability. Solutions like Kubernetes automate deployment, scaling, and management of containerized applications.*
CAUTION ALERT	*Don't confuse resource utilization monitoring or network security as the primary concern—while important, they don't address the need for automated scaling and update management.*

QUESTION 6

Answer - A) Configure ExpressRoute for private network connectivity.

Option B - Incorrect. Using a shared access signature (SAS) token may not provide the necessary network-level security for accessing cognitive services from on-premises servers. Option C - Incorrect. Setting up a VPN gateway for secure tunneling may provide connectivity but may not offer the same level of performance and reliability as ExpressRoute. Option D - Incorrect. Implementing Azure Key Vault for storing authentication credentials does not address the network-level security requirements for accessing cognitive services. Option E - Incorrect. Exposing the cognitive services endpoints to the public internet may pose security risks and is not recommended for on-premises access.

EXAM FOCUS	*You should configure ExpressRoute for private network connectivity between on-premises servers and Azure Cognitive Services. This provides fast, secure, and private connections without exposing services to the public internet.*
CAUTION ALERT	*Avoid using a shared access signature (SAS) token for this purpose—it only manages access permissions, not secure connectivity between networks.*

QUESTION 7

Answer - [A] Azure Monitor Logs.

Azure Monitor Logs - Leveraging Azure Monitor Logs enables real-time monitoring and analysis of Azure AI service usage, providing insights into resource utilization patterns and facilitating optimization efforts for cost efficiency and performance. Options B, C, D, and E may have relevance but do not specifically address real-time monitoring of Azure AI service usage.

EXAM FOCUS	*You need to leverage Azure Monitor Logs for real-time monitoring of Azure AI resource usage. This tool provides comprehensive insights into service performance, enabling resource allocation and cost optimization.*
CAUTION ALERT	*Stay clear of relying solely on Azure Application Insights or Azure Resource Graph—while useful, they don't provide the full depth of real-time analysis and monitoring you need for resource management.*

QUESTION 8

Answer - [B] Implement Transport Layer Security (TLS) encryption.

Implement Transport Layer Security (TLS) encryption - TLS encryption ensures data confidentiality, integrity, and authenticity during communication between Azure AI services, protecting sensitive information from interception and tampering, unlike options A, C, D, and E, which may compromise data security.

EXAM FOCUS	*Make sure to implement TLS encryption for secure communication between Azure AI services. This ensures data protection during transmission and meets compliance requirements for secure service interaction.*
CAUTION ALERT	*Avoid plaintext communication or disabling encryption, even for performance gains—this compromises data integrity and security, putting sensitive information at risk.*

QUESTION 9

Answer - D) Enable Managed Service Identity (MSI) for App3 and assign RBAC permissions to Azure AD.

Option A - Incorrect. Storing client secrets may introduce additional security risks and administrative overhead. Option B - Incorrect. While Azure AD authentication is a valid approach, enabling MSI with RBAC permissions directly meets the requirement with minimal administrative overhead. Option C - Incorrect. OAuth 2.0 authentication with Azure AD may introduce unnecessary complexity and does not leverage MSI for authentication. Option E - Incorrect. Azure AD SSO may provide centralized authentication but may not align with the requirement to use Azure AD directly.

EXAM FOCUS	*You should enable Managed Service Identity (MSI) for App3 and assign RBAC permissions to Azure AD. This reduces administrative overhead and ensures least-privilege access to services.*
CAUTION ALERT	*Stay alert—generating client secrets or configuring OAuth 2.0 introduces unnecessary complexity and security risks. MSI with RBAC provides a simpler, secure alternative.*

QUESTION 10

Answer - [B] Implementing Azure Functions with Azure Queue Storage for asynchronous image processing.

Azure Functions with Azure Queue Storage allow for scalable and asynchronous image processing, enabling efficient handling of large volumes of uploads with low latency. Options A, C, D, and E may introduce unnecessary complexity or may not provide the same level of efficiency for image moderation.

EXAM FOCUS	*You need to implement Azure Functions with Azure Queue Storage for asynchronous image moderation. This approach scales efficiently to handle large volumes with low latency, ideal for platforms experiencing high daily image uploads.*
CAUTION ALERT	*Avoid relying on virtual machines or complex Kubernetes setups if you aim for quick scaling and low operational complexity—Azure Functions are more suitable for this scenario.*

QUESTION 11

Answer - [B] Ensuring compliance with HIPAA regulations for handling sensitive patient information and data privacy.

Compliance with HIPAA regulations is essential when adjusting AI models based on performance feedback in healthcare scenarios to ensure regulatory compliance and protect patient privacy and sensitive information. Options A, C, D, and E focus on different privacy and security techniques but may not directly address the regulatory requirements specific to healthcare data handling.

EXAM FOCUS	*Always remember to ensure compliance with HIPAA regulations when handling healthcare data. It's critical to use security features and privacy techniques like RBAC and Azure Private Link to protect patient data during AI model updates.*
CAUTION ALERT	*Stay alert—while using advanced techniques like federated learning or homomorphic encryption are useful for privacy, they may not directly satisfy HIPAA regulatory compliance for handling healthcare data. Focus on regulatory frameworks.*

QUESTION 12

Answer - A) Provision a Metrics Advisor resource and define data sources for monitoring.
C) Define key metrics and anomaly detection thresholds to trigger alerts for potential issues.

Option B - Incorrect. Custom moderation policies are typically used for content moderation and may not be applicable for configuring data monitoring solutions. Option D - Incorrect. Azure Cognitive Search is useful for indexing and searching structured data but may not directly relate to configuring and managing Metrics Advisor for data monitoring. Option E - Incorrect. While automated actions can enhance system response, they may not be categorized as necessary for configuring and managing the monitoring solution itself.

EXAM FOCUS	*You should define key metrics and anomaly detection thresholds in Azure Metrics Advisor to trigger alerts for potential issues. This ensures timely identification of performance deviations and improves monitoring.*
CAUTION ALERT	*Avoid confusing data monitoring with indexing search data—Azure Cognitive Search is for search purposes, not monitoring. Also, custom moderation policies are unrelated to performance metrics.*

QUESTION 13

Answer - [C] Option C (Configure Azure Private Link to establish private communication channels between Azure AI services) addresses the security concern by ensuring encrypted and isolated data transmission between services within a private network.

Options A, B, D, and E provide security measures but do not directly address the specific concern of encrypting data transmission between Azure AI services. Option A focuses on encryption key management, Option B is about authentication, Option D deals with access control, and Option E involves network isolation.

EXAM FOCUS	*You need to recommend Azure Private Link to securely transmit data between AI services within a private network. This ensures end-to-end encryption and compliance with security standards.*
CAUTION ALERT	*Avoid assuming that Azure Key Vault or RBAC alone will fully address secure transmission concerns—these handle key management and access control but don't encrypt data during transmission between services.*

QUESTION 14

Answer - [A, D] Options A and D are crucial for optimizing object detection performance in the context of public safety surveillance. Minimizing false positives (Option A) helps reduce unnecessary alerts, while enhancing object localization accuracy (Option D) ensures precise identification of potential security threats.

Options B, C, and E may be less critical for this scenario. Maximizing recall rate (Option B) focuses on detecting all relevant objects, reducing model complexity (Option C) may sacrifice detection accuracy, and increasing inference speed (Option E) prioritizes efficiency over precision, which may compromise threat detection accuracy.

EXAM FOCUS	*You should focus on minimizing false positives and improving object localization accuracy when optimizing an object detection model for public safety. These ensure that real threats are detected without overwhelming users with unnecessary alerts.*
CAUTION ALERT	*Stay clear of over-prioritizing recall or reducing model complexity, as these may compromise detection accuracy in a critical safety context.*

QUESTION 15

Answer - [B] Check if the custom vision model has been properly trained and published.

Option B - Verifying the permissions of the Azure AI Vision resource (Option A) is important but may not directly resolve the issue related to the model. Reviewing the configuration settings (Option C) might help, but it may not be the root cause of the error. Ensuring container environment access to the API endpoint (Option D) is necessary but assumes the infrastructure is correctly set up. Upgrading the Azure AI Vision resource (Option E) may not address the issue if the model itself is not properly configured. Checking if the custom vision model has been properly trained and published (Option B) is essential as the error indicates a problem with the model's availability, which this option addresses.

EXAM FOCUS	*Always check if the custom vision model has been trained and published properly before troubleshooting deployment issues. Ensure models are available to avoid errors.*
CAUTION ALERT	*Stay alert—while verifying permissions or upgrading resources is important, missing a trained and published model is often the root cause of "Model not found" errors in deployment scenarios.*

QUESTION 16

Answer - [A) Log Analytics workspace, E) An Azure Storage account]

Enabling diagnostic logging in Azure AI Services requires a Log Analytics workspace and an Azure Storage account.
B) Azure Cosmos DB - While useful for other purposes, it's not a prerequisite for diagnostic logging.
C) Azure Key Vault - Azure Key Vault is not directly related to enabling diagnostic logging for Azure AI Services.
D) Azure SQL database - Diagnostic logging does not require an Azure SQL database.

EXAM FOCUS	*Make sure to set up a Log Analytics workspace and an Azure Storage account to enable diagnostic logging for Azure AI Services. These are essential for capturing and analyzing logs efficiently.*
CAUTION ALERT	*Avoid confusing the need for Cosmos DB or Key Vault—these services are not required for enabling diagnostic logging in Azure AI. Focus on storage and logging-specific tools.*

QUESTION 17

Answer - [B) K-fold cross-validation]

K-fold cross-validation partitions the dataset into k subsets and performs training and evaluation k times, ensuring robustness in model evaluation for object detection tasks.
A) Holdout validation may not adequately represent the dataset's variability, especially for smaller datasets.
C) Leave-one-out cross-validation may be computationally expensive and less suitable for larger datasets.
D) Stratified cross-validation is more appropriate for classification tasks with imbalanced class distributions.
E) Time series cross-validation is specific to temporal data and may not apply to object detection scenarios.

EXAM FOCUS	*You should use K-fold cross-validation to reliably evaluate the performance of custom object detection models. It's a widely accepted technique that helps ensure the model generalizes well across different data*

CAUTION ALERT	*splits.* *Avoid using Leave-one-out cross-validation for large datasets—it can be computationally expensive and less efficient for object detection models.*

QUESTION 18

Answer - [B] Retrieval of search results based on specified criteria.

Option B - This API request is aimed at retrieving search results from the specified index based on the provided search criteria. Indexing of documents (Option A) occurs separately and involves adding documents to the search index. Analysis of search performance metrics (Option C) is not performed through this endpoint. Translation of search queries (Option D) and synthesis of search results (Option E) are unrelated to the primary purpose of this request.

EXAM FOCUS	*You can expect a search result retrieval from POST API requests targeting the search.windows.net endpoint. This fetches relevant documents from the Azure Cognitive Search index.*
CAUTION ALERT	*Don't confuse this API with indexing—indexing and retrieving are separate processes. This API is for search queries, not for adding new data to the index.*

QUESTION 19

Answer - B) Azure Cognitive Services - Computer Vision

Option A - Azure AI Video Indexer focuses more on extracting insights and metadata from videos rather than detailed object tracking and anomaly detection.
Option C - Azure Cognitive Services - Video Analyzer is geared towards real-time video processing and activity detection rather than object tracking.
Option D - Azure AI Vision Spatial Analysis is more suited for analyzing static images and does not offer comprehensive object tracking capabilities.
Option E - Azure Media Services primarily deals with video streaming and encoding rather than detailed video analytics for manufacturing processes.

EXAM FOCUS	*You should select Azure Cognitive Services - Computer Vision for detailed object tracking and anomaly detection in video footage. This service offers the best tools for precise monitoring of assembly lines.*
CAUTION ALERT	*Avoid assuming Video Indexer or Media Services will meet the object tracking requirements—they focus on metadata extraction and video streaming rather than object detection and analysis.*

QUESTION 20

Answer - E) Azure Machine Learning service

Option A - Azure Cognitive Services - Video Analyzer focuses on real-time video analysis but may lack the flexibility to incorporate custom AI models for wildlife monitoring.
Option B - Azure AI Vision Spatial Analysis is more suitable for detecting spatial patterns and movements in videos rather than analyzing wildlife behavior.
Option C - Azure AI Video Indexer is designed for extracting insights and metadata from videos but may not support the incorporation of custom AI models for wildlife analysis.
Option D - Azure Cognitive Services - Custom Vision is geared towards image classification tasks and may not provide real-time analysis capabilities required for wildlife monitoring.

EXAM FOCUS	*Make sure to recommend Azure Machine Learning service for projects requiring custom AI models for real-time video analysis, such as wildlife monitoring. It supports flexible model integration and scalability.*

CAUTION ALERT	*Stay clear of using services like Video Indexer or Spatial Analysis—these may not support custom models or real-time capabilities needed for monitoring complex behavior patterns in wildlife.*

QUESTION 21

Answer - [C] Renewing the service account credentials.

Option C - Renewing the service account credentials can resolve authentication errors caused by expired or invalid credentials. Refreshing authentication tokens (Option A) may help mitigate token expiration issues but does not address underlying credential problems. Reviewing API request parameters (Option B) is unlikely to directly resolve authentication errors. Implementing multi-factor authentication (Option D) or adding IP restrictions (Option E) may enhance security but may not directly address authentication errors.

EXAM FOCUS	*You should focus on renewing service account credentials to resolve authentication errors in Azure AI Speech Service. Expired credentials often cause these issues, and refreshing them ensures uninterrupted access to the service.*
CAUTION ALERT	*Stay alert and don't confuse this with API token issues. Renewing the service account credentials addresses the root cause rather than token refresh settings.*

QUESTION 22

Answer - [B] Custom entity models.

Custom entity models can be trained on specific data, allowing them to adapt to noise and inconsistencies in the text, thus improving extraction accuracy. Named entity recognition (NER) may struggle with noisy data as it relies on predefined entity categories. Sentiment analysis focuses on identifying sentiment, not entity extraction. Machine learning can be used to train custom models but is not inherently focused on mitigating challenges in entity extraction. Rule-based matching may lack the flexibility to handle noisy data effectively.

EXAM FOCUS	*Make sure to use custom entity models when dealing with noisy text data. Training a model specific to your dataset helps adapt to inconsistencies and improves the accuracy of entity extraction.*
CAUTION ALERT	*Avoid relying on standard Named Entity Recognition (NER) when the text is noisy. Predefined categories often don't perform well in inconsistent datasets.*

QUESTION 23

Answer - [C] Custom language detection models.

Custom language detection models can be trained and fine-tuned to accurately identify languages across diverse datasets, making them suitable for multilingual content moderation. Pre-trained models may lack specificity for certain languages or domains. Rule-based, frequency-based, and lexicon-based approaches may not effectively handle the complexity of language detection in a multilingual environment.

EXAM FOCUS	*You need to prioritize custom language detection models for multilingual content moderation. These models allow for higher accuracy when moderating diverse language content and handling domain-specific language variations.*
CAUTION ALERT	*Stay clear of solely using pre-trained models for language detection in complex multilingual environments. Pre-trained models may not handle certain languages or dialects accurately.*

QUESTION 24

Answer - [A] Face detection

Option A - Face detection is specifically designed to identify and locate human faces within images, making it the most appropriate choice for detecting the presence of people. Image analysis (Option B) and OCR (Option C) are not tailored for this task. Object detection (Option D) identifies various objects, including people, but face detection provides a more precise solution for this specific requirement. Spatial analysis (Option E) focuses on spatial relationships rather than individual objects.

EXAM FOCUS	*Always remember that Face detection is the optimal Azure AI Vision feature for detecting people in images. It offers precise identification of human faces, improving accuracy in people detection tasks.*
CAUTION ALERT	*Avoid using Object detection if your goal is specifically identifying people. While object detection can recognize people, face detection is more suited for this task.*

QUESTION 25

Answer - B) <break> tag

Option A - The <audio> tag is used to include pre-recorded audio files in the speech output, not for inserting pauses between words.
Option B - Correct. The <break> tag is used to insert pauses of varying lengths between words in the synthesized speech output.
Option C - The <prosody> tag is used to modify the pitch, rate, and volume of speech but does not insert pauses between words.
Option D - The <sub> tag is used for substituting one word or phrase with another and is not related to inserting pauses.
Option E - The <emphasis> tag is used to indicate emphasis or stress on specific words, not to insert pauses.

EXAM FOCUS	*You need to use the <break> tag in SSML when inserting pauses between words in synthesized speech. It allows for fine control over the length of pauses, essential for clear and natural-sounding output.*
CAUTION ALERT	*Don't confuse the <prosody> tag with the <break> tag. While prosody adjusts the tone and volume, it doesn't insert pauses.*

QUESTION 26

Answer - [D] Azure Cognitive Services Speech Service

Option D is the correct choice as Azure Cognitive Services Speech Service offers speech-to-text conversion and can be used to implement intent recognition for processing voice commands in the smart home system. Options A, B, and C are unrelated to speech recognition. Option E refers to Azure OpenAI Service, which is not specifically tailored for speech recognition.

EXAM FOCUS	*Keep in mind that Azure Cognitive Services Speech Service is your best option for speech recognition and intent processing in voice-controlled systems. It integrates both speech-to-text and intent recognition capabilities.*
CAUTION ALERT	*Stay clear of using Azure Cognitive Services Translator Text for intent recognition. It focuses on translation, not processing voice commands for intent understanding.*

QUESTION 27

Answer - [C] Network congestion impacting data transmission to and from the Azure AI Translator service.

Option C - Network congestion can significantly impact the speed of data transmission, leading to delays in translation responses, especially in real-time scenarios. Insufficient permissions (Option A) may cause authentication errors but are unlikely to affect response times. Incompatibility between frontend technology and SDK (Option B) may cause integration issues but should not directly impact translation speed. Insufficient memory (Option D) might cause performance issues but is less likely to affect response times. Similarly, an outdated SDK version (Option E) may lead to compatibility issues but is not the primary cause of translation delays.

EXAM FOCUS	*Make sure to consider network congestion when diagnosing delays in real-time translation using Azure AI Translator. Poor network performance can significantly affect response times, particularly in latency-sensitive applications.*
CAUTION ALERT	*Stay cautioned—this issue is rarely related to memory allocation or SDK version. These factors may affect overall performance but are unlikely to be the primary cause of response delays.*

QUESTION 28

Answer - [B] Availability of language models

Explanation: The availability of accurate and diverse language models is crucial for high-quality speech translation to effectively cater to various languages and dialects. Options A, C, D, and E are not directly related to achieving high-quality speech translation.

EXAM FOCUS	*You should ensure that accurate language models are available to maintain high-quality speech translation across diverse languages. High-quality models are key to effective multilingual customer service.*
CAUTION ALERT	*Avoid overlooking the importance of language model availability when designing speech translation services. Without robust models, translation quality will suffer.*

QUESTION 29

Answer - [A] Include a diverse set of training phrases for each intent

Explanation: A) Including a diverse set of training phrases for each intent ensures robust intent recognition and improves the accuracy of entity extraction. B) Relying solely on customer feedback may result in biased or incomplete intent definitions. C) Limiting entities may lead to information loss and reduce the model's ability to understand user inputs accurately. D) Prebuilt models may not capture domain-specific intents and entities effectively. E) Ignoring entity extraction overlooks valuable information in user queries, affecting the overall understanding of customer requests.

EXAM FOCUS	*Always remember to include a diverse set of training phrases for each intent in your language understanding model. This ensures the model can accurately recognize a wide range of user inputs across different regions and contexts.*
CAUTION ALERT	*Don't confuse the need for diversity in training phrases with relying solely on customer feedback. Using only feedback may narrow your model's understanding.*

QUESTION 30

Answer - [B] Implement an image preprocessing pipeline in the app to enhance text visibility and then use Azure AI Computer Vision's OCR API for text extraction.

Option B - Implementing an image preprocessing pipeline within the app allows for enhancing text visibility in images before utilizing Azure AI Computer Vision's OCR API for accurate text extraction, ensuring better results compared to direct OCR. Option A may lead to inaccuracies if text visibility is poor in the original images. Option C introduces unnecessary translation overhead and complexity. Option D requires significant effort in model development and training, which may not be necessary for text extraction tasks. Option E, while feasible, adds complexity without addressing the issue of poor text visibility in images.

EXAM FOCUS	*You should implement image preprocessing before using the OCR API from Azure AI Computer Vision. Preprocessing enhances text visibility, leading to better text extraction results from captured images.*

CAUTION ALERT	*Avoid using Azure Translator or custom models for basic text extraction tasks. This introduces unnecessary complexity and doesn't directly improve text recognition.*

QUESTION 31

Answer - [A), B), and D)] - Implementing automated anomaly detection, setting up alerts, and scheduling regular performance testing align with best practices for continuous monitoring and management while minimizing disruptions.

C) Incorrect - While Azure DevOps is essential for version control, it might not directly address the specific requirements of continuous monitoring and management of model performance in production.

EXAM FOCUS	*You should implement automated anomaly detection and set up alerts for model response times. Regular performance testing is essential to catch performance deviations early and ensure smooth operation in production.*
CAUTION ALERT	*Stay cautioned—using Azure DevOps for version control is important, but it does not directly handle monitoring or model performance issues in real-time production environments.*

QUESTION 32

Answer - [A), B), and D)] - Configuring regular backups, implementing versioning, and integrating automated testing ensure effective backup and recovery while addressing compliance and data protection requirements for the language model.

C) Incorrect - While Azure Key Vault provides secure storage, it might not directly ensure the effectiveness of backup and recovery strategies or compliance with data protection regulations specific to language model deployments in e-commerce applications.

EXAM FOCUS	*Make sure to configure regular backups of model checkpoints and implement versioning for quick recovery. Automated testing will ensure the backups are functioning and up-to-date.*
CAUTION ALERT	*Avoid relying solely on Azure Key Vault for data protection; it doesn't address the need for actual backup and recovery mechanisms in case of model failure.*

QUESTION 33

Answer - [B] Azure Speech Service > Speech API

Option B - Azure Speech Service with the Speech API allows audio transcription, converting audio files into text format, making it the most suitable choice for this requirement. Option A is incorrect as Cognitive Search is not designed for audio transcription. Option C is incorrect as the Text Analytics API does not support audio transcription. Option D is incorrect as Computer Vision is for image processing, not audio transcription. Option E is incorrect as Content Moderator is more focused on content moderation.

EXAM FOCUS	*Always remember to use Azure Speech Service with the Speech API for transcribing audio to text. This service is designed specifically for high-quality, scalable audio transcription.*
CAUTION ALERT	*Stay clear of using Azure Cognitive Search or Text Analytics API for audio transcription. These services are for text analytics and not designed for converting speech to text.*

QUESTION 34

Answer - [A) and E)] - Addressing gaps in knowledge coverage involves conducting regular audits and integrating third-party knowledge bases for comprehensive coverage.

Option A) - Correct: Regular audits help identify and fill knowledge gaps, ensuring the relevance and accuracy of the content. Option E) - Correct: Integrating third-party knowledge bases supplements internal content, enhancing coverage and diversity. Option B) - Incorrect: User profiling may improve personalization but does not directly address knowledge gaps. Option C) - Incorrect: Ignoring gaps may lead to incomplete and unreliable information. Option D) - Incorrect: Predicting knowledge gaps may be speculative and less effective than direct assessment. Option E) - Incorrect: Integrating third-party knowledge bases supplements internal content, enhancing coverage and diversity.

EXAM FOCUS	*You need to conduct regular audits and integrate third-party knowledge bases to fill gaps in your question-answering solution. This ensures comprehensive knowledge coverage.*
CAUTION ALERT	*Stay alert—ignoring minor gaps can lead to incomplete or unreliable information, which will negatively affect the accuracy of your knowledge base.*

QUESTION 35

Answer - [A), B), and C)] - Enhancing user experience through multi-turn capability involves implementing context-aware responses, sentiment analysis, and personalized recommendations.

Option A) - Correct: Implementing context-aware response generation ensures responses are relevant to the ongoing conversation. Option B) - Correct: Utilizing sentiment analysis allows for adapting interaction based on user emotions and responses. Option C) - Correct: Offering personalized recommendations enhances user engagement by catering to individual preferences. Option D) - Incorrect: While enabling seamless handoff to human agents is important for escalation, it may not directly enhance user experience through multi-turn capability. Option E) - Incorrect: Ensuring compatibility with communication channels is essential but does not specifically relate to enhancing user experience through multi-turn capability.

EXAM FOCUS	*Make sure to implement context-aware response generation and use sentiment analysis to adapt to the user's emotional state. This improves engagement in multi-turn dialogues.*
CAUTION ALERT	*Don't confuse multi-turn capabilities with handoff to human agents. The primary goal is to handle complex interactions seamlessly within the system before escalating to humans.*

QUESTION 36

Answer - [A, B, E] "mcr.microsoft.com/azure-cognitive-services/vision/classification"
"--memory 384 --cpus 6"
"--api-key {API_KEY}"

Option A provides the correct URI for the image classification model container. Option B sets memory and CPU limits. Option E specifies the API key required for authentication. Options C and D are not relevant for container deployment.

EXAM FOCUS	*Keep in mind that setting proper resource limits such as memory and CPUs when deploying a containerized model will ensure performance and scalability. An API key is required for proper authentication.*
CAUTION ALERT	*Avoid deploying models without setting resource limits or an API key; this can result in poor performance or security vulnerabilities.*

QUESTION 37

Answer - [A, C, D].

A) Setting up alerts for abnormal model behavior allows proactive identification and mitigation of issues, ensuring continuous effectiveness. C) Implementing version control for model updates facilitates tracking changes and rolling back to previous versions if necessary, ensuring reliability. D) Conducting periodic retraining with new data helps maintain the model's relevance and accuracy over time, enhancing effectiveness. B) While regular performance optimization is essential, it is not as critical for ensuring effectiveness and reliability in production. Establishing failover mechanisms primarily addresses availability concerns.

EXAM FOCUS	*You need to set up alerts for abnormal model behavior and retrain the model with fresh data to maintain relevance. Regular version control will allow easy rollback if issues arise.*
CAUTION ALERT	*Stay alert—optimizing performance without addressing model retraining or anomaly detection may still lead to performance degradation over time.*

QUESTION 38

Answer - [C, D].

C) Integrating natural language understanding enables the voice assistant to comprehend user intents and context, leading to more relevant and engaging responses. D) Managing latency ensures that the voice assistant responds promptly to user inputs, maintaining a seamless and responsive experience. A) While handling noisy environments is important for accurate voice recognition, it may not directly impact user engagement and satisfaction in all scenarios. B) Providing real-time feedback enhances user feedback but may not address deeper engagement challenges. E) Implementing multimodal interaction is beneficial but may not directly address the challenges of voice interaction design related to engagement and satisfaction.

EXAM FOCUS	*Always remember that integrating natural language understanding for context-aware responses and managing latency are key to improving user engagement in voice interactions.*
CAUTION ALERT	*Don't confuse handling noisy environments with enhancing user engagement. It's important, but latency and context-awareness play a more crucial role in user satisfaction.*

QUESTION 39

Answer - [B] MachineLearningManagementClient

Choice A - TokenCredentials: Incorrect. This choice represents the credentials class, not the client for interacting with Azure Machine Learning service.
Choice B - MachineLearningManagementClient: Correct. This choice represents the client class for managing resources in Azure Machine Learning service.
Choice C - MachineLearningClient: Incorrect. There's no such class named MachineLearningClient for interacting with Azure Machine Learning service.
Choice D - AzureMachineLearningCredential: Incorrect. This choice is not a valid class for interacting with Azure Machine Learning service.
Choice E - AzureMachineLearningClient: Incorrect. There's no such class named AzureMachineLearningClient for interacting with Azure Machine Learning service.

EXAM FOCUS	*You should use the MachineLearningManagementClient class to interact with the Azure Machine Learning service, ensuring proper management of resources and deployments.*
CAUTION ALERT	*Stay clear of confusing the TokenCredentials class with the client class—it's for authentication, not for managing the service itself.*

QUESTION 40

Answer - [B] Azure Language Understanding (LUIS).

B) Azure Language Understanding (LUIS) provides capabilities for building language understanding models with transparency and explainability features, enhancing trust with users. A) Azure Text Analytics offers sentiment analysis but does not specialize in explainability. C) Azure AI Translator service focuses on translation tasks and does not provide explainability features. D) Azure Cognitive Services offers various AI capabilities but may require additional customization for model explainability. E) Azure Machine Learning can be used for training models but may require additional techniques for model explainability.

EXAM FOCUS	*Keep in mind that Azure Language Understanding (LUIS) provides explainability features to ensure that model decisions are transparent, which is crucial in customer-facing applications.*
CAUTION ALERT	*Avoid using services like Azure AI Translator or Text Analytics for explainability. These are not built with decision transparency in mind for complex models.*

QUESTION 41

Answer - [C] Configure indexers with appropriate batch sizes and concurrency settings.

C) Configuring indexers with appropriate batch sizes and concurrency settings allows for optimizing data ingestion performance by controlling the volume of documents processed in each batch and the degree of parallelism, ensuring efficient indexing of documents stored in Azure Blob Storage. A) While parallelization using Azure Data Factory may improve overall throughput, configuring indexers directly within Azure Cognitive Search provides more granular control over ingestion performance. B) Optimizing document metadata is important but may not directly address the performance of data ingestion into the search index. D) Azure Queue Storage is useful for decoupling components in distributed systems but may introduce additional complexity and overhead for data ingestion. E) Caching mechanisms primarily impact document retrieval latency and may not directly improve data ingestion performance.

EXAM FOCUS	*You should configure indexers with appropriate batch sizes and concurrency settings to control document ingestion performance in Azure Cognitive Search. This ensures efficient indexing and minimizes performance bottlenecks.*
CAUTION ALERT	*Avoid relying solely on parallelization via Azure Data Factory, as it may lack the granular control needed to optimize batch processing within Azure Cognitive Search.*

QUESTION 42

Answer - [C] Azure.AI.Speech.SpeechSynthesizer.CreateSpeechSynthesizer()

Option A is incorrect because Microsoft.CognitiveServices.Speech.SpeechSynthesis.SpeechSynthesizer.CreateSpeechSynthesizer() is not the correct method for creating a SpeechSynthesizer object in the Azure AI Speech service. Option B is incorrect because Microsoft.Azure.CognitiveServices.Speech.SpeechSynthesizer.CreateSynthesizer() is not the correct method for creating a SpeechSynthesizer object. Option D is incorrect because Azure.CognitiveServices.Speech.SpeechSynthesis.SpeechSynthesizer.CreateSynthesizer() is not the correct method for creating a SpeechSynthesizer object. Option E is incorrect because Microsoft.Azure.CognitiveServices.Speech.SpeechSynthesis.SpeechSynthesizer.CreateSpeechSynthesizer() is not the correct method for creating a SpeechSynthesizer object. Option C is the correct choice as CreateSpeechSynthesizer() is the method for creating a SpeechSynthesizer object in the Azure.AI.Speech namespace.

EXAM FOCUS	*Always remember to use the correct namespace, Azure.AI.Speech, and method CreateSpeechSynthesizer() when implementing the text-to-speech feature. Using the wrong method or namespace will lead to errors.*
CAUTION ALERT	*Stay cautioned—incorrect methods or namespaces such as Microsoft.Azure.CognitiveServices.Speech will not create the SpeechSynthesizer object. Ensure you use the exact namespace for Azure Speech.*

QUESTION 43

Answer - [A] Implement retry logic within indexers.

A) Implementing retry logic within indexers allows for automatic retries in case of transient errors, ensuring robust error handling and continuous indexing even in the presence of intermittent issues. B) Manually re-running indexers after resolving errors is not efficient and may lead to delays in data ingestion and indexing. C) Increasing the indexer timeout duration may address specific timeout issues but does not provide comprehensive error handling for all types of errors. D) Configuring alerting for indexer failures is important for monitoring but does not directly handle errors during indexer execution. E) Optimizing data source connections for reliability is essential but may not address all potential errors encountered during indexer execution.

EXAM FOCUS	*Make sure to implement retry logic within indexers for Azure Cognitive Search. This handles transient errors effectively and ensures continuous indexing without manual intervention.*
CAUTION ALERT	*Avoid relying solely on manual re-runs for resolving indexer errors, as this is inefficient and may cause data ingestion delays, especially with large volumes of data.*

QUESTION 44

Answer - [D] Store structured data in relational tables.

D) Storing structured data in relational tables is recommended for efficient retrieval and analysis, especially for structured data such as patient records and medical documents, as it provides a structured format that facilitates querying and reporting. A) Storing structured data as plain text files may not be optimal for efficient retrieval and analysis, especially for structured data that requires querying based on specific fields or attributes. B) Utilizing object storage for structured data projection may lack the structured format required for efficient querying and reporting compared to relational tables. C) While JSON format is suitable for semi-structured data, it may not offer the same level of efficiency for querying and analysis of structured data as relational tables. E) Using XML format for structured data storage may introduce complexities and overhead in data retrieval and analysis compared to relational tables, especially for the healthcare organization's requirements.

EXAM FOCUS	*You need to store structured data in relational tables within Knowledge Store to ensure efficient querying and analytics. This format provides a structured approach that meets healthcare organization requirements for efficient data retrieval.*
CAUTION ALERT	*Stay clear of using plain text files or object storage for structured data in healthcare scenarios, as they can hinder efficient querying and may not comply with regulatory standards.*

QUESTION 45

Answer - C) ExtractKeyPhrases()

Option A - Extract(): This is a hypothetical method and not part of the Azure AI Language service SDK.
Option B - AnalyzeText(): This is a hypothetical method and not part of the Azure AI Language service SDK.
Option D - IdentifyPhrases(): This is a hypothetical method and not part of the Azure AI Language service SDK.
Option E - KeyPhraseExtraction(): This is a hypothetical method and not part of the Azure AI Language service SDK.
Option C is correct because ExtractKeyPhrases() is used to analyze text and extract key phrases in Azure AI Language service.

EXAM FOCUS	*Make sure to use ExtractKeyPhrases() when working with Azure AI Language service to extract key phrases from text. This method is specifically designed for this task and ensures accurate extraction.*
CAUTION ALERT	*Avoid using non-existent methods like IdentifyPhrases() or KeyPhraseExtraction(), as they are not part of the Azure AI Language SDK. Using the wrong method will lead to runtime errors.*

QUESTION 46

Answer - [C] Accuracy: The percentage of correct predictions made by the model on unseen data.

C) Accuracy directly reflects the model's ability to make correct predictions, ensuring it meets business requirements.
A) While latency is important, it may not directly impact the quality of predictions.

B) Throughput is related to model scalability but does not guarantee accurate predictions.
D) Memory usage is a technical metric and may not directly correlate with prediction quality.
E) Cost is important but does not directly measure model performance in terms of prediction accuracy.

EXAM FOCUS	*Always remember to prioritize accuracy when monitoring Azure OpenAI models in production. Accuracy directly impacts business outcomes and is the key metric for measuring model effectiveness.*
CAUTION ALERT	*Don't confuse technical metrics like latency or memory usage with accuracy. While important for performance, they do not directly measure the model's prediction quality.*

QUESTION 47

Answer - [D] Automating code generation triggered by specific events in the development workflow.

D) Automating code generation triggered by specific events ensures seamless integration with CI/CD processes, enhancing efficiency and reducing manual intervention.
A) Manual approval introduces delays and may disrupt the CI/CD pipeline.
B) Standalone integration may cause inconsistencies and complicate pipeline management.
C) Version control tracks changes but does not automate integration.
E) Code reviews add overhead and may not align with automated deployment goals.

EXAM FOCUS	*You need to automate code generation triggered by specific events in your CI/CD pipeline. This integration reduces manual steps and ensures consistency in the deployment process.*
CAUTION ALERT	*Stay clear of manual approval for generated code in CI/CD pipelines, as it slows down the process and may introduce human error, impacting deployment timelines.*

QUESTION 48

Answer - E) Statement II, Statement III

Option A - Statement I: Azure AI Translator service primarily supports translation between written languages, not spoken languages, making Statement I false.
Option B - Statement II: Azure AI Translator service indeed allows translation of text and documents, making Statement II true.
Option C - Statement III: Azure AI Translator service does not provide sentiment analysis, making Statement III false.
Option D - Statement I: Azure AI Translator service primarily supports translation between written languages, not spoken languages, making Statement I false.
Option E is correct because Statement II is true and Statement III is false.

EXAM FOCUS	*Make sure to recognize that Azure AI Translator service supports text and document translation, but not sentiment analysis. This ensures you select the correct service based on your task needs.*
CAUTION ALERT	*Avoid confusing Azure AI Translator with services that provide sentiment analysis. Translator focuses solely on translation and does not offer text analytics features like sentiment analysis.*

QUESTION 49

Answer - [A, B] Implementing an automated monitoring system to track model performance metrics and trigger retraining when performance degrades. Regularly updating the model with new customer inquiry data to capture evolving language patterns and trends.

A) An automated monitoring system helps detect performance degradation, prompting timely retraining to maintain model relevance.
B) Regular updates with new data capture evolving language patterns, ensuring the model remains aligned with

customer inquiries.
C) Periodic audits are valuable but may not address real-time model drift or ensure continued relevance.
D) Ensemble learning combines models but may not directly address model drift and relevance.
E) Reinforcement learning adapts to feedback but might be overkill for managing model drift in this context.

EXAM FOCUS	*Keep in mind that implementing an automated monitoring system and retraining regularly with fresh customer inquiry data is crucial to prevent model drift in Azure OpenAI. This maintains the model's relevance.*
CAUTION ALERT	*Stay alert—failing to monitor performance or retrain the model can result in degraded accuracy and irrelevance over time, negatively affecting business outcomes.*

QUESTION 50

Answer - [B] Incorporating a context-awareness module to enhance relevance.

A) While a reward mechanism can incentivize coherent responses, it may not directly ensure relevance. C) Adjusting the temperature parameter may help with variability but may not specifically address coherence and relevance. D) Transfer learning may improve performance but may not directly address coherence and relevance issues. E) Pre-trained language models are valuable but may not specifically address the challenges mentioned.

EXAM FOCUS	*You should incorporate a context-awareness module to ensure coherence and relevance in the generated responses for a virtual assistant. This helps the model retain meaningful interactions with users.*
CAUTION ALERT	*Don't confuse adjusting the temperature parameter with solving coherence issues. While it controls variability, it may not address deeper problems related to context and relevance in responses.*

PRACTICE TEST 9 - QUESTIONS ONLY

QUESTION 1

You are developing a multilingual chatbot to assist customers with inquiries about a global product lineup. The chatbot needs to understand user queries in different languages, provide relevant responses, and maintain context across conversations. Additionally, the chatbot should seamlessly integrate with existing customer support systems.
Which Azure AI service or combination of services would be most suitable for this multilingual chatbot scenario?
Select all answers that apply.

A) Azure Cognitive Services Text Analytics
B) Azure Cognitive Services Language Understanding (LUIS)
C) Azure Bot Services
D) Azure AI Translator service
E) Azure Cognitive Services QnA Maker

QUESTION 2

Your organization is developing a virtual language tutor application that listens to students' spoken sentences, evaluates pronunciation, and provides feedback. The application should also generate spoken responses to students' queries and explanations.
Which Azure AI service should you choose to fulfill these requirements effectively?
Select all answers that apply.

A) Azure AI Speech to Text
B) Azure AI Text Analytics
C) Azure AI Language Understanding (LUIS)
D) Azure AI Text to Speech
E) Azure AI Translator Text

QUESTION 3

When deploying a custom language understanding model, which Azure CLI command should be used to publish the model for consumption?

```
A) az language-understanding model publish
B) az language-understanding model deploy
C) az language-understanding model create
D) az language-understanding model activate
E) az language-understanding model enable
```

QUESTION 4

You are building a web application that utilizes Azure AI Computer Vision services to analyze images uploaded by users. Which authentication method should you implement to ensure that the application can securely access the image analysis capabilities?

A) OAuth 2.0
B) API key
C) Azure Active Directory (AAD)
D) Shared access signature (SAS)
E) JWT token

QUESTION 5

Your team is deploying an Azure AI service that involves sensitive data processing. Which security measure is most appropriate to protect the account keys used by the service?

A) Storing keys in plaintext configuration files
B) Using encryption at rest for key storage
C) Sharing keys via email for backup
D) Hardcoding keys in source code
E) Rotating keys periodically

QUESTION 6

You are deploying an Azure AI solution that includes Azure Machine Learning services for model training. Your organization requires that access to the machine learning workspace is restricted to specific Azure Virtual Machines (VMs) in Azure. What should you do?

A) Implement Azure Active Directory (AAD) authentication for the VMs.
B) Configure network security groups (NSGs) for the VMs.
C) Use Azure Key Vault for storing access tokens.
D) Enable Managed Identity for the VMs.
E) Set up a custom route table for the VMs.

QUESTION 7

Your team is tasked with implementing strategies for proactive incident management in Azure AI solutions. What approach should you adopt to proactively identify and address potential incidents before they impact service availability?

A) Reactive incident response based on user complaints
B) Manual log analysis during scheduled maintenance windows
C) Predictive analytics and anomaly detection
D) Waiting for system failures to occur before taking action
E) Implementing incident management policies after service disruptions

QUESTION 8

As part of your Azure AI service management strategy, you need to ensure compliance with security standards and regulations. Which consideration should influence your decision-making process when implementing security measures for Azure AI implementations?

A) Ignoring security standards for faster deployment
B) Maximizing exposure to security vulnerabilities
C) Adhering to industry-specific security regulations
D) Sharing sensitive information publicly
E) Disabling security features for ease of use

QUESTION 9

You have an Azure App Services web app named App4. You need to configure App4 to use Azure AD authentication while minimizing administrative effort and adhering to the principle of least privilege. What should you do?

A) Enable Azure Active Directory (Azure AD) authentication and configure App4 to use it.
B) Implement OAuth 2.0 authentication with Azure AD and grant App4 access to Azure AD.
C) Enable Managed Service Identity (MSI) for App4 and assign RBAC permissions to Azure AD.
D) Configure App4 to use Azure AD single sign-on (SSO).

E) Generate a client secret and store it securely for App4 authentication.

QUESTION 10

Your organization is implementing image moderation for a healthcare platform that allows users to upload medical images for analysis. What is a critical consideration for ensuring compliance and privacy when moderating medical images?

A) Implementing end-to-end encryption for data transmission between client and server.
B) Ensuring compliance with HIPAA regulations for handling sensitive medical data.
C) Restricting access to moderated images to authorized healthcare professionals only.
D) Encrypting metadata associated with medical images to prevent unauthorized access.
E) Implementing multi-factor authentication for users uploading medical images.

QUESTION 11

Your company has deployed a decision support system (DSS) for analyzing customer feedback and sentiment to improve marketing strategies. Which Azure AI service should you leverage to continuously update and retrain the sentiment analysis model based on evolving customer trends?

A) Azure Cognitive Services Text Analytics for sentiment analysis and natural language processing.
B) Azure Machine Learning service for building, training, and deploying machine learning models.
C) Azure Speech service for transcribing and analyzing customer call recordings.
D) Azure Translator service for multilingual sentiment analysis and translation.
E) Azure Video Indexer for analyzing customer sentiment in video content.

QUESTION 12

You are tasked with implementing a text moderation solution on Azure AI Content Safety for a social media platform. What steps should you take to ensure effective content filtering and moderation?

A) Define custom content filtering rules based on specific community guidelines and policies.
B) Utilize Azure AI Language to analyze sentiment and context for more nuanced content moderation.
C) Implement real-time monitoring and alerts to detect and respond to inappropriate content promptly.
D) Use Azure Cognitive Search to index and search through historical moderation data for analysis and review.
E) Configure automated responses to flag and remove content that violates moderation policies automatically.

QUESTION 13

Your team is developing a decision support solution for a financial institution to detect fraudulent transactions in real-time. The solution requires integrating AI models for anomaly detection and risk assessment based on transaction patterns and historical data. Which Azure AI service should you choose to implement the core functionality of fraud detection in this scenario?

A) Azure Cognitive Search
B) Azure AI Content Moderator
C) Azure AI Metrics Advisor
D) Azure Machine Learning
E) Azure AI Video Indexer

QUESTION 14

Your team is tasked with developing an AI-driven solution for an agricultural company to automate crop monitoring and pest detection using aerial imagery. The solution aims to improve crop yield by identifying pests and diseases early. Considering the challenges of aerial imagery analysis, which technique should you employ to enhance object detection

accuracy?
Select all answers that apply.

A) Feature fusion
B) Context aggregation
C) Multi-scale object detection
D) Domain adaptation
E) Semi-supervised learning

QUESTION 15

While integrating Azure AI Services into a CI/CD pipeline, you encounter an authentication error when accessing the AI resources. What steps should you take to troubleshoot and rectify this issue?

A) Verify the credentials used for authentication.
B) Check if the correct API version is being used in the CI/CD pipeline.
C) Review the network security settings to ensure access to Azure services.
D) Ensure that the Azure AI Service resource is provisioned in the same Azure region as the CI/CD pipeline.
E) Upgrade the Azure AI Service resource to a higher tier.

QUESTION 16

You are provisioning an Azure OpenAI service resource. You need to ensure that the resource is only available to applications that are hosted in your Azure subscription. Which network security setting should you configure?

A) All networks
B) All networks, and a network security group to control traffic
C) Disabled, and allow a private endpoint connection to establish access
D) Selected networks

QUESTION 17

Your team is optimizing a custom object detection model trained on Azure AI Vision for detecting anomalies in satellite images. Which use case-specific optimization technique should you prioritize to enhance model performance?

A) Transfer learning from pre-trained models
B) Implementing non-maximum suppression
C) Utilizing region-based convolutional neural networks (R-CNN)
D) Applying class-specific post-processing filters
E) Employing anchor box optimization

QUESTION 18

While developing a language understanding model using Azure AI Language, you come across an API request with the command: `PUT https://<resource-name>.cognitiveservices.azure.com/luis/authoring/v3.0/apps/<app-id>/versions/0.1/train`. What action does this request perform?

A) Publishing the language understanding model.
B) Training the language understanding model.
C) Importing data into the language understanding model.
D) Evaluating the language understanding model.
E) Exporting the language understanding model.

QUESTION 19

As part of a research project, your team needs to analyze drone footage captured over agricultural fields to monitor crop health and identify areas requiring attention. The solution should leverage machine learning models to classify different types of crops, detect pest infestations, and assess overall vegetation health. Which Azure AI service would you recommend for developing and deploying custom computer vision models to achieve these objectives effectively, considering the need for accurate image classification and object detection?

A) Azure AI Video Indexer
B) Azure Cognitive Services - Computer Vision
C) Azure Cognitive Services - Video Analyzer
D) Azure AI Vision Spatial Analysis
E) Azure Machine Learning

QUESTION 20

You are leading a team tasked with developing an AI-driven safety monitoring system for a construction site. The system needs to analyze live video streams from multiple cameras to detect potential safety hazards and alert on-site personnel in real-time. However, the team is facing challenges in ensuring the scalability of the live stream processing. Which Azure AI service should you recommend to address the scalability challenges and enable efficient analysis of live video feeds for safety hazard detection?

A) Azure AI Metrics Advisor
B) Azure Cognitive Services - Video Analyzer
C) Azure Cognitive Services - Face API
D) Azure AI Video Indexer
E) Azure AI Vision Spatial Analysis

QUESTION 21

You are experiencing latency issues with the Azure AI Form Recognizer service integrated into your application. Which step should you take to investigate and address the latency problems?

A) Analyze network latency metrics using Azure Monitor.
B) Increase the concurrency limit for API requests.
C) Decrease the timeout duration for API requests.
D) Review and optimize the service endpoint configuration.
E) Scale up the underlying infrastructure hosting the AI service.

QUESTION 22

In your AI solution, you need to extract entities from text data with a high degree of domain specificity. Which technique would be most effective for this scenario?

A) Named entity recognition (NER)
B) Custom entity models
C) Entity resolution
D) Language detection
E) Rule-based matching

QUESTION 23

Your company is developing a global news aggregation platform that curates articles from various sources. To enhance user experience, the platform needs to automatically detect and tag the language of each article. Which Azure AI service should you integrate into the platform to achieve accurate and efficient language detection?

A) Azure Text Analytics
B) Azure Translator
C) Azure Language Understanding (LUIS)
D) Azure AI Language
E) Azure Cognitive Search

QUESTION 24

You are developing an application that needs to analyze images for the presence of text and extract that text for further processing. Which Azure AI Vision feature should you utilize to accomplish this task?

A) Face detection
B) Object detection
C) Image analysis
D) Optical character recognition (OCR)
E) Spatial analysis

QUESTION 25

You are developing a speech synthesis application that needs to pronounce a specific word phonetically in the synthesized speech output. Which SSML tag should you use for this purpose?

A) <phoneme> tag
B) <break> tag
C) <prosody> tag
D) <say-as> tag
E) <sub> tag

QUESTION 26

Your team is building a language understanding model for a healthcare chatbot application. The model needs to accurately interpret user queries related to medical symptoms and provide relevant information. Which feature of Azure Cognitive Services Language Understanding (LUIS) should you prioritize to enhance intent recognition in this scenario?

A) Creating and training intents
B) Adding prebuilt entities
C) Importing labeled data for training
D) Designing and evaluating the conversation flow
E) Integrating with Azure Bot Service

QUESTION 27

You are investigating an issue with an Azure app that uses Azure AI Speech for real-time speech-to-text conversion. Users report inaccuracies in transcribed text, especially in noisy environments. What could be a potential cause of this inaccuracy?

A) Inadequate sampling rate for capturing audio input.
B) Lack of microphone access permissions granted to the app.
C) Insufficient training data for the Azure AI Speech model.
D) Limited bandwidth allocated to the Azure AI Speech service.
E) Outdated version of the Azure AI Speech SDK being used in the app.

QUESTION 28

Your organization plans to implement speech translation technology to facilitate communication between teams located in different regions. Which use case best aligns with the application of speech translation in this scenario?

A) Real-time transcription of board meetings
B) Translation of technical documentation
C) Automated language localization in software
D) Interactive language learning platforms
E) Sentiment analysis of customer feedback

QUESTION 29

Your organization is deploying a language understanding model for a banking application to enable users to perform transactions through voice commands. What is a key consideration for integrating the language model with the banking application to ensure security and compliance?

A) Store user transaction data in plaintext format to simplify integration with the language model
B) Implement end-to-end encryption for communication between the banking application and the language model
C) Share user authentication tokens between the banking application and the language model to streamline access
D) Use public APIs for integrating the language model with the banking application to accelerate development
E) Exclude compliance checks in the integration process to avoid delays

QUESTION 30

You are tasked with building an Azure app that will leverage Azure AI Decision service for personalized content recommendation based on user preferences and behavior. The app must be scalable and capable of handling a large number of concurrent users. How should you design the solution to meet these requirements effectively?

A) Implement a centralized decision-making module within the app that processes user data and generates recommendations using Azure AI Decision service in real-time.
B) Utilize Azure AI Decision service's built-in recommendation engine with pre-defined recommendation strategies for different user segments.
C) Develop a microservices architecture where each user's interaction triggers a separate decision request to Azure AI Decision service for personalized recommendations.
D) Integrate Azure AI Decision service with Azure Functions to create serverless decision-making workflows that scale automatically based on demand.
E) Use Azure AI Decision service's reinforcement learning capabilities to continuously optimize recommendation strategies based on user feedback.

QUESTION 31

You are responsible for updating a language understanding model used in an e-commerce platform to adapt to evolving customer preferences and trends. What strategies should you employ to update the model without disrupting the service and ensure seamless integration with existing systems?
Select all answers that apply.

A) Implement rolling updates to gradually introduce changes and minimize downtime
B) Version the model and maintain backward compatibility for existing integrations
C) Conduct A/B testing to validate the performance of the updated model
D) Utilize Azure API Management for seamless migration between model versions
E) Perform canary deployments with user segmentation for phased rollout of updates

QUESTION 32

You are tasked with managing the language understanding model for a legal firm's document analysis system. The model must accurately extract key legal concepts and clauses from various legal documents. What considerations should you prioritize when designing backup and recovery mechanisms to safeguard against data loss or corruption, while ensuring adherence to legal and regulatory requirements governing data privacy and confidentiality?
Select all answers that apply.

A) Implement secure off-site backups of model weights and configurations to prevent data loss in case of on-premises failures
B) Encrypt all backup data stored in Azure Blob Storage and enforce role-based access controls to restrict unauthorized access
C) Maintain a version history of model changes and establish a rollback process to revert to previous states if necessary
D) Conduct regular audits of backup procedures and document compliance with legal and regulatory frameworks
E) Implement a disaster recovery plan with predefined procedures for restoring model functionality in case of catastrophic events or emergencies

QUESTION 33

You are tasked with implementing a chatbot feature in your Azure app that can understand natural language and respond to user queries. Which Azure service and API combination should you use to achieve this functionality?

A) Azure Cognitive Search > Language API
B) Azure Speech Service > Speech API
C) Azure AI Language Service > Language Understanding (LUIS) API
D) Azure Computer Vision > Vision API
E) Azure Content Moderator > Decision API

QUESTION 34

What strategies should Azure AI engineers employ for iterative testing and improvement of a question answering solution?
Select all answers that apply.

A) Implement A/B testing to compare different versions of the knowledge base
B) Deploy automated regression testing for continuous validation
C) Introduce periodic updates without comprehensive testing
D) Utilize simulated user queries for scenario-based testing
E) Rely on manual testing for all updates and changes

QUESTION 35

What techniques can Azure AI engineers employ to design effective multi-turn conversation flows in a question answering solution, considering both technical and usability aspects?
Select all answers that apply.

A) Implement context persistence for seamless transition between turns
B) Design intuitive prompts for guiding user interactions
C) Incorporate error handling mechanisms for robustness
D) Integrate feedback loops for continuous improvement
E) Ensure accessibility and inclusivity across diverse user groups

QUESTION 36

Your task involves deploying a custom speech-to-text model in an Azure container. Which options should you include in

the bash statement to accomplish this task successfully?
Select all answers that apply.

```
A) "mcr.microsoft.com/azure-cognitive-services/speech/speech-to-text"
B) "--memory 256 --cpus 4"
C) "--accept"
D) "--region eastus"
E) "--api-key {API_KEY}"
```

QUESTION 37

As part of updating a custom NLP model deployed on Azure, your team is considering versioning strategies. Which approach ensures efficient management of model versions while minimizing disruptions to production?
Select all answers that apply.

A) Utilize Azure Machine Learning pipelines for automated versioning
B) Maintain separate deployment environments for each model version
C) Implement blue-green deployment for seamless transition between versions
D) Roll out updates gradually to a subset of users for testing
E) Use Azure DevOps for continuous integration and deployment (CI/CD)

QUESTION 38

Your team is developing a voice assistant solution for a healthcare IoT platform, integrating Azure Cognitive Services for voice recognition and processing. To ensure compliance with data privacy regulations, what action should you prioritize during development?
Select all answers that apply.

A) Implement end-to-end encryption for voice data transmission
B) Utilize Azure Key Vault for managing voice data encryption keys
C) Incorporate role-based access control (RBAC) for data access
D) Implement anonymization techniques for protecting user identity
E) Conduct regular security audits for voice assistant vulnerabilities

QUESTION 39

You are building a chatbot application that integrates Azure Language Understanding (LUIS) for natural language understanding. Choose the appropriate class for initializing the LUIS client in the provided code snippet.

```
var luisClient = new LUISRuntimeClient(new ApiKeyServiceClientCredentials("<LUIS_API_KEY>"))
{ Endpoint = "<LUIS_ENDPOINT>" };
```

```
A) LUISClient
B) LUISRuntimeClient
C) LUISCredentials
D) LUISOptions
E) LUISRuntimeCredentials
```

QUESTION 40

Your organization is developing a document intelligence solution to extract data from legal documents for analysis. Regulatory compliance and responsible AI practices are critical in handling sensitive legal information. Which Azure AI service should you integrate into the solution to ensure compliance and responsible AI practices?

A) Azure Text Analytics
B) Azure Language Understanding (LUIS)
C) Azure AI Translator service

D) Azure Cognitive Services
E) Azure AI Document Intelligence

QUESTION 41

Your team is implementing Azure Cognitive Search to index and search documents containing sensitive information, such as customer details and financial records. As the Azure AI engineer responsible for security considerations, you need to ensure that connections to data sources are securely established to protect sensitive data from unauthorized access. Which security measure should you prioritize when configuring data source connections for Azure Cognitive Search?

A) Implement encryption in transit for data transfer
B) Utilize managed identities for authentication
C) Restrict access to data sources using IP firewall rules
D) Encrypt data at rest in the data source
E) Enable role-based access control (RBAC) for data sources

QUESTION 42

Your application needs to analyze user sentiments using Azure Cognitive Services Text Analytics. Which code snippet should you use to authenticate with the Text Analytics service?

```
A) var credential = new AzureKeyCredential(apiKey);
B) var credential = new TextAnalyticsApiKeyCredential(apiKey);
C) var credential = new TextAnalyticsServiceClient(apiKey);
D) var credential = new AzureTextAnalyticsCredential(apiKey);
E) var credential = new TextAnalyticsClient(apiKey);
```

QUESTION 43

Your team is responsible for monitoring the performance and efficiency of indexers in Azure Cognitive Search to ensure optimal search index updates. Which metric should you prioritize monitoring to assess the performance of indexers?

A) Latency of indexer execution
B) CPU utilization during indexing
C) Number of documents indexed per unit time
D) Network bandwidth consumption
E) Disk I/O operations during indexing

QUESTION 44

Your team is implementing an Azure Cognitive Search solution for a financial institution to index a vast repository of financial documents. The institution requires efficient querying and analysis capabilities for the projected data stored in Knowledge Store. What is a best practice for optimizing query performance in Knowledge Store for financial documents?

A) Minimize the use of query filters to reduce query complexity
B) Implement aggressive caching mechanisms for projected data
C) Design indexes to include all fields from projected documents
D) Utilize partitioning to distribute projected data across multiple storage accounts
E) Implement pre-processing steps to optimize data before projection

QUESTION 45

When working with Azure AI Computer Vision service to detect objects in an image, which method should you use?

```
A) DetectObjects()
B) IdentifyObjects()
C) AnalyzeImage()
D) ObjectDetection()
E) RecognizeObjects()
```

QUESTION 46

Your team is developing a customer support chatbot using Azure OpenAI Service. The chatbot needs to generate contextually relevant responses based on customer inquiries. Which technique should you prioritize to ensure the chatbot generates coherent and relevant text?

A) Fine-tuning the language model on customer support transcripts.
B) Adjusting temperature parameter for controlled text generation.
C) Implementing beam search for better response selection.
D) Using reinforcement learning to optimize chatbot responses.
E) Adding randomness to responses for natural conversation flow.

QUESTION 47

Your team is developing an AI-powered creative platform leveraging Azure OpenAI Service to generate images based on textual descriptions. You need to ensure that the generated images maintain high quality and relevance. Which approach should you prioritize to evaluate the quality of the generated images?

A) Implementing human evaluation of generated images for subjective quality assessment.
B) Measuring image fidelity and coherence using structural similarity metrics.
C) Utilizing automated image recognition algorithms to assess visual consistency.
D) Conducting sentiment analysis on user feedback regarding the generated images.
E) Applying style transfer techniques to refine the appearance of generated images.

QUESTION 48

When integrating Azure AI Vision service for image analysis, which combination of statements is correct?

A) Statement I: Azure AI Vision service supports face recognition.
B) Statement II: Azure AI Vision service enables object detection in images.
C) Statement III: Azure AI Vision service offers text translation functionalities.
D) Statement I, Statement II
E) Statement II, Statement III

QUESTION 49

As part of a project to fine-tune an Azure OpenAI model for sentiment analysis, you are exploring strategies for incremental learning and model adaptation. What approach should you consider to facilitate gradual updates to the model without requiring extensive retraining?
Select all answers that apply.

A) Employing transfer learning by fine-tuning the model on new sentiment analysis tasks while retaining knowledge from previous training.
B) Implementing a federated learning framework to allow distributed updates from multiple data sources while preserving data privacy.
C) Leveraging online learning techniques to update the model in real-time based on incoming data streams without

offline retraining.

D) Using active learning methods to selectively query additional labeled data for specific sentiment analysis scenarios.

E) Applying model distillation to extract knowledge from the fine-tuned model and transfer it to a smaller, more efficient architecture for incremental updates.

QUESTION 50

In a scenario where your organization is fine-tuning an Azure OpenAI model for generating product descriptions based on images, what strategies could help mitigate overfitting during the fine-tuning process?

A) Increasing the model complexity to capture more features
B) Regularizing the model with techniques like dropout or weight decay
C) Fine-tuning the model on a smaller subset of the training data
D) Reducing the learning rate to slow down convergence
E) Ensembling multiple models trained on different subsets of the data

PRACTICE TEST 9 - ANSWERS ONLY

QUESTION 1

Answer - [B, D] Azure Cognitive Services Language Understanding (LUIS), Azure AI Translator service

Option A - Azure Cognitive Services Text Analytics: Primarily used for sentiment analysis and key phrase extraction, not for understanding user queries in different languages.
Option C - Azure Bot Services: Although capable of building chatbots, it lacks robust multilingual support and context retention across languages.
Option E - Azure Cognitive Services QnA Maker: Designed for creating question-and-answer bots and does not provide extensive multilingual support or context retention features.
Option B - Azure Cognitive Services Language Understanding (LUIS): Allows for building language understanding models to comprehend user intents and entities in different languages.
Option D - Azure AI Translator service: Provides translation capabilities essential for understanding user queries and responding in multiple languages, facilitating the development of a multilingual chatbot.

EXAM FOCUS	*You need to combine Azure Cognitive Services Language Understanding (LUIS) and Azure AI Translator for multilingual chatbots. LUIS ensures context retention while Translator enables language comprehension and responses.*
CAUTION ALERT	*Avoid relying on Azure Bot Services alone for multilingual scenarios, as it lacks built-in language support and context retention across languages.*

QUESTION 2

Answer - [A, D] Azure AI Speech to Text, Azure AI Text to Speech

Option B - Azure AI Text Analytics: Used for text analysis tasks such as sentiment analysis, not suitable for evaluating pronunciation.
Option C - Azure AI Language Understanding (LUIS): Designed for intent recognition in conversational AI applications, not suited for evaluating pronunciation.
Option E - Azure AI Translator Text: Translates text between languages, not suitable for evaluating pronunciation.

EXAM FOCUS	*Make sure to use Azure AI Speech to Text for evaluating pronunciation and Azure AI Text to Speech for generating spoken responses. These services are tailored for voice and speech applications.*
CAUTION ALERT	*Don't confuse Azure Text Analytics or LUIS with pronunciation tasks; these services focus on text analysis and intent recognition, not evaluating or generating speech.*

QUESTION 3

Answer - A) az language-understanding model publish

Option B - Incorrect. This command is not used for publishing models but rather for deploying them to specific endpoints. Option C - Incorrect. This command is used for creating new models, not for publishing existing ones. Option D - Incorrect. This command does not exist in the Azure CLI for language understanding models. Option E - Incorrect. This command does not exist in the Azure CLI for language understanding models.

EXAM FOCUS	*Always remember to use the command az language-understanding model publish when deploying a custom LUIS model. This command is essential to make your model available for consumption.*
CAUTION ALERT	*Stay cautioned against using incorrect commands like az language-understanding model deploy, which could lead to deployment errors or delays.*

QUESTION 4

Answer - C) Azure Active Directory (AAD)

Option B - Incorrect. API keys may not provide the necessary user authentication and access control for securely accessing image analysis capabilities. Option D - Incorrect. Shared access signatures are typically used for granting limited access to resources and may not provide comprehensive user authentication for a web application. Option E - Incorrect. JWT tokens are typically used for secure transmission of information but may not provide comprehensive user authentication for accessing Azure AI services.

EXAM FOCUS	*You should implement Azure Active Directory (AAD) for secure access to Azure AI services like Computer Vision. AAD provides strong authentication and access control.*
CAUTION ALERT	*Stay clear of API keys or shared access signatures (SAS) for critical services, as they lack the security and fine-grained control that AAD offers.*

QUESTION 5

Answer - [E] Rotating keys periodically.

Rotating keys periodically - Regularly rotating keys enhances security by limiting the exposure window in case of key compromise. Options A, B, C, and D pose significant security risks and are not recommended practices for protecting account keys.

EXAM FOCUS	*Always consider key rotation as part of your security strategy for sensitive data processing. Periodically rotating keys minimizes the risk of exposure in case of compromise.*
CAUTION ALERT	*Avoid storing or sharing keys in plaintext or insecure mediums like email or source code, as this can lead to critical security breaches.*

QUESTION 6

Answer - B) Configure network security groups (NSGs) for the VMs.

Option A - Incorrect. Implementing Azure Active Directory (AAD) authentication for the VMs may provide user authentication but does not directly restrict access to the machine learning workspace. Option C - Incorrect. Using Azure Key Vault for storing access tokens does not restrict access to the machine learning workspace from specific VMs. Option D - Incorrect. Enabling Managed Identity for the VMs is not directly related to restricting access to the machine learning workspace. Option E - Incorrect. Setting up a custom route table for the VMs does not directly restrict access to the machine learning workspace.

EXAM FOCUS	*Make sure to configure network security groups (NSGs) to control access to Azure Machine Learning workspaces. NSGs restrict traffic and ensure that only authorized VMs can access resources.*
CAUTION ALERT	*Stay cautioned—enabling Managed Identity does not restrict network access. Use NSGs for restricting access based on IP addresses or specific VMs.*

QUESTION 7

Answer - [C] Predictive analytics and anomaly detection.

Predictive analytics and anomaly detection - Proactively identifying potential incidents through predictive analytics and anomaly detection allows for early intervention and preventive measures, minimizing service disruptions and ensuring continuous availability of Azure AI solutions. Options A, B, D, and E are reactive approaches that may lead to service downtime and user dissatisfaction.

EXAM	*You need to implement predictive analytics and anomaly detection for proactive incident management.*

FOCUS	*This allows you to identify potential issues before they impact service availability.*
CAUTION ALERT	*Avoid relying on reactive approaches like waiting for failures or user complaints, as this can lead to downtime and user dissatisfaction.*

QUESTION 8

Answer - [C] Adhering to industry-specific security regulations.

Adhering to industry-specific security regulations - Ensuring compliance with industry-specific security regulations demonstrates commitment to data protection and regulatory compliance, mitigating legal and financial risks associated with non-compliance, unlike options A, B, D, and E, which may result in security breaches and compliance violations.

EXAM FOCUS	*Always prioritize adherence to industry-specific security regulations when implementing security measures for Azure AI solutions, ensuring compliance and avoiding legal risks.*
CAUTION ALERT	*Stay clear of disabling security features or ignoring standards for the sake of convenience, as this can lead to vulnerabilities and non-compliance issues.*

QUESTION 9

Answer - C) Enable Managed Service Identity (MSI) for App4 and assign RBAC permissions to Azure AD.

Option A - Incorrect. While Azure AD authentication is a valid approach, enabling MSI with RBAC permissions directly meets the requirement with minimal administrative overhead. Option B - Incorrect. OAuth 2.0 authentication with Azure AD may introduce unnecessary complexity and does not leverage MSI for authentication. Option D - Incorrect. Azure AD SSO may provide centralized authentication but may not align with the requirement to use Azure AD directly. Option E - Incorrect. Storing client secrets may introduce additional security risks and administrative overhead.

EXAM FOCUS	*You should enable Managed Service Identity (MSI) and assign Role-Based Access Control (RBAC) permissions to minimize overhead and adhere to least privilege principles for App4 authentication.*
CAUTION ALERT	*Stay cautioned—storing client secrets or using OAuth 2.0 may introduce unnecessary security risks and administrative complexity in managing access.*

QUESTION 10

Answer - [B] Ensuring compliance with HIPAA regulations for handling sensitive medical data.

Compliance with HIPAA regulations is crucial for handling sensitive medical data appropriately, ensuring privacy and security in image moderation. Options A, C, D, and E focus on security measures but may not specifically address regulatory compliance for healthcare data.

EXAM FOCUS	*Ensure HIPAA compliance when handling medical images in healthcare platforms by implementing strong encryption and following strict data protection practices.*
CAUTION ALERT	*Avoid neglecting compliance with healthcare regulations like HIPAA. Failure to follow regulations can result in data breaches and legal consequences.*

QUESTION 11

Answer - [B] Azure Machine Learning service for building, training, and deploying machine learning models.

Azure Machine Learning service provides capabilities for building, training, and deploying machine learning models, making it suitable for continuously updating and retraining the sentiment analysis model based on evolving customer trends in the decision support system. Options A, C, D, and E focus on different Azure AI services but may not provide the same level of model customization and retraining capabilities required for this scenario.

EXAM FOCUS	*You should use Azure Machine Learning for continuously retraining models as customer trends evolve. ML models require periodic retraining to remain accurate and relevant to changing behaviors.*
CAUTION ALERT	*Avoid relying solely on predefined models like Text Analytics for dynamic, evolving datasets. These models may not adapt well to shifts in customer trends.*

QUESTION 12

Answer - A) Define custom content filtering rules based on specific community guidelines and policies.
C) Implement real-time monitoring and alerts to detect and respond to inappropriate content promptly.

Option B - Incorrect. While sentiment and context analysis can enhance moderation, it may not be sufficient as the sole method for content filtering. Option D - Incorrect. While historical data analysis is valuable, it may not directly contribute to real-time content moderation. Option E - Incorrect. While automated responses can aid in content removal, they may not be suitable for all scenarios and should be used cautiously to avoid false positives.

EXAM FOCUS	*Make sure to define custom filtering rules that reflect the community's guidelines and policies. Real-time monitoring and alerts will help detect and mitigate inappropriate content faster.*
CAUTION ALERT	*Stay clear of over-reliance on sentiment analysis for content moderation. While useful, it doesn't cover specific inappropriate content detection as effectively as custom rules.*

QUESTION 13

Answer - [D] Option D (Azure Machine Learning) is the most suitable choice for implementing AI models for anomaly detection and risk assessment based on transaction patterns and historical data in a real-time fraud detection system.

Options A, B, C, and E are not specifically designed for fraud detection functionality in real-time transaction monitoring. Option A focuses on text search and analytics, Option B is for content moderation, Option C deals with metrics monitoring, and Option E is for video analysis and insights extraction.

EXAM FOCUS	*Always remember that Azure Machine Learning is key for implementing AI-driven fraud detection. It allows for real-time anomaly detection using historical and live data to identify fraud patterns.*
CAUTION ALERT	*Don't confuse services like Metrics Advisor with fraud detection. Metrics Advisor focuses on monitoring metrics rather than real-time anomaly detection in transactions.*

QUESTION 14

Answer - [B, C] Options B and C are essential techniques for enhancing object detection accuracy in aerial imagery analysis for crop monitoring and pest detection. Context aggregation (Option B) allows the model to incorporate surrounding information, improving object recognition, while multi-scale object detection (Option C) enables detection of objects at different resolutions, addressing challenges posed by varying sizes and scales of pests and diseases.

Options A, D, and E may have limited applicability or effectiveness in the context of aerial imagery analysis. Feature fusion (Option A) may not adequately leverage contextual information, domain adaptation (Option D) may be challenging due to the unique characteristics of aerial imagery, and semi-supervised learning (Option E) may not provide sufficient labeled data for effective training.

EXAM FOCUS	*You need to apply context aggregation and multi-scale object detection to enhance object detection in aerial imagery. These techniques account for spatial and scale variations in complex imagery.*
CAUTION ALERT	*Avoid relying on basic object detection models alone. Aerial imagery often requires multi-scale techniques due to differences in object size and scale.*

QUESTION 15

Answer - [A] Verify the credentials used for authentication.

Option A - Checking the credentials used for authentication is crucial as incorrect or expired credentials can lead to authentication errors. Confirming the API version (Option B) is important but may not directly resolve authentication issues. Reviewing network security settings (Option C) is essential but may not be the cause of the authentication error. Ensuring the Azure AI Service resource is in the same region as the CI/CD pipeline (Option D) is relevant for performance but may not directly solve the authentication problem. Upgrading the Azure AI Service resource (Option E) is not necessary to address authentication errors.

EXAM FOCUS	*Make sure to verify the authentication credentials first when encountering access issues in a CI/CD pipeline. Expired or incorrect credentials are common causes of access errors.*
CAUTION ALERT	*Stay alert to other network-related issues, but the first step should always be credential verification. Incorrect credentials are often the root cause of these errors.*

QUESTION 16

Answer - [D) Selected networks]

Configuring the network security setting to "Selected networks" ensures that the Azure OpenAI service resource is only available to applications hosted in your Azure subscription.
A) All networks - This would make the resource accessible from any network, which doesn't meet the requirement.
B) All networks, and a network security group to control traffic - While this could be a valid option, it doesn't specifically limit access to applications hosted in your Azure subscription.
C) Disabled, and allow a private endpoint connection to establish access - This setting would disable all network access, which is not aligned with the requirement.

EXAM FOCUS	*You need to configure "Selected networks" to ensure only applications within your Azure subscription can access the OpenAI service. This enhances security by limiting exposure.*
CAUTION ALERT	*Avoid leaving access open to all networks or using settings like "Disabled." These choices either expose resources to public networks or prevent legitimate access.*

QUESTION 17

Answer - [C) Utilizing region-based convolutional neural networks (R-CNN)]

Region-based convolutional neural networks (R-CNN) are specifically designed for object detection tasks and excel in detecting anomalies in satellite images by capturing detailed spatial information.
A) Transfer learning can provide a good starting point for training, but it may not address the unique characteristics of anomaly detection in satellite images.
B) Non-maximum suppression helps in removing redundant bounding boxes but may not directly enhance anomaly detection performance.
D) Class-specific post-processing filters may be beneficial but may not address the inherent challenges of anomaly detection.
E) Anchor box optimization is more relevant for improving localization accuracy but may not be the primary optimization technique for anomaly detection.

EXAM FOCUS	*You should prioritize using region-based convolutional neural networks (R-CNN) to enhance anomaly detection in satellite imagery. R-CNNs excel in spatial and object-based tasks.*
CAUTION ALERT	*Stay clear of non-specialized techniques like simple post-processing or anchor box optimizations. These may not be sufficient for complex satellite anomaly detection.*

QUESTION 18

Answer - [B] Training the language understanding model.

Option B - This API request initiates the training process for the language understanding model associated with the specified application and version. Publishing the model (Option A) occurs after training is completed. Importing data (Option C), evaluating the model (Option D), and exporting the model (Option E) are separate operations not performed by this request.

EXAM FOCUS	*You should recognize that the PUT API request initiates training of a language understanding model in LUIS. Training is required before models can make accurate predictions.*
CAUTION ALERT	*Stay cautioned against confusing training with publishing or evaluating. These are distinct steps that must occur after training is completed.*

QUESTION 19

Answer - E) Azure Machine Learning

Option A - Azure AI Video Indexer is more focused on extracting insights and metadata from videos rather than developing custom computer vision models.
Option B - While Azure Cognitive Services - Computer Vision offers pre-trained models, it may not provide the flexibility required for custom model development and training.
Option C - Azure Cognitive Services - Video Analyzer is geared towards real-time video processing rather than training custom computer vision models.
Option D - Azure AI Vision Spatial Analysis is suitable for analyzing spatial data but may not offer the customization options needed for complex crop health analysis.

EXAM FOCUS	*Always consider Azure Machine Learning for developing custom computer vision models that require flexibility in training and fine-tuning. It supports complex image classification tasks like crop monitoring.*
CAUTION ALERT	*Avoid using pre-built vision services like Video Indexer for custom model development. While useful for metadata extraction, they lack flexibility for training custom models.*

QUESTION 20

Answer - B) Azure Cognitive Services - Video Analyzer

Option A - Azure AI Metrics Advisor is designed for monitoring and analyzing metrics data and may not provide the real-time video analysis capabilities required for safety hazard detection.
Option C - Azure Cognitive Services - Face API is tailored for facial recognition and detection, not real-time analysis of safety hazards in construction sites.
Option D - Azure AI Video Indexer is more suited for extracting insights and metadata from videos rather than real-time analysis for safety monitoring.
Option E - Azure AI Vision Spatial Analysis focuses on detecting spatial patterns and movements in videos but may not provide the scalability required for analyzing multiple video streams simultaneously.

EXAM FOCUS	*Make sure to choose Azure Video Analyzer for scalable real-time video analysis in safety monitoring systems. It can efficiently process multiple video streams and detect hazards.*
CAUTION ALERT	*Stay cautioned against using services like Face API or Video Indexer. These services focus on specific tasks (like face detection or metadata extraction) and lack scalability for real-time hazard detection.*

QUESTION 21

Answer - [A] Analyze network latency metrics using Azure Monitor.

Option A - Analyzing network latency metrics using Azure Monitor can help identify bottlenecks or issues affecting network performance, which may be contributing to latency problems. Increasing concurrency limits (Option B) might exacerbate issues without addressing the root cause. Decreasing timeout durations (Option C) could lead to more request failures without solving latency issues. While reviewing and optimizing endpoint configurations (Option D) and scaling up infrastructure (Option E) can be beneficial, they may not directly pinpoint or resolve network latency issues.

EXAM FOCUS	*You should start by analyzing network latency using Azure Monitor. This will help identify bottlenecks before making other changes like scaling infrastructure or increasing concurrency limits.*
CAUTION ALERT	*Avoid increasing concurrency limits without first identifying the root cause of the latency. This could worsen performance rather than improve it.*

QUESTION 22

Answer - [B] Custom entity models.

Custom entity models can be trained and fine-tuned to specific domains, ensuring that entities relevant to the domain are accurately extracted. Named entity recognition (NER) may not capture domain-specific entities effectively without customization. Entity resolution deals with disambiguating references to entities, not directly related to domain specificity. Language detection identifies the language but does not address domain specificity. Rule-based matching may not capture the nuances of domain-specific entities.

EXAM FOCUS	*Make sure to use custom entity models when dealing with highly specific domains. This will allow for better accuracy in entity extraction tailored to your data.*
CAUTION ALERT	*Stay clear of relying solely on Named Entity Recognition (NER) for domain-specific tasks as it may miss important entities not covered by the pre-built models.*

QUESTION 23

Answer - [A] Azure Text Analytics.

Azure Text Analytics provides robust language detection capabilities, allowing the platform to accurately detect and tag the language of each article for efficient organization and retrieval in a global news aggregation platform. Azure Translator focuses on translation tasks, not language detection. Azure Language Understanding (LUIS) is used for intent classification and entity recognition, not language detection. Azure AI Language is a broad category covering various natural language processing services but does not specifically specialize in language detection. Azure Cognitive Search is designed for indexing and searching text data, not language detection.

EXAM FOCUS	*Always remember to use Azure Text Analytics for language detection in text-heavy platforms. It's built for text processing and provides accurate language tagging.*
CAUTION ALERT	*Don't confuse Azure Translator with Text Analytics. Translator is designed for translation tasks, not for detecting the language of the input text.*

QUESTION 24

Answer - [D] Optical character recognition (OCR)

Option D - Optical character recognition (OCR) is specifically designed to extract text from images, making it the most suitable choice for analyzing images for the presence of text and extracting that text for further processing. Face detection (Option A) and object detection (Option B) focus on identifying faces and objects, respectively. Image analysis (Option C) and spatial analysis (Option E) do not specialize in text extraction.

EXAM FOCUS	*You need to use the Optical Character Recognition (OCR) feature of Azure AI Vision to extract text from images effectively. It is specifically designed for this task.*

CAUTION ALERT	*Avoid using other features like image analysis or object detection, as they do not specialize in extracting text from images.*

QUESTION 25

Answer - A) <phoneme> tag

Option A - Correct. The <phoneme> tag is used to specify the phonetic pronunciation of a word in the synthesized speech output.
Option B - The <break> tag is used to insert pauses between words, not to specify pronunciation.
Option C - The <prosody> tag is used to modify the pitch, rate, and volume of speech but does not specify pronunciation.
Option D - The <say-as> tag is used to insert dynamic content, such as numbers or dates, into the speech output.
Option E - The <sub> tag is used for substituting one word or phrase with another and is not related to specifying pronunciation.

EXAM FOCUS	*Make sure to use the <phoneme> tag in SSML to control how words are pronounced in speech synthesis. This ensures phonetic precision in the output.*
CAUTION ALERT	*Stay cautioned against using <prosody> or <break> tags for pronunciation. These tags control aspects like pitch and pauses but do not alter phonetic pronunciation.*

QUESTION 26

Answer - [A] Creating and training intents

Option A is the correct choice as creating and training intents is crucial for defining the different actions or tasks that the language understanding model should be able to recognize based on user queries. Options B, C, D, and E are unrelated to enhancing intent recognition.

EXAM FOCUS	*Always consider creating and training intents in LUIS for accurate recognition of user queries. Intents are the backbone of how LUIS understands user input.*
CAUTION ALERT	*Stay alert to the importance of training intents correctly. Incorrect or incomplete training will lead to poor performance in recognizing user queries.*

QUESTION 27

Answer - [C] Insufficient training data for the Azure AI Speech model.

Option C - Insufficient training data for the Azure AI Speech model can lead to inaccuracies in transcribed text, particularly in handling variations such as noise in the audio input. Inadequate sampling rate (Option A) may affect audio quality but is less likely to cause transcription inaccuracies. Lack of microphone access (Option B) might prevent audio input but is not related to transcription accuracy. Limited bandwidth (Option D) can affect data transfer speeds but should not directly impact transcription quality. An outdated SDK version (Option E) may cause compatibility issues but is not the primary cause of transcription inaccuracies.

EXAM FOCUS	*You should evaluate whether your Azure AI Speech model has been trained on sufficient data, especially for noisy environments. Training data volume is crucial for handling complex audio inputs.*
CAUTION ALERT	*Don't confuse transcription errors caused by insufficient training data with hardware or bandwidth issues. Poor training is often the primary cause of inaccuracies.*

QUESTION 28

Answer - [A] Real-time transcription of board meetings

Explanation: Speech translation can facilitate real-time communication between teams speaking different languages during meetings, enhancing collaboration. Options B, C, D, and E are not directly related to facilitating communication between teams located in different regions.

EXAM FOCUS	*Keep in mind that real-time transcription and translation are ideal use cases for speech translation in a global setting. It enhances collaboration by breaking language barriers in live communications.*
CAUTION ALERT	*Stay clear of thinking that speech translation is suitable for static content like documentation or localization. It's meant for dynamic, real-time communication.*

QUESTION 29

Answer - [B] Implement end-to-end encryption for communication between the banking application and the language model

Explanation: B) Implementing end-to-end encryption ensures secure communication between the banking application and the language model, protecting sensitive user transaction data. A) Storing data in plaintext poses a security risk and violates compliance regulations. C) Sharing authentication tokens may compromise user privacy and security. D) Using public APIs may expose sensitive banking data to unauthorized access. E) Excluding compliance checks disregards regulatory requirements and increases the risk of non-compliance.

EXAM FOCUS	*Make sure to implement end-to-end encryption between the banking app and language model to ensure secure communication of sensitive transaction data.*
CAUTION ALERT	*Avoid storing sensitive user data in plaintext or relying on shared authentication tokens, as this could compromise the security and compliance of the system.*

QUESTION 30

Answer - [C] Develop a microservices architecture where each user's interaction triggers a separate decision request to Azure AI Decision service for personalized recommendations.

Option C - Developing a microservices architecture where each user's interaction triggers a separate decision request allows for scalable and personalized content recommendations, ensuring efficient handling of concurrent users and optimizing resource utilization. Option A introduces potential scalability and performance bottlenecks with centralized decision-making. Option B limits flexibility and customization compared to custom recommendation strategies. Option D, while scalable, may incur unnecessary overhead with serverless function invocations for each user interaction. Option E adds complexity and may not be necessary for initial recommendation tasks.

EXAM FOCUS	*You need to consider a microservices architecture where each user request triggers a separate decision from Azure AI Decision service, ensuring scalability and individualized recommendations.*
CAUTION ALERT	*Avoid building a centralized decision-making module. This creates a bottleneck and reduces the app's ability to handle a large number of concurrent users efficiently.*

QUESTION 31

Answer - [A), B), and D)] - Implementing rolling updates, versioning, and utilizing Azure API Management enable seamless updates and integration while minimizing disruptions and ensuring backward compatibility.

C) Incorrect - While A/B testing is important for validating model performance, it might not directly address the challenge of updating the model without disrupting service and ensuring seamless integration.

EXAM FOCUS	*You should implement rolling updates, versioning, and use Azure API Management to ensure smooth updates and backward compatibility when updating language models without disrupting the service.*
CAUTION ALERT	*Stay clear of deploying updates without version control or backward compatibility as it can cause integration issues and service disruption.*

QUESTION 32

Answer - [B), C), and D)] - Encrypting backup data, maintaining version history, and conducting regular audits ensure effective backup and recovery mechanisms while addressing legal and regulatory requirements for data privacy and confidentiality in legal document analysis.

A) Incorrect - While off-site backups can provide redundancy, they might not offer the same level of security and compliance assurance as encrypted backups stored in Azure Blob Storage with restricted access controls.

EXAM FOCUS	*Make sure to encrypt backup data, maintain a version history, and conduct regular compliance audits to safeguard legal data and ensure privacy and confidentiality.*
CAUTION ALERT	*Avoid relying solely on off-site backups without proper encryption and access control, as this can lead to unauthorized data access and legal compliance issues.*

QUESTION 33

Answer - [C] Azure AI Language Service > Language Understanding (LUIS) API

Option C - Azure AI Language Service with the Language Understanding (LUIS) API allows for the creation of language understanding models, enabling chatbots to understand natural language and respond to user queries effectively. Option A is incorrect as Cognitive Search is not suitable for language understanding tasks. Option B is incorrect as the Speech Service is for speech-to-text and text-to-speech conversion. Option D is incorrect as Computer Vision is for image processing, not language understanding. Option E is incorrect as Content Moderator is more focused on content moderation.

EXAM FOCUS	*You need to use Azure AI Language Service with LUIS API to enable your chatbot to understand natural language queries effectively. This is the most suitable API for language comprehension tasks.*
CAUTION ALERT	*Stay alert to the limitations of services like Cognitive Search or Speech Service—they are not meant for natural language understanding in chatbot applications.*

QUESTION 34

Answer - [A), B), and D)] - Strategies for iterative testing and improvement include A/B testing, automated regression testing, and simulated user queries for scenario-based testing.

Option A) - Correct: A/B testing allows comparison between different versions of the knowledge base, aiding in decision-making for improvements. Option B) - Correct: Automated regression testing ensures continuous validation and prevents regressions. Option D) - Correct: Simulated user queries enable scenario-based testing, providing insights into real-world performance. Option C) - Incorrect: Introducing updates without comprehensive testing may introduce errors and degrade performance. Option E) - Incorrect: Relying solely on manual testing is time-consuming and may overlook potential issues.

EXAM FOCUS	*Always remember to use A/B testing, automated regression testing, and simulated user queries to iteratively improve question-answering models and prevent performance regression.*
CAUTION ALERT	*Don't confuse relying solely on manual testing or skipping comprehensive testing. This can introduce undetected errors, compromising system reliability.*

QUESTION 35

Answer - [A), B), and C)] - Designing effective multi-turn conversation flows involves implementing context persistence, intuitive prompts, and error handling mechanisms.

Option A) - Correct: Implementing context persistence ensures a seamless transition between conversational turns, maintaining context. Option B) - Correct: Designing intuitive prompts guides user interactions effectively, enhancing user experience. Option C) - Correct: Incorporating error handling mechanisms improves robustness by addressing user queries effectively, even in case of errors. Option D) - Incorrect: While integrating feedback loops is important for continuous improvement, it may not directly relate to designing effective multi-turn conversation flows. Option E) - Incorrect: Ensuring accessibility and inclusivity is crucial but may not directly address designing effective multi-turn conversation flows.

EXAM FOCUS	*You should implement context persistence, intuitive prompts, and error handling to design effective multi-turn conversation flows, ensuring a smooth and user-friendly experience.*
CAUTION ALERT	*Avoid overlooking error-handling mechanisms. Missing these can result in a poor user experience, especially when interactions encounter unexpected queries.*

QUESTION 36

Answer - [A, B, C] "mcr.microsoft.com/azure-cognitive-services/speech/speech-to-text"
"--memory 256 --cpus 4"
"--accept"

Option A specifies the correct URI for the speech-to-text model container. Option B sets memory and CPU limits. Option C accepts necessary agreements during deployment. Options D and E are not relevant for container deployment.

EXAM FOCUS	*Always consider using the correct container image (speech-to-text), CPU and memory limits, and accept terms during container deployment to ensure your speech-to-text model functions smoothly.*
CAUTION ALERT	*Stay clear of neglecting resource limits and API agreements during deployment. This can lead to performance issues and failed deployments.*

QUESTION 37

Answer - [A, C, D].

A) Utilizing Azure Machine Learning pipelines automates versioning and facilitates efficient management of model versions. C) Implementing blue-green deployment allows for seamless transition between versions with minimal disruption to production. D) Rolling out updates gradually to a subset of users for testing mitigates risks and ensures smooth transitions. B) Maintaining separate deployment environments for each model version may lead to resource duplication and complexity. Using Azure DevOps for CI/CD is beneficial but does not specifically address versioning strategies.

EXAM FOCUS	*Make sure to leverage versioning strategies like blue-green deployment and gradual rollouts to minimize disruptions during model updates, ensuring smooth transitions.*
CAUTION ALERT	*Avoid separate environments for each version, which can lead to resource wastage and complexity. Keep updates automated and gradual.*

QUESTION 38

Answer - [A, B, C].

A) Implementing end-to-end encryption for voice data transmission ensures that sensitive information remains protected during communication between the voice assistant and backend services. B) Utilizing Azure Key Vault for managing encryption keys enhances security by providing centralized key management and protection. C) Incorporating role-based access control (RBAC) restricts access to voice data based on user roles, reducing the risk of unauthorized access and ensuring compliance with regulations. D) While anonymization techniques protect user identity, they may not directly address compliance requirements related to data privacy regulations. E) Conducting regular security audits is important but may not directly ensure compliance with data privacy regulations for voice assistant development.

EXAM FOCUS	*You should prioritize end-to-end encryption, secure key management, and role-based access controls when developing voice recognition solutions to ensure compliance with data privacy regulations.*
CAUTION ALERT	*Stay alert to the risk of exposing sensitive voice data without encryption or access control mechanisms, which could lead to privacy breaches.*

QUESTION 39

Answer - [B] LUISRuntimeClient

Choice A - LUISClient: Incorrect. This choice is not a valid class for interacting with LUIS service.
Choice B - LUISRuntimeClient: Correct. This choice represents the client class for interacting with LUIS service at runtime.
Choice C - LUISCredentials: Incorrect. This choice is not a valid class related to LUIS client initialization.
Choice D - LUISOptions: Incorrect. This choice represents options for configuring the LUIS client, not the client itself.
Choice E - LUISRuntimeCredentials: Incorrect. This choice is not a valid class for initializing LUIS client.

EXAM FOCUS	*Keep in mind that using LUISRuntimeClient is essential for initializing and interacting with LUIS for runtime queries. This class provides the necessary functions for processing language models in real time.*
CAUTION ALERT	*Avoid confusing LUISRuntimeClient with other classes like LUISClient, which may lead to errors in setting up the language understanding process.*

QUESTION 40

Answer - [E] Azure AI Document Intelligence.

E) Azure AI Document Intelligence provides capabilities for handling sensitive document data with regulatory compliance and responsible AI practices, ensuring the secure extraction of data from legal documents. A) Azure Text Analytics focuses on text analysis but may not provide specialized features for regulatory compliance in legal documents. B) Azure Language Understanding (LUIS) is used for understanding user intents and entities in text and does not specialize in document intelligence. C) Azure AI Translator service is focused on translation tasks and does not address regulatory compliance in document processing. D) Azure Cognitive Services offers various AI capabilities but may require additional customization for document intelligence and regulatory compliance.

EXAM FOCUS	*Make sure to use Azure AI Document Intelligence for handling sensitive legal documents as it provides specialized capabilities for regulatory compliance and responsible AI practices.*
CAUTION ALERT	*Avoid using general AI services that do not specialize in document processing for legal contexts. This could lead to compliance and security risks.*

QUESTION 41

Answer - [A] Implement encryption in transit for data transfer.

A) Implementing encryption in transit ensures that data transferred between Azure Cognitive Search and data sources is securely encrypted, protecting sensitive information from interception during transmission. B) While utilizing managed identities enhances security, it primarily addresses authentication concerns rather than encryption during data transfer. C) IP firewall rules may restrict access but do not directly address encryption of data during transit. D) Encrypting data at rest in the data source enhances data security but does not specifically address encryption during transit between

Azure Cognitive Search and data sources. E) Role-based access control (RBAC) governs access to Azure resources but does not directly relate to encryption of data during transmission.

EXAM FOCUS	*You should prioritize encryption in transit when handling sensitive data to ensure data integrity and security during transfer between Azure Cognitive Search and data sources.*
CAUTION ALERT	*Stay clear of relying solely on authentication methods like managed identities, as they do not address the encryption of data during transmission. Always secure data in motion.*

QUESTION 42

Answer - [B] var credential = new TextAnalyticsApiKeyCredential(apiKey);

Option A is incorrect because AzureKeyCredential is not the correct class for authenticating with the Text Analytics service. Option C is incorrect because TextAnalyticsServiceClient is not the correct class for authentication. Option D is incorrect because AzureTextAnalyticsCredential is not the correct class for authentication. Option E is incorrect because TextAnalyticsClient is not the correct class for authentication. Option B is the correct choice as TextAnalyticsApiKeyCredential is the class for authenticating with the Text Analytics service using an API key.

EXAM FOCUS	*Keep in mind that using the correct authentication class, such as TextAnalyticsApiKeyCredential, is essential to interact with Azure Cognitive Services securely and avoid access issues.*
CAUTION ALERT	*Avoid confusing credential types like AzureKeyCredential, which are not intended for Text Analytics service authentication, leading to potential security risks.*

QUESTION 43

Answer - [C] Number of documents indexed per unit time.

C) Monitoring the number of documents indexed per unit time provides insights into the throughput and efficiency of indexer execution, allowing for the assessment of performance and identification of potential bottlenecks or issues. A) Latency of indexer execution is important but may not directly reflect overall performance or efficiency. B) CPU utilization during indexing may vary based on indexer implementation and may not directly correlate with performance. D) Monitoring network bandwidth consumption is important for resource utilization but may not directly indicate indexer performance. E) Disk I/O operations during indexing may be influenced by various factors and may not provide a comprehensive view of indexer performance.

EXAM FOCUS	*Always remember to monitor the number of documents indexed per unit time for performance insights. This metric directly reflects indexing efficiency and potential bottlenecks.*
CAUTION ALERT	*Don't confuse CPU utilization or network bandwidth as direct indicators of indexer performance; these may fluctuate due to unrelated factors without impacting indexing speed.*

QUESTION 44

Answer - [C] Design indexes to include all fields from projected documents.

C) Designing indexes to include all fields from projected documents helps optimize query performance by allowing efficient retrieval and analysis of data without the need for additional lookups or processing steps, especially for complex queries on financial documents. A) Minimizing the use of query filters may limit the flexibility of queries and may not address performance issues related to data retrieval and analysis. B) Implementing aggressive caching mechanisms may improve performance for repeated queries but may not address underlying issues related to data retrieval efficiency. D) Utilizing partitioning to distribute projected data across multiple storage accounts may improve scalability but may not directly optimize query performance for individual queries. E) Implementing pre-processing steps to optimize data before projection may introduce complexity and overhead without guaranteeing significant improvements in query performance compared to optimizing index design.

You should design indexes that include all necessary fields from projected documents to ensure fast, efficient queries, especially for large-scale financial documents.

Avoid relying on minimal query filters or simple caching without focusing on index optimization. This can result in slower performance for complex financial document queries.

QUESTION 45

Answer - A) DetectObjects()

Option B - IdentifyObjects(): This is a hypothetical method and not part of the Azure AI Computer Vision service SDK.
Option C - AnalyzeImage(): This is a hypothetical method and not part of the Azure AI Computer Vision service SDK.
Option D - ObjectDetection(): This is a hypothetical method and not part of the Azure AI Computer Vision service SDK.
Option E - RecognizeObjects(): This is a hypothetical method and not part of the Azure AI Computer Vision service SDK.
Option A is correct because DetectObjects() is used to detect objects in an image in Azure AI Computer Vision service.

EXAM FOCUS	*Make sure to use the DetectObjects() method in Azure Computer Vision for object detection tasks, as it is the API specifically designed for this function.*
CAUTION ALERT	*Stay alert to the existence of hypothetical methods like IdentifyObjects() or ObjectDetection(). These do not exist in the official SDK and could lead to implementation errors.*

QUESTION 46

Answer - [C] Implementing beam search for better response selection.

C) Beam search is a technique used to generate more accurate and contextually relevant responses by exploring multiple potential responses simultaneously.
A) Fine-tuning language models on specific data may improve relevancy but may not ensure coherent responses in all scenarios.
B) Temperature parameter adjustment controls the randomness of generated text but may not guarantee coherent responses.
D) Reinforcement learning can optimize responses but may require extensive training and might not guarantee coherence.
E) Adding randomness could lead to unpredictable responses, potentially undermining the coherence of generated text.

EXAM FOCUS	*You need to implement beam search to ensure the chatbot generates coherent and contextually relevant text. Beam search helps by evaluating multiple potential outputs simultaneously for optimal selection.*
CAUTION ALERT	*Stay cautioned when adjusting randomness or relying on extensive fine-tuning alone. These may not guarantee consistent coherence in chatbot responses without structured techniques like beam search.*

QUESTION 47

Answer - [B] Measuring image fidelity and coherence using structural similarity metrics.

B) Structural similarity metrics offer an objective measure to assess the quality and coherence of generated images, ensuring adherence to the desired standards.
A) Human evaluation is subjective and resource-intensive, not providing consistent assessment.
C) Automated image recognition algorithms may not capture the nuanced quality aspects crucial for creative outputs.
D) Sentiment analysis on user feedback might not directly correlate with image quality and relevance.
E) Style transfer techniques focus on altering the appearance of images and may not address fidelity and coherence concerns directly.

EXAM FOCUS	*You should prioritize using structural similarity metrics to objectively measure the quality of generated images, ensuring they meet the required fidelity and relevance standards.*
CAUTION ALERT	*Avoid depending on human evaluation or sentiment analysis alone, as these methods are subjective and may not provide consistent insights into the image quality.*

QUESTION 48

Answer - A) Statement I: Azure AI Vision service supports face recognition.

Option A is correct because Statement I is true.
Option B - Statement II: Azure AI Vision service enables object detection in images, making this statement true.
Option C - Statement III: Azure AI Vision service does not offer text translation functionalities, making this statement false.
Option D - Statement I: Azure AI Vision service supports face recognition, making this statement true.
Option E - Statement II: Azure AI Vision service enables object detection in images, making this statement true.

EXAM FOCUS	*Keep in mind that Azure AI Vision service supports face recognition and object detection but does not offer text translation functionalities. This distinction is critical for integrating the right services.*
CAUTION ALERT	*Stay clear of assuming Azure AI Vision includes text translation. This is a separate functionality handled by Azure AI Translator service, not Vision.*

QUESTION 49

Answer - [A, C] Employing transfer learning by fine-tuning the model on new sentiment analysis tasks while retaining knowledge from previous training. Leveraging online learning techniques to update the model in real-time based on incoming data streams without offline retraining.

A) Transfer learning allows the model to build on previous knowledge, facilitating incremental updates with new sentiment analysis tasks.
C) Online learning enables real-time updates, ensuring the model adapts to evolving sentiment trends without requiring offline retraining.
B) Federated learning focuses on privacy and distributed updates but may not facilitate incremental learning as directly.
D) Active learning queries additional data but may not address the need for continuous updates.
E) Model distillation aims to compress models rather than facilitate incremental updates.

EXAM FOCUS	*You should employ transfer learning and online learning techniques for incremental model updates, allowing the model to adapt to new data without requiring extensive retraining.*
CAUTION ALERT	*Stay alert to over-complicating updates with federated learning or active learning unless your use case specifically demands these methods. They might not directly facilitate incremental updates.*

QUESTION 50

Answer - [B] Regularizing the model with techniques like dropout or weight decay.

A) Increasing model complexity may exacerbate overfitting rather than mitigate it. C) Fine-tuning on a smaller subset could lead to underfitting rather than addressing overfitting. D) Reducing the learning rate might help converge more effectively but may not directly address overfitting. E) Ensembling can improve performance but may not specifically target overfitting.

EXAM FOCUS	*Make sure to apply regularization techniques like dropout or weight decay to prevent overfitting during model fine-tuning. These methods help maintain model generalization.*
CAUTION ALERT	*Avoid increasing model complexity or fine-tuning on smaller subsets of data. These strategies could exacerbate overfitting or lead to underperformance in real-world scenarios.*

PRACTICE TEST 10 - QUESTIONS ONLY

QUESTION 1

You are tasked with implementing a multilingual natural language processing (NLP) solution for your organization's customer service department.
The solution needs to support sentiment analysis, key phrase extraction, and language detection for customer inquiries in multiple languages.
Which Azure AI service or combination of services should you select to meet these requirements effectively?
Select all answers that apply.

A) Azure Text Analytics
B) Azure Language Understanding (LUIS)
C) Azure QnA Maker
D) Azure Translator Text
E) Azure Cognitive Search

QUESTION 2

Your team is tasked with developing a multilingual customer service chatbot for a global retail chain. The chatbot needs to understand and respond to customer queries in multiple languages, providing product information, handling returns, and processing orders. Additionally, it should integrate seamlessly with the company's CRM system to access customer information.
Which Azure AI service or combination of services should you select to meet these requirements effectively?
Select all answers that apply.

A) Azure AI Speech to Text
B) Azure AI Text Analytics
C) Azure AI Language Understanding (LUIS)
D) Azure AI Text to Speech
E) Azure AI Translator Text

QUESTION 3

To manage the billing details and pricing tier of an Azure AI service, which Azure CLI command should be used?

A) az cognitiveservices account billing
B) az cognitiveservices account pricing
C) az cognitiveservices account tier
D) az cognitiveservices account update
E) az cognitiveservices account configure

QUESTION 4

You are developing an IoT solution that utilizes Azure AI Speech services for real-time speech recognition. Which authentication method should you use to ensure that the IoT devices can securely access the speech recognition capabilities?

A) OAuth 2.0
B) Shared access signature (SAS)
C) Azure Active Directory (AAD)
D) Certificate authentication
E) API key

QUESTION 5

While monitoring an Azure AI resource, you notice an unexpected increase in latency. Which action is most appropriate for troubleshooting and resolving the latency issue?

A) Increasing resource allocation
B) Analyzing diagnostic logs
C) Rebooting the service instance
D) Disabling security measures temporarily
E) Ignoring the latency spike as transient

QUESTION 6

You are tasked with optimizing the performance of an Azure AI solution that utilizes Azure Cognitive Search. The solution is experiencing slow response times due to high query volumes. What action should you take to improve performance while minimizing costs?

A) Scale up the Azure Cognitive Search service tier.
B) Optimize search indexes to reduce unnecessary fields.
C) Increase the number of replicas for fault tolerance.
D) Enable caching for frequently accessed search queries.

QUESTION 7

Your team is reviewing options for configuring alerts and notifications for Azure AI resources. Which compliance consideration should influence your decision when setting up alerting policies?
Select all answers that apply.

A) Compliance with industry standards
B) Minimizing operational costs
C) Maximizing resource performance
D) Avoiding service interruptions
E) Enhancing user experience

QUESTION 8

Your organization is deploying Azure AI services across multiple environments and needs to manage authentication effectively. Which practice should you adopt to enhance authentication management for Azure AI resources?

A) Use default authentication mechanisms provided by Azure
B) Implement custom authentication solutions without encryption
C) Rotate authentication keys periodically
D) Store authentication tokens in plaintext files
E) Share authentication credentials openly within the organization

QUESTION 9

You need to set up authentication for an Azure App Services web app named App5. The app must authenticate using Microsoft Entra ID with minimal administrative effort and adhere to the principle of least privilege. What should you do?

A) Configure App5 to use Azure AD single sign-on (SSO).
B) Enable Managed Service Identity (MSI) for App5 and assign RBAC permissions to Microsoft Entra ID.
C) Implement OAuth 2.0 authentication with Azure AD and grant App5 access to Microsoft Entra ID.
D) Enable Azure Active Directory (Azure AD) authentication and configure App5 to use it.
E) Generate a client secret and store it securely for App5 authentication.

QUESTION 10

You are designing an image moderation solution for a news website that frequently publishes articles with embedded images. The platform aims to prevent the dissemination of inappropriate or misleading visual content. What is a key strategy for addressing challenges in distinguishing contextually sensitive imagery during moderation?

A) Implementing image recognition models trained on a diverse dataset of news-related visuals.
B) Leveraging natural language processing (NLP) techniques to analyze accompanying article text.
C) Integrating sentiment analysis algorithms to gauge the emotional context of images.
D) Collaborating with subject matter experts to develop nuanced moderation criteria.
E) Using blockchain technology to verify the authenticity of news images.

QUESTION 11

Your organization is implementing a decision support system (DSS) for analyzing social media data to identify emerging trends and consumer preferences. What technique should you employ to ensure the DSS remains up-to-date and relevant in a rapidly evolving social media landscape?

A) Implementing real-time data streaming with Azure Event Hubs for continuous ingestion of social media data.
B) Utilizing Azure Cognitive Search for indexing and querying social media content based on relevance.
C) Configuring Azure Logic Apps for automated workflows and event-driven triggers from social media platforms.
D) Employing Azure Databricks for collaborative analytics and machine learning on social media datasets.
E) Using Azure Functions for serverless event-driven compute and automated data processing tasks.

QUESTION 12

You are building a document intelligence solution on Azure AI Document Intelligence to extract data from legal documents. What actions should you take to ensure accurate data extraction and processing?

A) Provision a Document Intelligence resource and select prebuilt models tailored for legal document processing.
B) Train a custom document intelligence model using a diverse set of labeled legal documents for specific data extraction tasks.
C) Implement optical character recognition (OCR) to extract text and structured data from scanned legal documents accurately.
D) Utilize Azure Cognitive Search to index and search through extracted data for retrieval and analysis.
E) Define skillsets with custom skills to enhance data extraction capabilities for legal document processing.

QUESTION 13

You are leading a team of Azure AI engineers tasked with implementing a decision support solution for a manufacturing company to optimize production processes and reduce downtime. The solution requires real-time analysis of sensor data from industrial equipment to detect anomalies and predict maintenance needs. Which Azure AI service should you select to fulfill the requirements of this scenario?

A) Azure AI Document Intelligence
B) Azure AI Video Indexer
C) Azure Cognitive Search
D) Azure Machine Learning
E) Azure AI Metrics Advisor

QUESTION 14

You are leading a team developing an AI solution for a retail company to automate shelf monitoring and product replenishment using shelf-mounted cameras. The solution requires accurate object detection to identify out-of-stock items and optimize shelf layout. Considering the dynamic retail environment, which approach should you adopt to

ensure robust object detection performance?
Select all answers that apply.

A) Ensemble learning
B) Adaptive thresholding
C) Dynamic region proposal networks
D) Progressive resizing
E) Spatial pyramid pooling

QUESTION 15

You are implementing a text moderation solution with Azure AI Content Safety. However, during testing, you encounter an issue where certain inappropriate content is not being flagged correctly. What steps should you take to improve the accuracy of the text moderation?

A) Train a custom model specifically tailored to identify the inappropriate content.
B) Adjust the sensitivity threshold of the Azure AI Content Safety service.
C) Increase the size of the Azure AI Content Safety resource.
D) Incorporate additional metadata features into the text analysis.
E) Upgrade the Azure AI Content Safety resource to a higher tier.

QUESTION 16

You have an Azure OpenAI solution. The solution uses a specific GPT-35-Turbo model version that was current during initial deployment. Auto-update is disabled. Sometime later, you investigate the deployed solution and discover that it uses a newer version of the model. Why was the model version updated?

A) Auto-update is always enabled.
B) Auto-update is enabled automatically when a new version is released.
C) Model versions are updated automatically when the version is older than five version updates.
D) The model version reached its retirement date.

QUESTION 17

You are developing a custom object detection model for monitoring wildlife habitats using Azure AI Vision. Which compliance consideration should you prioritize while deploying the model in this scenario?

A) GDPR compliance for data privacy
B) HIPAA compliance for healthcare data
C) COPPA compliance for children's privacy
D) FERPA compliance for educational data
E) Environmental regulations for wildlife protection

QUESTION 18

You are working on a computer vision solution using Azure AI Vision. While configuring the service, you encounter an API request with the command: POST https://<resource-name>.cognitiveservices.azure.com/vision/v3.0/read/core/asyncBatchAnalyze. What is the purpose of this request?

A) Analyzing images for object detection.
B) Extracting text from images asynchronously.
C) Analyzing video streams for spatial analysis.
D) Detecting faces and emotions in images.
E) Generating captions for images.

QUESTION 19

Your organization is building an AI-powered security solution that analyzes video feeds from surveillance cameras installed in a busy urban area. The solution needs to accurately detect and track vehicles, pedestrians, and unusual activities in real-time to alert law enforcement agencies. Which Azure AI service should you primarily rely on to develop the necessary computer vision models for object detection and tracking in this scenario, considering the requirement for high accuracy and real-time processing capabilities?

A) Azure AI Video Indexer
B) Azure Cognitive Services - Computer Vision
C) Azure Cognitive Services - Video Analyzer
D) Azure AI Vision Spatial Analysis
E) Azure Machine Learning

QUESTION 20

Your organization is developing an AI-based live event monitoring system for ensuring crowd safety and security during large-scale gatherings. The system requires analyzing live video streams from multiple cameras to detect crowd density, identify suspicious behavior, and respond to emergencies promptly. Which Azure AI service should you recommend to implement real-time alerting and response based on the analysis of live video streams for crowd safety and security management?

A) Azure Cognitive Services - Face API
B) Azure AI Metrics Advisor
C) Azure Cognitive Services - Video Analyzer
D) Azure AI Vision Spatial Analysis
E) Azure Machine Learning service

QUESTION 21

You are troubleshooting errors occurring in the Azure AI Content Moderator service integrated into your application. Which action should you prioritize to diagnose and resolve the errors effectively?

A) Enabling detailed diagnostic logging for the AI service.
B) Implementing robust error handling and reporting mechanisms.
C) Reviewing and updating API request payloads and formats.
D) Analyzing historical performance data for the service.
E) Contacting Azure support for assistance with debugging.

QUESTION 22

You are tasked with building an AI solution for a legal firm to extract entities from legal documents written in multiple languages. Which approach should you recommend to ensure accurate entity extraction while handling the language diversity effectively?

A) Named entity recognition (NER)
B) Language detection
C) Custom entity models
D) Machine translation
E) Rule-based matching

QUESTION 23

You are developing an AI-driven document management system for a multinational corporation. The system needs to support documents in multiple languages and automatically categorize them based on language for efficient organization and retrieval. Which Azure AI service should you leverage to implement language detection and classification in the document management system?

A) Azure Translator
B) Azure Text Analytics
C) Azure AI Language
D) Azure Language Understanding (LUIS)
E) Azure Cognitive Search

QUESTION 24

You are working on an application that requires analyzing images to identify and understand the spatial relationships between various objects. Which Azure AI Vision feature should you use to fulfill this requirement?

A) Face detection
B) Object detection
C) Image analysis
D) Optical character recognition (OCR)
E) Spatial analysis

QUESTION 25

You are implementing a speech-enabled application that requires converting written text into natural-sounding speech output. Which SSML tag should you use to specify the language and accent of the synthesized speech?

A) <phoneme> tag
B) <voice> tag
C) <prosody> tag
D) <lang> tag
E) <sub> tag

QUESTION 26

Your company is deploying a virtual assistant for an e-commerce platform to assist customers with product searches and recommendations. The virtual assistant must accurately understand user queries to provide relevant responses. Which strategy should you employ to ensure effective intent recognition in this scenario?

A) Utilizing Azure Cognitive Services Form Recognizer for query analysis.
B) Implementing context switching to handle multi-turn conversations.
C) Training the language model with a diverse dataset of user queries.
D) Integrating Azure Cognitive Services Computer Vision for image recognition.
E) Using Azure Cognitive Services Translator Text for language translation.

QUESTION 27

You are troubleshooting an issue with an Azure app that utilizes Azure Cognitive Search for indexing and querying a large dataset of documents. Users report slow response times when executing complex search queries. What could be a potential reason for this performance issue?

A) Insufficient Azure Cognitive Search unit count provisioned for the app.
B) Inadequate query optimization implemented in the app's search functionality.
C) Limited indexing frequency configured for the Azure Cognitive Search service.
D) Outdated version of the Azure Cognitive Search SDK being used in the app.
E) Insufficient permissions granted to the Azure Cognitive Search service.

QUESTION 28

Your team is developing a speech translation solution for a global healthcare conference. They aim to ensure that sensitive medical information remains confidential during translation. Which Azure service should be utilized to address this privacy concern?

A) Azure Key Vault
B) Azure Cognitive Services
C) Azure Speech Studio
D) Azure Translator Text
E) Azure Confidential Computing

QUESTION 29

Your team is tasked with updating a language understanding model used in a healthcare chatbot to assist patients with appointment scheduling. What strategy should your team employ to ensure seamless updates to the language model while minimizing disruption to the chatbot's functionality?

A) Deploy updates during peak usage hours to maximize user engagement
B) Notify users of upcoming updates and provide guidance on using new features
C) Implement updates without testing to expedite the deployment process
D) Roll back updates immediately if any issues are reported by users
E) Ignore user feedback during the update process to avoid delays

QUESTION 30

You are developing an Azure app that will utilize Azure AI Language for sentiment analysis of customer reviews. The app must provide near real-time sentiment analysis with high accuracy. How should you implement the sentiment analysis functionality to achieve these requirements?

A) Use Azure AI Language's pre-built sentiment analysis model with batch processing of customer reviews at regular intervals.
B) Implement a custom deep learning model using Azure AI Language for sentiment analysis, trained on historical customer review data.
C) Utilize Azure AI Language's real-time sentiment analysis API for on-the-fly analysis of customer reviews as they are submitted.
D) Integrate Azure AI Language with Azure Stream Analytics for continuous sentiment analysis of incoming customer review data streams.
E) Develop a sentiment analysis module within the app that processes customer reviews locally before sending them to Azure AI Language for final sentiment analysis.

QUESTION 31

Your team has deployed a language understanding model for a travel booking application, and you need to monitor its performance and usage patterns in production to ensure optimal service delivery. What metrics and techniques should you prioritize for effective performance monitoring and management of the model?
Select all answers that apply.

A) Monitor latency and throughput of model responses
B) Track error rates and identify common failure patterns
C) Utilize distributed tracing to identify bottlenecks in service calls
D) Analyze user feedback and sentiment to gauge model effectiveness
E) Implement throttling mechanisms to control resource usage and prevent overload

QUESTION 32

Your team is responsible for managing the language understanding model deployed in a government agency's citizen service chatbot application. The model must handle sensitive citizen inquiries while adhering to strict security and compliance standards. What automated processes and technologies should you implement to streamline backup and recovery operations for the language model, ensuring data integrity and compliance with government regulations?
Select all answers that apply.

A) Integrate Azure Automation runbooks to schedule regular backups of model configurations and training data
B) Implement Azure Policy to enforce backup retention policies and compliance standards for model backups
C) Utilize Azure Functions to trigger automated recovery procedures in response to predefined incidents or failures
D) Configure Azure Security Center policies to monitor backup activities and detect unauthorized access attempts
E) Employ Azure Machine Learning pipelines to automate testing and validation of backup data integrity and recovery processes

QUESTION 33

Your organization is developing an Azure app that requires identifying and extracting specific keywords from large volumes of text data. Which Azure service and API combination should you use for this task?

A) Azure Cognitive Search > Language API
B) Azure Content Moderator > Decision API
C) Azure AI Language Service > Text Analytics API
D) Azure Translator Text > Language API
E) Azure Computer Vision > Vision API

QUESTION 34

How can Azure AI engineers incorporate user queries for real-world testing of a question answering solution effectively?
Select all answers that apply.

A) Implement user feedback forms for collecting query data
B) Analyze user interactions with the knowledge base for insights
C) Integrate user queries into automated test scripts for validation
D) Ignore user queries and rely on simulated data for testing
E) Engage users in focus groups for qualitative feedback

QUESTION 35

When leveraging machine learning for dynamic conversation paths in a question answering solution, what considerations should Azure AI engineers keep in mind to ensure effective implementation?
Select all answers that apply.

A) Train models with diverse conversational datasets for better generalization
B) Regularly update models to adapt to evolving user preferences
C) Implement reinforcement learning for optimizing conversation flow
D) Monitor model performance and adjust hyperparameters accordingly
E) Ensure transparency and accountability in model decision-making

QUESTION 36

Your organization plans to deploy a custom sentiment analysis model using Azure containers. Which options should you include in the bash statement to deploy the Sentiment Analysis container successfully?
Select all answers that apply.

```
A) "mcr.microsoft.com/azure-ai/sentimentanalysis"
B) "--memory 512 --cpus 4"
C) "--accept"
D) "--region westus"
E) "--api-key {API_KEY}"
```

QUESTION 37

Your organization is deploying a custom NLP model on Azure to extract key information from legal documents for compliance purposes. Which security measure should be implemented to protect sensitive data processed by the model?
Select all answers that apply.

A) Implement Azure Confidential Computing for secure data processing
B) Apply role-based access control (RBAC) for restricting data access
C) Use Azure Key Vault for storing and managing encryption keys
D) Enable Azure Active Directory authentication for model access
E) Implement data anonymization techniques to obfuscate sensitive information

QUESTION 38

Your company is developing a voice assistant solution for a hospitality management system, leveraging Azure Cognitive Services for voice recognition and natural language understanding. To evaluate user engagement and satisfaction with the voice interface, what approach should you adopt?
Select all answers that apply.

A) Implement sentiment analysis for user feedback interpretation
B) Conduct usability testing with real users for feedback collection
C) Utilize Azure Application Insights for voice assistant performance monitoring
D) Analyze user interaction logs for behavior pattern recognition
E) Deploy A/B testing for comparing voice assistant variations

QUESTION 39

You are developing an application that uses Azure Key Vault to manage and access secrets securely. In the provided code snippet, which class should you use to authenticate with Azure Key Vault?
var credential = new DefaultAzureCredential();

```
A) AzureKeyVaultCredentials
B) KeyVaultClient
C) KeyVaultCredentials
D) DefaultAzureCredential
E) AzureKeyVaultClient
```

QUESTION 40

Your team is developing a knowledge mining solution to extract insights from research papers in the medical field. Ensuring fairness and avoiding bias in the extraction process is crucial for maintaining the integrity of the insights. Which Azure AI service should you use to address bias and ensure fairness in knowledge mining from research papers?

A) Azure Text Analytics
B) Azure Language Understanding (LUIS)
C) Azure AI Translator service
D) Azure Cognitive Services
E) Azure Cognitive Search

QUESTION 41

Your organization is deploying an Azure Cognitive Search solution to index and search a large volume of documents stored in various repositories, including Azure Blob Storage, Azure SQL Database, and Azure Data Lake Storage. As the Azure AI engineer responsible for creating data sources, you need to ensure seamless integration and automation of data ingestion from these diverse sources into the search index. Which Azure service should you leverage to automate data ingestion workflows efficiently across different data repositories?

A) Azure Data Factory
B) Azure Logic Apps
C) Azure Functions
D) Azure Event Grid
E) Azure Batch

QUESTION 42

You are implementing a feature in your application that requires language understanding using Azure Cognitive Services Language Understanding (LUIS). Which code snippet should you use to create a LUIS runtime client?

```
 A) var client = new LuisRuntimeClient(new ApiKeyServiceClientCredentials(apiKey));
 B) var client = new LuisRuntimeClient(apiKey);
 C) var client = new LanguageUnderstandingRuntimeClient(new
ApiKeyServiceClientCredentials(apiKey));
 D) var client = new LanguageUnderstandingRuntimeClient(apiKey);
 E) var client = new LuisClient(apiKey);
```

QUESTION 43

Your organization is implementing Azure Cognitive Search to index a large dataset consisting of millions of records. As part of the deployment, you need to devise a strategy for indexing data incrementally while ensuring efficient updates to the search index. Which approach should you adopt to achieve incremental data indexing in Azure Cognitive Search?

A) Rebuild the search index periodically with updated data
B) Configure indexers to perform full data re-indexing
C) Implement delta indexing to capture only changed or new data
D) Manually trigger indexers for incremental updates
E) Utilize Azure Functions to handle incremental data ingestion

QUESTION 44

Your organization is deploying an Azure Cognitive Search solution to index a diverse range of documents, including text files, PDFs, and images. As part of the implementation, you need to ensure that the projected data stored in Knowledge Store is optimized for analytics and machine learning tasks. What is a recommended approach for leveraging projected data from Knowledge Store for analytics and machine learning?

A) Store projected data in a proprietary format for specialized analytics tools
B) Extract features from projected data and store them in separate tables for analysis
C) Implement custom serialization methods for projected data storage
D) Utilize pre-trained machine learning models for direct analysis of projected data
E) Integrate projected data with Azure Machine Learning pipelines for analysis and model training

QUESTION 45

In Azure AI Document Intelligence service, which method should you use to train a custom document intelligence model?

```
A) TrainModel()
B) CreateModel()
C) BuildModel()
D) TrainCustomModel()
E) DevelopModel()
```

QUESTION 46

You are developing an AI-powered content generation system for a news publishing platform using Azure OpenAI Service. Which parameter should you adjust to ensure the generated news articles maintain a balance between novelty and relevance?

A) Learning rate: Controls the rate at which the model adapts to new data.
B) Diversity: Adjusts the diversity of generated text to introduce new ideas.
C) Beam width: Determines the number of candidates considered during text generation.
D) Prompt length: Specifies the length of input provided to the language model.
E) Epochs: Defines the number of training iterations for the language model.

QUESTION 47

Your company is building an AI-driven marketing platform using Azure OpenAI Service to generate images for advertising campaigns based on textual descriptions. As part of the development process, you need to ensure compliance with copyright regulations and ethical considerations. Which strategy should you prioritize to address these concerns when using the DALL-E model for image generation?

A) Verifying the licensing status of input image datasets and ensuring proper attribution for generated images.
B) Implementing watermarking techniques to protect the ownership of generated images.
C) Reviewing and adhering to usage guidelines provided by the DALL-E model's terms of service.
D) Conducting regular audits to monitor the usage and distribution of generated images across marketing channels.
E) Utilizing image hashing algorithms to detect potential copyright infringements in the generated images.

QUESTION 48

When deploying Azure AI Content Moderator service for content moderation, which combination of statements is accurate?

A) Statement I: Azure AI Content Moderator service provides text moderation capabilities.
B) Statement II: Azure AI Content Moderator service supports image recognition.
C) Statement III: Azure AI Content Moderator service offers language translation functionalities.
D) Statement I, Statement II
E) Statement I, Statement III

QUESTION 49

You are fine-tuning an Azure OpenAI model to generate product recommendations based on customer preferences for an e-commerce platform. Which tool or process should you leverage to evaluate the impact of different fine-tuning strategies on recommendation accuracy and diversity?
Select all answers that apply.

A) Implementing counterfactual evaluation techniques to simulate the impact of alternative fine-tuning strategies on historical user interactions.
B) Utilizing recommendation evaluation metrics, such as precision and recall, to quantify the performance of the fine-tuned model.
C) Conducting user studies or surveys to gather qualitative feedback on the relevance and diversity of recommendations generated by the fine-tuned model.
D) Employing adversarial testing to identify vulnerabilities and biases in the fine-tuned model's recommendation outputs.
E) Integrating reinforcement learning to dynamically adjust fine-tuning parameters based on real-time feedback from user interactions.

QUESTION 50

Your team is fine-tuning an Azure OpenAI model to generate responses for a customer support chatbot. In order to maintain ethical standards and prevent harmful or inappropriate responses, what compliance considerations should be integrated into the fine-tuning process?

A) Implementing profanity filters to censor inappropriate language
B) Conducting regular audits on the generated responses for bias and sensitivity
C) Training the model on diverse datasets to promote inclusivity
D) Securing the model checkpoints to prevent tampering
E) Monitoring user interactions to detect and flag harmful responses

PRACTICE TEST 10 - ANSWERS ONLY

QUESTION 1

Answer - [A, D, E] Azure Text Analytics, Azure Translator Text, Azure Cognitive Search

Option B - Azure Language Understanding (LUIS): Primarily used for building conversational AI solutions and intent recognition, not suitable for sentiment analysis or key phrase extraction.
Option C - Azure QnA Maker: Designed for creating question-answering bots, not for sentiment analysis or key phrase extraction.
Option A - Azure Text Analytics: Offers sentiment analysis, key phrase extraction, and language detection, making it suitable for the requirements.
Option D - Azure Translator Text: Provides language detection and translation capabilities, aligning with the multilingual aspect of the scenario.
Option E - Azure Cognitive Search: Designed for building search solutions and lacks specific NLP capabilities like sentiment analysis and key phrase extraction.

EXAM FOCUS	*You need to use Azure Text Analytics for sentiment analysis and key phrase extraction, and Azure Translator for multilingual support. Cognitive Search can assist with indexing and searching.*
CAUTION ALERT	*Avoid using LUIS and QnA Maker, as they are not designed for sentiment analysis or key phrase extraction.*

QUESTION 2

Answer - [C, E] Azure AI Language Understanding (LUIS), Azure AI Translator Text

Option A - Azure AI Speech to Text: Converts speech to text, not suitable for multilingual chatbot interactions.
Option B - Azure AI Text Analytics: Used for text analysis tasks such as sentiment analysis, not suitable for chatbot interactions.
Option D - Azure AI Text to Speech: Converts text to spoken audio, not directly relevant for chatbot interactions.

EXAM FOCUS	*Make sure to leverage Azure LUIS for intent recognition and Azure Translator for handling multiple languages in the chatbot. These services are key for building multilingual, intelligent customer service bots.*
CAUTION ALERT	*Don't confuse Text Analytics with LUIS. Text Analytics is for analysis, while LUIS is for conversational AI.*

QUESTION 3

Answer - D) az cognitiveservices account update

Option A - Incorrect. This command does not exist in the Azure CLI for managing billing details. Option B - Incorrect. This command does not exist in the Azure CLI for managing pricing tiers. Option C - Incorrect. This command does not exist in the Azure CLI for managing service tiers. Option E - Incorrect. This command does not exist in the Azure CLI for configuring billing details.

EXAM FOCUS	*Always remember to use az cognitiveservices account update to manage billing details and pricing tiers. This command updates existing services with new configurations.*
CAUTION ALERT	*Stay clear of commands like az cognitiveservices account billing or az cognitiveservices account pricing as they do not exist.*

QUESTION 4

Answer - B) Shared access signature (SAS)

Option A - Incorrect. OAuth 2.0 is typically used for user authentication and may not be suitable for authenticating IoT devices. Option C - Incorrect. Azure Active Directory (AAD) may be overly complex for authenticating IoT devices and may not provide the necessary flexibility. Option D - Incorrect. Certificate authentication may be overly complex for IoT devices and may not provide the necessary flexibility. Option E - Incorrect. API keys may not provide the necessary security measures for authenticating IoT devices and accessing speech recognition capabilities.

EXAM FOCUS	*You should use Shared Access Signatures (SAS) for IoT device authentication with Azure Speech services, as this method is specifically designed for securing IoT connections.*
CAUTION ALERT	*Avoid using OAuth 2.0 or Certificate Authentication, as they are more suited for user authentication and may complicate IoT implementations.*

QUESTION 5

Answer - [B] Analyzing diagnostic logs.

Analyzing diagnostic logs - Examining diagnostic logs can provide insights into potential causes of latency spikes, such as resource exhaustion or network issues, enabling targeted troubleshooting and resolution. Options A, C, D, and E either do not address the underlying issue or may exacerbate the problem.

EXAM FOCUS	*Make sure to analyze diagnostic logs when investigating latency issues. Logs provide insight into potential bottlenecks, network issues, or resource exhaustion.*
CAUTION ALERT	*Stay alert to temporary fixes like rebooting the instance or ignoring spikes. These may not address the root cause.*

QUESTION 6

Answer - B) Optimize search indexes to reduce unnecessary fields.

Option A - Incorrect. Scaling up the service tier may improve performance but can increase costs significantly. Option C - Incorrect. Increasing the number of replicas improves fault tolerance but may not directly address slow query response times. Option D - Incorrect. While caching can improve performance for frequently accessed data, it may not be the most effective solution for optimizing search queries.

EXAM FOCUS	*Keep in mind that optimizing search indexes by removing unnecessary fields can greatly enhance performance while minimizing costs.*
CAUTION ALERT	*Avoid scaling up the service tier unless absolutely necessary, as this can significantly increase costs without addressing index inefficiencies.*

QUESTION 7

Answer - [A, D] Compliance with industry standards; Avoiding service interruptions.

Compliance with industry standards - Ensuring alerting policies align with industry standards helps maintain regulatory compliance and data security, reducing the risk of penalties or legal consequences. Avoiding service interruptions - Configuring alerts to prevent service interruptions supports continuous availability and operational stability of Azure AI resources, enhancing overall service reliability and user satisfaction. Options B, C, and E may be relevant but do not specifically address compliance considerations related to alerting policies.

EXAM FOCUS	*You should prioritize compliance with industry standards and ensure alerting policies help avoid service interruptions, particularly in regulated industries.*

CAUTION ALERT	*Stay clear of focusing solely on operational costs or performance without considering compliance requirements.*

QUESTION 8

Answer - [C] Rotate authentication keys periodically.

Rotate authentication keys periodically - Periodically rotating authentication keys enhances security by reducing the risk of unauthorized access and credential misuse, unlike options A, B, D, and E, which may expose Azure AI resources to security vulnerabilities and unauthorized access.

EXAM FOCUS	*Always remember to rotate authentication keys periodically to minimize security risks and protect Azure AI resources.*
CAUTION ALERT	*Avoid storing authentication tokens in plaintext files or sharing credentials openly, as this introduces significant security risks.*

QUESTION 9

Answer - B) Enable Managed Service Identity (MSI) for App5 and assign RBAC permissions to Microsoft Entra ID.

Option A - Incorrect. Azure AD SSO may provide centralized authentication but may not align with the requirement to use Microsoft Entra ID. Option C - Incorrect. OAuth 2.0 authentication with Azure AD may not directly support Microsoft Entra ID and may introduce unnecessary complexity. Option D - Incorrect. Azure AD authentication may not directly support Microsoft Entra ID and may introduce additional configuration overhead. Option E - Incorrect. Storing client secrets may introduce additional security risks and administrative overhead.

EXAM FOCUS	*You need to enable Managed Service Identity (MSI) for the app and assign RBAC permissions to Microsoft Entra ID to ensure minimal administrative effort and least privilege.*
CAUTION ALERT	*Avoid relying on client secrets or complex OAuth 2.0 implementations that introduce additional administrative overhead and security concerns.*

QUESTION 10

Answer - [D] Collaborating with subject matter experts to develop nuanced moderation criteria.

Collaborating with subject matter experts ensures that moderation criteria consider the nuanced context of news imagery, addressing challenges in distinguishing contextually sensitive content effectively. Options A, B, C, and E focus on different approaches but may not provide the same level of contextual understanding as collaboration with experts.

EXAM FOCUS	*Make sure to collaborate with subject matter experts to define nuanced moderation criteria, especially when moderating sensitive visual content for news platforms.*
CAUTION ALERT	*Stay clear of relying solely on automated image recognition or sentiment analysis, as they may miss subtle contextual clues in news-related visuals.*

QUESTION 11

Answer - [A] Implementing real-time data streaming with Azure Event Hubs for continuous ingestion of social media data.

Implementing real-time data streaming with Azure Event Hubs enables continuous ingestion of social media data, ensuring that the decision support system remains up-to-date and relevant in a rapidly evolving social media landscape by capturing emerging trends and consumer preferences in real-time. Options B, C, D, and E focus on different Azure services but may not provide the same level of real-time data ingestion and processing capabilities required for this scenario.

EXAM FOCUS	*You should prioritize implementing real-time data streaming with Azure Event Hubs to continuously capture emerging trends and consumer preferences from social media data.*
CAUTION ALERT	*Stay alert to focusing only on batch processing, as it may not capture fast-evolving trends in social media, making your DSS outdated quickly.*

QUESTION 12

Answer - A) Provision a Document Intelligence resource and select prebuilt models tailored for legal document processing.
C) Implement optical character recognition (OCR) to extract text and structured data from scanned legal documents accurately.

Option B - Incorrect. While training a custom model can be beneficial, prebuilt models tailored for legal documents are likely optimized and require less effort for implementation. Option D - Incorrect. While Azure Cognitive Search can be useful for indexing and searching data, it does not directly relate to data extraction from legal documents. Option E - Incorrect. Defining custom skills may enhance extraction capabilities, but selecting prebuilt models and implementing OCR are more direct solutions for accurate data extraction from legal documents.

EXAM FOCUS	*Make sure to use prebuilt models tailored for legal documents and implement OCR to extract text accurately. This will save time and ensure high accuracy for document extraction tasks.*
CAUTION ALERT	*Avoid relying solely on Azure Cognitive Search for extraction—it's mainly for indexing and searching, not extraction. Ensure your choice is optimized for the task.*

QUESTION 13

Answer - [D] Option D (Azure Machine Learning) is the most suitable choice for implementing AI models to analyze sensor data, detect anomalies, and predict maintenance needs in real-time production processes.

Options A, B, C, and E are not specifically designed for real-time analysis of sensor data and predictive maintenance in industrial settings. Option A deals with document processing, Option B is for video analysis, Option C focuses on text search and analytics, and Option E is for metrics monitoring.

EXAM FOCUS	*You need to leverage Azure Machine Learning for real-time analysis of sensor data and anomaly detection in manufacturing processes. This service provides advanced capabilities for predictive maintenance.*
CAUTION ALERT	*Don't confuse Azure AI Metrics Advisor with Machine Learning; Metrics Advisor is for monitoring, while Machine Learning is needed for real-time predictive models.*

QUESTION 14

Answer - [C, D] Options C and D are suitable approaches for ensuring robust object detection performance in a dynamic retail environment with shelf-mounted cameras. Dynamic region proposal networks (Option C) adaptively adjust object detection regions based on scene characteristics, while progressive resizing (Option D) allows the model to handle objects of varying scales effectively.

Options A, B, and E may have limited effectiveness or applicability in this scenario. Ensemble learning (Option A) may not address the challenges of dynamic environments, adaptive thresholding (Option B) may be less effective in complex scenes, and spatial pyramid pooling (Option E) may not adequately capture scale variations in object sizes on shelves.

EXAM FOCUS	*Always remember to use dynamic region proposal networks and progressive resizing for detecting out-of-stock items on shelves. These approaches help improve object detection under varying conditions in retail*

environments.

CAUTION ALERT *Stay clear of methods like adaptive thresholding, which may not perform well in dynamic, complex environments like retail stores.*

QUESTION 15

Answer - [B] Adjust the sensitivity threshold of the Azure AI Content Safety service.

Option B - Training a custom model (Option A) could improve accuracy but may require significant time and resources. Increasing the size of the Azure AI Content Safety resource (Option C) might not directly impact accuracy and could lead to unnecessary costs. Incorporating additional metadata features (Option D) can enhance analysis but might not specifically address the issue of inaccurate content flagging. Upgrading the Azure AI Content Safety resource (Option E) is not necessary initially. Adjusting the sensitivity threshold (Option B) is the most appropriate action as it allows fine-tuning of the moderation process to improve accuracy.

EXAM FOCUS	*You can consider adjusting the sensitivity threshold of Azure AI Content Safety to better detect inappropriate content. Fine-tuning thresholds is a quick way to enhance the solution's accuracy.*
CAUTION ALERT	*Avoid increasing the resource size or upgrading tiers without first adjusting the sensitivity, as this might result in unnecessary costs without improving detection accuracy.*

QUESTION 16

Answer - [B) Auto-update is enabled automatically when a new version is released.]

With auto-update disabled, the model version would only be updated automatically when a new version is released.
A) Auto-update is not always enabled; it depends on the configuration.
C) There's no specific threshold of five version updates for automatic model version updates.
D) Retirement dates may trigger updates, but it's not the only reason for automatic updates.

EXAM FOCUS	*Keep in mind that even with auto-update disabled, model versions in Azure OpenAI Service can be updated automatically when new versions are released.*
CAUTION ALERT	*Don't confuse auto-update behavior with retirement triggers. Model versions can still be updated when new ones are released, regardless of retirement timelines.*

QUESTION 17

Answer - [E) Environmental regulations for wildlife protection]

Prioritizing environmental regulations ensures that the deployment of the object detection model for monitoring wildlife habitats aligns with legal and ethical considerations related to wildlife protection.
A) GDPR compliance is more relevant to personal data protection and may not directly apply to wildlife monitoring.
B) HIPAA compliance pertains to healthcare data and is not applicable in this scenario.
C) COPPA compliance focuses on children's online privacy and is not relevant to wildlife monitoring.
D) FERPA compliance relates to educational data privacy and is not applicable in this context.

EXAM FOCUS	*You should prioritize compliance with environmental regulations when deploying object detection models for wildlife monitoring. This ensures your solution aligns with legal and ethical requirements.*
CAUTION ALERT	*Avoid focusing on regulations like GDPR or HIPAA in this scenario—they are not relevant for wildlife monitoring but are crucial in other industries.*

QUESTION 18

Answer - [B] Extracting text from images asynchronously.

Option B - This API request is used to asynchronously analyze images and extract text from them. Object detection (Option A), spatial analysis of video streams (Option C), face detection and emotion analysis (Option D), and caption generation (Option E) are unrelated to the primary function of this endpoint.

EXAM FOCUS	*Make sure to understand that the API request asyncBatchAnalyze is designed for asynchronous text extraction from images using Azure AI Vision. This is key for batch processing scenarios.*
CAUTION ALERT	*Stay alert to mixing up endpoints designed for different tasks. Object detection, face detection, and captioning require different APIs.*

QUESTION 19

Answer - B) Azure Cognitive Services - Computer Vision

Option A - Azure AI Video Indexer focuses more on extracting insights and metadata from videos rather than real-time object detection and tracking.
Option C - Azure Cognitive Services - Video Analyzer is geared towards real-time video processing but may not provide the level of customization needed for complex object detection tasks.
Option D - Azure AI Vision Spatial Analysis is more suited for analyzing spatial data and may not offer the real-time processing capabilities required for surveillance applications.
Option E - While Azure Machine Learning allows custom model development, Azure Cognitive Services - Computer Vision offers pre-trained models and APIs optimized for real-time object detection tasks.

EXAM FOCUS	*You should rely on Azure Cognitive Services - Computer Vision for object detection and tracking in surveillance applications. This service is well-suited for real-time analysis with high accuracy.*
CAUTION ALERT	*Don't confuse Azure Video Indexer or Vision Spatial Analysis with Computer Vision—they serve different purposes and may not be optimized for object detection and tracking.*

QUESTION 20

Answer - C) Azure Cognitive Services - Video Analyzer

Option A - Azure Cognitive Services - Face API is designed for facial recognition and detection, not real-time analysis of crowd behavior and security management.
Option B - Azure AI Metrics Advisor is geared towards monitoring and analyzing metrics data and may not provide the real-time video analysis capabilities required for crowd safety and security management.
Option D - Azure AI Vision Spatial Analysis focuses on detecting spatial patterns and movements in videos but may not offer specific features for crowd behavior analysis and real-time alerting.
Option E - Azure Machine Learning service provides a platform for building custom AI models but may require additional development effort for real-time video analysis in crowd safety and security management scenarios.

EXAM FOCUS	*You need to use Azure Cognitive Services - Video Analyzer for real-time monitoring of live video feeds in crowd safety management. This service is designed for real-time video processing and alerting.*
CAUTION ALERT	*Avoid relying on services like Face API or Metrics Advisor for crowd safety—they are more specialized for facial recognition and metric monitoring, not live video safety analysis.*

QUESTION 21

Answer - [B] Implementing robust error handling and reporting mechanisms.

Option B - Implementing robust error handling and reporting mechanisms enables the application to capture and process errors effectively, facilitating diagnosis and resolution. While enabling diagnostic logging (Option A) can provide additional insights, it may not be as immediate or actionable as robust error handling. Reviewing API request payloads (Option C) and analyzing performance data (Option D) are important but secondary to effective error handling. Contacting Azure support (Option E) may be necessary in some cases but should not replace proactive error handling within the application.

EXAM FOCUS	*You should implement robust error handling and reporting mechanisms early to capture issues and debug efficiently. It helps to isolate errors and react quickly during integration.*
CAUTION ALERT	*Avoid relying solely on contacting Azure support or focusing on logging without an error handling process in place. This delays effective troubleshooting and prolongs resolution.*

QUESTION 22

Answer - [C] Custom entity models.

Custom entity models can be trained to recognize legal entities across different languages, providing better accuracy compared to generic techniques like NER or rule-based matching. Language detection is helpful in identifying the language used but does not directly aid in entity extraction. Machine translation may introduce errors and may not preserve entity integrity. Rule-based matching may not handle language nuances and legal terminologies effectively.

EXAM FOCUS	*Make sure to train custom entity models for the legal domain across multiple languages to improve accuracy. This approach is more effective than relying on generic models for legal-specific extractions.*
CAUTION ALERT	*Stay alert to using rule-based matching as it may miss out on legal terminologies and variations in different languages, leading to lower extraction accuracy.*

QUESTION 23

Answer - [E] Azure Cognitive Search.

While Azure Translator and Azure Text Analytics offer language detection capabilities, Azure Cognitive Search provides language detection and classification features specifically designed for document management systems, allowing efficient organization and retrieval of documents based on language. Azure AI Language is a broad category covering various natural language processing services but does not specifically specialize in language detection. Azure Language Understanding (LUIS) is used for intent classification and entity recognition, not language detection. Azure Cognitive Search is designed for indexing and searching text data, including language detection.

EXAM FOCUS	*You need to leverage Azure Cognitive Search for document language detection and classification, which can enhance document organization and retrieval across multilingual environments.*
CAUTION ALERT	*Stay cautioned about using Azure Translator solely for language detection. It's more suited for translation and won't provide the needed indexing and retrieval capabilities.*

QUESTION 24

Answer - [E] Spatial analysis

Option E - Spatial analysis is specifically designed to detect and understand the spatial relationships between objects within images, making it the most suitable choice for this requirement. Face detection (Option A), object detection (Option B), and OCR (Option D) are not tailored for analyzing spatial relationships. Image analysis (Option C) focuses on broader image processing tasks rather than spatial analysis.

EXAM FOCUS	*Keep in mind that Azure AI Vision's Spatial Analysis feature is designed specifically for detecting spatial relationships, making it the right tool for this task.*
CAUTION	*Avoid using general object detection or image analysis for spatial relationships—they focus on detecting*

ALERT	*objects but don't interpret their relationships in space.*

QUESTION 25

Answer - B) <voice> tag

Option A - The <phoneme> tag is used to specify the phonetic pronunciation of a word, not the language or accent of speech.
Option B - Correct. The <voice> tag is used to specify the language, accent, and gender of the synthesized speech output.
Option C - The <prosody> tag is used to modify the pitch, rate, and volume of speech but does not specify language or accent.
Option D - The <lang> tag is used to specify the language of text content, not the language or accent of speech output.
Option E - The <sub> tag is used for substituting one word or phrase with another and is not related to specifying language or accent.

EXAM FOCUS	*Always remember to use the <voice> tag to define language, accent, and gender of speech output when developing multilingual speech-enabled applications.*
CAUTION ALERT	*Don't confuse the <phoneme> tag with specifying language—it's used only for pronunciation adjustments, not for defining speech attributes like accent or language.*

QUESTION 26

Answer - [C] Training the language model with a diverse dataset of user queries.

Option C is the correct choice as training the language model with a diverse dataset of user queries is essential for effective intent recognition, ensuring that the virtual assistant can accurately understand a wide range of user intents. Options A, B, D, and E are unrelated to intent recognition.

EXAM FOCUS	*You should train the language model with a diverse set of user queries to ensure effective and accurate intent recognition in a customer-facing virtual assistant.*
CAUTION ALERT	*Avoid depending on Azure Cognitive Services Form Recognizer or Translator Text for intent recognition, as they are meant for different tasks like form analysis and translation.*

QUESTION 27

Answer - [B] Inadequate query optimization implemented in the app's search functionality.

Option B - Inadequate query optimization within the app's search functionality can lead to slow response times, especially for complex queries, as the search engine may not efficiently process and retrieve relevant results. Insufficient unit count (Option A) might impact scalability but is less likely to cause performance issues for individual queries. Limited indexing frequency (Option C) can affect data freshness but should not directly affect query performance. An outdated SDK version (Option D) may lead to compatibility issues but is not the primary cause of slow response times. Insufficient permissions (Option E) may result in authentication errors but are unlikely to impact query execution speed.

EXAM FOCUS	*You need to optimize the search query structure for complex searches in Azure Cognitive Search to improve performance and response time, especially for large datasets.*
CAUTION ALERT	*Stay alert to overlooking query optimization while increasing resources. Simply adding units won't necessarily improve query performance if the search logic is inefficient.*

QUESTION 28

Answer - [E] Azure Confidential Computing

Explanation: This service ensures that sensitive data remains encrypted and confidential during processing, addressing privacy concerns in speech translation. Options A, B, C, and D do not specifically address privacy concerns in speech translation.

EXAM FOCUS	*You should use Azure Confidential Computing to ensure sensitive healthcare data remains protected during processing in your speech translation solution.*
CAUTION ALERT	*Avoid relying on basic encryption mechanisms or standard Azure services that don't specifically guarantee confidentiality during active processing.*

QUESTION 29

Answer - [B] Notify users of upcoming updates and provide guidance on using new features

Explanation: B) Notifying users of updates and providing guidance ensures transparency, manages expectations, and minimizes user confusion or frustration during the transition. A) Deploying updates during peak usage hours risks disrupting user interactions and may lead to negative experiences. C) Implementing updates without testing increases the likelihood of errors and service disruptions. D) Promptly rolling back updates without investigation may exacerbate issues and undermine user trust. E) Ignoring user feedback disregards user experience and may result in missed opportunities for improvement.

EXAM FOCUS	*Always notify users of any upcoming updates to chatbot models and provide clear guidance on new features, ensuring minimal disruption in chatbot functionality.*
CAUTION ALERT	*Stay clear of updating without testing or ignoring user feedback during updates. Doing so may degrade the user experience and result in unresolved errors.*

QUESTION 30

Answer - [C] Utilize Azure AI Language's real-time sentiment analysis API for on-the-fly analysis of customer reviews as they are submitted.

Option C - Utilizing Azure AI Language's real-time sentiment analysis API ensures near real-time sentiment analysis of customer reviews with high accuracy, meeting the app's requirements effectively. Option A's batch processing approach may introduce delays and is not suitable for near real-time analysis. Option B requires significant effort in model development and training, which may not guarantee high accuracy compared to pre-built models. Option D involves continuous analysis of data streams but may not offer the immediacy required for near real-time analysis. Option E adds unnecessary complexity by implementing local processing before utilizing Azure AI Language's capabilities.

EXAM FOCUS	*Make sure to use Azure AI Language's real-time sentiment analysis API for near real-time processing, ensuring the app delivers fast and accurate sentiment results for customer reviews.*
CAUTION ALERT	*Avoid using batch processing for sentiment analysis if real-time results are required—it introduces delays and won't meet the performance requirements of your app.*

QUESTION 31

Answer - [A), B), and C)] - Monitoring latency, error rates, and utilizing distributed tracing are essential for identifying performance bottlenecks and ensuring optimal service delivery.

D) Incorrect - While analyzing user feedback and sentiment is valuable, it might not directly address the technical aspects of performance monitoring and management in production.

EXAM FOCUS	*You should monitor latency, error rates, and use distributed tracing for proactive performance management of the model. Identifying bottlenecks early helps maintain optimal performance in production.*
CAUTION ALERT	*Stay clear of neglecting error rate tracking or relying solely on user feedback, as this will not provide complete insights into model performance issues.*

QUESTION 32

Answer - [A), B), and C)] - Integrating Azure Automation runbooks, enforcing backup retention policies, and utilizing Azure Functions for automated recovery procedures streamline backup and recovery operations while ensuring compliance with government regulations.

D) Incorrect - While Azure Security Center policies can monitor backup activities, they might not directly contribute to streamlining backup and recovery operations or ensuring compliance with government regulations specific to citizen service chatbot applications.

EXAM FOCUS	*Make sure to integrate automated backup and recovery processes like Azure Automation and Azure Functions to meet government compliance standards. This ensures regular backups and recovery readiness.*
CAUTION ALERT	*Avoid overlooking backup retention policies. Ensure backup data complies with legal and security requirements by enforcing Azure Policy to monitor retention standards.*

QUESTION 33

Answer - [C] Azure AI Language Service > Text Analytics API

Option C - Azure AI Language Service with the Text Analytics API is designed for extracting key phrases and entities from text data, making it the best choice for identifying and extracting keywords. Option A is incorrect as Cognitive Search is more suited for indexing and searching text data. Option B is incorrect as Content Moderator is focused on content moderation. Option D is incorrect as Translator Text is for translation tasks, not keyword extraction. Option E is incorrect as Computer Vision is for image processing, not text analysis.

EXAM FOCUS	*You need to use Azure AI Language Service and its Text Analytics API for extracting keywords from large datasets efficiently. This API is optimized for text analysis tasks such as key phrase extraction.*
CAUTION ALERT	*Stay alert to confusing Azure Cognitive Search with text analysis tasks. Cognitive Search is for indexing and searching, not for analyzing and extracting key phrases.*

QUESTION 34

Answer - [A), B), and C)] - Incorporating user queries for real-world testing involves implementing user feedback forms, analyzing interactions with the knowledge base, and integrating queries into automated test scripts for validation.

Option A) - Correct: User feedback forms facilitate the collection of query data, providing valuable insights for testing and improvement. Option B) - Correct: Analyzing user interactions offers qualitative insights into the effectiveness of the knowledge base. Option C) - Correct: Integrating user queries into automated test scripts ensures systematic validation and coverage of real-world scenarios. Option D) - Incorrect: Ignoring user queries neglects valuable real-world data and may lead to biased testing results. Option E) - Incorrect: Focus groups may provide qualitative feedback but are less scalable and systematic than automated methods for incorporating user queries.

EXAM FOCUS	*You should include user queries in automated test scripts and analyze real-world interactions to validate the effectiveness of your question-answering solution. This ensures it handles diverse real-world scenarios.*
CAUTION	*Avoid ignoring user queries or relying entirely on simulated data for testing. Simulated data may not*

ALERT	*accurately represent real-world use cases and will lead to biased results.*

QUESTION 35

Answer - [A), B), and D)] - Leveraging machine learning for dynamic conversation paths involves training with diverse datasets, regular updates, and monitoring performance.

Option A) - Correct: Training models with diverse datasets ensures better generalization and adaptability to various user scenarios. Option B) - Correct: Regularly updating models helps keep them aligned with evolving user preferences and conversational trends. Option C) - Incorrect: While reinforcement learning can optimize conversation flow, it may not be the primary consideration for ensuring effective implementation. Option D) - Correct: Monitoring model performance and adjusting hyperparameters ensure optimal performance and responsiveness to user inputs. Option E) - Incorrect: Ensuring transparency and accountability is important but may not directly relate to leveraging machine learning for dynamic conversation paths.

EXAM FOCUS	*Always remember to regularly update machine learning models with diverse conversational datasets. This practice ensures dynamic conversation paths remain relevant and provide accurate responses.*
CAUTION ALERT	*Don't confuse reinforcement learning as the main method for improving conversation flow. The primary focus should be on model training and regular updates for better performance.*

QUESTION 36

Answer - [A, B, E] "mcr.microsoft.com/azure-ai/sentimentanalysis"
"--memory 512 --cpus 4"
"--api-key {API_KEY}"

Option A specifies the correct URI for the Sentiment Analysis container. Option B sets memory and CPU limits. Option E specifies the API key required for authentication. Options C and D are not relevant for container deployment.

EXAM FOCUS	*Make sure to include the correct container image URI, memory, CPU specifications, and API key when deploying a sentiment analysis model. This ensures that your deployment is optimized and authenticated.*
CAUTION ALERT	*Stay clear of skipping the memory and CPU specifications when deploying containers, as incorrect settings can lead to poor performance or deployment failure.*

QUESTION 37

Answer - [A, B, C].

A) Implementing Azure Confidential Computing ensures secure data processing within a trusted execution environment, safeguarding sensitive information. B) Applying role-based access control (RBAC) restricts data access to authorized personnel, enhancing security. C) Using Azure Key Vault for storing encryption keys adds an additional layer of security to protect sensitive data. D) Enabling Azure Active Directory authentication improves access control but does not directly protect sensitive data processed by the model. E) Data anonymization techniques may be beneficial for privacy but are not sufficient to protect sensitive data in this scenario.

EXAM FOCUS	*You need to implement Azure Confidential Computing and role-based access control to ensure sensitive data in compliance-related models is protected during processing and access is restricted.*
CAUTION ALERT	*Avoid neglecting the importance of storing encryption keys securely in Azure Key Vault. Without secure key management, sensitive data is at risk.*

QUESTION 38

Answer - [A, B, C, D].

A) Implementing sentiment analysis allows for interpreting user feedback and gauging overall satisfaction with the voice interface. B) Conducting usability testing with real users provides valuable insights into user experiences and preferences, aiding in improving engagement and satisfaction. C) Utilizing Azure Application Insights enables monitoring voice assistant performance and identifying areas for enhancement to boost engagement. D) Analyzing user interaction logs helps recognize behavior patterns and identify areas for optimization to enhance user engagement and satisfaction. E) While A/B testing can be beneficial, it may not directly measure user engagement and satisfaction with the voice interface and may focus more on feature comparison.

EXAM FOCUS	*Keep in mind that analyzing user interaction logs and sentiment analysis can provide valuable insights into user engagement with voice assistants, ensuring your solution evolves based on real-world usage.*
CAUTION ALERT	*Don't confuse A/B testing with analyzing user satisfaction. While A/B tests compare versions, they don't provide enough insight into the overall user experience with voice interfaces.*

QUESTION 39

Answer - [D] DefaultAzureCredential

Option A, AzureKeyVaultCredentials, is incorrect because it doesn't represent the class used for authentication with Azure Key Vault. Option B, KeyVaultClient, is also incorrect as it's used for interacting with Azure Key Vault, not for authentication. Option C, KeyVaultCredentials, is incorrect because it's not the class used for credential management. Option E, AzureKeyVaultClient, is incorrect as it's not a valid class for authentication. Option D, DefaultAzureCredential, is the correct choice as it provides a default credential solution for authentication with Azure services, including Key Vault.

EXAM FOCUS	*Always remember to use DefaultAzureCredential for authenticating securely with Azure Key Vault, as it simplifies authentication by supporting multiple credential types.*
CAUTION ALERT	*Stay alert to using hardcoded credentials in your application code, which can lead to security risks. Always rely on secure authentication methods like DefaultAzureCredential.*

QUESTION 40

Answer - [E] Azure Cognitive Search.

E) Azure Cognitive Search provides capabilities for knowledge mining while offering features to address bias and ensure fairness in the extraction process from research papers. A) Azure Text Analytics focuses on text analysis but may not provide specialized features for fairness in knowledge mining. B) Azure Language Understanding (LUIS) is used for understanding user intents and entities in text and does not specialize in knowledge mining. C) Azure AI Translator service is focused on translation tasks and does not address bias in knowledge mining. D) Azure Cognitive Services offers various AI capabilities but may require additional customization for fairness in knowledge mining.

EXAM FOCUS	*You should leverage Azure Cognitive Search to ensure fairness in knowledge mining processes, addressing bias when extracting insights from research papers.*
CAUTION ALERT	*Stay cautioned about assuming all AI services handle bias automatically. Be proactive in assessing fairness during the extraction process, especially in sensitive fields like medical research.*

QUESTION 41

Answer - [A] Azure Data Factory.

A) Azure Data Factory provides comprehensive capabilities for orchestrating data pipelines, supporting various data sources, and enabling efficient automation of data ingestion workflows across diverse repositories, making it the ideal choice for automating data ingestion into Azure Cognitive Search. B) Azure Logic Apps offer workflow automation but may not provide native support for data transformation and complex data ingestion scenarios. C) Azure Functions are suitable for event-driven serverless computing but may lack the built-in capabilities for orchestrating complex data ingestion workflows. D) Azure Event Grid is a publish-subscribe event routing service and may not directly support data ingestion workflows across different data repositories. E) Azure Batch is designed for large-scale parallel and high-performance computing tasks but may not be optimized for data ingestion workflows involving diverse data sources.

EXAM FOCUS	*Make sure to use Azure Data Factory for automating data ingestion workflows from diverse sources like Azure Blob Storage, Azure SQL Database, and Azure Data Lake Storage. Its ability to orchestrate pipelines makes it ideal for complex integrations.*
CAUTION ALERT	*Stay clear of relying on services like Azure Functions or Logic Apps alone for complex data ingestion. These are better suited for simpler event-driven tasks and may lack robust data transformation capabilities.*

QUESTION 42

Answer - [A] var client = new LuisRuntimeClient(new ApiKeyServiceClientCredentials(apiKey));

Option B is incorrect because LuisRuntimeClient expects an instance of IServiceClientCredentials, not a string apiKey. Option C is incorrect because LanguageUnderstandingRuntimeClient is not the correct class for creating a LUIS runtime client. Option D is incorrect for the same reason as Option C. Option E is incorrect because there is no class named LuisClient for creating a LUIS runtime client. Option A is the correct choice as LuisRuntimeClient requires an instance of ApiKeyServiceClientCredentials for authentication.

EXAM FOCUS	*Always remember to use the correct authentication method when creating a LUIS runtime client. You need to pass the API key credentials correctly, as shown in the option using LuisRuntimeClient and ApiKeyServiceClientCredentials.*
CAUTION ALERT	*Avoid using incorrect class names or passing the API key directly into the client constructor. This will result in runtime errors, and it won't work with LUIS services.*

QUESTION 43

Answer - [C] Implement delta indexing to capture only changed or new data.

C) Implementing delta indexing allows for capturing only changed or new data since the last indexing operation, enabling efficient incremental updates to the search index without reprocessing the entire dataset. A) Rebuilding the search index periodically with updated data is not efficient for large datasets and may result in unnecessary processing overhead. B) Configuring indexers to perform full data re-indexing involves reprocessing the entire dataset, which is resource-intensive and may not be suitable for incremental updates. D) Manually triggering indexers for incremental updates is not scalable and may introduce delays in indexing processes. E) While Azure Functions can be used for various automation tasks, they may not provide native support for delta indexing and incremental updates in Azure Cognitive Search.

EXAM FOCUS	*You should implement delta indexing in Azure Cognitive Search for large datasets. This approach updates only changed or new data, improving efficiency without having to re-index the entire dataset.*
CAUTION ALERT	*Avoid relying on full re-indexing, as it is resource-intensive and inefficient for large datasets. Incremental indexing is the best practice for handling high volumes of data updates.*

QUESTION 44

Answer - [E] Integrate projected data with Azure Machine Learning pipelines for analysis and model training.

E) Integrating projected data with Azure Machine Learning pipelines allows for seamless integration of data analysis and model training tasks, leveraging the scalability and flexibility of Azure AI services for analytics and machine learning workflows. A) Storing projected data in a proprietary format may limit interoperability and integration with standard analytics tools and platforms, complicating the analysis process. B) Extracting features from projected data and storing them in separate tables may introduce data redundancy and complexity, leading to potential inconsistencies in analysis results. C) Implementing custom serialization methods may increase development effort and maintenance overhead without offering significant advantages over standard data storage formats for analytics and machine learning tasks. D) Utilizing pre-trained machine learning models for direct analysis of projected data may not fully leverage the capabilities of Azure AI services for customized analysis and model training specific to the organization's requirements.

EXAM FOCUS	*Keep in mind that integrating projected data with Azure Machine Learning pipelines allows seamless data processing for analytics and model training. It optimizes workflows and uses the flexibility of Azure's AI services.*
CAUTION ALERT	*Don't confuse using proprietary data formats or custom serialization for storing projected data with optimizing for analytics. This can introduce unnecessary complexity and limit flexibility.*

QUESTION 45

Answer - D) TrainCustomModel()

Option A - TrainModel(): This is a hypothetical method and not part of the Azure AI Document Intelligence service SDK.
Option B - CreateModel(): This is a hypothetical method and not part of the Azure AI Document Intelligence service SDK.
Option C - BuildModel(): This is a hypothetical method and not part of the Azure AI Document Intelligence service SDK.
Option E - DevelopModel(): This is a hypothetical method and not part of the Azure AI Document Intelligence service SDK.
Option D is correct because TrainCustomModel() is used to train a custom document intelligence model in Azure AI Document Intelligence service.

EXAM FOCUS	*You need to use the TrainCustomModel() method when training a custom document model in Azure AI Document Intelligence. This method is designed specifically for custom document model training.*
CAUTION ALERT	*Stay alert to using incorrect method names like CreateModel or BuildModel. These are not valid in Azure AI Document Intelligence and will result in errors.*

QUESTION 46

Answer - [B] Diversity: Adjusts the diversity of generated text to introduce new ideas.

B) Diversity parameter influences the novelty of generated text by adjusting the range of ideas introduced.
A) Learning rate affects the speed of model adaptation but does not directly control novelty.
C) Beam width affects the search space during text generation but may not directly impact novelty.
D) Prompt length influences the context provided to the model but does not control novelty.
E) Epochs determine the training duration but do not specifically address the balance between novelty and relevance.

EXAM FOCUS	*Always remember to adjust the diversity parameter in Azure OpenAI Service for balancing novelty and relevance in generated content. It helps maintain freshness in output without losing context.*
CAUTION ALERT	*Stay cautioned against over-adjusting parameters like beam width or learning rate, as they do not directly control the novelty of the generated text.*

QUESTION 47

Answer - [C] Reviewing and adhering to usage guidelines provided by the DALL-E model's terms of service.

C) Adhering to usage guidelines provided by the DALL-E model's terms of service ensures legal compliance and ethical use of the generated images.
A) Verifying licensing status and attribution addresses copyright concerns but may not cover all ethical considerations.
B) Watermarking protects ownership but does not address potential copyright violations in the input or generated images.
D) Audits help monitor usage but may not prevent copyright violations proactively.
E) Image hashing detects infringements but may not be sufficient to ensure compliance with model terms of service.

EXAM FOCUS	*Make sure to review and adhere to the DALL-E model's terms of service. This ensures that your company follows legal and ethical guidelines when generating images for advertising campaigns.*
CAUTION ALERT	*Avoid assuming that implementing watermarking or audits alone ensures compliance. These are supportive strategies but do not replace understanding and following the model's terms of service.*

QUESTION 48

Answer - D) Statement I, Statement II

Option A - Statement I: Azure AI Content Moderator service indeed provides text moderation capabilities, making this statement true.
Option B - Statement II: Azure AI Content Moderator service supports image recognition, making this statement true.
Option C - Statement III: Azure AI Content Moderator service does not offer language translation functionalities, making this statement false.
Option D is correct because both Statement I and Statement II are true.
Option E - Statement III: Azure AI Content Moderator service does not offer language translation functionalities, making this statement false.

EXAM FOCUS	*You should use Azure AI Content Moderator for text and image moderation capabilities. It offers tools to handle inappropriate content across various formats.*
CAUTION ALERT	*Stay clear of confusing content moderation with language translation. Azure AI Content Moderator does not offer translation functionalities, so be cautious when selecting the service for the right purpose.*

QUESTION 49

Answer - [A, C] Implementing counterfactual evaluation techniques to simulate the impact of alternative fine-tuning strategies on historical user interactions. Conducting user studies or surveys to gather qualitative feedback on the relevance and diversity of recommendations generated by the fine-tuned model.

A) Counterfactual evaluation allows assessing the impact of fine-tuning strategies retrospectively, providing insights into recommendation accuracy and diversity.
C) User studies capture qualitative feedback on recommendation relevance and diversity, complementing quantitative evaluation metrics.
B) Recommendation metrics quantify performance but may not fully capture diversity or qualitative aspects.

D) Adversarial testing focuses on identifying vulnerabilities rather than assessing recommendation impact.
E) Reinforcement learning adjusts parameters but may not directly evaluate recommendation diversity or accuracy.

EXAM FOCUS	*You should use counterfactual evaluation techniques and user studies to assess the impact of fine-tuning strategies on recommendation accuracy. These techniques help simulate and gather feedback on how recommendations evolve.*
CAUTION ALERT	*Avoid assuming that recommendation metrics like precision and recall alone can provide a full view of recommendation diversity. They are limited to performance metrics and don't capture user experience or novelty.*

QUESTION 50

Answer - [B] Conducting regular audits on the generated responses for bias and sensitivity.

A) Profanity filters are important but may not address broader ethical concerns. C) While training on diverse datasets is valuable, it may not directly ensure ethical standards. D) Securing checkpoints is essential for security but does not directly relate to ethical considerations. E) Monitoring user interactions helps detect harmful responses but may not prevent them during fine-tuning.

EXAM FOCUS	*You need to conduct regular audits to monitor the generated responses for bias and sensitivity. This ensures the AI chatbot operates ethically and prevents harmful outputs.*
CAUTION ALERT	*Stay clear of thinking that profanity filters or security measures alone address ethical issues. While important, they don't prevent biases or other inappropriate content in the fine-tuning process.*

ABOUT THE AUTHOR

Step into the world of Anand, and you're in for a journey beyond just tech and algorithms. While his accolades in the tech realm are numerous, including penning various tech-centric and personal improvement ebooks, there's so much more to this multi-faceted author.

At the heart of Anand lies an AI enthusiast and investor, always on the hunt for the next big thing in artificial intelligence. But turn the page, and you might find him engrossed in a gripping cricket match or passionately cheering for his favorite football team. His weekends? They might be spent experimenting with a new recipe in the kitchen, penning down his latest musings, or crafting a unique design that blends creativity with functionality.

While his professional journey as a Solution Architect and AI Consultant, boasting over a decade of AI/ML expertise, is impressive, it's the fusion of this expertise with his diverse hobbies that makes Anand's writings truly distinctive.

So, as you navigate through his works, expect more than just information. Prepare for stories interwoven with passion, experiences peppered with life's many spices, and wisdom that transcends beyond the tech realm. Dive in and discover Anand, the author, the enthusiast, the chef, the sports lover, and above all, the storyteller.

Made in United States
Orlando, FL
03 April 2025

60109377R00162